Scandinavia in the Middle Ages 900–1550

Medieval Scandinavia went through momentous changes. Regional power centres merged and gave birth to the three strong kingdoms of Denmark, Norway, and Sweden. At the end of the Middle Ages, they together formed the enormous Kalmar Union comprising almost all lands around the North Atlantic and the Baltic Sea. In the Middle Ages, Scandinavia became part of a common Europe, yet preserved its own distinct cultural markers.

Scandinavia in the Middle Ages 900–1550 covers the entire Middle Ages into an engaging narrative. The book gives a chronological overview of political, ecclesiastical, cultural, and economic developments. It integrates to this narrative climatic change, energy crises, devastating epidemics, family life and livelihood, arts, education, technology and literature, and much else. The book shows how different groups had an important role in shaping society: kings and peasants, pious priests, nuns and crusaders, merchants, and students, without forgetting minorities such as Sámi and Jews. The book is divided into three chronological parts 900–1200, 1200–1400, and 1400–1550, where analyses of general trends are illustrated by the acts of individual men and women.

This book is essential reading for students of, as well as all those interested in, medieval Scandinavia and Europe more broadly.

Kirsi Salonen is Professor of Medieval History at the University of Bergen, Norway. Her previous publications include *Papal Justice in the Late Middle Ages. The Sacra Romana Rota* (2016); and she is the co-editor of *Scandinavia and the Vatican Archives* (2022).

Kurt Villads Jensen is Professor of Medieval History and Director of the Centre for Medieval Studies at Stockholm University, Sweden. His previous publications include *Crusading at the Edges of Europe. Denmark and Portugal c.1000–c.1250* (2017); and he is the co-author of *The Rise and Fall of the Danish Empire* (2022).

Scandinavia in the Middle Ages 900–1550

Between Two Oceans

Kirsi Salonen and Kurt Villads Jensen

LONDON AND NEW YORK

Designed cover image: © Photo Kirsten Trampedach 2007, Public Domain.
Kirkeudsmykninger.euman.net

First published 2023
by Routledge
4 Park Square, Milton Park, Abingdon, Oxon OX14 4RN

and by Routledge
605 Third Avenue, New York, NY 10158

Routledge is an imprint of the Taylor & Francis Group, an informa business

© 2023 Kirsi Salonen and Kurt Villads Jensen

The right of Kirsi Salonen and Kurt Villads Jensen to be identified as authors of this work has been asserted in accordance with sections 77 and 78 of the Copyright, Designs and Patents Act 1988.

All rights reserved. No part of this book may be reprinted or reproduced or utilised in any form or by any electronic, mechanical, or other means, now known or hereafter invented, including photocopying and recording, or in any information storage or retrieval system, without permission in writing from the publishers.

Trademark notice: Product or corporate names may be trademarks or registered trademarks, and are used only for identification and explanation without intent to infringe.

British Library Cataloguing-in-Publication Data
A catalogue record for this book is available from the British Library

Library of Congress Cataloging-in-Publication Data
Names: Salonen, Kirsi, author. | Jensen, Kurt Villads, author.
Title: Scandinavia in the middle ages 900–1550: between two oceans / Kirsi Salonen & Kurt Villads Jensen.
Description: Abingdon, Oxon; New York: Routledge, 2023. |
Includes bibliographical references and index. |
Identifiers: LCCN 2022037894 (print) | LCCN 2022037895 (ebook) |
ISBN 9780367558703 (hardback) | ISBN 9780367558697 (paperback) |
ISBN 9781003095514 (ebook)
Subjects: LCSH: Scandinavia—History—To 1397. | Scandinavia—Economic conditions—To 1500. | Church history—Middle Ages, 600-1500. | Christianity—Scandinavia—History—To 1500. | Middle Ages.
Classification: LCC DL61 .S256 2023 (print) |
LCC DL61 (ebook) | DDC 948/.02—dc23/eng/20220816
LC record available at https://lccn.loc.gov/2022037894
LC ebook record available at https://lccn.loc.gov/2022037895

ISBN: 978-0-367-55870-3 (hbk)
ISBN: 978-0-367-55869-7 (pbk)
ISBN: 978-1-003-09551-4 (ebk)

DOI: 10.4324/9781003095514

Typeset in Sabon
by codeMantra

Published with the kind support of

Sven och Dagmar Saléns vetenskaps- och kulturstiftelse
The Department of Archaeology, History, Cultural Studies and Religion,
  Bergen University
The Department of History, Stockholm University

Contents

List of Maps xii
List of Illustrations xiii

Introduction 1

PART I
900–1200: Formation 5

1 **Coming of the Kingdoms** 7
   The Kingdoms and Conversion 7
   Denmark: Conquest and Christianisation – Swift or Slow? 10
   The North Sea Empire 14
   Norway: The Long Land Unified by Christianity 17
      Saint Olaf 18
   Sweden: The Kingdoms of the Goths and of the Sveas 21
   Iceland: The Lands without Kings 22
   Greenland: Northerners in a New Environment 24
   The Period of Civil Wars 26
   An Especially Violent Period in Scandinavian History? 32
   Royal Administrators 33
   Military Organisation 35
   Watch Towers and Castles 37

2 **Coming of Christ** 40
   Before Christianity 40
   Western Christianity 900–1200 41
   The Danish Church 900–1200 41
   The Norwegian Church 900–1200 47
   The Icelandic Church 900–1200 51
   The Swedish Church 900–1200 52
   The Finnish Church 900–1200 55
   The Long Arms of the Papacy 57

The General Church Councils 57
  The Papal Curia 58
  Papal Representatives 58
  Ecclesiastical Administration at Local Level 59
  Inquisition 61
 Ecclesiastical Norms 62
 Ecclesiastical Justice 65
 Sin and Absolution 67
 Clerical Stand and Monastic Orders 69
  Monastic Orders 71
  Canons Regular 73
  Military Orders 75
  Mendicants 77
  Embarking Upon the Monastic Lifestyle and the Choice of the Right Order 81
  Monasteries and Medieval Society 82

3 **Tilling the Land – The Local Economy**   84
 The Spread of Agriculture 84
 Population and Family Structure 87
 Life in the Countryside 88
 Agriculture, Fishing, and Hunting 89
 The Self-Sufficient Economy and Local Market 93

4 **Cultural Tradition and Transition**   96
 Romanesque Architecture 96
 Romanesque Arts 100
 The Coming of Writing 104
  Oral Tradition – Scaldic and Eddic Poetry and Sagas 105
  Liturgical Literature 106
 Mortality, Illnesses, and Life Expectance 107
 Food and Drink 111
 Clothing 113

PART II
1200–1400: Consolidation and Restructuring   117

5 **Dominion over the Seas**   119
 Military Revolution and Expansion into the Baltic 119
 Naval Revolution 120
 Expansion in the Baltic 122
  The Danish Baltic Empire 123
  A Traitor: The Black Count Henry of Schwerin 127

Swedish Colonisation and Crusades 129
Expansion into the North Atlantic – The Norwegian Dominium 130
Killing Kings 133
Inter-Scandinavian Marriages and Raids 137
Models for Governance 139
Legal Development 143
    From Oral to Written, from Provincial to National Laws 144
    Issues Regulated by Law 150
    Legal Practice 152
1319 – The Year That Everything Changed 153
Denmark Pawned and Redeemed 156
Wars with the Hansa, and among the Scandinavian Kingdoms 157

6 Consolidation of the Church   160
The Western Church 1200–1400 160
The Danish Church 1200–1400 160
The Norwegian Church 1200–1400 163
The Icelandic Church 1200–1400 165
The Swedish Church 1200–1400 166
The Finnish Church 1200–1400 169
Saints 170
Relics 175
Pilgrimage 176
Crusades 180

7 Economic Growth and Fall – Urbanisation and Agrarian Crisis   184
Urbanisation 184
Towns on the Coast 186
Urban Environment 186
Trade in Towns: Local and International 191
The Monetary Economy 191
Progress and Prosperity: Technological Innovations of the 13th Century 193
The Economic Crisis of the 14th Century 196
    The Plague 196
    The Climate Change 199
    The Agricultural Crisis 199
    The Lack of Labour 200

8 Cultural Universalism   202
Gothic Architecture 202
Gothic Arts 206
Literature 212
Education and Learning 218
    Local Education 218

University Education 219
Scandinavian University Students 222
Student Life 224

PART III
1400–c. 1550: Power in Crises — 227

9 Rise and Fall of the Kalmar Union — 229
The Scandinavian Union – The Apogee of Scandinavian Power, or a Colossus with Clay Feet? 229
Licence to Crusade – Even Against Christians 230
The Early Union in International Politics 233
Conflict and Commerce 237
The Bloodbath and the Shining Light of the Gospel 240

10 Fall of the Church — 244
The Western Church 1400–1550 244
The Danish Church 1400–1550 245
The Norwegian Church 1400–1550 247
The Icelandic Church 1400–1550 249
The Swedish Church 1400–1550 250
The Finnish Church 1400–1550 254
Church and Everyday Life – Sacraments Signposting the Christian Life 255
  Birth and Baptism 255
  Adolescence and Confirmation 257
  Lifelong Practice: Eucharist and Confession 257
  Adulthood and Marriage 260
  Priests, Monks, and Nuns: Ordination 265
  Old Age: Preparations for Death and the Last Unction 266
The Rhythm of Life 267

11 Economic Expansion – The International Market Economy — 270
The Hanseatic League 270
The Internationalisation of Commerce: Transnational Commercial Networks and Routes 272
Harvesting Lakes and Seas: Professional Fishing in Scandinavia 275
The Mining Industry 280
International Banking and Money Transfer 281
Guilds 283

12 A Revolution in Communication — 286
Late Gothic Architecture 286
Late Gothic Arts 288

Literature – the Printing Revolution 291
Medieval Music in Scandinavia 297

The Medieval Legacy 301

Sources and Literature 303
Databases 303
Journals 303
Sources 303
Literature 304

Index 307

Maps

1	Scandinavia in the Middle Ages	8
2	The medieval provinces of Scandinavia	11
3	Scandinavian migration and settlements in the North Atlantic	25
4	Church provinces in Scandinavia	60
5	The juridical districts in medieval Scandinavia	146
6	Hanseatic cities and trading routes in Scandinavia around 1370	274
7	The Scania fish market at Falsterbo	279

Illustrations

1.1 The Kuli-stone, raised when Christianity had been 12 winters in Norway. Unfortunately, the stone is undated. Now in the Scientific Museum in Trondheim   9
1.2 Trelleborg, the type of Viking fortress from around 970   12
1.3 Jelling Rune Stone, probably from the 980s, on which King Harald Bluetooth claims to have conquered all Denmark and Norway and made the Danes Christian. Pictured here is a modern copy from the Danish National Museum with a reconstruction of the original painting   14
1.4 Silver coin issued by King Sweyn Estridsen in 1047, presenting him as an emperor and receiving the banner of victory from an angel. It is a direct copy of a coin issued by the Byzantine emperor   16
1.5 Saint Olaf with his typical attributes: the long Nordic axe in his hand and the defeated dragon under his feet. Very often it is crowned, as here, and most likely symbolises the pagan kings of Norway, forced into adopting Christianity. Sculpture in the altar piece in Saint Mary's Church, Bergen, late 15th century   20
1.6 Þingvellir, the general assembly place in medieval Iceland. The peculiar geological formation is a result of the meeting of the North American and the Eurasian tectonic plates. In practice, this creates an enormous theatre background that amplifies sound and makes individual voices audible even for a very large group   23
1.7 Saint Bendt's Church, Ringsted, was the Danish royal burial church from 1131 until 1319. In 1170, Canute Lavard was canonised here in a solemn ceremony, and his grandson, Canute VI, was crowned king and co-regent with his father Valdemar I, in an attempt to secure the succession to the throne. A new and larger church had begun being built for this occasion, one of the earliest brick buildings in Scandinavia, but in 1170 probably only the choir and the central crossing had been finished   29
1.8 The relics of Saint Eric of Sweden, which are today still kept in the cathedral at Uppsala. They were investigated by anthropologists in 2014, and it is clear from the marks on his bones that he had been hit by sword and had had his head cut off, all well in accordance with the description of his martyrdom contained in the medieval description of his life. Eric had organised a crusade to Finland in the mid-1150s together with Bishop Henry from Uppsala, who

	became the Finnish patron saint. The crusade, referred to as the first Swedish crusade to Finland, is known from much later sources and scholars have questioned whether it actually ever took place. There is no reason to doubt, however, that a cult for Eric developed shortly after his death	32
2.1	Ansgar, the 'Apostle of the North', was allowed to build a church in Hedeby and, around the middle of the 9th century, another one in Ribe on the west coast of Denmark. Missions to Scandinavia had begun to become organised. We do not know exactly what the churches looked like, but a replica has been made for the Viking Centre in Ribe which gives an impression of the interior of the very first, wooden churches in Scandinavia	43
2.2	Poppo, the missionary bishop, baptising the Danish King Harald Bluetooth. The golden relief is from an early 12th-century altar decoration from the Church of Tamdrup and illustrates the legend of Denmark's Christianisation. It probably formed part of an attempt (which never succeeded) to have Harald, as Denmark's first Christian king, recognised as a saint and to create a cult for him	44
2.3	Archbishop Absalon of Lund († 1201), the missionary bishop eager for the crusades against the Slavic peoples south of the Baltic Sea, depicted here in full armour and with a small axe in his hand in the centre of Copenhagen. The equestrian statue by the famous artist Vilhelm Bissen was made to commemorate the 700th anniversary of Absalon's death but was delayed and only inaugurated in 1902	47
2.4	Selje monastery on the west coast of a small island off the Norwegian coast. Some of the early Scandinavian monasteries from the 12th century tried to promote Christianity through isolation and contemplation rather than active missionary work among people	50
2.5	Church behind pagan graves. Old Uppsala became an episcopal see in the 1130s and in 1164 it was raised to an archiepiscopal see, which was moved to present-day Uppsala in the 1270s. Old Uppsala had been a numinous centre for centuries. The landscape is dominated by the three enormous burial mounds from the 6th century and literally hundreds of minor mounds and burial sites. Uppsala was also, according to the historian Adam of Bremen, the centre for a pagan cult and temple. The new Christian faith received authority from connecting to the old pagan belief system	54
2.6	Bishop Henry began the mission to the Finns but was chased over the frozen ice of Lake Köyliö by the peasant Lalli. Henry had visited Lalli's house and taken food from his wife; Lalli took revenge by killing Henry with his axe. This story is late and legendary, but became important within the national romanticism of the 19th century, when Lalli became a symbol for Finnish independence	56
2.7	Letter of indulgence from 1517, issued by the famous papal legate and indulgence seller in Scandinavia Johannes Angelus Arcimboldus. Tens and probably hundreds of thousands of these letters were printed in the later Middle Ages. Space was left open to add the names of the recipients of the indulgence. The letter here	

	was issued to Swenwngh Helghessen and Swanogh Olaffzdotther with their children in Heyredal in Norway	70
2.8	The hospital in Aalborg was founded in 1431 by the wealthy Lady Maren Hemmingsdatter but burned down only three years later. The new hospital that replaced it was incorporated into the order of the Holy Spirit in 1451. The buildings are still standing and are among the oldest medieval houses preserved in Scandinavia. Its charitable function has continued, and today the hospital is a retirement home with a governing board that represents both ecclesiastical and lay administration, including the bishop and the mayor of Aalborg	80
3.1	Plan of a typical medieval village in Scandinavia	86
3.2	Milk was a very important part of nutrition everywhere in medieval Scandinavia and would have been processed into butter or cheese to be stored and transported. To churn milk into butter was hard work and a transformation of one element into another, and was therefore considered especially vulnerable to abuse by evil forces. Here a witch is churning, her small demon is vomiting up the milk it has sucked and stolen from the neighbours' cows, and a devil is helping while the head of its tail eagerly licks up the drops of butter. Fourteenth-century wall painting, Söderby-Karl church, Sweden	91
3.3	The catch around the big fishing market in Scania was famous from at least the 12th century and throughout the Middle Ages. The herring could be taken up directly by hand, and the fish shoals were allegedly so thick that a spear put into the water would not sink	93
4.1	The stave church in Fantoft. Originally built c. 1150 in the parish of Fortun, Norway, and moved to its present location in 1883. It was burned down by an arsonist in 1992. Fantoft church was completely rebuilt and gives a fine impression of how the 12th-century wooden churches in Norway would have looked when they were new	97
4.2	Høm church is a typical example of the small Romanesque churches that were built on the Scandinavian countryside during the 12th century. The apse has the original small window that let the sun shine directly on the crucifix on the alter. The tower was added during the later Middle Ages	98
4.3	Christ in majesty, surrounded by the four Evangelist symbols, sitting on the globe and ready to judge the whole world. Vä church in Scania, 1120s	102
4.4	The Runic alphabet was still known and continued to be used for some hundred years in short messages or prayers and amulets and can also sometimes be found on liturgical items. Runes could be used for writing in Latin, but were also common in daily life messages in the local languages, a kind of medieval SMS. Hundreds of small wooden sticks with short messages have been found, as this one from Bergen. It reads *unthu mær ankthær gunnildr kys mik*: 'Love me, Gunhild, I love you. Kiss me'	104

xvi *List of Illustrations*

4.5 Surgery was a well-developed and sophisticated art in the Middle Ages. Hard manual labour with few worker protections or regulations resulted in a high risk for injuries with broken bones, and warfare with its ensuing physical traumas was relatively common, so practical surgery was in high demand. This skull has been trepanned, which is opened to remove from the brain a tumour, coagulated blood, or pieces of bones after a heavy blow to the skull. The patient survived and lived for years after the operation, because the circular hole made by the drill had begun to close. The skull, from around 1500, was found near Pälkäne church, Finland. Now in the National Museum of Finland, Helsinki   109

4.6 Shortly after 1350, this young man was killed with heavy blows to the skull and dumped into a moor with a pole hammered through his heart, either to keep the body down to conceal the crime or to prevent his ghost from coming back and haunting his murderers. He was found in 1936 with his clothes unusually well preserved by the acidic water of the moor. The clothes were locally made but followed the latest European fashion at the time. Pictured here is a modern reconstruction   114

4.7 Wealthy people dressed in colours, but excessive luxury could be interpreted as a sign of a sinful personality. The young dandy with the hat and very pale complexion and the fool in gold and red are the evil ones mocking Jesus on His way to being crucified. Detail from altarpiece c. 1470, local work, Törnevalla church Sweden, now in the National Historical Museum, Stockholm   115

5.1 Bishop's crozier and bishop's ring, found in a late 13th-century grave in Gardar, Greenland. The gold ring is relatively simple for a bishop of the time, but the crozier, made of walrus ivory, probably locally on Greenland, is elaborately decorated and on a level with most other croziers of western Europe at the time. The connections to western Europe were still good in the late 13th century, but the Norse settlements in Greenland had begun to be threatened   132

5.2 King Eric Ploughpenny was invited to peace negotiations with his brother Abel in 1250, but was killed by Abel's armed men and taken out and dumped into the water of schleswig Fjord. His body was later found and transferred to the church in Ringsted, where his martyrdom was depicted in wall-paintings from the 1290s   134

5.3 Birger Jarl of Sweden († 1266), crusader, kingmaker, warrior, and diplomat. Medieval chronicles claimed that he founded Stockholm, though modern archaeologists dispute this – the town was already in existence earlier. However, Birger Jarl was strongly influential in directing Swedish perspectives towards the Baltic and in furthering new infrastructure for the rapidly increasing Swedish industry, especially within iron production

Based on his skull, a reconstruction of the face of Birger Jarl was made in the early 21st century, showing a face full of expression and emotion. It is very different from the 13th-century depiction of him from his burial place in the Varnhem monastery, which is dignified with long and carefully arranged hair and ducal crown.

Reconstruction Oscar Nilsson. Photo skull and reconstruction Medeltidsmuseet, Stockholm. Published with the permission of Medeltidsmuseet. Varnhem sculpture: Photo Axel Forssén, c 1920, Public Domain ... 138

5.4 Punishments in medieval Scandinavia could be severe, because they were firmly believed to deter others from committing crimes. Magnus Ericsson's national law-code from c. 1350 is divided into sections according to different crimes. The one on theft opens with a picture of a hanged man and two inscriptions, in Old Swedish: 'Aga bondens barn i tid, då kommer det ej hit' and the other 'Han levde utan aga, därför har han denna plåga' ('Chastise the children of peasants from early on, so they do not end here', and the other, 'He lived without discipline, therefore he ended in this trouble'.) ... 149

6.1 Saint Birgitta, pointing to a book in her hand. Next to her is the missionary Saint Sigfrid with the three heads of his nephews in a basket. Altar from 15th century, Möja church, Sweden, now in the National Historical Museum, Stockholm ... 181

7.1 The storage and trading houses of the medieval Hanseatic League along the water front at Bryggen in Bergen. The wooden houses are not medieval but reflect the architecture and the layout of the original structures relatively precisely. Excavations in the area have yielded a huge range of material illustrating many aspects of everyday life ... 188

7.2 Mills revolutionised the energy sector in medieval Scandinavia. Pictured here is an illustration from the mid-16th century with a big watermill and some windmills around Stockholm
   Olaus Magnus, *Historia de gentibus septentrionalibus*, Rome 1555. *Public domain* ... 195

7.3 Danse macabre. The skeletons have risen from their graves and dance together with the living to remind us that we shall all die. The motif became especially popular after the Black Death in the mid-14th century. Pictured here is an image by the artist Bernt Notke († 1509). The painting was originally 30 m long, but only c. 7.5 m exist today. It is in the church of Saint Nicholas in Tallinn, but Bernt Notke also worked in Scandinavia, e.g., in Århus and in Stockholm
   Art Museum of Estonia, Tallinn. Public domain ... 198

8.1 Stavanger cathedral. The older Romanesque church burned in 1272, and the new cathedral was built in Gothic style and probably finished already shortly after 1300. It was inspired by northern English church architecture; pictured here is the square choir to the east, with large windows and flanked by two towers ... 203

8.2 Håkonshallen, the Hall that King Haakon of Norway had made in the mid-13th century, as part of the Bergen fortification but also for official occasions. Its entire upper floor consists of the great banquet hall, measuring 33 × 13 m and 17 m high from the floor to the top of the ceiling. It was taken into use for the first time on 11 September 1261 for the wedding of the King's son Magnus. It

8.3 Biblia Pauperum, the late medieval collection of woodcuts of biblical scenes with short explanations, came in many different editions. It was used as a model for decorating churches everywhere in western Europe, including in Scandinavia. Pictured here is a page with Jesus rising from the grave and with the two Old Testament typological prefiguration of the resurrection: Samson removing the town gates of Gaza just as Jesus had opened the gates to the land of death, and Jonas raising out of the mouth of the whale-fish just as Jesus had risen from the grave   207

8.4 The late medieval pictorial programmes in Scandinavian churches often closely followed the international models in the Biblia Pauperum, as Jonas in the whale-fish here in Söderby-Karls church, Sweden, demonstrates. The wall paintings are from the very late 15th century; characteristic for the period is the *horror vacui*, the fear of empty spaces, meaning that all space must be filled with colour and pictures or patterns. The green and bright red were also very common towards the end of the Middle Ages   208

8.5 Stained glass windows had probably been common in Scandinavian churches, but few have survived to the present day; almost all of those that have survived are on the island of Gotland. Pictured here is the Ascension of Christ, first half of 13th century, Dalhem church   210

8.6 Crucifix using Limoges technique, 13th century. From Nävelsjö church in Sweden, today at the National Historical Museum, Stockholm   212

8.7 Pilgrim badge from the grave of Saint Thomas Becket in Canterbury. He had been killed by the men of King Henry II of England in 1171 and became a very popular saint, in Scandinavia as well as England. He was a symbol of the liberty of the Church, and gave hope that religious piety was, in the end, stronger than political violence. The badge here, with a depiction of Thomas Becket and the ampulla for consecrated water and a tiny drop of his blood, are modern replicas, as bright and fine as the medieval ones were when they were new   213

9.1 King Christian II's siege of Stockholm 1520, showing the attack and bombardment from ships, the peace agreement, and the crowning of Christian as King of Sweden. Below, festivities with tournaments and immediately afterwards the Stockholm Bloodbath are pictured. Swedish nobles and two bishops have been decapitated on the central square, and their heads have been collected in big barrels. The illustration was ordered in the 1520s by Gustav Vasa and was an early example of the new use of printing for propaganda. The picture is known today only from this copy, a copper engraving from 1676   242

10.1 Nidaros cathedral was an important pilgrimage site throughout the Middle Ages because of the grave of Saint Olaf and the many miracles that were recorded to have happened here. The saint was

	buried in a chapel at the eastern end of the cathedral, which is an exact copy, centimetre by centimetre, of the rotunda with Jesus' empty grave at the Church of the Holy Sepulchre in Jerusalem	248
10.2	Church tabernacle, 14th century, 2.17 m high, in the church of Rimbo, Sweden. The chalice for the wine and the paten for the bread were kept securely under lock and key in a tabernacle when not in use during mass, as were the wafers of the Eucharist that had been consecrated but not eaten because they were now the real and physical flesh of Christ according to the theology of transubstantiation. They needed to be secured against theft and used as amulets or in magic rituals	259
10.3	Table of consanguinity from the jurisprudent Cardinal Henry of Segusio's (also known as Hostiensis) *Summa Aurea*. The picture presents the multitude of different kinds of blood relations that impeded the contracting of a marriage. The Fourth Lateran Council in 1215 set the limit for the forbidden relations to 4th degree of consanguinity	262
11.1	Lisa von Lübeck, a reconstruction from 2004 of a ship from 1470 of the Carrack type, which replaced the Cog as the big transport ship in the Baltic and the Atlantic	271
11.2	Fish could be dried either by hanging them on stocks or by being laid out on the cliffs along the shore. Pictured here is an illustration from the mid-16th century when this procedure of conserving fish was already very old Olaus Magnus, Historia de gentibus septentrionalibus, Rome 1555. Public domain	277
11.3	Iron production required high heat and constantly working bellows, driven by water power. This technology was already well developed in Sweden in the 13th century and continued to work along the same principles for centuries. Pictured here is an illustration from the mid-16th century	281
12.1	Clock, Lund cathedral, mentioned for the first time in 1422. The big astronomical clocks were time machines, constructed to show the time, the date, the saint's name of each day, the day's position in the movable liturgical year of the church, lunar phases, sunrise and sunset, and the position of the day within the zodiac system, for hundreds of years. It struck a bell four times or at least once per hour, and some clocks had small figures that came out when the bell was struck, playing music or blowing trumpets and then disappearing inside the clock again. The four figures in the corner of the upper clock are famous astronomers, one from antiquity, one medieval Spanish king, and two Muslims. The harsh anti-Islamic polemics of medieval Christians did not prevent them from using the superior science of Muslim researchers, also in Scandinavia. The clock was completely restored in 1923 and can now show information for every day until 2123	287
12.2	The Danish Doctor Harpestreng wrote in the mid-13th century about medicine and cooking, which for him were closely connected.	

On this page, he explains how to treat green cabbage (*Kaal*) with water or wine; it can then be used to heal infected wounds ('green wounds') and to treat cancer. It is an effective pain killer, heals bad eyes, assists digestion, and reduces swollen milt. It is even effective against hair loss and becoming bald

MS NKS 66 oktav, p. 45, Royal Library Copenhagen. Public domain   293

12.3 *Ars moriendi*, the Art of Dying. It was translated into Swedish in 1514 with the subtitle, 'How you can learn to die in a way to secure the blessedness of the soul'

This file is licensed under the Creative Commons Attribution-Share Alike 4.0 International license   296

Introduction

The northern people have stimulated the interest and imaginations of historians for a long time, beginning with the Byzantine historian Jordanes. He wrote around 550 that Scandinavia – *Scandza* – was the hive of peoples, from which the Goths and others, leaving their cold homes, swarmed like bees throughout all Europe, fighting, conquering, and carving out for themselves new kingdoms. It is not clear what Jordanes exactly meant by *Scandza* in terms of geographic scope, since he had no personal knowledge of the Nordic territories.

The lands and the peoples of the north became more widely known in the Middle Ages, and later medieval authors were able of describing Scandinavia and Scandinavians with increasing detail: the *vita* of the missionary Ansgar, from c. 870, mentioned his travels to Denmark and Sweden and the founding of churches, but not much else. Adam of Bremen writing in the early 1070s also knew of Iceland in the Northern Atlantic, Greenland far away in the west, and even Finland or Sápmi, but to him the latter areas were clearly semi-mythical.

From the 12th century onwards, the Scandinavians began to write their own history. The sagas contain detailed stories about the events in Scandinavia, and c. 1200 the Danish historian Saxo Grammaticus wrote his *Gesta Danorum*, in which he narrates the Danes' medieval history. Numerous medieval and early modern authors have then followed this tradition and written about Scandinavia and its history.

Scandinavian medieval history is still relevant and interesting to students and scholars, and the amount of modern research literature on different aspects of medieval Scandinavia is enormous. There are thousands of research articles and hundreds of monographs and anthologies, both bigger and smaller, written in local languages as well as English, German, French, and so on. This book is one in the continuum. It is intended as a textbook for graduate students and everybody interested in the history of Scandinavia in the Middle Ages, and it aims to give readers a comprehensive overview.

In this book, Scandinavia is understood in a very broad sense. It is not only about the medieval history of the three kingdoms in the Scandinavian Peninsula, Denmark, Norway, and Sweden, but it has also tried to include the eastern parts of the Scandinavian kingdoms around the Baltic, Finland, and northern Estonia, and in west Iceland, Greenland, and the islands in the North Atlantic. The northern parts of Scandinavia inhabited by the Sámi, who continued to live according to their own culture but had many contacts with the other Scandinavians, have also been included in this book.

The title of the book, *Between Two Oceans*, stresses Scandinavia's strong dependence on the sea. In strict geographical terms, Scandinavia is placed around, not

DOI: 10.4324/9781003095514-1

between, the Atlantic Ocean and the Baltic Sea. Nevertheless, these two vast waters provided access to different natural resources and to very different neighbouring cultures. Scandinavia was formed in the meeting of these two oceans.

Medieval Scandinavia did not emerge suddenly from nothing. It developed in continuation from earlier history and never in isolation from, but in close contact with, the rest of Europe. We could have begun this book with strong connections to the Roman Empire in the first Christian centuries. We could have begun it with the great climatic catastrophe in 536, when the sun was covered for years leading to mass death and emigration and new beginnings for societies, religions, and languages, also in Scandinavia.

We have, however, decided to begin around 900. It is only really then that a remarkable and dynamic expansion took place everywhere in Western Europe, including in Scandinavia. Populations began to grow much faster, new land was put under plough, and new villages were founded across the region. This expansion necessitated new forms of organisation and cooperation, within local communities as well as over larger entities. The idea of kingdoms began taking form during this time, with the introduction of Christianity providing further influence and impetus. This is where we begin our history of Scandinavia in earnest, although we do touch briefly upon earlier events if they are necessary for understanding what happened during the period covered here.

We have chosen to divide the book into three chronological sections wherein we cover the political, ecclesiastical, economic, and cultural development of each period in separate chapters. The first section considers the period of state formation and Christianisation from c. 900 to c. 1200; the second that of the political, ecclesiastical, and economic consolidation of c. 1200–c. 1400; and the last section presents the period from c. 1400 until the dissolution of the Kalmar Union and the international Catholic Church, which was replaced by national Lutheran churches.

All periodisation in history is artificial and can be criticised, and particular choices often reveal more about the historian than about the historical past. We too needed to make our choices and decided upon a structure simply to make the narrative readable, but also to underline that the Middle Ages were a changing and dynamic period in history. Traditional historiography has often operated with the idea of a static Middle Ages where things did not change, or did so only very slowly. Instead, we want to point to decisive turning points in Scandinavian history: around 1200, when a technological and military revolution took place and a new religious climate emerged within the church; and around 1400, when an entirely new political situation arose with all Scandinavia united in the Kalmar Union, and new economic and mental orientations were developed as the region recovered from the great pandemic and mass death of the mid-14th century.

Nevertheless, some medieval phenomena were still relevant to all three periods and show some fundamental structures that changed little. We have chosen not to repeat them in all three sections but to consider them in the chronological section containing their most important developments. For example, town life and urbanisation are included in the second section because in this period the growth of urbanisation in Scandinavia was at its strongest and we discuss the everyday life of Christians in the last section because most of the relevant sources are from that period. It has not been possible to completely avoid factual repetition, and in many places, we have done so intentionally to supply essential information to those only reading certain chapters of this book.

Two persons cannot master all aspects of the Middle Ages or be expert on all the regional variations. This book stands upon the shoulders of numerous other scholars: on their research and writings, and on discussions with them over many years. The manuscript has been read and commented upon by Helle Vogt (Copenhagen), Christian Lovén (Stockholm), and Leidulf Melve (Bergen). We are grateful for their many suggestions and corrections which have made this book without doubt much better, but we alone are responsible for all mistakes remaining. We have also drawn extensively on friends and family for helping with private pictures, namely Pia Bengtsson Melin, Tina Rodhe, Mona Bager Jensen, Anna-Stina Hägglund, and Niilo Jauhola. In addition, several institutions have kindly provided us with pictures of items from their collections. Last, but not least, we would like also to thank warmly Jussi Kinnunen for all the maps.

Part I
900–1200
Formation

1 Coming of the Kingdoms

The Kingdoms and Conversion

Viking Age Scandinavia consisted of several power centres with rulers who fought or supported each other in rapidly shifting alliances. They were part of a huge network spanning the northern hemisphere from England and the Atlantic isles, and across the Baltic, all the way to Novgorod, Kiev, and Byzantium. There were earlier attempts at unification, but it was only in the 10th and 11th centuries that regions in Denmark, Norway, and Sweden became gathered under single rulers, and the first contours of the three kingdoms became visible. It was a slow and complicated process requiring the creation of new power structures and royal administrations, spurring a continuum of conflicts in the long 12th century, traditionally called 'civil wars'. The result of this process was a clearer concept of a kingdom as a more distinct centre for power compared to that of any magnate. The rulers were no longer first among equals, but kings elevated above all others. In all countries, kings strived to ensure their heirs' right to the throne, often in brutal competition with magnates.

Scandinavian historians have been mesmerised by the State. When did it arrive? How did it develop? State formation has been an important framework for interpreting medieval history – and indeed later periods. This is however a difficult task because there is no clear-cut understanding of what 'the State' is, what state formation actually means and what kinds of stages it entailed. One of the explanatory frameworks used by historians defines four different periods of state formation: in pre-state societies (c. 400–950), territorial states (c. 950–1200), administrative states (c. 1200–1450), and dynastic states (c. 1450–1650). Although this division is made for European societies in general, it fits with some moderation also Scandinavian state formation.

Christianity came to Scandinavia both by the persuasive words of humble preachers, and by the sword of mighty rulers. In either case, the Christian faith talked of the kingdom of heaven, but also of one on earth. Christianity offered an ideology and world view that suited a king, and this religion of the book could not exist without education and well-ordered procedures, the very first elements in creating an administration and an embryonic state. The political history of medieval Scandinavia is therefore closely connected to the conversion of rulers and peoples, while the conversion of hearts and minds of individuals may have followed later.

Christianisation was not a linear and irreversible process. It was the result of negotiations and cultural choices among political groups that cannot be fully traced

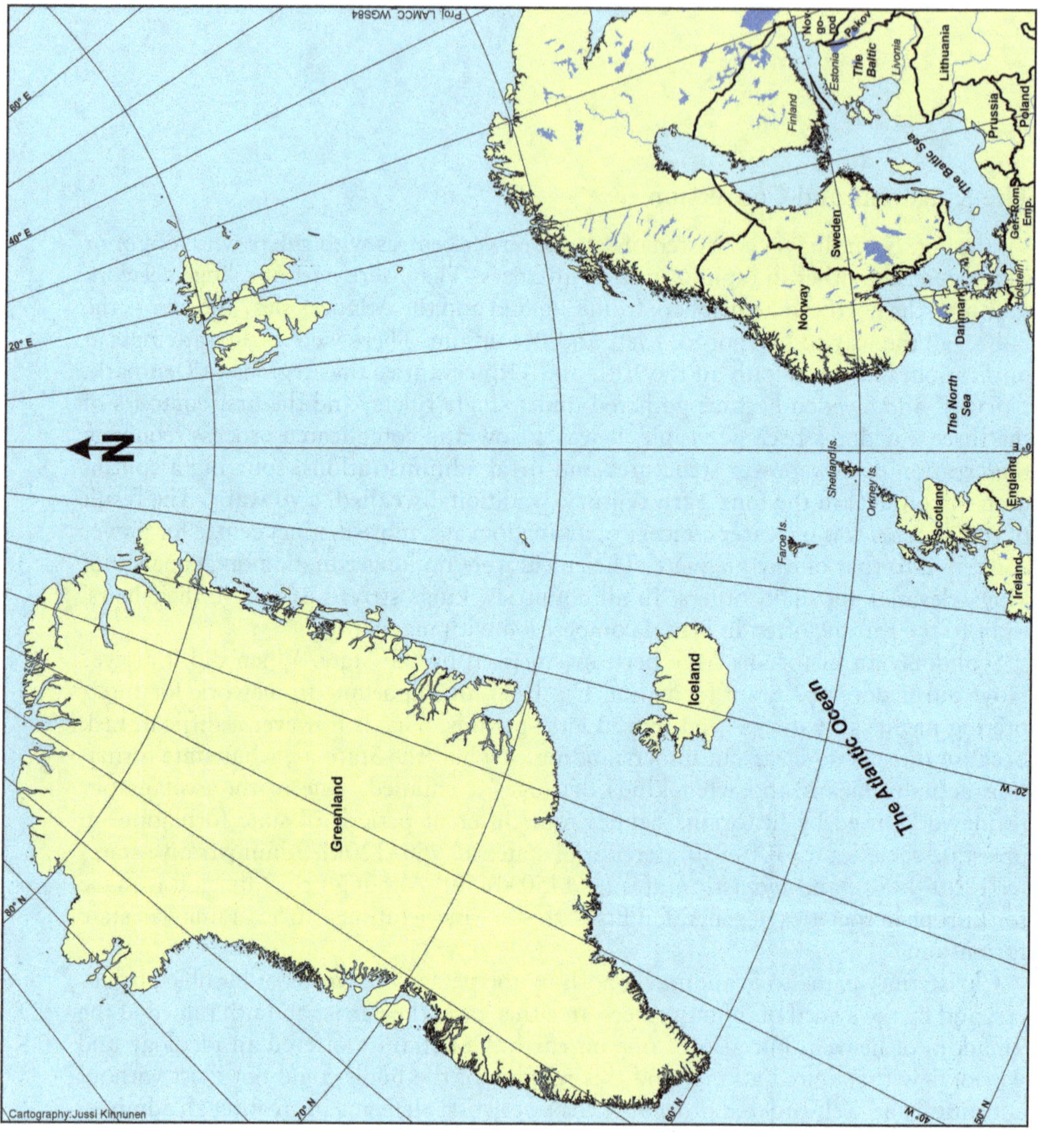

8 *900–1200: Formation*

Map 1 Scandinavia in the Middle Ages.
Map © Jussi Kinnunen, 2022.

due to the few sources left from this early period. Rulers adopted the Christian faith probably for a number of different reasons, and sometimes their successors considered it more profitable to choose another strategy, gaining followers by propagating the old religion. Changing one's religion according to political necessity was not uncommon.

Due to the importance of Christianity for Scandinavian state formation, historians have tried to determine a date, a specific historical moment, for the conversion of the Scandinavian peoples. For Denmark the year 965 has been proposed, when according to the Saxon chronicler Widukind from Corvey King Harald accepted baptism, or the 980s, when he had the large Jelling rune stone raised with the proud inscription that he had 'won for himself all Denmark and Norway and made the Danes Christians'. Finding a specific year for conversion has been less straightforward in Norway and Sweden. In Norway, on the island of Kuli off the coast not far away from Trondheim,

Illustration 1.1 The Kuli-stone, raised when Christianity had been 12 winters in Norway. Unfortunately, the stone is undated. Now in the Scientific Museum in Trondheim.

Photo Arne Kvitrud 2011. This file is licensed under the Creative Commons Attribution-Share Alike 3.0.

a runestone was found in 1810 with an inscription reading that Tore and Halvard raised the stone in commemoration of somebody with a now-unreadable name and that *Twelf vintr hafði kristendómr um rétt i Nóregi* – 'Twelve winters Christianity had secured justice in Norway'. Unfortunately, the stone is not dated and therefore it is not possible to determine from which year these 12 should be counted. Arguing from very different criteria, modern historians have suggested dating the Kuli-stone from the 10th to the early 11th century. It is possible that it was raised during the military missionising of King Olaf (r. 1015–1028), and if so in the 1030s. Correspondingly, on the Island of Frösön in Sweden, there is a runestone raised c. 1030–1050 claiming that Östman had made Christians of the Jämtländers. Nothing is known of Östman's identity, actual role or anything else. In Iceland, according to written evidence, the inhabitants accepted Christianity in the year 1000 by common decision at the central assembly. These sources attest to the importance of conversion in the formation of the power structure of the Scandinavian countries, regardless of the problems with dating the runestones precisely.

In the Viking Age, Denmark, Norway, and Sweden existed as geographical areas but not as kingdoms united under one single ruler. The idea of such a united political entity is a construct, made already by historians writing in the Middle Ages, mainly in the 13th century. Before c. 1000, Scandinavia was composed of a large number of smaller power centres under the tighter or looser control of local magnates. In sources from England or the European continent, some of these were called 'king of the Danes' or 'king of the Norwegians', but only seldom was their power recognised by everybody home in Scandinavia. They were not kings in the proper sense of the word, although conversion to the Christian faith helped them in the process of becoming so in the period from c. 1000 to c. 1200.

Denmark: Conquest and Christianisation – Swift or Slow?

The Christianisation of Denmark was an important step towards the unification, under one king, of areas that earlier had possessed some degree of independence. There had been several local power centres in Denmark with large chieftains' halls, some of which had existed for centuries, but archaeologists can show that many were destroyed or abandoned around the year 1000. Place names also indicate the existence of an older structure by which the geographical area of Denmark was divided into a number of 'lands'. To the west lay northern and southern Jutland, divided by the small *Kongeåen*, 'The King's Stream'. The main island is Zealand, while Lolland to the south is much smaller, and Halland is one of the territories to the east of Øresund which today forms the border between Denmark and Sweden. These names continued to be used in the Middle Ages – and still are today – for different provinces in Denmark, many with their own provincial laws and local court centres. Scania, Halland, and Blekinge belonged to the medieval kingdom of Denmark, becoming part of Sweden only in 1658. The southern part of Norway, Viken and Vestfold, was conquered by Harald Bluetooth and may actually have belonged to Danish rulers much earlier but became part of the Norwegian kingdom in the early 11th century. Although the borders between the three Scandinavian kingdoms originate in the early Middle Ages, they were not fixed but often disputed.

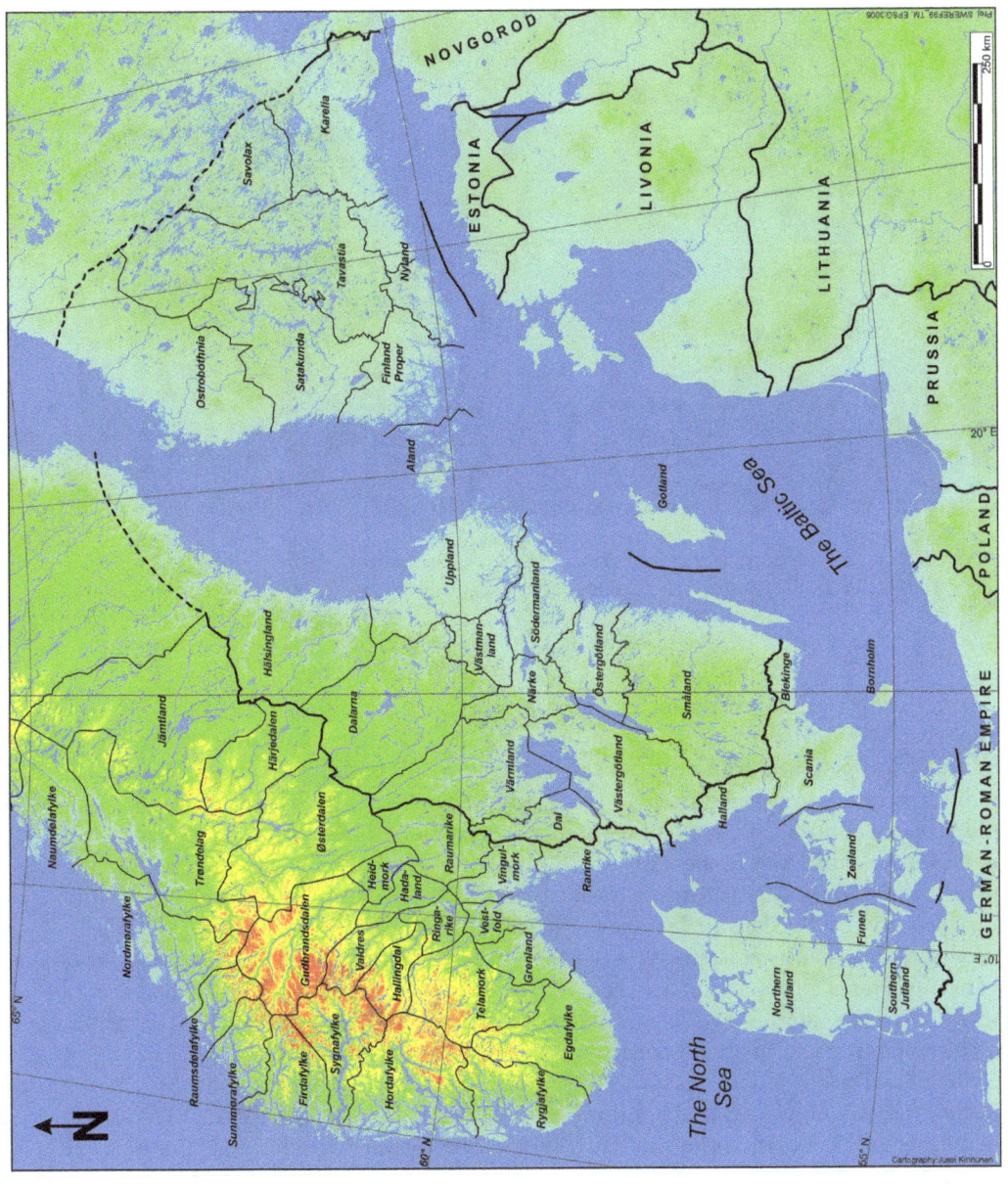

Map 2 The medieval provinces of Scandinavia.
Map © Jussi Kinnunen, 2022.

Illustration 1.2 Trelleborg, the type of Viking fortress from around 970.
Photo Thue C. Leibrandt, 2008. This file is licensed under the Creative Commons Attribution-Share Alike 3.0.

Some Danish rulers were already Christians in the 9th century. King Harald Klak, competing with others for power, found a strong ally in the German Emperor Lothar I, became his vassal, and was baptised at Ingelheim in 826 with the Emperor himself as godfather. Harald returned to Denmark with precious gifts, Christian missionaries, and military contingents. He had little success as a ruler, however. Forced into exile, he was installed by the Emperor as duke of a buffer zone north of the River Elbe to protect the Empire against attacks from other Danes. Nevertheless, some Christian presence was established in Denmark. A church was erected around 855 in Ribe, a town on the south-western coast of Denmark. Some of Harald Klak's successors were Christians, although most were not. Christianity only became established more firmly 150 years later under Harald Bluetooth, in the last decades of the 10th century, as the result of a well-planned conquest.

The most striking expression of King Harald's military machine is the so-called *Trelleborgs*: strongly fortified military caserns, perfectly circular, with four gates located precisely north-south and east-west – two in northern Jutland, one in the centre of the island of Funen, and two on Zealand in the west and east. In addition, there may have been a Trelleborg in Scania, and maybe one in southern Norway. Three of the Danish Trelleborgs are 120 m in diameter, one is 240 m, and one 136 m. Inside the circular walls, there were built large, totally regular houses in square formation. The Trelleborgs were erected in a very short time around 980, and with brutal efficiency. Terrain was levelled, local villages destroyed, the local population including children killed and dumped into their own wells, and the fort built on top of it all. The Trelleborgs were in use for a very short period, probably a maximum of 20 years. Their function has been very much debated, but the best explanation is that they were built as part of Harald's conquest and forced Christianisation of Denmark. It would also explain why no Trelleborg has been found in southern Jutland. Harald was already in command there, so no military fortifications were needed.

King Harald established a Danish royal power centre in Jelling in the southern parts of Jutland in the late 10th century. There, he totally re-organised the burial complex of his father, King Gorm the Old, who had been buried according to pagan rites in one of the largest burial mounds in Denmark, 8 m high. The mound was located exactly in the middle of a 356 m long ship-setting – a row of very big stones arranged in the shape of a big ship. Harald had another mound built at the southern end of the ship-setting, a new church erected in the middle between the two mounds, and the complex was surrounded by a palisade of thousands of oak-planks, all in all spanning 1,440 m and enclosing an area of 12.5 hectares. Access to Jelling was facilitated with new infrastructure, including the impressive bridge over the wetlands at Ravninge, c. 760 m long and 5 m broad, constructed with more than 1,000 oak poles, each c. 5 m tall. The bridge was built in 980, at the same time as the Trelleborgs. It was intended to impress visitors but also for moving Harald's military troops around very rapidly.

In a central position in the Jelling monument is a rune stone raised by King Harald to mark his importance. The stone is huge, and the Danish medieval historian Saxo claimed in the 12th century that installing the stone had been so difficult and required so much forced labour that the Danish people had rebelled against Harald. The stone not only commemorates Harald but also marks the conversion of the Danes. On one side is depicted the crucified Christ, fully dressed as was the tradition in northern Italian monumental crosses of the time and looking proudly and directly towards the viewer: not the suffering Christ but the king and conqueror, as the Germanic peoples of the period preferred to depict him. The cross is extended into an elaborate pattern of leaves: into the tree of life. On the other side of the stone is a lion – perhaps the Lion of Judah from the Old Testament, symbol of kings, of truth, and of Christianity – fighting against the snake, standing for evil and paganism. On the third side of the stone is the inscription that in modern times has been called Denmark's 'Birth certificate': 'Harald ordered these runes to be made in commemoration of Gorm, his father, and Thyra, his mother, the Harald who won for himself all Denmark and Norway and made the Danes Christians'. It is written in four horizontal lines, clearly resembling the parchment page of a Bible manuscript and not in the tradition of runic inscriptions with vertical lines.

Although Harald claimed the honour of converting the Danes, the process that had led to Danish rulers being firmly and undisputedly members of the Christian international community had been slow. In a short and decisive period around 980, however, King Harald Bluetooth's swift conquest of all Denmark made the process irreversible. Afterwards, paganism was no longer any realistic political alternative, although Harald's son Sweyn Forkbeard for a very short while attempted to rely on pagan allies.

Illustration 1.3 Jelling Rune Stone, probably from the 980s, on which King Harald Bluetooth claims to have conquered all Denmark and Norway and made the Danes Christian. Pictured here is a modern copy from the Danish National Museum with a reconstruction of the original painting.

Photo: The National Museum of Denmark, 2013. This file is licensed under the Creative Commons Attribution-Share Alike 2.0 Generic. Black background removed.

The North Sea Empire

After Harald Bluetooth had united Denmark, his successors began to expand the country towards the west. The expansion began during the rule of Harald's son, Sweyn Forkbeard, who had rebelled against his father in circumstances not clear from the meagre sources and became the new ruler. In the early 990s, Sweyn began a series of annual, large-scale military expeditions against England, either with himself as a sole leader or in cooperation with the Norwegian rulers. The result was immense income from the tribute that English kings paid each year to make the invaders return home, but also fierce resistance. In 1002, King Æthelred the Unready of England (r. 978–1016) tried to solve the problem by a large-scale ethnic cleansing of all Danes in England, newcomers as well as those who had lived there for generations. Sweyn intensified the military pressure on England, and in 1013, he equipped a very large fleet in which each commander's ship was marked with golden emblems showing lions, birds, roaring dragons breathing fire, and mad bulls. England was conquered, but Sweyn died only two months later and left his kingdoms on both sides of the North Sea to his sons, Harald (r. 1014–1018?) and Canute the Great (r. 1019–1035).

Canute secured his control over England and also after 1018 over Denmark. This North Sea empire's broad political and economic basis, embracing England, Norway, and Denmark, significantly enhanced Canute's royal authority. He issued also coins in Scandinavia with an English inspiration, minted by masters from England. These were not intended for common use but for certain high-level economic transactions and tributes and also as propaganda for Canute's kingship. Such ideological expressions of power were typical of Canute's rule. He began to use the title of emperor, either the Latin *imperator* or the Byzantine *basileus*. To stress the divine sanctioning of his rulership, his court poets composed laudatory songs comparing Canute to the Byzantine emperor or even to God.

After Canute's death in 1035, England and Denmark were divided between two warring rulers and their successors. In 1066, the Norwegian King Harald Hardrada attempted to conquer England but fell in the Battle of Stamford Bridge, and three weeks later the whole of England was taken by William the Conqueror of Normandy. Danish rule over England was definitively over although at the time no one could certainly know that. The Danes staked a claim to England later in the 11th century and on several more occasions until at least the mid-14th century.

In 1047, Canute's sister's son Sweyn Estridsen became king in Denmark after living in Sweden and siding with one pretender to the Norwegian throne against another – an illustration of how interwoven the Scandinavian dynasties were in the Middle Ages. Although other medieval rulers used a patronym, Sweyn Estridsen was called after his mother Estrid and not after his father Ulf, because that stressed his connection to royal blood. It was not totally uncommon in the early medieval period to take one's name from the mother if she was of a higher social status than the father.

Sweyn re-organised the ecclesiastical structure in Denmark with a division of the country into dioceses, and he continued Canute's display of proud royal ideology and the connection to the Holy See. On large heavy silver coins that Sweyn issued in 1047, he was depicted as an emperor receiving the banner of victory from an angel. It was actually a direct copy of a gold coin issued by the Byzantine emperor some five years earlier, so Sweyn was posing as an emperor. He also became a vassal of Saint Peter, which meant that not only he had taken a special oath to support and protect the pope but also that he had become a member of a western European network of important rulers who, too, were papal vassals.

Sweyn was unusually fond of women, even for a Dane (as the medieval chronicler Adam of Bremen put it), which was mentioned and lamented by contemporary ecclesiastical authors. He had numerous sons, all apparently born out of wedlock. After his death in 1076, five of his sons succeeded him as king over the following almost 60 years. One of Sweyn's sons was Canute IV, who attempted to raise an army to reconquer England a couple of times without success, and who was killed during a rebellion of magnates on 10 July 1086. He had tried to collect the royal fleet in northern

Illustration 1.4 Silver coin issued by King Sweyn Estridsen in 1047, presenting him as an emperor and receiving the banner of victory from an angel. It is a direct copy of a coin issued by the Byzantine emperor.
Photo Rasmus Holst Nielsen 2020, The National Museum of Denmark. Reproduced with permission.

Denmark to sail out for England, but something went awry and he was chased all the way down the peninsula of Jutland and over Funen to Odense. He sought refuge in the Church of Saint Alban but his persecutors entered and killed him while he was praying in front of the altar. Canute was buried in Odense, and miracles were soon reported from his grave. Canute was the first royal saint in Europe to be recognised by the pope. A large new cathedral began to be built over his grave, and he became a very important legitimatisation for the royal dynasty during the Middle Ages, as well as the national patron saint of Denmark. Canute was married to Adele of Flanders and through her was connected to a large circle of papal vassals. Canute's son was christened Charles, a name unknown in Danish royal families but which stressed the connection through Adele back to the iconic Emperor Charlemagne († 814). In 1119, Charles became count of Flanders and was even offered the throne of the crusader kingdom of Jerusalem in 1123, which he renounced.

Another of Sweyn's sons was Eric Ejegod. He began to look eastwards in his expansion policy, fighting the pagan Wends in the Baltic. He made also two journeys to the pope for political as well as religious reasons, during which he succeeded in having Pope Paschal II recognise his half-brother Canute IV as saint and canonise him in 1100. Eric Ejegod also became the first European king – as far as we know – to set out on an expedition to Jerusalem after the crusaders had conquered the city in 1099. Eric never reached Jerusalem because he died on his way in 1103 in Cyprus, and was buried there, but his Queen Bodil did. She died in Jerusalem and was buried on the Mount of Olives, in the Church of the Holy Virgin Mary.

The connection to England was ended, and the future expansion from Denmark tended more towards the east via the Baltic Sea than the west over the North Sea. Connections to Germany became stronger. There were rivalries between the many sons of Sweyn but no large-scale armed conflicts. That changed after 1131 when different claimants to the royal title raised large armies against each other, beginning a 25-year civil war.

Norway: The Long Land Unified by Christianity

Norway was divided into more or less autonomous regions, often with a common seat of justice (*thing*) and in principle with one local ruler, although the situation was in practice much more volatile. To judge from place names, there may have been perhaps 15 important power centres along the coast, of which several merged during the 9th century. As in Denmark, some were called *land* – Hordaland, Rogaland, Hålogaland, some *riki* meaning realm or country, as in Ringeriki, and others *lag* meaning an area with the same law and juridical system, such as Trøndelag. Some of these areas lay on the coast and communication between them was relatively easy by ship; others lay inland and further to the east and were more difficult to access.

Norwegian contacts with Christian areas probably stretched back to late antiquity and include connections to southern Europe. The connections across the North Sea to Christian England and Ireland, however, were well established and regular from an early period, as was the relationship with Byzantium and its imperial guard. These connections may explain why, to judge from graves, there seem to have been small Christian communities in Norway from a very early period, perhaps already from the 9th century.

The first Christian king of Norway, Haakon the Good († c. 960) was raised in England at the court of King Adalstein, where he established important political connections with western Europe in general and received baptism. He returned to Norway around 935 with clerics from England and began building churches and tried to establish himself as king after his father, Harald Fairhair. More details of Haakon are known only from sagas written down almost 300 years after his death. They recount that King Haakon the Good was compelled to negotiate with strong regional rulers and participate in their ritual beer drinking and sacrificial eating of horse meat, where he allegedly tried in secret to make the sign of the cross over the cups before emptying them. Some sources also claim that he actually became a practising pagan. It is impossible to know for certain whether or not this is true, but it fits with the general pattern of Scandinavia's Christianisation as a long and hesitant process. There are several similar examples from Scandinavia and the areas around the Baltic of rulers who converted to Christianity and a little later returned to paganism. Some did it repeatedly. It may have taken place due to personal religious conviction, but it also political reasons.

Christianity was established first in the southern and western parts of Norway, while the north and east had much stronger pagan societies. One of the important regions was Trøndelagen in the middle of Norway, its centre being where the town of Nidaros (later: Trondheim) was founded, but stretching far to the north. The earls of Lade ruled in Trøndelagen, playing an important role in the 10th century as defenders of paganism against the new Christian cult. From time to time they extended their rule to larger parts of Norway, sometimes in alliance with rulers from Denmark. Haakon Sigurdsson († 995) succeeded to the Earldom of Lade around 962 and made an alliance with King Harald Bluetooth of Denmark which secured him the power, throughout all Norway, to refuse tribute and military assistance to the Danish king.

Earl Haakon was king in all except name. In 983, Harald Bluetooth led an army against the German emperor and burned down Hamburg, with the assistance of Earl Haakon, albeit also with Slavic troops. According to later sources, King Harald demanded that Haakon convert to Christianity and had him baptised, which Haakon strongly resented. Back in Norway, he defeated Harald's army at the Battle of Hjørungavåg (in the 980s), and Norway was divided again into a southern part under Danish rule, with a centre in Viken around present-day Oslo, and a northern part controlled by the earls of Lade with a centre in Trøndelagen.

Earl Haakon was killed by the locals in Trøndelagen, apparently for his tough governance and other political reasons, although other sources indicate that it may also have been because of his great fondness for women, especially other men's wives. His family and sons were forced into exile elsewhere in Scandinavia or in England. After Haakon's death in 995, Olaf Tryggvason was also elected king in Trøndelagen and now controlled all of Norway. He had had a military career in England, where he had been baptised and expressed his clear aim of ruling over Norway in its entirety, all of whose inhabitants he would introduce to Christianity, by any means, including it would seem by simply forbidding paganism. Olaf Tryggvason's short rule was ended after he lost a naval battle at Svold, probably in the year 1000, probably in Øresund, to a coalition of the kings of Denmark and of Sweden, and the new Earl of Lade. When Olaf realised that there was no longer a chance of victory, he took his treasure chest under his arm and jumped into the water where he drowned, according to later sources. Olaf Tryggvason had provoked powerful pagan movements, not least in Trøndelagen, and disturbed the mutual toleration whereby Christians and pagans had to an extent been living peacefully together. His men attacked pagan temples and razed them to the ground. He had churches built and brought missionaries to Norway, issued coins with cross motifs like other Christian rulers in western Europe, and laid the foundation for the ensuing Christianisation under Olaf Haraldsson, who was to become Saint Olaf – *rex perpetuus Norvegiae*, 'the everlasting king of Norway'. Without Olaf Tryggvason's preparatory work, it would have been much harder for Olaf Haraldsson to succeed in introducing Christianity.

Saint Olaf

Olaf Haraldsson's aim was to unite Norway, at least according to the sagas and sources written down at least 200 years after Olaf's lifetime. These sources have a clear tendency to romanticise the past by making missionary kings more focused on and devoted to Christianity than they may actually have been. Many of these sources were also composed in troubled times when several factions were fighting each other in Norway, and the authors may have sought comfort in knowing that the many wars of the conversion period came to a good end and that the righteous and Christian ruler succeeded. While the sagas may contain some correct information that had been transmitted orally for generations, they should nevertheless be used with caution.

Olaf was from Vestfold in southern Norway, embarking on a successful international military career around the year 1000. He fought in England for the English king, and he fought against the English king together with the king of Denmark. In 1012, he and the Danish King Sweyn Forkbeard promised not to attack England in return for a tribute of 17,900 kg of silver – an enormous sum that according to modern economic historians could have bought Olaf 225,000 cows back in Norway. Olaf spent 1013–1014 in Rouen in Normandy, whose duke had Scandinavian ancestry. He was baptised in Rouen and returned to Norway in 1015, apparently firmly set on becoming king and introducing Christianity. He was accepted as ruler in one local district after the other, and because of his family background, with relatives in many places in Norway, he could attract followers not only in its western parts, and along the coast all the way to Hålogaland far north of Trøndelagen, but also in the east. The Earl of Lade lost a battle against Olaf in 1016 after which Trøndelagen's inhabitants hailed Olaf as king.

Olaf was the first king to aim at stricter control over his lands. For the earlier Norwegian kings, ruling a territory had meant receiving tributes and access to military forces, but they lacked a firm grip upon the land and inhabitants. To this end, Olaf used two main instruments. One was local administration. He brought in his own people to do the practical work, for they were dependent on him and therefore much more loyal than the old aristocratic families. It was a double-edged sword, however, for it was a policy that stirred discontent and opposition to him amongst the old local chieftains. Olaf's second instrument was the Christian Church with its missionary bishops and priests, possessing few or no local connections and totally reliant on his protection. Moreover, the Christian Church had a hierarchical structure which covered and connected the entire kingdom, in contrast to the older paganism with its local cult sites.

King Olaf forbade paganism and declared Christianity as the only permitted religion. Just like his predecessor, Olaf seems to have propagated his faith with harsh means and large-scale confiscation of opponents' property: of the 16 known large estates belonging to local pagan rulers, 15 had become royal property by the later Middle Ages. This policy was certain to provoke reaction, and in 1026–1027 troops gathered from the southern part of Norway and from Trøndelagen. Olaf had to flee from Norway in 1028, seeking refuge with his brother-in-law, Jaroslav of Kiev. Two years later, after King Canute's regent in Norway drowned on his way back from England, Olaf seized the opportunity and returned with a group of followers, marched through Sweden over the mountains, and met a Norwegian army at Stiklestad, some 100 km inland upon the Trondheim Fjord. Olaf was killed in the battle on 29 July 1030, struck by three blows from a spear, an axe, and a sword.

The result of the Battle at Stiklestad is in fact surprising. It became the single most decisive event in securing the Christianisation of Norway, although it was fought against Olaf and his forced conversion, and led by several pagan local chieftains. A year after Olaf's death, his tomb was opened, his body was found fine and uncorrupted, and his hair and nails to have grown. He had fresh red cheeks, and a sweet odour filled the air – exactly in the same way as in the opening of any saint's grave. Miracles began to happen. Olaf's body was transferred to the church of Saint Clement in Nidaros. Olaf became a saint, promoted by the Church through liturgy and meticulous registering of miracles. Soon began the construction of a large new stone church around the shrine of Olaf, so that it had the space to receive all the pilgrims who began to come to visit the place and pray.

Olaf's illegitimate young son, Magnus, was fetched from Kiev by leading Norwegians and chosen as king because of his father's holiness – perhaps also to get rid of King Canute's son and regent in Norway, Sweyn, who was 'a child in age, and a child in mind' as the historian Snorri wrote much later; and even more, to get rid of Sweyn's mother, Alfiva, an unpleasantly effective administrator and tax collector. The two

Illustration 1.5 Saint Olaf with his typical attributes: the long Nordic axe in his hand and the defeated dragon under his feet. Very often it is crowned, as here, and most likely symbolises the pagan kings of Norway, forced into adopting Christianity. Sculpture in the altar piece in Saint Mary's Church, Bergen, late 15th century.

Photo © Niilo Jauhola, 2022.

had to leave Norway in 1035, and Magnus ruled all his father had had without question of it being a Christian kingdom. In 1042, Magnus also became king of Denmark; the two kingdoms were united under one ruler but not for long.

Magnus continued the missionary work, but in the south. He fought the pagans around the River Oder, the present-day border between Germany and Poland, and the pagan Wends in the border area between Denmark and northern Germany. Before a battle at Lyrskov Moor in southern Jutland in 1043, he saw his father in a dream promising him victory, and on the day of the battle, the Christian army heard the sound of the big church bell in Nidaros where Olaf was buried. Thus strengthened and comforted, Magnus threw away his armour and fought in a bare shirt, swinging his father's large Nordic battle axe *Hel*, and won a decisive victory. At the end of the day, 15,000 pagans lay dead upon the swampy moor – all this according to Adam of Bremen, writing around 1070. Magnus' missionary enthusiasm and symbolic use of his saintly father can also be confirmed from other sources. He began issuing coins showing Jerusalem and Saint Olaf with his saintly attribute, the big battle axe. Magnus also founded churches dedicated to Olaf in the religious border areas, including two on the island of Falster which in the 1040s probably still had a mixed pagan-Christian population.

In Norway, Magnus was suddenly confronted with demands from a powerful person, Saint Olaf's half-brother Harald Hardrada, Harald the Hard Ruler. He had fought together with Olaf at Stiklestad but had survived and escaped via Sweden to Constantinople, where he had served the Byzantine emperor in the Nordic elite guard, the Varangian Guard. Harald had been to Jerusalem, had fought for the emperor on Sicily, and had defended the northern part of the empire against peoples from the steppes, gaining the respectful Byzantine appellation *Burner of the Bulgars*. He returned to Norway around 1045 with immense riches and in 1046 agreed with Magnus that they would rule Norway together. Magnus may not have been happy with this solution but he avoided an open war, and when he died in 1047 without heirs, Harald became the sole ruler.

Harald Hardrada completed the unification of Norway begun more than a hundred years earlier. He had the local magnates killed, or pacified in other ways, not least in the problematic Trøndelagen whose tradition of independence and rebellion was no longer a problem after Harald's intervention. Harald also finally subdued the eastern part of Norway: the interior which was much harder to access and control than the lands along the coast, accessible by ships. During a series of military campaigns involving burning and confiscation of property, the eastern parts of Norway also fell under the control of the king. Harald fell in 1066 at the Battle of Stamford Bridge some 8 km east of York, in the last Scandinavian attempt to conquer England. After Harald's death, his descendants ruled in a period that was relatively peaceful compared to the preceding time of conversion, and to the long period of civil wars that began in 1130.

Sweden: The Kingdoms of the Goths and of the Sveas

In the 10th century, Sweden also was composed of several entities possessing some degree of local jurisdiction and rule. The three main regional entities were Östergötland and Västergötland, the two lands of the Goths east and west of the large Lake Vättern, and Svealand with its long Lake Mälaren leading out to the Baltic Sea at present-day Stockholm. To the north of Svealand stretched the enormous and thinly populated areas containing Hälsingland, Ångermanland, Jämtland, and places that in the later Middle Ages together became known as Norrland. Each of these regions was subdivided into several minor units, many also called -*land*, such as Västmanland and Södermanland that were parts of Svealand.

Unlike in Denmark and Norway, Christianisation played a different role in Swedish state formation and the development of royal power. There had been a Christian mission in the two Götalands and Svealand since the 9th century, but due to the lack of a strong central power, a centrally imposed top-down conversion in aid of state formation did not take place contemporaneously. Nonetheless, kings who had converted to Christianity or were sympathetic towards the new religion had an important role in the formation of the Swedish kingdom. According to Archbishop Rimbert of Bremen († 888), a Swedish delegation in 829 actually asked the Frankish Emperor Louis the Pious to send missionaries to Sweden because there were so many Christians there. He did, and the missionaries were well received by King Biörn in Birka, but we know nothing of what happened afterwards.

The German Chronicler Adam of Bremen associates the Christianisation of Sweden with King Eric Segersäll, the Victorious († c. 995), who had fought against the pagan re-convert King Sweyn of Denmark. King Eric had won and driven Sweyn into exile in England, Adam claimed. As ruler of Christian Denmark, Eric Segersäll converted, but when he returned to Sweden to fight the other claimants to power, he lapsed into paganism. As many scholars have argued, King Eric's rule over Denmark and Sweyn's apostasy may be a total fabrication of Adam, but the story shows how a conversion to Christianity could happen for political purposes. Had Eric attempted to be king of Denmark after Harald Bluetooth, he would have gained a stronger position by becoming Christian.

Eric was succeeded on the Swedish throne by his son Olof Skötkonung († 1022. The etymology of the name is uncertain, but probably connected to *skat*, 'taxation'). Olof was baptised by a missionary bishop of English origin. He seems to have been recognised as the ruler over both Götalands and Svealand, and he began issuing coins in Sigtuna, which was an important international trading hub and a centre for the mission in Uppland.

The religious situation in Sweden, especially in Svealand, was much more fluid than in Denmark and Norway. The Swedes adhered to old pagan practices for a longer time and demanded the same of their rulers. In Svealand, it was decided at a general meeting in the mid-11th century that Christ was stronger than other gods, but that the pagan cult should continue and that kings had to participate in the pagan sacrifice. When King Inge the Elder († 1110?) refused to do so, he was expelled by Blot-Sweyn – Sweyn the Sacrificer – and had to flee to Västergötland, which seems to have been thoroughly Christian at that time. This happened shortly before 1100. King Inge later returned, fought against Sweyn and killed him, re-established Christian rule, and continued to invite missionaries from England.

Military enterprises with pagan agendas continued into the 12th century but became rare. In the early 1120s, a joint Danish-Norwegian-Polish crusade was launched against Småland, with the justification that the population had lapsed from their faith and returned to paganism. The campaign had the approval of one of the highest international Church authorities, Abbot Peter the Venerable of Cluny, but was no great military event. The three armies came at different times and were not coordinated, and apparently never came to real fighting. Nevertheless, the pagan movements seem to have disappeared from that area soon after. The episode is, however, illustrative of how Christian rulers in Scandinavia could unite politically to promote religion; this would become very common after 1100 in the many crusades in the Baltic against the pagans living along its southern shores and to the east.

Iceland: The Lands without Kings

The earliest settlers in Iceland were probably occasional hermits from Ireland seeking wilderness and isolation in order to meditate and pray undisturbed. They came to the Faroe Islands and to Iceland before the 9th century, and perhaps long before. The first settlers from Scandinavia recorded that they found items from these Irish *papar*, priests or monks, but archaeological traces of their presence are few and unclear.

Iceland was empty when the first Norwegians came to the island in 874. The Scandinavian settlement in the Atlantic was possible economically and practically because of changes in technology and climate, but it began as a conservative opposition to the new and increasing centralised royal power. Families and petty chieftains left their homes so as to be able to continue a traditional system without king or any single leader, but with a fragile power equilibrium between big men and their clans. They actually succeeded in preserving this political system until the 1260s, moreover in spite of conversion to Christianity. The religion that in Scandinavia had been used to support the idea of a king and increasing royal power, was applied in Iceland to strengthen a much more decentralised society.

According to sources from c. 300 years later, the first Norwegian to settle in Iceland was Ingólfr Arnarson, whose farm was built where Reykjavik now is. Archaeological evidence supports the date. Ingólfr may have left Norway because of the first attempts to introduce Christianity there by force. That was certainly the reason for the arrival of several of the settlers in the following generations. Some came from Norway, others from the Viking colonies in Ireland and probably also in Scotland.

Iceland was organised around big farms spread out over the island. These were connected by a net of personal alliances confirmed by marriage agreements and the obligation to aid allies in avenging the many feuds seemingly endemic to medieval Icelandic society. In 930, the chieftains agreed to establish the *althing*, the general assembly, which was meant to meet once a year at Þingvellir (Thing fields), to settle disputes and make decisions. The romantic nationalism of the 19th and 20th centuries cast it as a kind of proto-democracy; in reality, it was the meeting place for chieftains with armed retainers in a strictly hierarchical society. However, it was still a very different administrative and political system to the kingdoms of Scandinavia. The chieftains in Iceland never developed a permanent administrative sector with officials comparable to that of the kingdoms, and military forces were smaller and organised on a much more local level than the large royal *ledungs* of Norway, Sweden, or Denmark.

From 964, power in Iceland was divided between 39 chieftains, *goðar*, whose office was hereditary. One of their main functions was to meet at the *thing* and dispense justice, but also to negotiate and solve conflicts, and to help economically. All free men were obliged to choose a chieftain to support and be supported by, but in principle, they could change to another if they wanted. During the 12th century, power was

Illustration 1.6 Þingvellir, the general assembly place in medieval Iceland. The peculiar geological formation is a result of the meeting of the North American and the Eurasian tectonic plates. In practice, this creates an enormous theatre background that amplifies sound and makes individual voices audible even for a very large group.

Photo Diego Delso, delso.photo, License CC-BY-SA.

concentrated among five or six families who each controlled several offices, and feuding escalated. Some sought to enhance their position by alliances with the Norwegian king. This resulted in a civil war in the first half of the 13th century, culminating in the Battle of Örlygsstaðir on 21 August 1238 between the clan of the Sturlungar and two others, the Ásbirningar and the Haukdælir. Numbers from the Middle Ages are uncertain, but the Sturlungar should have been able to muster around 1,000 men against their opponents, 1,700. The armies were big from an Icelandic perspective, albeit not on a broadly Scandinavian or European scale, but only around 50 men actually died. The Norwegian King Haakon IV († 1263) had supported different chieftains in the Icelandic struggles including the famous saga-writer Snorri Sturluson. He had become a vassal of King Haakon but later changed side, and Haakon was behind Snorri's assassination in 1241; this gave the King a bad reputation in Icelandic history writing, in the Middle Ages and today, but paved the way for Iceland submitting to Haakon's authority in 1262 and becoming part of Norway.

Church and local lay power went hand in hand in Iceland, to an extent that was unusual not only in Scandinavia but in Europe generally speaking. After the Icelanders had decided to convert to the Christian faith, the chieftains in Iceland had a decisive influence on the appointments of bishops to the two episcopal sees on the island, Skálholt and Hólar, and of heads of monasteries until the Norwegian king took power, despite attempts both by Icelandic ecclesiastics and the papal curia to guard the Church's liberty. The chieftains wanted to use ecclesiastical positions for the benefit of their own kin but also to control the income from the ecclesiastical properties they had founded or donated themselves. This fight for income, Icelandic *staðamál*, had parallels everywhere in Scandinavia and western Europe, but because of the decentralised structure in Iceland, it may perhaps have lasted longer and involved ecclesiastics more directly in feuding than in other countries possessing a ruler with more centralised power. On the other hand, bishops in Iceland were chieftains, or so closely connected to them that they probably became a more integrated part of the political establishment than in other parts of Scandinavia. Until 1264 in Iceland, the Church was not dependent upon secular rulers, but churchmen ruled with them.

Greenland: Northerners in a New Environment

In 982, the first settlers arrived in southern Greenland from Iceland and soon after from Norway. At that time, it does not seem that the Inuit Dorset culture in the north of Greenland and arctic Canada had yet come so far south, so in practise, the Norse colonists arrived in an empty land.

The Scandinavian settlement of Greenland began with Eric the Red, who had been declared an outlaw in Iceland around 982 for committing murders. He had no other option than to leave the island and find new land to settle. In the preceding years, some ships had drifted off course and landed on islands that must have been Greenland's southern part, and they had managed to survive and return with astounding tales about it. Nevertheless, it was a daring act of Eric to try to find this unknown land in the hope that he could carve out a living there. The climate had begun to become milder around the year 1000 with temperatures slowly rising, but Greenland's eastern coast was still packed with ice all year round. Eric settled inside one of the fjords on the western coast and returned to Iceland in 985 to convince more people to join him

Coming of the Kingdoms 25

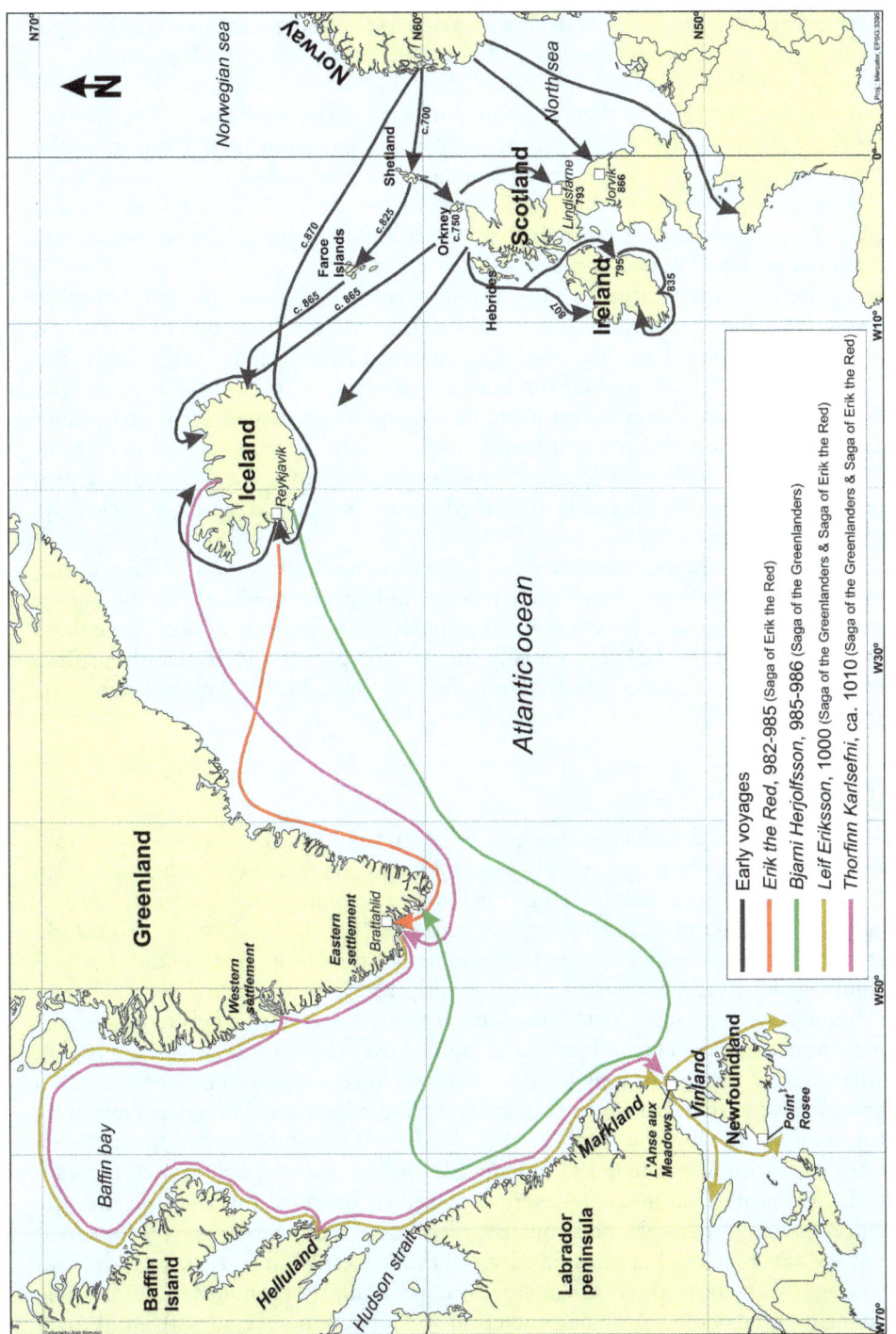

Map 3 Scandinavian migration and settlements in the North Atlantic.
Map © Jussi Kinnunen, 2022.

to the new land of opportunities. To persuade them that it was a fertile and inviting land he called it 'Greenland', explained the Icelandic historian Ari Þorgilsson († 1148) in his *Íslendingabók* from the 1120s. It was written several generations after the event but is one of the oldest sources we have about Greenland's Nordic colonisation.

In Greenland, the Scandinavians established themselves in two settlements, the Eastern and the Western Settlement, both located on the west coast. The Eastern Settlement furthest to the south was the largest, the more northern Western Settlement, around present-day Nuuk, much smaller. Over the following centuries, more Scandinavian colonies were established. Signs of between 400 and 600 farms and settlements have been found, but many were very small. The total Norse population in Greenland probably never exceeded 4,000.

Eric the Red and many others among the early settlers had been pagans, but those later were Christian. According to one Norwegian source from the 12th century, the settlements in Greenland were soon Christianised from Iceland. Sagas from after 1200 recounts that Eric's son Leif the Lucky was baptised in Norway at King Olaf Trygvasson's court, and after his return to Greenland he persuaded his mother, Thjodhild, to convert and build the first church in Greenland at their farmstead of Bratthalid. Eric was not enthusiastic about abandoning his faith, but Thjodhild denied him access to their bed as long as he remained pagan, 'which did not please Eric', and he became Christian.

Eric and other chieftains on Greenland built churches and chapels at their farms, and as in Iceland they kept control over income and appointments of priests, but we have no sources to recount how it worked in practice in the early period. Greenland got its episcopal see in 1124, but already in 1117 (or perhaps 1121) a bishop, Eric, was sent to Greenland and continued from there to missionise in America, where he disappeared.

The Period of Civil Wars

For decades in the mid-12th century, there were feuds and warfare between individuals who all wanted to be kings, or between ambitious members of mighty clans. Such was the case in the Scandinavian countries, just as in many other places in Europe. In England, 'The Anarchy' under King Stephen lasted for almost 20 years, from 1135 to 1153. In Germany, wars between the members of the Hohenstaufen and the Welf dynasties began in 1125 and lasted until the early 13th century.

Are internal wars good or bad? Historians have agreed that this period was one of the important societal changes, but have disagreed over the reasons these wars began, and what exactly the results may have been. Some have stressed internal factors. An earlier economic system based on plunder and tribute kept most magnates relatively content, as long as they could follow their leader on profitable expeditions. When the kings increasingly attempted to monopolise the control over armies and incomes in the 12th century, the magnates were deprived of much of their wealth and began fighting among themselves and against the king. Other historians have looked at some of the same factors but stressed external influences. With Christianity, the idea of the king as far above the magnates became particularly pronounced, and strong neighbouring kings could provide protection for rebellious magnates from abroad. In the older historiographical tradition, these internal wars were definitely bad: they were civil wars that disrupted the smooth workings of king and state. More recent historiography, however, has seen these wars as good, or at least as necessary during this transitional period in order to create a new and more centralised society with a stronger king.

In Denmark, the internal wars began in 1131 when the Christmas peace ended on 7 January. Magnus, the son of King Niels, killed Canute Lavard, the son of the former King Eric Ejegod. Canute's brother Eric Emune raised a rebellion against Magnus and King Niels and gathered supporters. In 1134, the two armies met in a big battle at Fotevik in Scania. Magnus fell and King Niels fled, surprisingly to Canute Lavard's principal town, Schleswig, where he was killed by its citizens. Eric Emune's Danish troops had been assisted by a contingent of 300 mounted warriors sent by the German Emperor Lothar III, and the Battle at Fotevik is the first known example of large-scale employment of cavalry in Scandinavia. It was a big battle and became mythical even in its own time. We do not know how many ordinary soldiers fell, but five bishops and perhaps as many as 60 clerics were killed.

King Eric Emune, in his turn, was killed at a general assembly only three years later, in 1137, by a spurious person called Black Plough. Eric was succeeded by his sister's homonym son, Eric Lam, who almost immediately had to wage a war against another uncle. Eric Lam abdicated in 1146, entered the Benedictine monastery in Odense, and soon after died. This did not mean an end to war, because 'Danes excel in one thing only, that is civil wars', as the contemporary historian Helmold of Bosau in Germany remarked. During the following 11 years, there were almost constant wars between three members of the royal families: Sweyn, Canute, and Valdemar. They allied in shifting constellations variously with the German kings, pagan Wendic rulers from northern Germany, other Scandinavian kings and magnates, and with or against each other. Valdemar – son of Canute Lavard – had been firmly supported by his uncle Sweyn but changed side in the early 1150s and married Sofia, the sister of Canute Magnussen, who was the son of the Magnus who had killed Valdemar's father. She was an extremely pretty woman, contemporary sources explained, but the manoeuvre was also politically very advantageous for Valdemar.

In 1157, the three competing parties agreed to meet in Roskilde in order to settle affairs peacefully and divide Denmark amongst them. Sweyn arrived a little late at the meeting because he had had to rest from the heavy smoke in the sauna, he explained. In reality, he had arranged and instructed his men. During the negotiations, they suddenly drew their hidden swords and began killing, cleaving the head of Canute Magnussen, but Valdemar managed to escape in the tumult. The *Blood-feast in Roskilde*, as the event was later called, did not in the end help Sweyn. Later the same year Valdemar led an army into Jutland against Sweyn who fled and was unceremoniously killed with an axe by a peasant on the moor of Grathe. The dead king has since been designated as Sweyn Grathe in Danish historiography. His grave was long unknown, but in 2015, archaeologists found what seems to be the remnants of a chapel on the place where he was killed. The main result of the battle was that after 26 years of warfare Valdemar became the sole ruler of all Denmark, and the country was again united.

With internal fights over, the Danish military energy was turned outwards. During his reign from 1157 until his death in 1182, Valdemar I systematically dispatched armies against the Wends in northern Germany every year or second year. He also intervened in Norwegian affairs in 1165 and 1170 to support one Norwegian king against others.

Despite his focus on territories outside Denmark, there were attempted rebellions against King Valdemar. His relative Duke Buris long supported him but in 1166 refused to pay homage to Valdemar's young son Canute (later: VI) as a co-regent. Nobody can serve two masters, Buris explained, adding that only Germans do that. In 1167, Buris was accused of conspiring with Norwegians to become Danish king himself; he was imprisoned and, according to later sources, blinded and castrated to prevent him from taking over power in Denmark. In another case the king was perhaps more lenient; two relatives of Archbishop Eskil of Lund had conspired against Valdemar but were allegedly forgiven, and only exiled in 1176.

In 1170, Valdemar I was at the peak of his power. Only two years earlier, his troops had conquered the strongest pagan fortress and cult centre in northern Europe, Arkona on the island of Rügen, and Pope Alexander III had agreed to canonise Valdemar's father, Canute Lavard. The canonisation was celebrated at a long, lavishly ornate liturgy at the so-called 'Church Feast at Ringsted' in June 1170. Canute's bones were put in a shrine that was placed on the high altar of the enormous newly built church. At the same time, Valdemar's seven-year-old son Canute was crowned king. His destiny – his coming reign – was thus closely connected to the blessing of the saint after whom he had been named, and the entire ceremony was an attempt to establish the principle of primogeniture (that the oldest legitimate son of the king should inherit the throne). In practice, this principle came to work relatively well in the Middle Ages but became law only much later, in 1660.

Norwegian historians often work inside a Civil War era time-frame of 1130–1240, but wars were more intensive in some periods than in others and encompassed larger or smaller areas. In Norway, it was also a dangerous business to be a king. Of 14 rulers in 1130–1202, only one died peacefully in bed; the other 13 fell in battle or were executed as prisoners of war.

The Norwegian tumults began when Magnus, the son of King Sigurd Jorsalafare 'the Crusader' († 1130), succeeded his father to the Norwegian throne but his rule was contested by Harald Gille. Harald had come from Ireland and claimed that he was the son of the Norwegian King Magnus Barefoot († 1103) who had fallen in battle against the Irish, and was thereby half-brother to King Sigurd Jorsalafare. Harald Gille had to prove his royal descent by ordeal, by appealing to divine justice and miracles. He walked barefooted over seven or nine hot glowing plough irons and showed three days later that his feet were unharmed. His claim was thus recognised by large groups, and so he could summon support and began to wage war in 1134. At Christmas, Magnus Sigurdsson was beleaguered in Bergen and probably had a presentiment of what was in store for him. Harald Gille waited out the Christmas peace. When it ended on 7 January 1135, he captured Magnus, blinded and castrated him, had one of his feet cut off to make him unfit to rule, and placed him in a monastery in Nidaros.

Harald Gille's joy was only short lived. The next year Sigurd Slembe, who claimed to be his half-brother, challenged his rule and succeeded in killing Harald, who had spent the night with his mistress and not at home with his queen; having carelessly boasted about his plans, he thus revealed where he could be found and ambushed. Local magnates then chose two of Harald's sons as kings. In the ensuing war, Sigurd Munn tried to bolster his authority by having Magnus the Blind taken out of monastery to become co-regent. In 1139, Magnus fell in battle; Sigurd was caught, tortured, and died.

Illustration 1.7 Saint Bendt's Church, Ringsted, was the Danish royal burial church from 1131 until 1319. In 1170, Canute Lavard was canonised here in a solemn ceremony, and his grandson, Canute VI, was crowned king and co-regent with his father Valdemar I, in an attempt to secure the succession to the throne. A new and larger church had begun being built for this occasion, one of the earliest brick buildings in Scandinavia, but in 1170 probably only the choir and the central crossing had been finished.
Photo Orf3us 2016. This file is licensed under the Creative Commons Attribution 3.0 Unported license.

Norway had now two, and for periods three, kings ruling at the same time but with power bases in different areas of the country. In 1155, happened the same as in Denmark: two kings united against the third. Sigurd Munn and Eystein allied against Inge the Hunchback but with little luck. Sigurd fell in 1155, Eystein in 1157, and Inge became the sole ruler, if not for long. Sigurd's retinue declared one of his sons the new king, and Inge fell in another war in 1161. The new king had already fallen a year later to the next leader, Erling, and his son Magnus.

Erling's problem was that he did not have a king for a father, but luckily his wife Kristin did. She was the daughter of King Sigurd Jorsalafare. Erling had himself been on crusade and fought against Muslims in the Holy Land and Sicily. Their son Magnus had royal blood and was born in lawful marriage in contrast with almost all other royal candidates. In 1163 (or 1164), the seven-year-old Magnus Erlingsson was crowned king in Bergen by the archbishop of the recently established Norwegian metropolitan see of Nidaros. Magnus was the first king in Scandinavia to be crowned, and he was the first in Norway to use the title 'King by the grace of

God'. The coronation marked a strong act of cooperation between the king and the Church, and Magnus issued a promise to respect the latter's liberty. Beyond this, Magnus in fact donated the entire realm of Norway to the Church, or rather to God. The dating of this so-called coronation letter has been hotly debated by Norwegian historians but it was most probably issued in connection with the coronation in 1163.

> On this blessed Day of Resurrection, I donate myself with the kingdom forever to God and to the venerable martyr King Olaf, to whom I totally and fully, second only to God, with special veneration donate the kingdom of Norway. And I will lead this kingdom as long as it pleases God, as the inheritance after the venerable martyr Olaf – lead it under his governance, as his vicar, and as having it from him.

The law of succession from the time of the coronation stipulated that there should be only one king in Norway and that he should be a legitimate son of the king, normally the eldest, 'if he is not too evil or too stupid'. A council of magnates, ecclesiastics, and the royal personal guard, the *hird*, should decide who amongst the sons was eldest and suited to ruling, and if a disagreement arose, the Church had the decisive vote.

This meant, on parchment, an enormous strengthening of the royal position and a regulation of affairs promising more order and fewer wars. To strengthen his sons' position, Erling had the sons of several other kings killed, which may in fact have been counter-productive and not benefitting the credibility of his own son. In reality, after his coronation in 1163, King Magnus Erlingsson had to fight against different competitors to the throne every second or third year. His opponents attracted warriors with very different backgrounds. Some had lost status and influence during the many wars and were mocked as *birkebeinar*, the 'birchlegged', because they were so poor that they had no shoes but wrapped birchbark around their feet. In a battle in 1177, many of them were brutally slaughtered or scattered, and seemed to be of little further danger – but then they found a new leader to rally around, the charismatic King Sverre of mysterious background.

Sverre claimed to be the illegitimate son of King Sigurd Munn and a Norwegian woman, although he had been brought up and educated by the bishop of the Faroe Islands and had even been consecrated as priest, 'but he was not a good priest' – all this according to the contemporary narrative of his life, the *Sverre's saga*, which he proof-read himself. The veracity of the account has been doubted, many details seem wrong, and it may be a fabrication of Sverre's, but it served a purpose. He could claim direct royal descent in contrast to Magnus Erlingsson, and also some kind of semi-ecclesiastical status when he later came into harsh dispute with the bishops.

In 1177 Sverre came to Norway and began leading the *birkebeinar* against King Magnus' men, and was hailed as king. In 1179, he lined his men up in Nidaros and promised them the position and income of the men they would kill in the ensuing battle. Erling fell with many of his personal guard and Sverre took over a large part of his fleet, meaning he could now operate along the coast and meet Magnus on a more equal footing. Sverre was accepted as king by ever more people and offered to share Norway with Magnus, who declined. Magnus had a hold in the southern part of Norway and support from the Danish king but fell in a naval battle against Sverre in 1184.

In the nearly 20 years following, until his death in 1202, Sverre ruled and re-organised the army and administration, fighting against a coalition with strong support from the bishops, the *baglars*, named after the bishop's staff. The fighting between *birkebeinar* and *baglars* also came to characterise the early 13th century.

The Swedish political history of the 12th century is marred by a regrettable lack of sources. From Denmark and especially Norway, by contrast, long and detailed narratives have survived until our own day. While they are biased and problematic to use, they nevertheless convey details and past opinions about individuals, and often some of their information can be confirmed by other contemporary documents. Nothing similar from Sweden is known of in this period. Its political history is therefore sketchy and vague, but luckily some details can be extracted from other Scandinavian sources or from often laconic remarks in later sources.

Inge the Elder, who fought against Blot-Sweyn, had a base in Västergötland and perhaps also Svealand. When he died in 1110 or 1111, he was succeeded by two brothers. One was also called Inge, and he was killed in Östergötland, by poison according to a later list of Swedish kings. The other was Magnus, who was elected king by the Götar around 1125. He was the son of King Niels of Denmark but had a claim to succeed to the throne in both Götalands after his mother, Queen Margaret Fridkulla, daughter of King Inge the Elder. Magnus tried to strengthen his rule by fighting paganism and confiscating the large cultic copper hammers from a pagan temple, but we do not know where these were located. Meanwhile, a certain Ragnvald, of whose background we know nothing, became king of Svealand and tried to extend his reign to Västergötland but was killed, probably around 1130. Magnus, on the other hand, was not accepted in Svealand. As mentioned above he fell in the battle at Fotevik in 1134.

Magnus' rule had been contested by Sverker the Elder, a pious man with a keen eye for women of power. Sverker had been elected king in the very early 1130s, and after Magnus he ruled both Götalands and Svealand. He married the Danish King Niels' widow Ulfhild after Niels' death in 1134 although he had already seduced her while Niels was alive. After her death, around 1150, he married Magnus' widow Rikissa, who meanwhile had been married to the Russian King Volodar of Minsk – another example of the strong Scandinavian-Russian connections of this period. Sverker seems to have had a close cooperation with the bishop of Linköping, and he and Queen Uflhild were active in the founding of the Cistercian monasteries of Alvastra and Nydala. King Sverker also worked to establish an independent Swedish archiepiscopal see in 1153, parallel to the Norwegian one in Nidaros but did not succeed. The plan was probably to place it in Linköping, but that would have been unacceptable to the population in Svealand. Sverker also reigned at the same time as Eric Jedvarsson, perhaps making it impossible to agree on where to site an archbishopric.

On Christmas morning 1156, Sverker was killed in his sleep by a servant who took care of his horses. He had been persuaded or paid by Magnus Henriksson, another member of the Danish royal dynasty who declared himself king in Sweden in 1160. Magnus was himself killed by Sverker's son Karl in 1161, but not before he had succeeded the year before in killing King Eric Jedvarsson, who became the national patron saint of Sweden.

Different regions had had different kings. After 1161, Karl Sverkersson became the sole ruler apparently over all three Swedish lands. However, in 1167, Canute, the son of Saint Eric, sailed out to Visingsö in Lake Vättern and killed Karl. Canute fought for several years against Karl's two sons, but in the early 1170s, he became the sole king and ruled, apparently relatively peacefully, until he died in 1196. Sweden had finally become a united kingdom.

Illustration 1.8 The relics of Saint Eric of Sweden, which are today still kept in the cathedral at Uppsala. They were investigated by anthropologists in 2014, and it is clear from the marks on his bones that he had been hit by sword and had had his head cut off, all well in accordance with the description of his martyrdom contained in the medieval description of his life. Eric had organised a crusade to Finland in the mid-1150s together with Bishop Henry from Uppsala, who became the Finnish patron saint. The crusade, referred to as the first Swedish crusade to Finland, is known from much later sources and scholars have questioned whether it actually ever took place. There is no reason to doubt, however, that a cult for Eric developed shortly after his death.
Photo Mark A. Wilson, 2007. Public domain.

An Especially Violent Period in Scandinavian History?

Historians have understood all these conflicts and regicides in the mid-12th century as being civil wars among claimants to the thrones and their followers, and as unusually bloody. The few sources we have from the earlier periods do not truly invite a depiction of peaceful societies that afterwards slid into chaos, nor did bloody wars between kings and rulers disappear after the 12th century. The period was possibly not very much worse than any other in the Scandinavian Middle Ages. Nevertheless, conflicts were common and have been explained by historians in different ways.

One explanation stresses the role of families or different lineages within them. The kings of Sweden from c. 1150 into the 13th century, for example, belonged to the kin of Sverker or of Eric. Swedish and Scandinavian history in this period is often depicted as driven by rivalry between two or more family dynasties, but in reality, the individuals and their followers had all kinds of connections across these lines. Loyalties were on many levels, fluid, and changeable, with intermarriages common.

Another explanation stresses the importance of the introduction of the new principle of primogeniture (that the oldest son succeeded his father). According to the earlier system, all sons and their descendants had a claim on the throne and one was elected by the magnates. The Danish example is striking: five sons of King Sweyn Estridsen became kings, one after the other, from 1076 until 1134. In the meantime, they all had had sons who lined up to take over after a father or an uncle. The attempts in all Scandinavian countries to have the magnates pay homage to the ruling king's son and accept him as co-ruler, while the father was still alive, were to the end of breaking away from this system. Primogeniture developed in close contact with the Church: with coronation ceremonies, with the elevation to kingship by the grace of God, and with the insistence that the king be born in legitimate wedlock. All this encroached upon the traditional rights of the princely aristocracy and was resisted with violence.

However, we can also look at the history of the first medieval centuries in Scandinavia from the other way around. Internationally, the 12th and 13th centuries were a great period for social science and new theories of governance according to which the people – represented by the magnates, in medieval understanding – should have the authority to choose their ruler. If he was tyrannical, the people could depose him or kill him outright. Throughout the Middle Ages there continued the struggle between two understandings of authority: from above, of the king by blood and by the grace of God; and from below, as chosen by the people. We don't know whether these discussions were generally known in Scandinavia in the 12th century, but it is very likely, and they may have given legitimacy to the many groupings fighting against a king. The Swedish provincial laws state that the people could choose their king, and dispose of him again.

Compared to earlier periods, the mid-12th century is probably not markedly more violent, as far as the few sources allow us to judge. Violence was an endemic part of societies that consisted mainly of competing networks and where kings only gradually became strong enough to effectively monopolise the use of violent power.

Royal Administrators

A reason for the troubled times of the 12th century may also have been changes in the economic situation of the big magnates and their families. Earlier, they had had access to huge incomes from plundering and from leading private or semi-private armies on what are known as Viking raids. By the 12th century, however, they had become more dependent upon serving a king, who acquired ever more power and control over military resources. The magnates therefore invested in and favoured their own candidates for king. This explanation finds some support in the fact that Scandinavian kings needed the support of the great men to survive, but also that some of them tried to pull themselves away from the aristocratic clasp, favouring lesser powerful individuals whom they could better control. The rulers began to become more independent from the magnates by creating a class of *ministeriales*, lesser officials in royal service, like kings in Germany and other European rulers. Contemporaries noted this, with disapproval if belonging to or connected to the old elites. The historian Saxo wrote dismissingly of King Sweyn Grathe, he took away honours from the nobles and gave them to his nod dolls, he rejected the magnates and famous ones and gathered around him ugly and effeminate ordinary men to demonstrate his power, ... and so that they should ascribe their good fortune solely to the benevolence of the king, not to their family background.

King Sverre of Norway began his career by gathering around him followers who were not from the old and powerful families, and who gained the condescending epithet of *birkebeinar* to stress their poverty and primitivity.

The creation of the ministerial class was also necessary because the kings needed administrators at the local level, for collecting taxes and income from royal possessions and for keeping law and order. To achieve this goal the kings could ally with old elites, or create new ones. The distinction between the two groups was probably not sharp, and individuals could move between them over time. Some of the titles of these royal offices go far back, while others came later with the expansion and diversification of administration.

Villicus or *vilicus* was a steward who managed the property of a ruler. The term was used in Roman antiquity and also in the Bible in the Parable of the Unjust Steward (Luke 16:1–13), in both cases designating a person unfree but with great responsibility. Villicus corresponds most probably to the Nordic title *bryde*, which is known from runestones from as early as the 10th century, but it is not known what function the early bryde had. It is assumed by historians that villici or bryde were unfree servants in an earlier period, but there are in fact no good sources for this. In the later period, the villici were high-ranking administrators, witnessing royal charters and acting as the king's local representatives on royal domains. Some were villicus of important towns and royal castles, and some led contingents of the royal army. The Swedish use of the Latin villicus is later than the Danish, the earliest known example being from 1267, and it became especially frequent after 1300. At that time, at the latest, the term's application had become broader and could be used for persons on very different social and economic levels. In Norway, the corresponding royal administrator or steward of royal farms was termed *ármann*. According to the Norwegian provincial laws, the ármann was appointed by the king and responsible for organising the thing assemblies and summoning the navy or the army. When the king was travelling around in the country, he would lodge with the local ármann.

In many other places, such as England or France, the rulers delegated power to their vassals, to whom they gave noble titles. In Scandinavia, by contrast, the *jarls* (earls or dukes) were traditionally local elites and rulers of large regions, with great power and often closely married into the royal dynasties, but not necessarily royal vassals. The Scandinavian kings attempted to gain control over the titles and reserve them for members of the royal family as a temporary position for the heir to the throne, such as the duchy of Schleswig, or as appanage to younger sons. In Norway, the use of the title of earl was forbidden by law in 1308, 'because there were so many problems with this title'. The next level of Norwegian elites were the *lendermen* – men with land. They seem to have had a local power basis but were chosen or appointed by the king to represent him and work together with the ármann. A corresponding group in Denmark were the *stallars* or *stabularii* who were responsible for the royal stables and therefore had important military functions, often appearing in the sources in groups of three to five. The first known mention of them is as witnesses in the oldest preserved Danish charter, a huge royal donation for the founding of Lund Cathedral in 1085. The stallars as high-ranking royal officers were replaced around 1200 and after by the marshals, a title similarly connected to the horses. For the rest of the Middle Ages, stallar was a title used for important functions a bit lower on the social ladder: for stewards with high responsibility in the service of bishops and big aristocrats.

The *drost* or *dapifer* in Latin is a title that began to be used in Denmark and Norway shortly after 1200, and a little later in Sweden. Although the basic meaning of dapifer is 'responsible for the kitchen', the drost was throughout the Middle Ages the most powerful royal official. He had important military functions, often including control with some of the strongest royal castles, and important roles within the royal legal system. In the 14th and 15th centuries, the drost could act on behalf of the king in the case of the ruler's minority or absence.

From the 12th century onwards, the Scandinavian kings created new elites from among the laymen but also relied on cooperating with the ecclesiastical apparatus. In the second half of the 12th century, Scandinavian kings had their private chapels with royal chaplains, who in addition to their spiritual functions took care of the king's correspondence and increasingly also of accountancy and the royal treasury. Mainly responsible for this part of the administration was the royal chancellor, normally a bishop, but much of the staff belonged to the royal chapel. The first known chancellor in Denmark was Bishop Radulf of Ribe in the 1160s.

By around 1200, the status and power of local Scandinavian elites had diminished, and kings had succeeded in creating an administration through which they could control their kingdoms – to a lesser or greater extent, varying significantly over time. This development was a major step towards royal independence from the local elites. The old functions of royal villicus, ármenn, stallare, and lendermen disappeared or lost influence, and were replaced by other offices with new titles.

Military Organisation

The king's main function was to make war: whether to create peace and defend the people against outside aggressors, to avenge old injustices, because of love for foreign women, or very often simply because it was good and honourable. For warfare, it was necessary that the kings could rely on a well-functioning military organisation.

Scandinavia became heavily militarised during the Middle Ages. Earlier Viking Age raids had been large and efficient, but during the 11th and 12th centuries, Scandinavian societies became systematically re-organised and tuned to providing larger and stronger military forces, increasingly under the control of the kings. The great strength of the Viking armies had been their ships, and the fleets continued to be essential to all Scandinavian military thinking. The geography itself demanded it, with archipelagos outstretched along the thousands of kilometres of coastlines of the Scandinavian peninsula and Finland, and with the lines of communication across the sea to the Atlantic Isles. Ships became longer and bigger, but technology and styles of boat did not change much before c. 1200.

An integral part of medieval Scandinavian warfare was the royally controlled conscription of the navy – the *ledung* system. Its principle was very simple: every country was divided into units, each of which had to provide one ship for the fleet. These units were subdivided into smaller units each of which had to provide one warrior for the ship. In Denmark these were called *hafne*, 'harbours'. The Norwegian *fylke*, 'gathering', and the Swedish *skeppslag*, 'ship-groups', were much larger, while the Swedish *hundare*, 'hundred', amounted to 100 men and four ships. The exact meaning of these terms is highly debated in modern research. Provincial laws from the early 13th century contain detailed instructions as to who was obliged to serve onboard, how often, and for how long. Free men had to participate and were fined if they sent a slave instead of coming in person, or even worse, the slave was confiscated and the owner had to carry the economic loss himself. There appears to have been a system of turn-taking so that a free man would normally join the navy every third year on summer expeditions, except if the country was attacked. In that case, all had to take part in the defence of the land. Many were exempt for various reasons, and many paid a tax for staying home.

How efficient the ledung was is hard to say. When the navy was summoned and before it could set out, the first couple of weeks were spent on training the men in warfare and probably also in understanding commands and working as a unit. Such praxis does not indicate a very professional group of warriors. Nevertheless, it illustrates that all free men were expected to have weapons and to be ready to use them. The ledung must also have had an important ideological function by making the idea of war a part of daily life, even in the smallest, remotest community. The ships were kept locally over the winter and maintained and prepared for the next summer's expedition. The many Danish placenames with *snekke*, 'longship', must indicate where these boathouses were located. In Norway, several large medieval *naust*, 'boathouses', have been excavated along the coast. Norwegian laws gave detailed prescriptions for how the ledungsnaust should be organised and what it should contain. Kings and magnates additionally had boathouses for the ships of their personal clique of retainers. In Norway, the large and extremely expensive square sails of the ledung-ships were stored on the attics of the local churches, and we must expect that this was also the case in other Scandinavian countries.

The age of the ledung system is hard to determine. It may have been inspired by a corresponding Anglo-Saxon military organisation, the *fyrd*, and introduced into Scandinavia during the 10th century or even earlier when kings gained greater power and could command more territory and men. Some historians have argued that the royally controlled ledung was only introduced in the second half of the 12th century, and all naval expeditions before that were privately organised. This position has, however, been severely criticised by other historians with special reference to Norwegian sources which clearly indicate the existence of an early royal navy.

The Scandinavian warship, the longboat or snekke, was a technologically advanced construction developed and refined over centuries. A number of these refinements ensured manoeuvrability and speed. Since the ships had no deep keel, they could sail in very shallow water and get exceptionally close to the coast or up even minor rivers. This made the packing of goods and ballast crucial to maintain balance when sailing. The ships were driven by big sails, either made of wool, which was strong and elastic, or of flax which was more difficult to work and lasted a shorter time, but resulted in a lighter sail. The tackling and ropes were made of plant or tree fibres, or of animal hair or skin, horsetails, hides, and so on. Ropes from walrus hide were as strong as modern steel wires and used for anchor ropes, mostly in Norway with its easier access to artic animals, but also elsewhere in Scandinavia.

In case of no wind, in difficult waters with reefs and stones, or in battle, the ships could be moved by rowing. In warfare, any ship could be used, but the fast, slim battle ships would normally have had from about 20 oars up to perhaps 40. The big ships of the king and magnates could be over 30 m long and have 60 oars, so the warriors rowing them sat very close together and must have been very well trained in coordinating their movements exactly, as archaeological experiments have shown. According to Snorri Sturluson in the mid-13th century, the Norwegian King Olaf Tryggvason's ship, called *Long Snake*, was 43 m long.

Watch Towers and Castles

When enemies approached, it was important to be prepared to meet them and therefore to be forewarned as early as possible. The first mention of a warning system in Norway dates from the 10th century, and in Sweden and Denmark from the 14th and 15th centuries. However, placenames show that such a system is much older and already well established in the early Viking Age. The system consisted of fires prepared on hills or high mountains which could be lit if enemies were observed, sending the signal from one fire to the next. There seem to have been main lines of warning to ensure large-scale mobilisation in case of major attacks, and minor lines to mobilise the local population. On the flat shores of the Danish isles, these fires were prepared next to watch towers for the scouts. It was the obligation of the local population to man the watch positions in turn, and to not show up or be negligent on duty was a capital offence, at least from the 14th century onwards.

Nordic words for these watch positions were *bavn* or *var(d)*, and very frequent as place or even family names – such as *Varberg* (watch-mountain) which later developed into a strong castle; *Vaxholm* (watch-island); *Baunehøj* (watch-mound); and *Baunsgaard* (watch-farm) which is still used as a family name.

Castles were often built close to the warning beacons. They essentially had three functions: variously to protect, to control the surrounding countryside, and to be centres for military aggression. These sites are often very difficult to date archaeologically, and most were constantly repaired, rebuilt, and expanded by using older structures and materials. Nevertheless, it is possible to suggest some important stages in the castles' development.

Until the first half of the 12th century, castles and fortifications were made from earth, often within huge wooden frames or 'boxes' and with wooden palisades and towers on top. They were placed where the terrain could help to give protection, on islands or small peninsulas in lakes, on hilltops, or up mountains. The hill could be artificially made – a *motte* as was known in western Europe since shortly before the year 1000 and introduced to England after the Norman invasion in 1066. Scandinavian examples include Danish Sigersholm on Zealand, probably from around 1100, 45 m in diameter and 6 m high, while some royal fortifications such as the Danish Trelleborgs from around 980 could be large, impressive structures on a sophisticated technological and logistical level. The majority were much smaller and adapted to fit into the surrounding landscape. Some were basically only fortified private homes and continued to be built throughout the Middle Ages.

After 1100, castles became much larger and stronger. The Bastrup-tower was built in stone in the very early 12th century on an 11 m high mound, itself almost 21 m in diameter and perhaps an impressive 50 m tall, with walls that were 6 m thick at the bottom. It was among the most magnificent and strongest towers in northern Europe at the time, heralding a new epoch in Scandinavia: of stone castles and fortified 'strong houses' in natural stone, and from the 1160s to 1180s sometimes in brick. New and much larger castles were built, and sometimes the old ones had to be moved to a location nearby with better space or with more solid foundations to support the heavier structure. Especially in southern Scandinavia, castles moved from up the rivers and fjords and down closer to the coastline. This had become necessary for logistical reasons. Castles still needed provisions, much of which arrived in ships that had become larger and could perhaps no longer sail up the small rivers. Another and perhaps more important reason was that the role of castles became increasingly aggressive. Armies and navies would gather in the castle's protected harbour before setting out on expeditions, or castles became strongholds from which important waterways could be controlled and protected against pirates and enemy troops.

In Denmark, strong new castles were built almost directly on the seashore by kings and their most trusted magnates in a very short period between 1150 and 1200. The castle on the small island of Sprogø in the middle of the Storebælt (Great Belt) was built c. 1160 by King Valdemar I, controlling access from the North Sea and Kattegat to the Baltic Sea. It was supported by two huge castles on land, Nyborg on Funen to the west, built c. 1170 by the king's nephew, and Tårnborg on Zealand to the East, also from c. 1170. The same period also saw built Kalundborg on Zealand, further north along the Great Belt, by a member of the Hvide family, high-rank magnates and strong supporters of King Valdemar. Kalundborg was unique also because of its Byzantine-inspired church possessing five towers and a geometrical form, with the same unit of measurement repeated in shifting mathematical patterns throughout the entire building. A little earlier, probably around 1160, the first Vordingborg castle on the south coast of Zealand was erected by King Valdemar I, becoming the gathering point for the ledung before the annual raids against the pagan Wends in northern Germany.

Along the southern coast of Sweden, a similar erection of strong castles took place in the decades around 1200, protecting the sailing routes along the coasts of the mainland and the two big islands of Öland and Gotland. The royal castle on the island of Visingsö in Lake Vättern was strongly built in a protected location, allowing it to control some of the important east-west roads of southern Sweden where they had to cross over the lake.

In Norway, a new castle was built in Bergen and heavily fortified during the 12th century. It became one of the favourite castles of Norwegian kings, even before the erection of the magnificent Hall of Haakon (*Håkonshallen*) in around 1250. Tønsberg on the coast of the long Oslo fjord was also probably already fortified as a stone castle by the 1160s, becoming during the civil wars an important stronghold of the *baglars* against the *birkebeinars*.

If attackers came, the local population could sometimes seek refuge in the churches. It is much discussed among researchers to what extent some churches were actually built to function as defensive structures, and whether they had battlements. After the mid-12th century, in any case, churches were increasingly constructed in stone and would normally be the most solid building in their respective villages.

Castles were for protection, as were ships and all other kinds of military equipment. Kings were peacemakers, a role which could even become a semi-official part of their titles. The Danish King Valdemar I, on the plaque accompanying him inside the grave, was designated as *pacis conseruator*, The Guardian of Peace. According to its medieval understanding, the aim of war was to create peace, and all warfare was fundamentally defence. This has sometimes confused modern historians who have taken medieval sources at face value and simply repeated their descriptions of attacks from pagans or other neighbours on Scandinavian rulers and concluded that these rulers had to establish defensive military organisations and structures to protect their countries. In reality, all military assets could obviously be used for defence as well as for aggression. In either case, war could strengthen the king's position if done successfully.

2 Coming of Christ

Before Christianity

Scandinavia had had knowledge of Christianity since late antiquity because many Scandinavians had served in the Roman army. There were strong connections to the Goths around the Black Sea, many of whom had already converted to Christianity in the 4th century. However, it is only during the Viking Age that the Christian faith began to reach the Nordic countries, gradually influencing and replacing their local religious habits. We know very little about Scandinavia's pre-Christian religions. No contemporaneous sources exist apart from some place names and symbols that are difficult to interpret, and almost all we know stems from later Christian sources, mainly from the 13th century. According to these, the old Norse religion was polytheistic with a number of gods, goddesses, elves, land-spirits, and other spirits, the best known of which are probably the god of thunder *Thor* with his magical hammer *Mjölnir*, along with *Odin* and his wife *Frigg*. The rituals of the old Norse religion are described as practices in which local kings and chiefs played an important role, for example by carrying out public acts of sacrifice. Some sources mention also temples, for example in Uppsala, but there is no concrete contemporary evidence and no certain archaeological findings for such cultic buildings.

The old Norse religion was not centralised, but there were numerous local variations of cults and deities. Neither did all inhabitants of the Nordic countries practice it. Those living in present-day Finland or Lapland had their own beliefs and deities that had nothing to do with the *Æsir* and the *Vanir* of the old Norse religion, albeit with some similarities due to frequent contacts. The traditional Sámi religion, for example, was polytheistic and its beliefs were closely connected to the land, to animism, and to contacting the supernatural. The rituals were carried out by shamans or *noaidi* and included playing drums, chanting and entering trances, maybe by consuming fly agaric. Thus, there was no strong, common religion in Scandinavia nor central cultic places at the time when the Christian religion arrived. The previous pantheistic religions made it easier to introduce new gods, and during the first Christian centuries, there was much mutual religious borrowing in both directions.

The arrival of Christian faith to the territory and the conversion of the inhabitants to Christianity is difficult to trace exactly but some patterns can be seen especially in burial patterns: the deceased were no longer cremated, nor were they buried with grave goods, and the graves were orientated east-west, the head of the deceased being placed in the west. A change in burial habits indicates often a change of religion, but it is not a totally certain rule.

Western Christianity 900–1200

Christianity became the dominant religion of Europe in the Middle Ages in its two main forms, the eastern Greek and western Latin branches. In 1054, these came to an open rift when ecclesiastical leaders no longer could agree on several important doctrinal issues such as the theological status of the Holy Spirit and the universal jurisdiction of the bishop of Rome – the pope – over the other bishops.

After the schism, the Roman popes began a programme of ecclesiastical reforms with active legislation that unified the earlier ecclesiastical practices, building an effective central administration, tightening the papacy's control over the Christian territories, and spreading the Christian faith to the pagan territories in the north and Muslim ones in the south. The reform movement of the period is known as the Gregorian Reform after Pope Gregory VII (r. 1073–1085), who initiated a process of renewal within the Church. He aimed at improving the moral integrity of the Catholic priests as well as ensuring the independence of the clergy from secular rulers and jurisdiction. The latter led to a long controversy about the right to appoint bishops and abbots between the papacy and the European rulers, particularly the German Emperor, known as the Investiture Controversy.

When the Nordic territories became subject to Christian mission, the Christian Church had not yet split into two. Scandinavians were influenced both by the Eastern and the Western Church, and many had deep personal knowledge of the Eastern Greek Church through serving in Constantinople. After the split in 1054, the newly Christianised territories in the north eventually adopted Western Christianity from England or from Germany and followed the Roman pope, who granted great privileges to those rulers willing to convert and spread Christian faith in their territories and beyond, for example in the form of crusades. Scandinavian rulers seized this offer and also used it for their own political aims, as was explained in the previous chapter.

The conversion of Scandinavia was a complicated and prolonged process which lasted for centuries. In Denmark, it was mainly a top-down process, while the Swedish equivalent can rather be defined as bottom-up, and the Christianisation of Norway was something in between. Nor was it a linear or irreversible process but rather a result of negotiations and cultural choices, on occasion reversing direction according to which option was considered politically more profitable.

The Danish Church 900–1200

The first knowledge of the Christian faith arrived in Denmark through the seaborne Vikings' cultural and commercial contacts. The Vikings had especially close contacts with England and northern France, both of which had already been Christianised by the 7th century, and from where they brought home the knowledge of this religion. However, it took some time before Denmark could be defined as a Christian territory. We know very little about the circumstances of the first Christian contacts, and solely from sources outside Scandinavia.

The first missionaries arrived in Denmark in the 8th century. The mission to the Danes was closely connected with activities in Friesland where English monks preached. In Denmark, they often met a violent end because the pitiless Vikings and their rulers were not eager to hear about the Christian God. According to a text written by Charlemagne's court theologian Alcuin, an English missionary named

Willibrord arrived in Denmark from Friesland around the year 700. He preached to the local people and was even received by the local king, who was 'wilder than any animal and hard as a stone'. The meeting with the ruler was not successful and Willibrord had to flee from Denmark, but he managed to bring with him 30 young boys whom he baptised and taught the principles of Christianity. The tactic of adopting and teaching Christianity to young men having knowledge of local languages and habits was a useful missionary strategy, well known in the Middle Ages. These men could later return to their native lands and spread the new faith much more efficiently than foreigners could. However, there is no information about how successful Willibrord's mission was. Apparently, he and his followers did not manage to create any permanent Christian communities in the Danish territory. But the first contacts had been made.

In the following century, missionary activities in Scandinavia became more serious. This was possible because the Church, supported by the rulers, had established a stronger position in northern Germany, and the missionaries could use these territories as a base when they went further north. The founding of a new town along the River Elbe shortly after 800, Hamburg (*Hammaburg*), was central to missionary activities. Together with another north German town, Bremen, Hamburg became an important ecclesiastical centre and gained the status of an archbishopric. Saint Ansgar (801–865), also known as the 'Apostle of the North', was appointed Archbishop of Hamburg-Bremen and took an active role in the Christianisation of Scandinavia, which was included in his archbishopric's vast territory.

The Danes, especially the would-be king Harald Klak, had had an important role in the establishment of missionary connections. After King Godfred's death in 810, Denmark entered a civil war and Harald was one of the pretenders. He turned to the Frankish Emperor Louis for political support for his claim to the Danish throne. In the Emperor's court, Harald met Archbishop Ebo of Reims who baptised him and his entourage and agreed to political and religious collaboration. To fulfil the agreement Harald returned to Denmark with Ansgar. Ansgar's ambitions of converting the Danes fell flat, however, when Harald failed to ascend the Danish throne, although around 829/830 Ansgar continued his mission further north, in Sweden. When he returned home, he was appointed Archbishop of Hamburg-Bremen as a reward for his attempts to evangelise the north. Although his mission to Denmark failed, Ansgar did not give up the idea of converting the Scandinavians and later resumed his missionary activities in Danish territory. The first concrete result of Ansgar's new contacts with Denmark was receiving a permit to build a church in Hedeby (the modern-day town of Schleswig) and appointing a permanent priest there to continue missionary activities. King Horik II of Denmark (r. 850s–860s/870s?) at first forbade Christian mission in his country, but later in his reign accepted Christianity as one of its religions. He even donated land to build a church in the town of Ribe. From the same time, there has survived the first papal letter regarding the Danish territory – the Danish mission had become officially recognised at the highest ecclesiastical level.

The Christian mission in Denmark began to bear fruit in the 10th century, during the reign of Gorm the Old (r. c. 936–c. 958) and especially his son Harald Bluetooth (r. c. 958–c. 986). The recently crowned German Emperor Otto I took an active role in the Christian mission, sending Archbishop Unni of Hamburg-Bremen to Gorm to discuss a political alliance and religious matters. Gorm did not become Christian

Illustration 2.1 Ansgar, the 'Apostle of the North', was allowed to build a church in Hedeby and, around the middle of the 9th century, another one in Ribe on the west coast of Denmark. Missions to Scandinavia had begun to become organised. We do not know exactly what the churches looked like, but a replica has been made for the Viking Centre in Ribe which gives an impression of the interior of the very first, wooden churches in Scandinavia.

Photo Hjart, 2019. This work is licensed under the Creative Commons Attribution-Non Commercial – No Derivatives 4.0 International License.

but Harald was more favourable and allowed Unni to missionise in the Danish territory. Unni must have created Christian communities in Denmark because three Danish bishops – Hored of Schleswig, Leofdag of Ribe, and Reginbrand of Århus – participated in the ecclesiastical council at Ingelheim in 948. Danish sources reveal nothing about these men, and modern historians have even doubted their existence, but most probably they would have been missionary bishops of some sort within Unni's entourage (perhaps without a permanent connection to their missionary dioceses). When Harald became Danish king after his father, he took the important step of accepting baptism – and following the example of other European rulers declared his realm Christian.

The legend of Poppo, a missionary monk in Denmark, relates to the Danish king's conversion. Poppo had tried to convince Harald of the Christian faith and eventually went as far as to promise to carry glowing steel to demonstrate the strength of his faith. On the following day, Poppo did so and when he showed his uninjured hand to Harald, the king was convinced and accepted baptism.

Illustration 2.2 Poppo, the missionary bishop, baptising the Danish King Harald Bluetooth. The golden relief is from an early 12th-century altar decoration from the Church of Tamdrup and illustrates the legend of Denmark's Christianisation. It probably formed part of an attempt (which never succeeded) to have Harald, as Denmark's first Christian king, recognised as a saint and to create a cult for him.

Photo Sven Rosborn 2012. This file is licensed under the Creative Commons Attribution-Share Alike 3.0 Unported license.

The Danish Church was strengthened by connections to England – the Danish Viking kings also ruled large territories in the British Isles that had already been Christian for centuries. King Canute the Great, who also ruled England, was the first Danish king to seek direct contact with the papacy. Following the example of many other European rulers, in 1027 Canute took a pilgrimage to Rome, travelling together with the German King Conrad II. Pope John XIX welcomed him and established official connections with Denmark, while Canute agreed that the Danes would pay the so-called Peter's Pence (a payment of one pence per household) to the papacy. Subsequently, the popes began to include the Danish kings in the list of European rulers to whom they sent all important circular letters, while the Danes began to turn to the pope when they had a complicated religious situation to solve.

Despite the close connections to England, the Danish Church was connected administratively to Hamburg-Bremen, a link that the German archbishops wanted to continue. Around the year 1050, King Sweyn Estridsen of Denmark tried to dissolve the connection but only managed to annoy Archbishop Adalbert who procured a papal letter announcing the German archbishopric's supremacy over Denmark. Pope Benedict IX (r. 1032–1048) also appointed Adalbert as a papal legate, granting him the privilege of being the only person to ordain bishops in the north.

The conflict with Hamburg-Bremen did not last long and during the second half of the 11th century the Danish rulers – in collaboration with Hamburg-Bremen – concentrated on creating a permanent ecclesiastical structure in Denmark. Danish territory was divided into eight dioceses that lasted until the Reformation: Lund, Schleswig, Ribe, Århus, Roskilde, Odense, Viborg, and Vestervig (later Børglum/Aalborg). Dalby, close to Lund, was also listed as a bishop's see but never properly developed into one, disappearing fairly soon afterwards. The dioceses were subsequently divided into parishes that were established at a fast pace all over the country.

Despite the often relatively good relationship with the archbishops of Hamburg-Bremen, the Danes rulers had not given up the idea about independence or their own archiepiscopal see. This was also politically important, and the Danish kings were active. Because the papal power was not strong enough, the popes needed a strong alliance. Until the second half of the 11th century, the popes allied with the German emperors and therefore opposed the Danish request. But when the bond between the papacy and the German empire was broken during the Investiture Controversy between the papacy and the German emperors (traditionally dated 1076–1122), Pope Paschal II agreed to the request of King Eric Ejegod, who visited the pope during his pilgrimage to Rome and the Holy Land. Thus, the Danish effort bore fruit and in 1104 Lund was elevated to an archbishopric, and Asser was appointed its first Archbishop. The ecclesiastical province of Lund was huge, consisting of all Danish, Norwegian, and Swedish territories including Greenland, Iceland, and the western islands. Eric Ejegod also received from the papacy another important concession when his murdered brother King Canute († 1086) was canonised. Denmark thus received a national saint.

The time of Archbishop Asser (r. 1089–1137) was an important one for the Danish Church, in which it received its final structure. The 12th century was also a period of economic growth, of which the Church received its part in the form of generous donations. With the support of the Danish aristocracy – among which was the powerful Hvide family – numerous churches and monasteries were built all over the country.

The Danish Church ended up in the middle of the Danish political crises of the 12th century. Asser was a close friend of King Eric Ejegod and the guardian of his children while Eric and his wife Bodil were on pilgrimage to Jerusalem. After King Eric's death en route in 1103, his brother Niels was elected king instead of one of Eric's sons, and the country entered a civil war. This controversy resulted in 1131 in the murder of one of Eric's eldest legitimate sons, Canute Lavard, who was later canonised like his namesake uncle. Asser took the side of the dead Canute and his brother Eric

Emune. The other side allied with German princes, and the archbishop of Hamburg-Bremen tried to obtain the Danish archiepiscopal see – but did not succeed because Eric Emune's troops won in the decisive Battle of Fotevik in 1134.

In 1137 Asser was succeeded in the see of Lund by his nephew Eskil, who had been educated in Germany and was a close friend of Bernard of Clairvaux, the great monastic reformer and leader of the Cistercian order. Eskil, who held the position of archbishop for 40 years (1137–1177), expended a lot of energy in implementing the principles of the Gregorian Reform, such as clerical celibacy, in the Danish Church, and introduced ecclesiastical law in Scania probably around 1171. This active Archbishop also intervened in internal Danish struggles and defended his archiepiscopal see from the Germans. Eskil had to give up some of his power over north, when in 1152/1153 the Norwegian province of Nidaros was established as independent. But the Swedish province remained under Lund's supremacy.

In the Danish political struggle, Eskil did not stand with Valdemar I the Great, who became the sole ruler in 1157. However, Valdemar was in good terms with the papacy because of his policy of active crusading in the Baltic See territory, and the Archbishop not only had to live with that but even go into exile for some years. Valdemar and Eskil made peace, and the Archbishop presided over the important celebration in the church at Ringsted in June 1170, in which he canonised King Valdemar's father, the murdered Canute Lavard, and crowned Valdemar's eldest legitimate son, the seven-year-old Canute, as co-ruler and heir of the throne.

Eskil obtained papal permission to abdicate from the archiepiscopal seat in 1177, which was such an unusual step that the papal letter confirming the right was added to the collection of canon law as an extraordinary exception from common practice. Eskil left Denmark and lived out his remaining years in the monastery of Clairvaux in France. The question of his successor at Lund was left open and to the canons of Lund to resolve. The Danish historian Saxo Grammaticus, working for Bishop Absalon of Roskilde, wrote that Eskil himself had in mind a suitable man for the position – none other than Bishop Absalon of Roskilde, a member of the powerful Danish aristocratic Hvide family. In him, the Danish Church would gain not only a politically powerful man but also one with a university education and large international ecclesiastical network. According to Saxo, Absalon first humbly declined the position but the canons of Lund persuaded him, and he was appointed. In reality, other sources show that the priests of Lund would have preferred Eskil being succeeded by someone else, but Absalon snatched the election and archbishopric with the help of King Valdemar.

Absalon's election marked an important break in the tradition of the Latin church, because with papal permission he also continued as bishop of Roskilde after being installed as Archbishop of Lund. Only in 1192 did he give up Roskilde. To hold two such high-ranking offices for 14 years was unheard of. Absalon was – like his predecessor – politically active and strongly supported his own family. For example, he let his relative Peder Sunesen be elected to the seat of Roskilde after him, while Absalon's successor to the see of Lund in 1201 was Peder's brother Anders Sunesen. Important parts of the Danish Church were thus now in the hands of the Hvide family, loyal to the Danish royal family. From the late 12th century onwards, the Danish Church worked closely together with Danish rulers. This could be seen especially in the Danish activity of spreading Christianity to nearby territories through regular crusades. Crusading activity had begun earlier, and King Valdemar I had become famous after his troops had conquered the important pagan temple of the Wends at Arkona on the island of Rügen in 1168.

Illustration 2.3 Archbishop Absalon of Lund († 1201), the missionary bishop eager for the crusades against the Slavic peoples south of the Baltic Sea, depicted here in full armour and with a small axe in his hand in the centre of Copenhagen. The equestrian statue by the famous artist Vilhelm Bissen was made to commemorate the 700th anniversary of Absalon's death but was delayed and only inaugurated in 1902.

Photo Calimo 2013. This file is licensed under the Creative Commons Attribution-Share Alike 3.0 Unported license.

The Norwegian Church 900–1200

In Norway, the first contacts with Christians took place via commerce and travel in the 9th century when the Vikings sailed to England and northern France, already Christianised for several centuries. As a result of this, some Norwegian chieftains accepted the new faith and were baptised. They invited missionaries and let them preach in Norway. The first contacts with Christianity were mainly limited to the coastal areas and merely built on individual contacts rather than any systematic or organised mission.

The late 12th-century saga tradition attributes the Norwegian conversion to two rulers: Haakon the Good (r. 934–961) and Olaf Tryggvason (r. 995–1000). According to the sagas, Haakon the Good was the first Norwegian ruler who attempted to convert the whole country to the Christian faith. The saga relates that Olaf had been Christianised around ten years prior to his ascension to the throne of Norway while staying in England and that during his reign, he forced a great number of Norwegians to convert to Christianity.

While archaeological findings and other information cannot fully corroborate the saga texts, it seems that the inhabitants of western Norway, ruled by Haakon and his nephews, learned of Christianity latest at that time. The connection with Christian England was important for the contemporary Christianisation of Norway. The basic idea behind the saga story of Haakon the Good's conversion is thus credible. English sources also mention a Sigefredus, bishop of the Norwegians (*Sigefredus Northmannorum episcopus*) during the rule of English King Edgar the Peaceful (r. 959–975). To be titled bishop to a people, the Norwegians, was typical for missionary bishops without a fixed episcopal see. Such bishops might have visited their bishoprics and missionised there, but their title might also have been only nominal. The Norwegian conversion was slow and some of Haakon's successors were Christian, some not. However, the archaeological evidence confirms that Christian burials became dominant in the western parts of Norway during the second half of the 10th century at the latest. By contrast, the territory of Trøndelagen was converted later, an event typically attributed to Olaf Tryggvason, who conquered the region and forced the inhabitants to accept baptism. He has also been given credit for promoting the conversion of Iceland, the Faroes, Orkney, and Shetland, as well as Greenland, by sending missionaries to these places. The northern area of Norway, Finnmark, remained non-Christian for a longer time, with the Christian influence spreading there during the 13th century.

During the 11th century, most of Norway was Christianised and the ecclesiastical system of administration was introduced to the country. The best known Christian king of Norway at that time was Olaf II Haraldsson (r. 1015–1028), Norway's patron saint. He managed to unite the country during his rule, and he was a supporter of the Christian faith to which he had converted in Normandy shortly before his conquest of Norway. His rule ended in civil wars, and he was killed in 1030 in the Battle of Stiklestad while he tried to reconquer Norway. His earthly remains were buried in Nidaros. We have no certain information about his importance to Norway's conversion, although he has typically been credited for it thanks to Grimkell, an English missionary in the retinue of Olaf. Only one year after Olaf's death, Grimkell had created a cult for him in Nidaros, turned the town into a pilgrimage centre, and had Olaf proclaimed a saint. Olaf's cult was extremely important for the consolidation of Christianity in Norway and for the country's unification.

For most of the 11th century, the Church in Norway remained in a phase of consolidation, with debate as to whether it should belong under the authority of the archbishops of York. Some Norwegian rulers supported the English connection because of the strong English influence during the conversion period. In 1053, however, Pope Leo IX (r. 1049–1054) placed Norwegian territory under the archbishops of Hamburg-Bremen.

We have no knowledge about established Norwegian dioceses before c. 1100. In the 1070s, Adam of Bremen mentions that the Norwegian dioceses did not have any fixed boundaries. However, the ecclesiastical structure had begun to take form at that time, because sources from shortly after 1100 mention three Norwegian dioceses: Oslo, Bergen, and Nidaros. It is probable that these three were established during the reign of Olaf III Kyrre (r. 1067–1093). The two other Norwegian dioceses, Hamar and Stavanger, are slightly younger. The diocese of Stavanger was separated from that of Bergen around 1125, and the diocese of Hamar from that of Oslo shortly after 1150.

The establishment of a permanent parish structure in Norway must be dated to the same period because fixed dioceses are not possible without the existence of well-defined parishes. The parish borders followed typically those of the *fylki*, which were districts of secular administration. In each fylke, there were usually multiple churches but with one of them considered the principal church of the district. The churches were built by local magnates, and wealthy persons could also have private churches or chapels. The system of tithes was also introduced to Norway alongside the formation of a parish structure.

In 1103/1104, Lund became a metropolitan see in the aftermath of the Investiture Controversy – the conflict between the papacy and the emperors over the powers to appoint bishops and abbots. When the popes tried to delimit German bishops' power in the North due to the conflict, Norwegian territory was included within the province of Lund, but when the Danish kings allied with the Germans, the popes sought to diminish Lund's influence and granted the Norwegians' wish for their own independent church province with its seat at Nidaros. In 1152, Pope Eugene III (r. 1145–1153) sent Cardinal Nicholas Breakspear to settle the question as papal legate to Norway. The Cardinal, later pope Hadrian IV (r. 1154–1159), established the province of Nidaros and consecrated Bishop Jon Birgersson of Stavanger as its first Archbishop in 1153. On the same occasion, the Cardinal ordered that from then on the Norwegians had to pay Peter's Pence to the papacy, also giving some general instructions as to how the cathedral chapters should be formed and how the cathedral canons should receive their income.

The province of Nidaros consisted of five Norwegian dioceses – Nidaros, Bergen, Hamar, Oslo, and Stavanger – as well as seven dioceses in the Norwegian realm's territory in the Atlantic – Orkney and Shetland, the Faroes, the Hebrides and Isle of Man, Iceland (two dioceses: Skálholt and Hólar), and Greenland (diocese of Gardar). The province of Nidaros was thus the largest province geographically in the whole Christian West, and it remained so until 1472 when the province of Saint Andrews in Scotland was created, and Orkney, Shetland, as well as the Hebrides and Isle of Man were transferred to its authority. From the point of view of the secular administration, some of these territories did not belong to the Norwegian realm for long. The Hebrides and the Isle of Man, for example, were already ceded administratively to Scotland in 1266.

According to the sagas, Christianity's arrival in Greenland was due to Olaf Tryggvason, who sent missionaries to all parts of his realm. There is very little information about early ecclesiastical events in Greenland, but a bishop is mentioned in 1112/1113. It is not known whether the diocese of Gardar was permanently founded at that time or for how long it continued to function. Historians have argued that there were probably not any Norwegian inhabitants in Greenland much after the turn of the 14th and 15th centuries, at which time there was no bishop in Gardar either.

The Scandinavians in Greenland made some expeditions to America, probably in search for timber, and a single remark in contemporary annals relates that a bishop of Greenland went to America in 1121. It was probably an attempt to extend the Christian mission yet further, although nothing is known of the bishop or his fate.

The early 12th century was not only the time for establishing dioceses and parishes, but it was the period when the first monasteries were founded in Norway. The first monastic order to arrive was the Benedictines with the foundation of the monastery of Nidarholm, in Nidaros, around 1100. A little later monasteries were founded in Bergen (Munkaliv) and on the island of Selje. Some decades later, other orders also began to spread to Norway. The first Cistercian monastery was founded in the 1140s by the bishop of Bergen in Lyse, close to the episcopal town. The first Augustinian monastery was established around 1150, with the Premonstratensian order arriving in Norway at the same time.

The period after the creation of the province of Nidaros was important for the Norwegian church, which during the rule of Archbishop Eystein Erlendsson (r. 1168–1180) significantly increased its power. The period was good for the Church because the Archbishop was on excellent terms with the Norwegian Jarl Erling and his son Magnus. The development of the Church and the country went hand in hand, and the Archbishop gained significant political influence by supporting the Jarl's suggestion of royal succession by primogeniture (so that the oldest son should become king after

Illustration 2.4 Selje monastery on the west coast of a small island off the Norwegian coast. Some of the early Scandinavian monasteries from the 12th century tried to promote Christianity through isolation and contemplation rather than active missionary work among people.

Photo Svein-Magne Tunli 2018. This file is licensed under the Creative Commons Attribution-Share Alike 4.0 International license.

his father). He also crowned the young King Magnus, the first Scandinavian king to be crowned.

Eystein played an important role in supporting the development and spreading of the cult of Saint Olaf of Norway, and Nidaros soon became an important international pilgrimage site. The Archbishop was also active in introducing the ecclesiastical reform of the late 12th century, known as the Gregorian Reform, into his province. This included the introduction of clerical celibacy and of the ecclesiastical law's complicated marriage regulations – the first of which was never really accepted among the Norwegian clergy who continued to marry or have concubines and produce offspring, as with clerics in many other territories. Eystein was also active in developing and centralising ecclesiastical administration to the hands of bishops and the archbishop. The period of Archbishop Eystein ended in 1180 when Sverre Sigurdsson killed King Magnus Erlingsson and assumed the Norwegian crown. He ended up in collision with the Archbishop, who as the supporter of the previous king lost his political influence and had to flee the country. He was soon joined by other Norwegian bishops who also had issues with King Sverre. When Pope Innocent III learned of what had happened in Norway, he excommunicated the King for obstructing the bishops. The situation remained unresolved during Sverre's reign (r. 1184–1202), and it was only his son King Haakon who was reconciled with the papacy and the Norwegian church.

The Icelandic Church 900–1200

The Christianisation of Iceland can easily be attributed to one specific event. The inhabitants of Iceland accepted the Christian faith in the year 1000 at their yearly assembly, *althing*. According to the saga sources, the Norwegian King Olaf Tryggveson had sent missionaries to the island who had converted some local chieftains. Some missionaries are known by name; one of them was Thangbrand, who according to the Icelandic sagas fought pagans armed only with a crucifix, and in the end killed two or three Icelanders who had made derogatory verses about Christianity.

All important issues concerning Iceland that might endanger the local peace had to be brought before the *althing*. Since the embracing of the Christian faith was a major issue and brought with it several consequences, for example regarding marriage and everyday habits, the Christian chieftains took it up at the *althing*. The participants agreed upon conversion and stipulated a time limit within which all inhabitants should give up old non-Christian habits and accept the new religion. The old habits that were permitted to continue for a couple of years included making offerings to ancestors or the local deity in private and eating horsemeat.

The story of Iceland's conversion through the missionising of the Norwegian king is interesting, and perhaps partially true – but it is also certain that the Icelanders had already learned of the Christian faith long before that through their trading networks in the Atlantic. English missionaries, not only Norwegian, also visited the island, as hermits had done occasionally in the previous centuries.

In the mid-11th century, Iceland was included within the territory of the archbishopric of Hamburg-Bremen, giving Icelanders direct contacts with the German see. In 1056 Isleif, the son of one of the chieftains who had suggested conversion at the *althing*, was consecrated in Bremen as the first Icelandic bishop. At that time Iceland did not have an episcopal see, so he acted as bishop from his own farm at Skálholt. Isleif's successor, his son Gizur, then turned Skálholt into a proper episcopal see.

In the early 12th century, when Scandinavia was separated from the Hamburg-Bremen see and Lund established as the metropolitan of the Nordic territories, Iceland came under Lund's authority. There were concrete contacts between Icelanders and Lund because Archbishop Asser consecrated Icelandic bishops, as well as suggesting Iceland's division into two bishoprics in 1106. Another diocese was founded in the northern area of the island, in Hólar. These two dioceses, Skálholt and Hólar, remained in use for the rest of the Middle Ages.

When the province of Nidaros was established in 1152/1153, Iceland became part of the Norwegian church. By that time, a kind of parish system had been created in Iceland. Local administration was based on the power of the local chieftains, *goðar*, who gathered regularly at the *althing*. The same structure was also adopted in the Icelandic church. Some chieftains combined the position of local ruler and priest, or appointed their sons as priests to the villages under their control. In Icelandic history, the civil and ecclesiastical administrations therefore worked very closely together, and the Church was really governed locally. The local chieftains additionally owned the churches where the congregation gathered (this practice is known also elsewhere, like for example in Germany, where this practice is known as the *Eigenkirche* system: the system of proprietary churches).

On the Norwegian mainland, the parish system had been differently established, with the churches not owned by the local magnates but more often built and maintained by their communities. The Norwegian archbishops tried to establish the same kind of system in Iceland too, and thus to diminish the power of the local secular chieftains within the Church. However, the reform attempt of the Norwegian Archbishop Eystein never succeeded due to the resistance of the chieftains who were accustomed to decide on ecclesiastical matters.

In addition to the formation of a parish structure on the island, some monastic institutions arrived in Iceland during the first Christian centuries. The Benedictines and the Augustinian canons were the first. The Benedictine order set foot on the island in the first half of the 12th century, establishing a number of monasteries including Þingeyraklaustur in Þingeyrar. The monastery was founded by Bishop Jón Ögmundsson in 1106, but it was inaugurated only in 1133 when its first abbot, Vilmundur Þórólfsson, was officially installed in office. The Augustinians established four houses in the diocese of Skálholt and one in the diocese of Hólar. Their first establishment was founded c. 1168 in Þykkivibær by Þorlákur Þorhallason, who had studied in Paris and became bishop of Skálholt in 1173. He died in 1193 and was soon venerated as saint, although he only gained official papal canonisation in 1984 when Pope John Paul II declared him the patron saint of Iceland.

The Swedish Church 900–1200

The Swedes too had already established their first contacts with the Christian faith before Sweden became an object for Christian mission. These took place during the many annual journeys the Swedes undertook to neighbouring territories whether to trade, wage war, or plunder. According to archaeological finds, these contacts began during the 8th century, and the objects found testify to contacts both with western and eastern Christianity. It is unclear whether Swedes who possessed Christian items can be considered Christians or whether they had only received these items from whatever source without appreciating their religious meaning.

However, in the 9th century, Sweden became a target for Christian mission. The stabilisation of the Church and political power in northern Europe made it possible to look towards new territories for conquest. An important event in this development was the founding of Hamburg, which became the centre of mission towards the north. The first person known by name to perform missionary work among the Swedes was Saint Ansgar, the Archbishop of Hamburg-Bremen (801–865). His saint's legend mentions two missions to Birka, which was the centre of trade in the territory of Lake Mälaren. For the first time, Ansgar arrived at Birka around 829/830 and stayed for a year and a half, while his second mission took place two decades later, around 852. Ansgar preached to the locals, some of which were already familiar with Christianity. He baptised several persons and began the building of three churches.

Although the author of Ansgar's *vita*, Archbishop Rimbert of Hamburg-Bremen († 888), tells of a successful mission in Birka, the Christian congregations were not permanent. The author of the well-known chronicles of the deeds of the archbishops of Hamburg-Bremen, Adam of Bremen, recounts in his chronicle from the 1070s that when Archbishop Unni of Hamburg-Bremen visited Birka in the mid-930s he could not find any traces of Christian worship in the town. According to Adam, however, Unni managed to re-establish Christian practices in Birka, although archaeological finds cannot confirm that.

The 10th century can be considered the first Christian century of Swedish ecclesiastical history. It is not certain how or why, but Birka lost its central position, and new places began to gain significance. At the same time, Christian burial habits began to spread in various parts of Götaland and Svealand. From the late 10th century onwards, English missionaries became active in Sweden. One of these was Saint Sigfrid, who arrived in the early 11th century. According to the later saint's legend from the 13th century, he first worked in Växjö, then continued his mission around Skara, later returning to Växjö. Another English missionary in Sweden was Eskil, said to have missionised in the region of Södermanland. He found martyrdom and was buried in Eskilstuna. Eskil was venerated as a saint, and so were many other contemporary missionaries such as Botvid, who is connected to Södertörn and Stockholm region (Botkyrka), and Staffan who was missionary in the Hälsingland region.

The first Swedish cathedral churches were built in places where the missionaries had been active – and in places around the burial and cult sites of the martyrised missionaries. Some of them are still ecclesiastical centres, while others have lost their significance. Skara is the oldest of the episcopal cities still in existence, and its territory originally covered the regions of Västergötland and Östergötland. Sigtuna, the second oldest ecclesiastical centre with a bishop from around the 1060s, was abandoned in the 1130s in favour of Gamla (Old) Uppsala – from where it was transferred to the present-day Uppsala in the 1270s. Other medieval diocesan centres were Linköping, Strängnäs, Västerås, Växjö, and Eskilstuna, although the last one ceased to be such relatively early. Turku, in present-day Finland, is the youngest of the Swedish medieval dioceses, established in the 13th century. Thus, the medieval Swedish dioceses were up until the Reformation (in alphabetical order): Linköping, Skara, Strängnäs, Turku, Uppsala, Västerås, and Växjö.

Each diocese was divided into parishes – autonomous entities with their own taxation, church building and parish priest, which according to Swedish medieval law their parishioners had to finance. The foundation of the Swedish parishes went hand in hand with the development of the local administration and increasing royal

54 900–1200: Formation

powers, especially since the Swedish kings of the 11th and 12th centuries often allied with the Church. The first patron saint of the realm was King Eric Jedvarsson, who was killed in Uppsala on 18 May 1160 by the Danish pretender Magnus Henriksson. The Swedes thus followed the model of the Norwegians and Danes who both had their royal patron saints, Saints Olaf and Canute respectively. But it was not just that the royals used the Church for political ends – the relationship was mutual. It was also important for the Swedish Church to be involved in royal coronations; since priests were typically literate and well educated, the kings often wanted to use them as counsellors or advisors. In fact, Swedish bishops automatically belonged to the council of the realm for the whole medieval period.

The Swedish church province was created as an independent administrative territory in 1164, when Uppsala was recognised as archiepiscopal centre. Why the archiepiscopal seat was located in Uppsala is not clear – it could as well have been another of the medieval Swedish dioceses. The first attempts to create a Swedish province had been in 1152–1153, when the papal legate Cardinal Nicholas Breakspear visited Scandinavia. For unknown reasons, however, he did not create a Swedish ecclesiastical

Illustration 2.5 Church behind pagan graves. Old Uppsala became an episcopal see in the 1130s and in 1164 it was raised to an archiepiscopal see, which was moved to present-day Uppsala in the 1270s. Old Uppsala had been a numinous centre for centuries. The landscape is dominated by the three enormous burial mounds from the 6th century and literally hundreds of minor mounds and burial sites. Uppsala was also, according to the historian Adam of Bremen, the centre for a pagan cult and temple. The new Christian faith received authority from connecting to the old pagan belief system.

Photo Leappel 2018. This file is licensed under the Creative Commons Attribution-Share Alike 4.0 International license.

province as he did in Norway with Nidaros. According to the Danish historian Saxo, writing around 1200, the Swedish aristocrats and ecclesiastical authorities could not agree upon the location of the archiepiscopal see. The Cardinal had certainly meant to create a Swedish province, since on his way back to the pope he visited Lund and left Archbishop Eskil a *pallium* intended for the Swedish Archbishop. A *pallium* is a long white narrow band of lambswool, symbolising the powers conferred by the pope upon the archbishop. The Cardinal instructed the Danish Archbishop to hand the *pallium* over to the Swedish archbishop when one was chosen. In 1164, the Swedish king, bishops, and the jarl finally decided that the Swedish bishop to receive the *pallium* should be Stefan of Uppsala. He became thus the first Swedish Archbishop.

During the 11th and 12th centuries, the Swedish Church spread and established its territorial borders, parishes, and dioceses. The Swedish Church did not only expand in the core Swedish areas but also played an important role in Swedish expansion to the east. Swedish rulers had a long tradition of making raids into the territories around the Baltic See. In the course of the 12th century, the Church became an important part of this expansion as the crusade ideology spread to northern Europe. According to his later saint's legend from shortly before 1300, the Swedish King Eric Jedvardsson led a crusade to Finland in the 1150s supported by a missionary Bishop Henry, which led to the conversion of the Finns and the inclusion of their territory in the Swedish realm.

Monastic institutions arrived in Sweden in the 12th century. At that time, the Benedictines and the Cistercians were the most widespread monastic orders, and also the first ones to set foot on Swedish territory. The Cistercians had a special significance for the Scandinavians because of the personal connections of Archbishop Eskil of Lund with Bernard of Clairvaux, the mighty leader of the Cistercian order. Due to the Archbishop's contacts and the support of King Sverker the Elder, the first Cistercian monastery in Scandinavia was founded in Alvastra in 1143. In the same year, another Cistercian monastery was also founded in Sweden, in Nydala, by Bishop Gisle of Linköping together with the king and local noblemen. After that, the Cistercian order spread across the country. Some of the older Benedictine monasteries were reformed and turned Cistercian, such as the nunnery in Vreta.

The Finnish Church 900–1200

Knowledge of the Christian faith reached the inhabited south-western shores of present-day Finland at the latest during the 11th century, via trade contacts. There are no contemporary written sources about this but the archaeological finds include numerous items of foreign provenance that evidence religious, cultural and economic exchange between the Finns and neighbouring populations, from both west and east.

The first signs of Christians and ecclesiastical organisation in Finland were to be found in the western coastal region of Satakunta and the territories around the later episcopal town of Turku. There is no certain information about the identity of the first Christians and how they learned about the religion, but since the Baltic Sea territory had been subject to activity by missionaries for a long time, it is no wonder if some also reached Finland's coastal regions.

According to medieval narratives from around 1300, Finland became Christianised when the Swedish King Eric led a crusade there in the 1150s. There are no contemporary historical sources about this crusade, and many historians have questioned its historicity because the earliest information on it derives from the later saints' legends of King Eric and the martyr Bishop Henry, who followed the king on the crusade. According to the bishop's legend and another vernacular tale of his death in Finland, Bishop Henry stayed in Finland and managed to convert Finns to the Christian faith, but was martyred by a local man. The Latin legend only mentions a man as the murderer, but the Finnish version reveals his name to be Lalli. It is possible that the first crusade to Finland never took place as told in the legend, but since the 12th century was a period of numerous crusades in the Baltic Sea region it is plausible that the Swedes made military attacks upon Finland, combining political expansion with missionary activities.

Until the 13th century, there was no permanent ecclesiastical administration in Finnish territory, the region being supervised by missionary bishops without a permanent residence. We have also only very sporadic and spurious information about people who held the title of Bishop of Finns, a certain Rodulfus and Folkvinus. However, archaeological finds show that Christian traditions began to be established in Finland during the 12th century when the first churches were also built. These were small, belonging to one family or village, and along with the surrounding graveyards sometimes built upon an older non-Christian burial place, showing a continuum with pre-Christian times.

Illustration 2.6 Bishop Henry began the mission to the Finns but was chased over the frozen ice of Lake Köyliö by the peasant Lalli. Henry had visited Lalli's house and taken food from his wife; Lalli took revenge by killing Henry with his axe. This story is late and legendary, but became important within the national romanticism of the 19th century, when Lalli became a symbol for Finnish independence.

Painting by C. A. Ekman, 1854. Public domain.

Unlike the other Scandinavian countries, knowledge of Christianity in Finland not only arrived from the west but there are also signs of eastern mission in Finnish-speaking territory: for example the first Christian words in Finnish, *pappi* (priest), *pakana* (pagan), and *risti* (cross), derive from Church Slavic.

The Long Arms of the Papacy

With the adoption of the Christian faith, the Scandinavians became a part of Western Christianity and accepted the bishop of Rome, the pope, as their spiritual overlord. According to the autocratic model of the Roman Catholic Church, the popes possessed powers in all fields of ecclesiastical administration, justice, dogma, and theology.

The administrative structure serving the pope was extremely effective. It had already begun to develop in the first Christian centuries, but the central administration known as the papal curia only became fully developed during the high Middle Ages, at the same time as the conversion of Scandinavia gained momentum. The ecclesiastical administration was affected through four different bodies: (1) the general Church councils; (2) the central administration of the Church; (3) papal representatives sent across Christendom; and (4) the local administrative hierarchy that spread throughout the Christian West.

The General Church Councils

The general church councils took the most important decisions regarding the Church, such as those concerning theological dogma or fundamental ecclesiastical jurisdiction. Hundreds of representatives – bishops, archbishops, metropolitans, cardinals, local rulers, and other influential Christians – were invited to the councils from all the Church's provinces.

The first medieval general church council was celebrated in the Lateran Church in Rome in 1123. It was followed by a series of ecumenical councils: the Second Lateran Council (1139), the Third Lateran Council (1179), the Fourth Lateran Council (1215), the First Council of Lyon (1245), the Second Council of Lyon (1274), the Council of Vienne (1311–1312), the Council of Constance (1414–1418), the Council of Basel, Ferrara and Florence (1431–1445), and the Fifth Lateran Council (1512–1517). The earlier councils concentrated on clerical discipline, political relations and developing canon law regulations, while the late medieval ones focused on fighting heresies and reforming the Church.

The most influential of the high medieval councils was the Fourth Lateran, convoked in Rome by Pope Innocent III which started on 11 November 1215. The Pope had already sent the invitations to the council in April 1213, which meant that a large number of participants from all over the Western Church had time to prepare for their attendance. It attracted 71 patriarchs, metropolitans or archbishops, 412 bishops, and 900 abbots and priors, as well as a large number of representatives of European rulers. Several Scandinavians also participated, even if Archbishop Anders Sunesen of Lund tried to excuse himself from attending. However, he was sharply reprimanded by his old study comrade, Pope Innocent III, and came all the way to Rome, gaining important privileges from the Pope afterwards.

The Papal Curia

The papal curia was complex. Due to the manifold tasks facing the popes from the 11th century onwards, they could no longer personally handle all cases referred to them but had to delegate their powers to trusted men. This led to the birth and differentiation of the various offices within the papal curia. All central papal offices were in existence by the 11th or 12th centuries at the latest, although the Church's administrative structure continued to develop to the late Middle Ages and beyond.

The medieval popes made decisions about the most important ecclesiastical matters – such as episcopal or abbatial appointments, or foreign policy – in presence of the cardinals, the most high-ranking ecclesiastics (besides the pontiff himself), who helped and advised him in regular meetings known as consistories. By contrast, the Church's everyday business was entrusted to the curial offices, each of which had its own tasks and whose officials worked under the guidance of a prelate, often a cardinal. Christians from all over the Christian West could turn to these offices with their requests to get issues handled by them.

Christians who needed a papal absolution, dispensation, privilege, licence, declaration, or another type of favour had to turn to the papal curia with a written petition called a supplication. The supplications were then directed to the right office and handled there. The papal curia processed hundreds of thousands of cases every year, and the papal archives that were opened for scholars in the 1880s include thousands of documents concerning medieval Scandinavia.

Papal Representatives

Although it was possible for the popes to rule Christendom from the Holy See, there were matters that required local knowledge unavailable within the curia. In such cases, the popes sent out a personal representative, chosen from high-ranking ecclesiastics, often cardinals, who usually had some knowledge of the local situation and languages. In the late Middle Ages, the use of papal representatives increased considerably, and there emerged a hierarchy of papal envoys: legates, judges delegate, nuncios, and collectors.

Legates were the most eminent group of papal representatives, appointed personally by the pontiff. They were very often cardinals sent abroad for settling important ecclesiastical matters such as presiding to local ecclesiastical synods or preaching crusades, or for a diplomatic mission. The most famous papal legates in Scandinavia have been Cardinal Nicholas Breakspear in the early 1150s and Cardinal William of Sabina in the late 1240s. Additionally, Archbishop Anders Sunesen of Lund was appointed as a papal legate in 1204.

The tasks of the papal nuncios were more general and practical. They were often of slightly inferior ecclesiastical rank (bishops or prelates), and they were typically sent to a certain territory for a certain period to take care of all the pope's errands there. Alongside the nuncios, the popes appointed collectors, who gathered the revenues donated to the Church. In the later Middle Ages, the roles of papal nuncio and collector were often combined. They also functioned as a kind of ambassador, an official representative of the very highest level, sometimes possessing little humility. 'They who receive the pope or his nuncio, receive Christ Himself', wrote Marinus de Fregano in 1474 when he was sent to Scandinavia as papal nuncio and collector.

Sometimes, the popes needed help in judging particularly difficult legal cases. For such purposes, the popes appointed legal experts called judges delegate. The practice of appointing judges delegate became common during the 12th century.

Ecclesiastical Administration at Local Level

Alongside the central administration of the Catholic Church, ecclesiastical administration was spread over the whole territory of Western Christendom according to a clearly defined hierarchical model. Its top was the pope, and directly under him were the ecclesiastical provinces. The Christian West was divided into well over one hundred provinces, each governed by a metropolitan or archbishop. Originally, the title of metropolitan referred to the bishops of the earliest episcopal towns such as Constantinople. In the high Middle Ages, the title was also given to those bishops who held the most important dioceses in a certain territory, but these titles were changed in the course of the 13th century to that of archbishop. Thus, there was practically no difference in the roles of metropolitans and archbishops, although the oldest archiepiscopal seats were often called metropolitan seats.

The province of Lund is a good example of such practice. In the first years of the 12th century, Lund became an independent province and the archbishop of Lund was elevated to metropolitan status. At that time the province of Lund encompassed the whole of Scandinavia including the islands in the north and Greenland, but Norway and Sweden were soon separated into their own ecclesiastical provinces. The Norwegian province of Nidaros was created in 1152/1153 and the Swedish province of Uppsala in 1164. The metropolitan archbishop of Lund acted for some time as a kind of *primus inter pares* including the two other Scandinavian archbishops, but Nidaros quickly became independent while the Swedish province remained, in theory, subordinate to the archbishop of Lund. In practice, however, he did not have any influence upon the Swedish Church.

The province of Lund covered the territory of the medieval Danish realm including Schleswig in the south-west, Jutland, and the isles of Funen and Zealand, as well as the regions of Scania, Blekinge, and Halland in the territory of present-day Sweden. In some periods, it also included Rügen and parts of Estonia. The Norwegian church province of Nidaros was the largest of all, covering a huge territory including southern Greenland, Iceland, the islands between Iceland, Scotland, and Norway (Faroe, Hebrides, Shetland, Orkney), the present-day Norway, and the regions of Härjedalen and Bohuslän which nowadays belong to Sweden. The Swedish province of Uppsala covered the area of present-day Sweden (excluding the territories within the Danish and Norwegian provinces) and Finland.

The ecclesiastical provinces in their turn were divided into smaller administrative territories called dioceses, which were led by bishops subordinate to the archbishops but acting independently. The territory of Western Christendom encompassed more than one thousand dioceses. The three Scandinavian church provinces were divided into almost thirty dioceses.

The dioceses were divided into smaller administrative units called parishes. Parish administration was entrusted to the parish priest. In principle, there could be a midlevel administration between the dioceses and parishes, called archdeaconries or rural deaconries. However, their significance was quite different in the Scandinavian countries than in England, Germany or Italy, for example. These mid-level administrative entities consisted of an undefined number of parishes, and their administration was

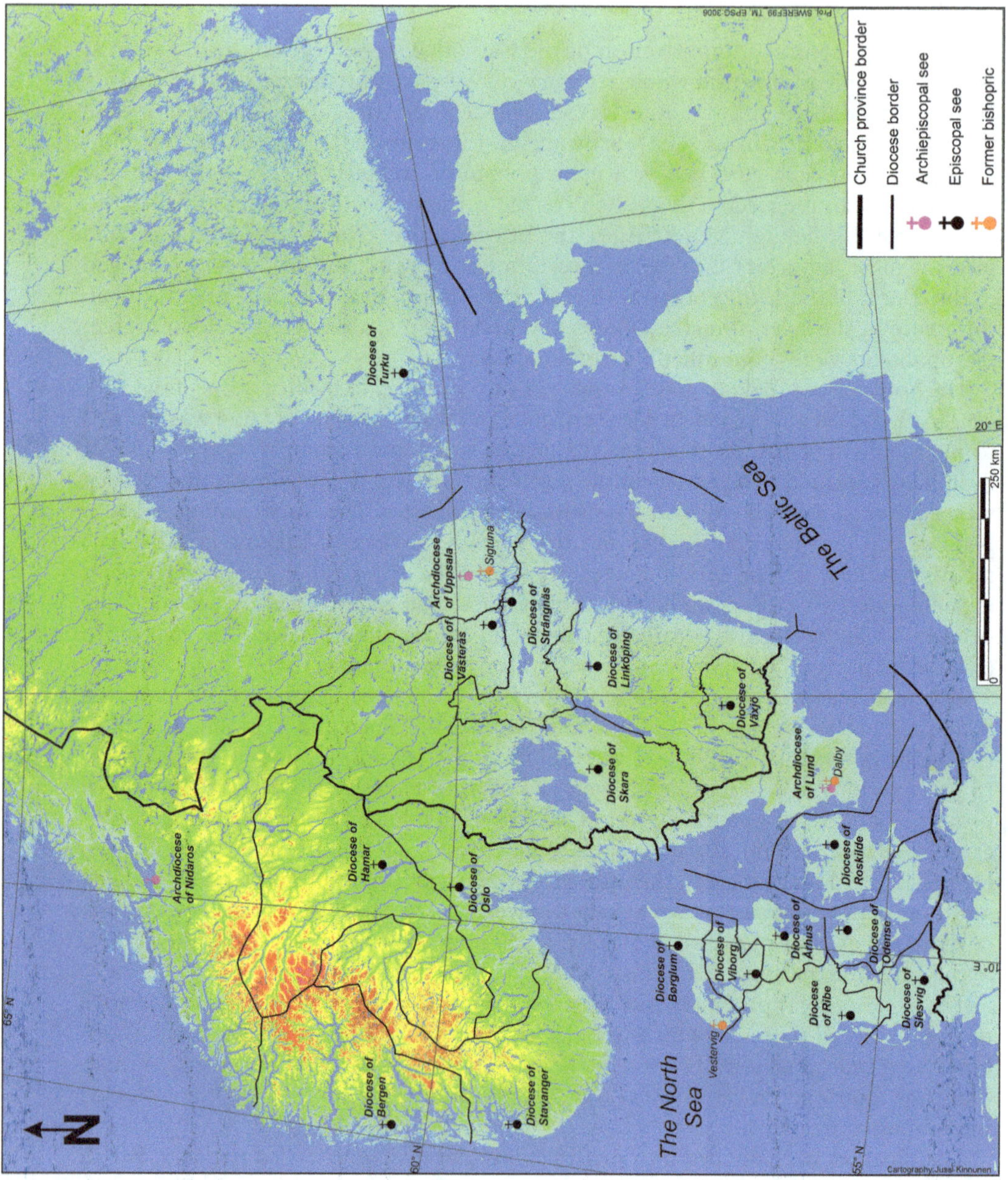

60 900–1200: Formation

Map 4 Church provinces in Scandinavia.
Map © Jussi Kinnunen, 2022

entrusted to one of the parish priests in the area, who could use the title of rural dean. However, this administrative layer varied much according to time and territory: for example in the diocese of Turku the rural deaconries functioned in practice only at the juridical level, while in Norway they had also economic and other functions such as the collection of tithes.

The Danish ecclesiastical province comprised c. 2,700 parishes, the province of Nidaros of almost 1,900 parishes, and the province of Uppsala c. 1,800 parishes. The parishes' sizes could vary substantially, depending upon an area's population density. In southern Scandinavia and on Gotland, there was only 3–4 km between the parish churches, but in northern Scandinavia sometimes hundreds of kilometres. In addition to the c. 6,400 parish churches, there were also other ecclesiastical buildings such as chapels in which chaplains could celebrate masses under the supervision of the parish priest. Monasteries, friaries, and nunneries were independent from the local ecclesiastical hierarchy and also had churches and chapels.

Through the ecclesiastical hierarchy, the Catholic Church possessed a direct line from the papal curia to every parish and each single Christian. If the popes wanted to advertise something important, such as the stipulation of a new canon law regulation or the announcement of the beginning of a new Jubilee year, they had a well-regulated system of correspondence. The papal letters declaring the will of the pontiff were sent in the same form to all archbishops; the latter passed the information on to the bishops, the bishops to all parish priests in their dioceses, and the parish priests on to their parishioners – and vice versa: individual Christians had the possibility to raise their own issues following the same path upwards to the papal curia.

Inquisition

The inquisition was an independent ecclesiastical institution which could act throughout the territory of Western Christendom. As an institution, the inquisition was founded only in 1542, by Pope Paul III (r. 1534–1549), but before that, the Dominican order in particular undertook the same task, namely to find, bring before the inquisitorial court, and sentence persons who were guilty of heresy. Heresy was the deliberate denial of fundamental dogmas of Christian faith, by individuals who knew what was right but chose to do what was wrong. Dogmas in the Middle Ages were often broadly defined; for example claiming that a papal decision was wrong, or simply not paying taxes to the Church, could be considered heresy. In principle, it was forbidden for inquisitors to use torture, but it did happen in some cases.

From 1231, popes or the leaders of the Dominican order could appoint inquisitors to control the purity of Christians' faith. In 1252, Pope Innocent IV (r. 1243–1254) authorised certain commissions to find possible heretics and bring them before episcopal tribunals. Both bishops and inquisitors could receive special papal authority to judge heresy cases. The inquisitors usually belonged to one of the mendicant orders, most often the Dominicans or Franciscans. Although the inquisitors acted mainly in Spain, southern France, and northern Italy, the long arm of the papal inquisition also reached Scandinavia. Written evidence shows that Dominicans and Franciscans in Scandinavia were appointed as inquisitors. One of them was Clemens Ragvaldus, the guardian of the Franciscan convent in Vyborg, close to the border with the schismatic Russians, who in the early 15th century received papal authority to act as inquisitor.

Since no historical sources testify to heresy investigations in eastern Finland, it is probable that this appointment was only nominal.

There are surprisingly few heresy cases from Scandinavia compared to the rest of Europe. One well-known example is that of the Swedish layman Botulf Botulfsson from the parish of Gottröra in Uppland. Archbishop Nils Allesson of Uppsala began to investigate Botulf's case in autumn 1303 after being told that after a communion the man had said that he did not believe the wine and bread to be the blood and body of Christ. When Botulf admitted his guilt and repented, the Archbishop was clement and sentenced Botulf to a penance of seven years. When the seven years had passed Botulf went to Uppsala, where the new Archbishop Nils Kettilsson absolved him. However, when Botulf returned to his parish church on Easter Sunday 1310, attending Mass and Communion for the first time since his sentence, the parish priest then asked him whether he now believed that the bread was the body of Christ. At this point, Botulf stated that if the bread were truly so, the priest would have eaten it all by himself a long time ago. He even continued that he did not want to have the body of Christ and compared the Communion to cannibalism. After this incident, Botulf was summoned to Uppsala again and at the trial admitted what he had said. When Botulf had not changed his mind after a year's imprisonment, the Archbishop adjudged Botulf an incorrigible heretic and handed him over to the secular judges, who were supposed to enforce the death penalty.

Ecclesiastical Norms

Since the ecclesiastical hierarchy encompassed all Christian territories in the same way, all Christians were considered equal in the eyes of the papacy – at least in theory. It is obvious that the rulers, the educated and the wealthy had different kinds of financial and cultural means to apply to the pope, but in principle, the poor and illiterate also had the same right.

During the Christian Church's first millennium it was not uncommon for ecclesiastical leaders of different dioceses or regions to reach very different conclusions in one and the same matter, and thus local ecclesiastical norms could deviate from each other significantly. From the end of the first millennium onwards, however, popes – in political alliance with the German Emperors – began to increase their control over the whole of Western Christianity. One means of this was unifying ecclesiastical legislation so that the same regulations were valid everywhere. The development and unifying of the ecclesiastical norms took place in two ways: first, church councils made decisions that were binding throughout Christendom; second, the popes could make decisions that were used as precedents everywhere and later included in ecclesiastical legislation.

Ecclesiastical legislation was very heterogeneous until the 11th century. At the turn of the 12th century, legal experts began to unify the various norms. When canon law was included in the curriculum of the universities and legal training became more professionalised, it was necessary to unify and gather ecclesiastical regulations into one corpus which would include all relevant norms. The first such collection, known as *Decretum*, was compiled around 1150 by the canon lawyer (and later bishop of the Italian diocese of Chiusi) Gratian. Gratian's *Decretum* spread over the whole of Western Christendom, and it was taught in the universities of Paris and Bologna at which Scandinavians also studied. One of the Scandinavians who very likely heard lectures on the *Decretum* in Paris was Anders Sunesen, later Archbishop of Lund and one of the most influential ecclesiastics in the north around 1200.

Ecclesiastical norms were however renewed and modified at the turn of the 13th century thanks to active and jurisprudent popes such as Alexander III (r. 1159–1181) and Innocent III (r. 1198–1216), and there was soon a need for an updated body of canon law. For this purpose, Bernardus of Pavia compiled a new collection between 1188 and 1192, *Breviarium extravagantium*, and in 1192 another one known as *Compilatio prima*. Bernardus' works were soon outdated because of the active legislative work of several popes. In 1230, Pope Gregory IX (r. 1227–1241) appointed one of the most brilliant legal experts of the time, the Dominican Raymundus de Penyaforte († 1275), to compile a new collection of canon law. His work is called *Liber extra*, but it is also known as the Decretals of Gregory because it was promulgated by the Pope in 1234. In 1298, *Liber extra* gained a sequel in the form of *Liber sextus*, the sixth book, which included the newest additions to the existing laws. Twenty years later, the so-called *Clementinae* (the decretals of Pope Clement V (r. 1305–1314) and decisions of the Council of Vienne in 1311–1312) were added to the previous collections and in turn supplemented by two later additions: *Extravagantes Ioannis XXII* comprising regulations made by Pope John XXII (r. 1316–1334) and *Extravagantes communes* consisting of the decretals of various later popes. These five collections formed the core of the medieval canon law, known as the *Editio Romana* of *Corpus Iuris Canonici*, which remained in force in the Catholic Church until 1917.

The manuscripts of the medieval collections of canon law were circulated and used in all parts of the Latin West, especially among lawyers and law students but also among learned clerics. Most Scandinavian bishops and higher dignitaries had a university education abroad and were familiar with canon law. We know, for example, that Bishop Thomas of Finland († 1248) had in his possession several central canonical and theological works and that Archbishop Anders Sunesen of Lund had a fine library including canonical manuscripts.

The canonical collections were typical law-books incorporating the regulations made at different times by different ecclesiastical authorities. Since legal matters were never straightforward and some regulations could be contradictory, the law-books were supplemented by works explaining and commenting upon the regulations, known as *glossae*, commentaries, or *summae*. The *glossae* were explanations, usually in the form of marginal notes, added to an important text such as the Bible or the central collections of canon law. The commentaries explained or commented upon specific canonical works or parts of them, such as Huguccio's († 1210) commentary upon the *Decretum*. The *summae* were intended to give a comprehensive treatment of an important topic and could be organised alphabetically or more often thematically.

In addition to the central ecclesiastical legislation, each ecclesiastical province or diocese had its local regulations fitted to local needs and circumstances. The provincial legislation was valid within the province in question, and the decisions about such norms were normally taken in the provincial councils regularly summoned by the archbishops. The diocesan legislation concerned only the territory of the diocese and decisions about it were taken in the yearly diocesan synods which were summoned by the local bishops.

Until the creation of the first church province of Lund, Scandinavia was administratively under the province of Hamburg-Bremen. Medieval sources, such as Adam of Bremen, relate that Scandinavian clerics participated in the councils organised in northern Germany. After the establishment of the Danish church province, the archbishops of Lund summoned the Scandinavian clerics to that town instead. There are no surviving sources concerning provincial councils before Archbishop Absalon held one in Lund in 1187. The Danish archbishops attempted to summon a provincial council every second year but did not always succeed due to political instabilities.

The large geographical territory of the Norwegian province made it impossible to celebrate provincial councils every year, although councils were summoned relatively regularly. The first notice of an ecclesiastical meeting in Norway is from 1163 in Bergen, in connection with the crowning of King Magnus Erlingsson, but there is no information about councils or any statutes they enacted for the next hundred years or so. In 1280, a provincial council was held in Bergen after which the ecclesiastics of the Norwegian church province gathered relatively regularly; many more statutes have been preserved from then until 1351, when the council took place in Nidaros. From the second half of the 14th century until the end of the Middle Ages there is only one preserved statute collection, from 1436, when the council was held in Oslo. In addition to Bergen, Nidaros and Oslo which were the usual venues of the Norwegian provincial councils, one council was held in Tønsberg in 1336.

The first known provincial council in Sweden was held in Skänninge in June 1248 under the auspices of the papal legate, Cardinal William of Sabina. After that, the next known provincial councils were celebrated in Tälje in 1276 and 1279. Around the turn of the century, during the archiepiscopacy of Nils Allesson, Swedish provincial councils were held regularly almost every year either in Arboga or Tälje, but the Archbishop's successors were not as active in this respect. We have information about a few councils, in 1327, 1341, and 1368, but there is very little information on the provincial councils of the late 14th century except that Archbishop Birger summoned several synods, unusually including one in Uppsala, with the rest in Tälje (1377–1381). From 1396, all known Swedish provincial councils were held either in Arboga (1396, 1412, 1417, 1423, and 1474) or in Söderköping (1436 and 1441).

The councils decided on the clerics' life and livings, on liturgical and dogmatic questions, and sometimes on pertinent political matters. The council of 1256 in the Danish town of Vejle opened with the declaration that 'the Danish Church is now so much persecuted by tyrants that …'. It decided that if a bishop was imprisoned, the perpetrators would automatically be excommunicated ipso facto, and if the king had been involved, all churches in the country should close and all services stop. Three years later, the Archbishop was caught and imprisoned by the king, and the council statute immediately became highly relevant – if not observed by all ecclesiastics in Denmark!

Diocesan synods were meetings summoned by the local bishop and celebrated in the episcopal towns. Canon law stipulated that the diocesan synods had to be held once a year, that it had the right to make decisions (called synodal statutes) concerning the diocese, and that each priest participating in the synod had to make a copy of the decisions for himself and pass the information on to his parishioners. The synods' purpose was to control the quality of the care of souls in the diocese, and the parish priests could ask questions of their superiors about ambiguous or difficult issues. The synod also functioned as a means of spreading information about new papal decisions or news from other parts of the Latin West and could moreover act as a tribunal if there were disciplinary issues concerning the clergy. Although the synods were summoned every year they did not necessarily make new statutes every time. In fact, there is relatively little information about the medieval Scandinavian synodal statutes. In the diocese of Turku, for example, the yearly diocesan synod was celebrated regularly the day after the celebration of the birthday of Virgin Mary (8 September), which brought the Finnish clergy to Turku's cathedral, dedicated to the Virgin. Despite the apparent frequency of its synods, medieval sources contain information on only two sets of synodal statutes from Turku. The earlier is from 1352 during the episcopacy of Bishop Hemming, and the other from 1492 when Magnus Nicolai (Särkilahti or Stjärnkors) was Bishop of Turku.

Ecclesiastical Justice

Canon law, alongside biblical norms, strictly regulated what Christians could do, both ecclesiastics and lay people, and what was forbidden. Ecclesiastical norms also stipulated who should take care of cases in which Christians had broken them. Because the popes could not oversee all juridical cases concerning the Church, they delegated their jurisdictional powers to the local ecclesiastical authorities. Since all provinces and dioceses differed, so too could the division of labour between parish priests, bishops, and archbishops, but in principle, all provinces followed the same hierarchical principle in judging crimes.

Unlike sins confessed in secrecy, ecclesiastical crimes were handled openly in ecclesiastical tribunals, where the judges sentenced those they had found guilty. Ecclesiastical tribunals dealt with a spectrum of different kinds of criminal act: first, all crimes committed by members of clergy, because according to the Church only an ecclesiastic was worthy to judge another. The aim of this regulation, called *privilegium fori*, was to defend clerics from possibly arbitrary treatment in lay tribunals. Second, the ecclesiastical jurisdiction handled all crimes that had something to do with the Church, dogma, or Christian worship, including falsifying ecclesiastical documents, heresy, homicide (when a cleric was either victim or perpetrator), arson, adultery, theft (from a cleric, church, or monastery) or witchcraft.

At the parish level, it was the role of the local parish priest to keep an eye on his parishioners and to note down if they committed crimes against the Church. However, the parish priests did not have the authority to judge or juridically punish their parishioners. This left very little means for priests to supervise their parishioners' behaviour. The only punitive means they had was to exclude Christians from the Eucharist or forbid their access to church, as the parish priest of Kokemäki in Finland did in 1468 to a parishioner who had not paid the tithes. He was prevented from entering the local church.

The parish priests, however, had a role in ecclesiastical justice; they could act as prosecutors in the ecclesiastical tribunals which were held in the parishes during the rural deans' regular visitations of the parishes under their jurisdiction. This practice was active in Sweden, Denmark, and some parts of Norway. We do not know for sure how often these visitations took actually place, but the statutes of the provincial council of Arboga in 1474 stipulate that the Swedish rural deans should visit each parish in their jurisdiction twice yearly. During the visitation, the rural dean was supposed to check the parish's property and economic situation as well as that the priest was conscientious in his profession and that he and the parishioners behaved according to ecclesiastical norms. In connection with the visitations, the rural dean acted as a judge and pronounced sentences upon parishioners guilty of breaking ecclesiastical regulations. The crimes handled in these tribunals were typically the use of enchantments or spells, adultery and other sexual misbehaviour, usury or illegal income, concealing of excommunications, working on holy days, or absence from ecclesiastical services. Priests could also be accused of not properly undertaking their clerical functions such as providing the last unction to dying persons or regularly celebrating the ecclesiastical services. Local ecclesiastical trials normally sentenced the guilty persons to fines but could also impose other ecclesiastical punishments such as excommunication (that excluded the person from ecclesiastical services or the community) or shameful penalties like sitting in the stock. The tribunals presided over by the rural deans were not necessarily very professional and there must have been variation between hearings in different parishes.

The bishops also had the obligation to regularly visit all parishes belonging to their diocese. According to canon law, the visits were to take place every year, but due to the long distances in Scandinavia local norms dictated that such visits should happen every three years. The episcopal visitation of a parish was similar to the visit of the rural dean: the bishop had to check the property and economy of the parish, that the priest fulfilled his duties, and that he and the parishioners respected ecclesiastical norms. The episcopal visitations also included a court session in the parish in which the parish priest acted as prosecutor, informing the bishop of his parishioners' misdeeds. The bishop heard the cases and eventual witnesses and made his judgement, but the sentences from these Scandinavian tribunals have usually not survived. The penalties imposed by the bishop were, however, the same as those imposed by the tribunals presided over by the rural dean: fines, excommunications, and punishments of shame. In the Scandinavian countries – unlike in many other Christian territories – trials in connection with episcopal visitations were the most common way of dispensing ecclesiastical justice. Sometimes, they were even combined with the district court sessions if they coincided with the visit of the bishop. This happened in northern Finland in 1445, when a court session was held in the parish of Ii in the presence of Bishop Magnus Tavast and the District Judge Olof Svärd.

In addition to the petty crimes handled in the court sessions during the visitations, the bishops had the authority to deal with other crimes, usually more severe, related to the Church. The more severe crimes were normally brought before the bishop in the episcopal town, where the bishop – or often someone to whom he had delegated his jurisdictional powers – was having court sessions. In other parts of the Christian West, these tribunals were professional and followed the juridical procedure stipulated in canon law, but we do not know exactly whether the Scandinavian courts worked in the same professional way. The difference with the locally held court sessions was moreover that the episcopal courts handled cases that had been brought before the court officially and based on a written complaint, not through an oral accusation by the parish priest. The episcopal courts in Germany or England also held sessions regularly, on the three weekly court days of Monday, Wednesday, and Friday. However, the Scandinavian dioceses were so sparsely populated that it was not necessary for a court to sit so frequently. The late 15th-century copy book of Bishop Hans Brask of Linköping suggests that the episcopal courts were summoned only when there was a need for it.

Although the Scandinavian episcopal courts functioned less frequently – and perhaps also less professionally – they took care of similar kinds of issues as their European counterparts. Most commonly, the episcopal courts resolved litigations related to marriages or rather cases in which the typically female plaintiff sued her fiancé for not marrying her despite numerous promises. Other relatively common case types involved economic quarrels, insults, or violence. The only court record surviving from

Finland concerns a case from 1492, in which the parishioners of Somero accused their local priest of ignoring his duties, although in the end the accusations also extended to the priest's violent, unpleasant behaviour and multiple quarrels with his parishioners.

Miscreant priests were not exceptional. Many medieval documents tell of clergymen who had not lived according to the priestly standards: pleasant behaviour, good manners, celibacy, and abstinence from various vices such as excessive use of alcohol or gambling. A good medieval example of the removal of priests from their office by episcopal decision was the case of Lars Sunesson Vit, from spring 1410. Lars was a notorious lecher who had begotten a number of children and deflowered a virgin and had often been involved in controversies with his parishioners. Additionally, he had ignored his priestly duties to his parishioners so that many had died without last unction, confession or other sacraments. The bishop removed Lars Vit from his office as priest.

According to the principles of the Catholic Church, Christians whose case had been judged at the local ecclesiastical courts could appeal to the next administrative level: from the rural deans' court to the episcopal court, from the episcopal to the archiepiscopal, and from there to the pope. The medieval documents also testify that the Scandinavians employed these options and that several Scandinavians appealed to the highest ecclesiastical court, the Sacra Romana Rota. At the turn of the 1490s, for example, the Rota handled the litigation between Bishop Niels Skave of Roskilde and the Cistercian monastery in Sorø over the possession of a farm.

Certain cases were not settled in the papal curia by the judges of the Rota, but rather the pope decided to commit them to judges delegate, who could ensure in situ that all documents and statements were correct. One such case was that of accusations made against Archbishop Johannes Gerechini of Uppsala. He was of Danish origin and worked as the chancellor of the Kalmar Union King Eric of Pomerania, who in 1408 appointed him Archbishop of Uppsala against the will of the locals. The cathedral chapter of Uppsala disliked the Archbishop from the beginning, but Johannes did not make any effort to make himself more popular. According to the sources, he lived a luxurious life, had relationships with women of dubious morals, kept a young local woman as a concubine, and begat two children. He was also known as somebody who did not hesitate to scare his opponents with violence. His economic situation always being bad, he borrowed money without the intention to pay it back, took bribes, and embezzled church property. These abuses led to an official complaint to Pope Martin V (r. 1417–1431) who commissioned the bishop of Riga to investigate. Against all odds, the bishop declared Johannes innocent, but the Archbishop drew his conclusions and abdicated from Uppsala in 1421. Five years later the Pope appointed him to the see of Skálholt in Iceland, where he arrived in 1429. His presence in Iceland was not much more appreciated than in Uppsala, and the locals soon grew weary and angry with him. The surviving sources do not give many details about his deeds in Iceland, but he must have engendered a great deal of hatred because on 20 July 1433, the locals took the law into their own hands, captured the bishop, stuffed him in a sack, and drowned him.

Sin and Absolution

Alongside the ecclesiastical system of criminal tribunals, the Church had a parallel system of justice for Christians who had committed sins. Instead of punishing evildoers, the idea of this institution was to bring them back into the community of Christians and function as a guarantee of their salvation. This institution was also organised hierarchically. At its lowest level, in the parishes, penitent Christian sinners had to turn to their parish priest and confess their sins. After the sacrament of confession the priest imposed a penance upon the sinner, who had to fulfil it before the absolution was valid. Sins confessed to the parish priests were usually less severe, such as cursing, opposing one's parents, or petty theft. The penance imposed by the father confessor upon such sinners was usually fasting, praying, or giving alms.

The parish priests had the authority to absolve their parishioners from almost all the different kinds of sins, but there were certain more severe ones that had to be brought to the local bishops. These included sodomy or incest. For example, in 1493, Bishop Magnus Nicolai of Turku absolved Gudmundus Gerss from Kimito, who had had sex with his wife's daughter and thus committed both incest and adultery.

Not even bishops had the power to absolve Christians from all sins. Certain sins like homicide, violence involving a priest (either as victim or perpetrator), or apostasy were considered so severe that only the pope could absolve the guilty. The popes had delegated these powers to the office called the Penitentiary. During the late Middle Ages, the Penitentiary granted hundreds of absolutions to Scandinavians who had committed such severe sins that they had to turn to the papacy.

Indulgence

Committing a sin turned Christians away from God. In order to return to Him, Christians had to confess their sins, do penance, and receive absolution. Afterwards, the sinner was accepted back into the congregation, although this did not guarantee access to heaven. After death, the sinner ended up in an intermediate state, Purgatory, where the soul would eventually be purified from the burden of sins accumulated in life.

The idea of Purgatory derives from the times of the early Church, but in the Middle Ages, the concept of Purgatory developed further as a physical place and was commonly accepted in Western Christendom by the late 12th century. According to dogma, the souls of dead Christians ended in Purgatory where an eternal fire burned them until they were freed from their sins and their souls could be admitted to Heaven. The length of time a soul had to spend in Purgatory depended upon the amount and gravity of the sins the person had committed during their lifetime. It was possible to shorten the time one's soul spent in Purgatory. One means was others' prayers for the deceased's soul. Another was to perform good deeds such as donations to the poor or ecclesiastical institutions or to undertake a pilgrimage in the name of the dead. The third way was through collecting indulgences.

A Christian could collect indulgences in various ways during his or her lifetime, for example by saying certain prayers, fasting, giving alms to the poor, donating to ecclesiastical institutions, visiting a holy place, participating in a religious celebration, or going on a crusade. By the high Middle Ages, the possibilities for collecting indulgences had increased significantly. When a church was consecrated, the local bishop usually granted an indulgence of 40 days to all participants. Similarly, it was possible to receive an indulgence of 40 days by visiting a parish church or monastery on the day of its patron saint.

A bishop could grant indulgences for 40 days at the most, but when five bishops granted it together, it became an indulgence of 200 days – the amount one cardinal could grant by himself. Cardinals could also grant joint indulgences. Only the pope could grant indulgences for longer periods. The popes rarely granted indulgences on their own initiative but typically at the request of a church or monastic institution. In addition to these individually granted indulgences, popes could grant special plenary indulgences on specific occasions such as to the visitors of the papal city during the Holy Years. Plenary indulgences were especially powerful because they entirely removed the burden of all sins the person had committed until receiving the indulgence.

By the late Middle Ages, the use of indulgences had become even more common and the Catholic Church began to finance its building and crusade activities by selling them, resulting in numerous protests, among the best known of which was that made by the German monk and theologian Martin Luther in 1517. The selling of indulgences was organised extremely professionally through numerous papal indulgence sellers who were sent all over the Christian West and also, in large numbers, to Scandinavia.

Clerical Stand and Monastic Orders

In the Middle Ages, people were classified socially into three different groups: those who fought, who prayed, and who worked – *bellatores*, *oratores*, and *laboratores*. This division is obviously very rough; the three groups were not homogeneous, and the important merchant class is absent. Members of the fighting or ruling class normally belonged to it by birth, and being born into the working class also normally meant that one would belong to it for life. By contrast, the group of clerics was open and an ecclesiastical career offered a possibility for skilled men – and also women – to rise in the social ladder, especially in the late Middle Ages.

A man became a member of the ecclesiastical estate when he received the lowest clerical orders, in Latin the *prima tonsura* – referring to clerics' obligation to shave some or all of their hair, which also functioned as a visible sign of their estate. Another way of joining was to take monastic vows, which were also open to women. Belonging to the clerical estate brought certain privileges but also obligations. The most important privilege was the so-called *privilegium canonis* or *privilegium fori* which protected clerics from laymen, and especially from lay justice; a person belonging to the clerical estate could only be judged in an ecclesiastical court. The obligations of the estate were also large. Members had to behave and dress to the honour of the Church. They were not allowed to drink excessively or gamble. They could not as act as inn-keepers, merchants, medical doctors, judges, or practice any other lay profession that could lead to someone's death or mutilation. Clerics were not allowed to act violently or to carry weapons. They had to wear the clerical dress or the habit of their order and take good care of their parish and parishioners.

Men and women living according to a monastic rule belonged to the clerical estate. There were several monastic rules or orders in the Middle Ages. Some spread all over the Latin Christendom, while some remained local. The religious communities can be divided into four main types: monastic orders, canons regular, military orders, and mendicants.

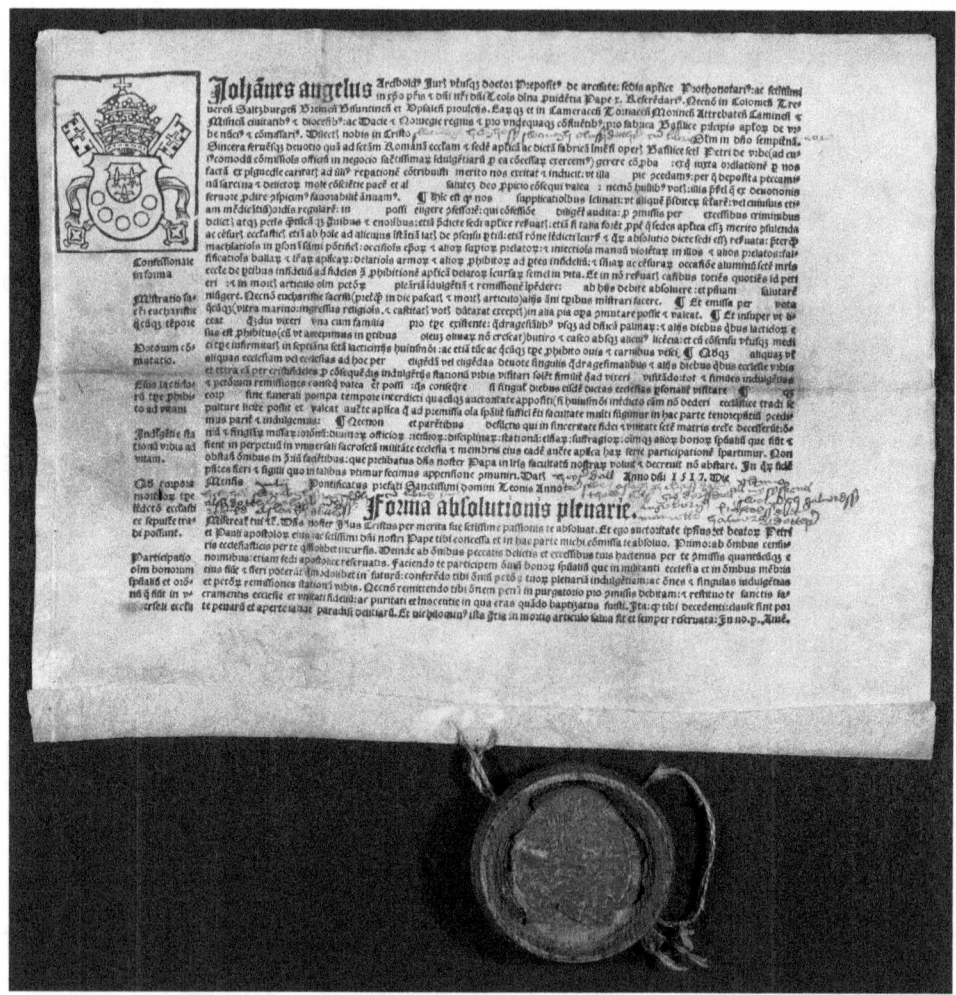

Illustration 2.7 Letter of indulgence from 1517, issued by the famous papal legate and indulgence seller in Scandinavia Johannes Angelus Arcimboldus. Tens and probably hundreds of thousands of these letters were printed in the later Middle Ages. Space was left open to add the names of the recipients of the indulgence. The letter here was issued to Swenwngh Helghessen and Swanogh Olaffzdotther with their children in Heyredal in Norway.
Royal Library, Copenhagen. With permission.

The two first types accepted both male and female members, the military orders were meant only for males although a few had parallel sister branches, while the mendicants were originally intended for men but very soon developed female branches as well.

When a man or a woman wanted to join a religious order, they first had to serve a trial period called a novitiate, which typically last for one year. If the novice was still willing to join the order after the trial period and become a monk or nun, he or she had to take the official monastic vows in a solemn ceremony. In some monasteries, the vows were confirmed in a written document and marked with a feast or donation.

There were three different monastic vows the novices had to take: poverty, chastity, and obedience. The vow of poverty did not mean that the monks and nuns necessarily had to live in poverty – some monasteries were extremely wealthy, and the monks and nuns had quite comfortable lives – but that they gave up the right to personal property. The vow of chastity meant that monks and nuns should not have sexual relationships, while the third vow of obedience bound monks and nuns for the rest of their lives to obey the superior of their monastery. There they were supposed to live according to the rule of their monastic order, and they were bound to the monastery they had entered. The superior of a male monastery was called an abbot while the nunneries were led by an abbess. The leaders of the mendicant convents were in their turn called priors or prioresses.

The abbot, prior, abbess, or prioress had to keep order in their monasteries and had the right to punish monks or nuns who did not obey the rule or the orders given by their superiors. Life in a monastery was not always easy, and coexistence in a closed society could create tensions between the members. Medieval sources offer hundreds of stories of monks and nuns who did not obey their monastic vows. Some monks even escaped from their monasteries after internal conflicts, such as Sueno Huso, a Cistercian monk from the Swedish monastery of Varnhem. He travelled to Rome in spring 1464 and asked for a papal absolution from excommunication because of apostasy – namely, that he had run away from his monastery. The reason for his apostasy was that his superior had imprisoned him, and he had escaped and left for Rome. The case of Sueno is particularly interesting because he had already turned to the pope before, requesting a licence to change monastery. At that time, he had been a monk in the German Birgittine monastery of Marienwold (Ratzeburg), which he had left after the German monks had mocked him because he could not sing in the right way. He then tried to return to Vadstena where he was not accepted but was allowed to transfer to the Birgittine monastery of Munkeliv in Bergen. However, he had apparently not done that but changed to the Cistercian order from where he had later escaped. It becomes clear that the monastic life did not suit everyone.

Monastic Orders

There were several monastic orders in the Middle Ages, the best known of them being the Benedictines, Cistercians, and Carthusians, all of whom had monastic houses in Scandinavia. In addition, there was one monastic order with especial Scandinavian ties, the Birgittines founded by Saint Birgitta of Sweden.

The Benedictines were the oldest monastic order, founded in the first half of the 6th century by Benedict of Nursia. The order was originally meant for men, but a mere hundred years or so later, it received a female branch. Life in the Benedictine monasteries was regulated by the Benedictine rule (*Regula Sancti Benedicti*) which the founder had formulated. Daily existence consisted of religious contemplation, praying, silence, poverty, work, and the communal life. The Benedictine order had already spread to the central areas of Europe by the high Middle Ages, and reached Scandinavia early. The Benedictine rule also became the model for other monastic orders, such as Silvestrins, Ambrosians, Olivetans, Trappists, and Camaldules, that did not come to the Nordic countries.

The first missionaries to Scandinavia in the first half of the 9th century belonged to the Benedictine order. Some of them arrived in Scandinavia from German territory, such as the 'Apostle of the North' Ansgar. The second wave of Benedictine missionaries arrived from England in the first half of the 11th century at the request of King Canute the Great. This mission resulted in the foundation of the first Benedictine monasteries in Scandinavia, such as the Allhelgon monastery (All saints) in Lund and the Selje abbey in Western Norway. The 11th and 12th centuries were the golden period of the Benedictines in Scandinavia, and the order spread fast. In Danish territory, some 30 Benedictine monasteries were founded, in Norway six, Iceland four, Greenland one, and in Sweden seven. The preponderance of Benedictine monasteries in Denmark is due to its earlier Christianisation.

The Cistercian order was closely related to the late 11th-century reform movement within the Benedictine order. Some monks began to demand stricter observance of the Benedictine rule and founded a new monastery in a place called Citeaux, Latin *Cistercium*, which gave name to the order (Lat. *Ordo Cisterciensis*, OCist.). Benedict's original idea of concentrating upon prayer and work (*ora et labora*) demanded isolation and peace, and Cistercian monasteries were places in the wilderness far away from cities. That was the self-image of Cistercians as presented in written sources; in reality, they often came to places that were already inhabited and with easy access to important natural resources.

The Cistercian order soon became very popular, thanks also to its charismatic leader Bernard of Clairvaux. Citeaux' first daughter monasteries were founded between 1113 and 1115, and in the following decades, the Cistercians spread rapidly all over Europe including to the newly Christianised territories in Scandinavia. In the Baltic countries, they became actively engaged in the crusading movement.

The first Scandinavian Cistercian monasteries were founded only three decades after the order's founding. Archbishop Eskil of Lund was a personal friend of Bernard of Clairvaux, and he welcomed the order to Scandinavia. Alvastra and Nydala in Sweden were the first monasteries, founded in 1143 by monks from Citeaux who also were involved in the founding of the first Danish Cistercian monastery, Herrevad in Scania, in 1144. The Cistercians came to Norway from England when the monks of Fountain Abbey founded Lysekloster in the diocese of Bergen in 1146. By the end of the 12th century, the number of Cistercian monasteries in Scandinavia had risen to around 30. The order never came to Iceland, the Atlantic islands, or Finland, although the monastery of Padise in northern Estonia had possessions in southern Finland. The success of the new order can also be seen in the closure and re-founding of some Benedictine monasteries as Cistercian, such as Veng (1165), Sorø (1162), and Esrom (c. 1160).

The Carthusians (Lat. *Ordo Cartusiensis*, OCart.) likewise demanded stricter observance of the Benedictine rule. They were founded in 1084 by Saint Bruno of Cologne, also receiving their name from their first monastery, that of Chartreuse near Grenoble in France. The Carthusians similarly spread relatively quickly in the early 12th century across France, Italy, and the German Empire, with Pope Alexander III confirming their rights in 1176, but the Carthusians never became popular in Scandinavia. There might have been a Carthusian monastery in Asserbo, Denmark, in the 1160s, but the information is uncertain. The only definite Carthusian house in Scandinavia was the monastery of Mariefred, which the Swedish Regent Sten Sture the Elder founded as late as in 1493 on his estates in Gripsholm. The Scandinavian monastery was male, but the order also had a female branch.

The Birgittine order (Lat. *Ordo Sanctissimi Salvatoris*, OSSalv.) was the fourth large monastic order and very important in Scandinavian history. It was founded by Birgitta Birgersdotter (1303–1373), a Swedish noblewoman, who through revelations from Christ gave advice not only to the Swedish King Magnus Ericsson but also to the Avignon popes. Birgitta left Sweden in 1349 in order to be in Rome during the Jubilee in 1350. She chose Rome as her residence and there developed her ideas of a monastic order in which men and women would inhabit the same monastery, albeit apart from each other. In 1370, Pope Urban V confirmed the monastic rule and the Birgittine order was officially founded. The first Birgittine monastery was erected in Sweden, in Vadstena, and from there the order spread over Europe: to England, Italy, Germany, Netherlands, and Estonia. In addition to Vadstena, there were four other Birgittine monasteries in Scandinavia: Naantali in Finland (founded in 1439), Maribo on Lolland (1418), Mariager in Jutland (1446), and Munkaliv in Bergen (1426). The Vadstena abbey became one of the most significant pilgrimage sites in Scandinavia since Birgitta, canonised in Rome in 1391, was buried there.

The idea of Birgitta was to create a double monastery, consisting of two convents occupying separate buildings, and separate parts of the church during services. The nuns' convent was to be led by an abbess and the monks' convent by a prior. According to the Birgittine rule, the abbess governed the whole monastery but the prior should help her with administration and daily business. Pope Urban V was not happy with the idea of double monastery because of the risk of controversies between the abbess and the prior and of temptations created by close contacts between nuns and monks. Historical sources testify to numerous moments of tension between the abbesses and the priors, but also that contacts between male and female members of the order sometimes made them forget their vows of chastity. For example, one of the Naantali monks had to seek pardon from the pope because he had had sexual relations with two nuns in the monastery.

Canons Regular

Canons regular were priests living in a community under a rule and often organised into religious orders. The most typical medieval religious orders of canons regular, which were also represented in Scandinavia, were the Augustinians and the Premonstratensians. The canons regular must be distinguished from the secular canons, who were priests attached to a church, typically in Scandinavia to a cathedral church. Unlike the canons regular, the secular canons did not take monastic vows nor did they live together under a monastic rule.

The majority of medieval canons regular followed the rule of Saint Augustine and were called Augustinian canons (lat. *Canonici Regulares Ordinis S. Augustini Congregationis*). The order took its name from Saint Augustine of Hippo in North Africa, who in his episcopal palace at the turn of the 5th century founded a community for priests serving in his cathedral. The priests of this community renounced their private property, agreed to live in chastity and obedience, assisted the bishop in the liturgical life of the cathedral, and took care of souls. From northern Africa, the idea of the Augustinian foundation spread first to France and Italy, and when Pope Gelasius at the end of the 5th century re-established the regular life of the Lateran Church in Rome on the Augustinian pattern, the order began to spread across Western Christendom. In 1059, the papacy officially approved the way of life of the canons regular.

By the end of the 11th century, the order had spread to recently converted regions like Scandinavia. The Scandinavian communities of Augustinian canons were organised according to ecclesiastical provinces and each community lived under the supervision of an abbot, provost, or prior appointed by the local bishop.

In the province of Lund, communities of priests attached to the cathedrals in Dalby, Viborg, and Vestervig assumed the Augustinian rule, while other communities, such as Eskilsø close to Roskilde and Tvilum in the diocese of Århus, were directly founded as Augustinian canons regular. Some of them continued their activities throughout the Middle Ages, while others functioned for a shorter time. Knowledge of Augustinian communities in the Norwegian church province is also scarce but Jonskloster in Bergen, the monastery of the Holy Spirit in Halsnøy, the monastery of Utstein close to Stavanger, and Helgeseter priory in Nidaros had Augustinian communities closely connected to the episcopal seats. Additionally, the monastery of Saint Olaf in Hamar may have belonged to the Augustinian order. From Greenland, we have information about an Augustinian community in Ketilsfjord.

In Iceland, the Augustinians had a central role. Around 1168, Saint Þorlákur Þórhallason founded the community of Þykkivibær in the diocese of Skálholt, and in the same diocese, there were three other Augustinian houses: Flatey-Helgafell, Viðey, and Skriða. In the other Icelandic diocese of Hólar, there was the community of Möðruvellir, which was administered by the bishop himself. A few early 13th-century Augustinian communities, like Skara cathedral chapter and Hagby in Uppland, are known from the Swedish church province, but they existed only for a short period. The female branch of the order had two houses in Denmark, in Viborg and Asmild, and the nunnery of Rain (Nonneseter) close to Nidaros might also have belonged to the Augustinian order.

The majority of the Scandinavian Augustinian communities followed the general line of the rule, but some, like Helgeseter in Norway or Helgefell in Iceland, might have been reformed on the model of the Victorines, a group of Augustinians from the school of Saint Viktor in Paris. The Victorines had a special significance for Denmark because Bishop Absalon of Roskilde invited his friend Vilhelm from the monastery of Saint Geneviéve in Paris to reform the Danish community of Eskilsø. After Vilhelm was elected as the abbot of the Eskilsø monastery, he moved the community to Æbelholt and turned it into a Victorine one. Æbelholt gained a daughter monastery in Kungälv, Kastellklostret. The Victorines collaborated closely with some Scandinavian bishops. Archbishop Eirik of Nidaros and Bishop Tore of Hamar were not only Victorines but also friends of Vilhelm of Æbelholt, who after his death became venerated as a local saint.

The Premonstratensians (lat. *Ordo Praemonstratensis*) were the other medieval order of canons regular, receiving its official name from the place where it was founded in 1120, Prémontré near Laon in France. The order is also known as Norbertines after its founder, Saint Norbert of Xanten, later Archbishop of Magdeburg and close friend of Bernard of Clairvaux. The Premonstratensians followed the rule of Saint Augustine but they had some additional regulations that rendered the life in the Premonstratensian monasteries more austere. The order received papal approval in 1126 after which it grew quickly and also obtained a sister order. The Premonstratensians were active in Scandinavian missionary activity and the conversion of the Wends of northern Germany and Poland. The order worked in close contact with parish churches and the care of souls was very important for the 'white brothers', as they were also called after the colour of their habit.

Archbishop Eskil of Lund invited the order to Scandinavia with the support of King Valdemar II of Denmark. The first Premonstratensian monastery was founded in Tommarp in Scania. Tommarp was a daughter monastery to Prémontré, and the foundation was confirmed in 1155 by Pope Hadrian IV. The order spread quickly in Scania, and monasteries were founded in Öved, Lund, and Vä, which later was transferred to Bäckarskog. During the last decades of the 12th century and the first decades of the 13th century, the order spread to other parts of Scandinavia too: in Børglum and Tønsberg in the 1190s and in the 1230s in Dragsmark in southern Norway. The only Scandinavian Premonstratensian nunnery was founded around 1215 in Vrejlev, northern Zealand, by Børglum. The Scandinavian Premonstratensian monasteries together formed one of the 30 medieval *circaries* (a Premonstratensian term for an ecclesiastical province) and it was called the circary of Dacia or the circary of Dacia and Norwegia. As can be deduced from the name of the province, the order never established itself in the Swedish province of Uppsala.

Military Orders

After the conquest of Jerusalem in 1099 via the first crusade (1096–1099), the crusaders founded a number of fighting monastic communities, so-called military orders, to assist pilgrims arriving in the Holy Land and to fight the Muslims in the territory. The idea of combining monastic life with military combat was new in Christianity and was only possible because of a new theology of war.

The best known military orders were the Templars, the Johannites, and the Teutonic order. They began their activities in the Holy Land but rapidly spread over Europe, continuing to operate in Europe after the Holy Land's loss to Muslims in 1291. These three orders were closely connected to the Holy Land's conquest, although there were a number of smaller, more local military orders in the Iberian Peninsula that were active in the *Reconquista*, such as the Calatrava, Alcantára, and Montesa. Additionally, upper-class circles in various countries founded their own small military orders, such as the order of the Dragon founded by the Hungarian King Sigismund von Luxembourg in 1408, and the order of Saint Michael founded by King Louis XI of France in 1469. In Scandinavia, the order of the Elephant was created around 1460 for the very uppermost stratum of the nobility of the Kalmar Union, with Saint Birgitta as a kind of patron, but without entailing any direct obligations to fight or to live in a monastic community.

Although the members of the military orders were originally fighters, the idea of the military orders was the same as for the traditional monastic ones. Their orders' members lived together under the same rules and were bound to obedience. Not all orders, however, expected their members to take the vows of chastity or poverty. The military orders admitted only male members, but several had parallel female orders which assisted through prayer without engaging in fighting.

Of the military orders, that of the Knights Templars (Lat. *Fratres militia Templi*) was the most famous. It was founded in 1119 in Jerusalem and had its headquarters on the Temple Mount. The order grew rapidly all over Europe, becoming rich and powerful with a large network of almost one thousand commanderies and castles across Europe and Near East. King Philip IV of France (r. 1285–1314) fostered envy and distrust towards the order and in collaboration with Pope Clement V (r. 1305–1314) managed to have them accused of heresy. In 1307, the order's most eminent members were arrested, tortured, and eventually burned. Its huge property holdings were confiscated, much of these donated to the Johannites, and the Templar order was officially dissolved. The Templars were well known in Scandinavia but never established any houses there. Nevertheless, there is today a huge mystical and fictional literature concerning the Templars and their secret treasure hidden somewhere in Scandinavia. It is very funny to read, but totally without any connection to medieval sources.

The Johannites, by contrast, gained a steady foothold in Scandinavian territory. The Johannites (Lat. *Religio sacre domus Hospitalis Sancti Johannis Hierosolimitani*) were the oldest of the military orders, originating as a Christian hospital founded in Jerusalem in the mid-11th century by merchants from Amalfi. The order had its rule confirmed by the pope in 1154 and was placed directly under the papal jurisdiction. Alongside caring for the sick, the order soon established a branch of military activity, and the fighting Johannite brothers became feared and respected soldiers just like the Templars. The order included priest brothers who took care of preaching and the care of souls, as well as lay brothers or servants. The order had sister convents for female members, where the sisters took care of the sick. The order spread quickly in the Crusader states and all over Europe. It had to give up its headquarters in Jerusalem after the Muslims conquered the Holy Land in 1291. In 1309, the order moved to the island of Rhodes and in 1522 to Malta. The Johannite order was led by a Grand Master, and its administration was arranged according to nations. The Scandinavian branch belonged to the German nation but formed its own priory (the prioratus of Dacia).

The first Johannite house in Scandinavia was founded around 1164 in Antvorskov close to Slagelse in Zealand, under the auspices of the Danish King Valdemar I the Great who himself was a fervent crusader. Antvorskov also became the motherhouse of all the Scandinavian Johannites. The order spread quickly over Scandinavia, so that by the 14th century, there were eight other Johannite houses in Denmark: Odense, Viborg, Ribe, Dueholm, Horsens, Lund, Svendstrup, and Maschenholt on Rügen. The first Johannite house in Sweden was established in Eskilstuna by the mid-1180s at the latest. For a long time, Eskilstuna remained the only Johannite house in Sweden, but in the second half of the 15th century, there were attempts to found new houses. The Swedish Johannites became part of the power struggle between Sweden and Denmark in the 15th century, and the house in Eskilstuna did not want to be subordinate to Antvorskov. The monks in Eskilstuna refused to receive a new prior sent from the Danish motherhouse and the conflict became violent, ending with the expulsion of the Danish prior and killing of his entourage.

In the 1470s, the Swedish council of the realm founded a hospital in Kronobäck and the Swedish Regent Sten Sture the Elder, who was close to the Johannites, allowed the building of a Johannite church in the old town of Stockholm. The Johannites founded one monastery in Norway, in Varne, in the 1190s. It remained the only Johannite establishment in Norway, but it was relatively big compared to other Scandinavian houses and as closely connected to the king's personal guard. Some wooden plates with the order's symbol, the Saint John's cross, have been found on Greenland, so possibly some Johannites have been fighting on the religious border even so far away. The Johannites in Scandinavia were close to the royal families and high nobility and were probably involved in crusades in the Baltic, Holy Land, and elsewhere, although sources are few.

The Teutonic order (Lat. *Ordo domus Sanctae Mariae Teutonicorum*) is the third large international military order. It was officially founded in the last years of the 12th century in Acre in the Holy Land, but by then, it had already existed for around a decade, running a hospital for German pilgrims. At the time of its official foundation, the order's purpose changed from care of the sick to fighting Muslims. It spread in eastern and northern Europe and became very important in the Baltic crusades from the 1220s alongside the small local order of the Sword Brethren – which in 1236 was incorporated into the Teutonic order. After the loss of the Holy Land in 1291, the order moved its headquarters to Marienburg in Prussia, present-day Malbork in Poland, from where it was led by the Grand Master.

The Teutonic order had only one house in Scandinavia, in Årsta in Sweden, mentioned in sources in 1308. It was probably not very big, but does show that members of the Swedish aristocracy were interested in supporting the Teutonic knights and the Baltic crusades. Although the Teutonic order did not settle in Scandinavia, it had strong connections to the area. The crusading conquest of Livonia (part of Estonia and Latvia) in the first half of the 13th century happened in competition and sometimes cooperation with King Valdemar II of Denmark, and in 1346, Valdemar IV sold the Danish possessions in Estonia to the order. As part of the agreement, King Valdemar's brother was to enter the order and become leader of its Livonian branch. Around 1400, the order gained huge political importance by cleansing Gotland of pirates and negotiating the struggle over its ownership between Queen Margaret and her opponent, Albert of Mecklenburg.

Mendicants

The word mendicant refers to all those religious orders whose main purpose was to live according to the original evangelical idea of poverty. There were a number of mendicant orders in the Middle Ages. The best known are the Franciscans, Dominicans, Augustine Eremites, and Carmelites. In addition, there were a large number of local mendicant orders, but not in Scandinavia.

The members of the mendicant orders took monastic vows like the members of other orders, but the mendicant life differed greatly from the typical monastic life. The mendicants took the vow of poverty much more seriously, and after joining the order their members lost all rights to private property and everything became common. The mendicant brothers were bound to their convents but did not have to stay within the monastery walls because of their calling to move, preach, and collect alms among Christians.

The Dominicans and the Franciscans worked actively for the eradication of heresy. Pope Gregory IX appointed members of the two mendicant orders as inquisitors in the mid-1230s. Originally, the mendicant idea was to fight the heresy by preaching the Gospel message among Christians and by setting a good example of a righteous life. When Pope Innocent IV established the inquisition in 1252 and authorised the limited use of torture by inquisitors to extract confessions from those suspected of heresy, the Franciscans along with the Dominicans were granted those rights too. It is not known whether the mendicants used those rights in Scandinavia.

The Franciscan order (Lat. *Ordo Fratrum Minorum*) was the oldest mendicant order. It was founded by Francis of Assisi (1181/1182–1226) at the beginning of the 13th century, and Pope Honorius III confirmed its rules in 1223. The Franciscans were also known as minorities, small brothers (from the order's Latin name) or grey friars because of their grey dress. Although the order was originally male it soon gained a female branch, the order of Saint Clare (Lat. *Ordo Sancte Clarae*), after the name of its founder Saint Clare of Assisi, a follower of Saint Francis. Additionally, the order admitted so-called penitential or tertiary brothers and sisters who did not take the permanent monastic vows but lived like the brothers or sisters in separate buildings. The order was divided into administrative territories called provinces, and the Scandinavian countries formed one province, that of Dacia. The provinces were led by the provincial prior who was elected by a provincial chapter that gathered regularly in one of the convents.

The Franciscan order spread rapidly all over the Latin Christian world in the 13th century, a period of strong economic growth and urbanisation, and most Franciscan convents were established in newly founded towns where the brothers found enough support for their begging lifestyle. The order spread to Scandinavia from the south in the 1230s. The first Scandinavian Franciscan convent was founded in 1232, in Ribe, followed by several others within a single decade. By the end of the Middle Ages, there were 26 Franciscan convents in Danish territory, administratively divided into five custodies: Ribe, Viborg, Odense, Roskilde, and Lund. Sweden received its first Franciscan convent in Visby in 1233, but the order did not spread as quickly in Sweden as in Denmark. The order let erect nine other convents during the 13th century. In Sweden, there were 16 Franciscan convents by the end of the Middle Ages, administratively divided into the custodies of Linköping and Stockholm. The first Franciscan convents in Norway were also founded during the 13th century, but the exact years of foundation are not known. The Norwegian convents included Tønsberg, Bergen, Konghelle, Marstrand, Oslo, and a convent founded later on in Nidaros, which all belonged to the sole Norwegian custody. The Franciscan order spread to Scandinavia in two waves: the first in the 13th century, and the second in the 15th century.

Originally, the Franciscans were supposed to live in extreme poverty but this requirement was relaxed when Pope Honorius III confirmed the order's rule in 1223. However, the question of the degree of poverty was not solved but became one that eventually caused the order to split into three branches. Those who wanted to follow the original, stricter idea of poverty were called the Observants. Those who supported the less strict principles were the Conventuals. The two different interpretations of poverty had already emerged in the 13th century and were officially recognised at the Church council of Constance in 1415, but it was only in 1517 that the Conventuals broke with the order and formed their own branch. The third branch is called the Capuchin, which in the 1520s became independent and called for a stricter observance of the original rule of Saint Francis. The Capuchins were formed so late that they never established themselves in Scandinavian territory, but the division of the Franciscan order into Conventuals and Observants had repercussions in Scandinavia in the late Middle Ages. Here, the fight within the order took a slightly different form than in any other Franciscan province; it began to follow the division between the supporters and opponents of the Kalmar Union king. The Swedish and Norwegian Franciscans voted for the Conventuals, while the Danish Franciscans wanted to follow the rule more strictly and opted for the Observants. This division did not have marked consequences in Swedish or Norwegian convents but the Danish convents went through quite substantial reform towards a stricter observance of the Franciscan rule. As a result, some Danish friars decided to change to Swedish convents or leave the order permanently.

The Dominicans were the second large mendicant order. The order was established in 1216 and named after its founder, Saint Dominic. It was also known as the order of preachers (Lat. *Ordo Fratrum Praedicatorum*). Conforming to mendicant ideology, the Dominicans also circulated publicly in Christian society, preaching and collecting alms for the order. They likewise could not own anything and were bound to celibacy and to the convent where they took their monastic vows. The Dominican order operated mainly in towns and cathedral cities. It was divided into administrative territories called provinces, and the Scandinavian countries formed the province of Dacia. The leaders of the Dominican provinces met once a year in a general chapter that assembled at previously agreed upon convent. Dominicans were keen on studying and are often known for the schools which they founded in their convents. Each province was to have at least one convent of higher learning together with its provincial lecturer. The order also stressed the importance of knowledge by sending its members to learn at other convents or even foreign universities. The Dominicans especially favoured the University of Paris where the order also had its own school. 'Books are the weapons of the Dominicans', wrote one of their general masters in the 13th century. Scandinavian Dominicans wrote extensive collections of sermons and some have survived till today, for example those by Matthias of Ribe from the beginning of the 14th century. They give a unique impression of the theological and moral lessons that Dominicans sought to convey to lay people in their public preaching.

The order had also a female branch, the 'second order'. Unlike the preaching friars, the Dominican nuns lived quietly in convents and did not have contacts with the outer world. The first Scandinavian Dominican nunnery was founded in Roskilde in 1263 by the daughters of the Danish King Eric IV Ploughpenny, Agnes and Jutta. Sweden received its first Dominican nunnery in 1281, at Skänninge, founded by Ingrid who had made several pilgrimages to Jerusalem, Santiago de Compostela, and elsewhere. There were other nunneries in Kalmar and Gavnø, and a convent of Saint Anna was planned for Finland, but in 1439, these plans were changed and a Birgittine abbey was instead erected in Naantali.

The Dominican order spread to Scandinavia soon after its founding. The first contacts between Scandinavians and the order took place through the University of Paris, where promising young men from the order and Scandinavian dioceses received their education. Through these contacts the Dominican order sent its first friars to the north in 1220. A few years later, in 1223, the first Scandinavian Dominican convent was established in Lund under the auspices of Archbishop Anders Sunesen, and the province of Dacia came into existence in 1228. The order spread in the course of the 13th century to all Scandinavian countries. By the end of the century, there were already 27 Dominican convents in Scandinavia: 15 in Denmark (including Estonia), three in Norway, and nine in Sweden. The Dominicans spread all over Scandinavia in the 13th century, after which very few new convents were erected. One of the latecomers was Vyborg, close to the Russian border.

The third mendicant order to arrive in Scandinavia was the Carmelites. This order (Lat. *Ordo Fratrum Beatae Mariae Virginis de Monte Carmelo*) had its origin in a community founded by French crusaders in the mid-12th century on Mount Carmel in the Holy Land, but it took some time before the order received its rule, confirmed by Pope Honorius III in 1226. The order's aim was to live in isolation, continuing the contemplative and apostolic life. After the Muslims had conquered the Holy Land where the order had been active, the Carmelites moved to Europe and changed their rule to fit to their new needs. The order gave up the idea of almost complete isolation and instead chose the monastic lifestyle, after which the Carmelite brothers could have broader contact with Christians just like the Franciscans and the Dominicans. Its members were known as the white friars because of their white dress.

The Carmelites arrived relatively late in Scandinavia. Their first establishment was founded in the Danish territory in the early 15th century, strongly supported by the Union King Eric of Pomerania. The first Carmelite convent was founded in Landskrona in the 1410s, and others followed slowly. The Carmelites originally allowed only male brothers, but from the mid-15th century onwards the order also accepted female members. However, all Scandinavian Carmelite convents were for males, and most of them were erected in eastern parts of Denmark. The order never became very significant in Scandinavia, although it had an especially large influence in the Danish Reformation since it stressed the activity of preaching, founded a collegium in 1519 in Copenhagen for this purpose. The collegium's leader was the well-known Danish reformer Poul Helgesen, and the collegium was the alma mater of many Danish reform-oriented priests.

The order of the Holy Spirit (Lat. *Ordo Sancti Spiritus*) had as its main mission the care of the sick. The order was founded c. 1195 in Montpellier, France, and spread soon to Rome where Pope Innocent III allowed it to build its hospital (nowadays the hospital of S. Spirito di Sassia) close to Saint Peter's Basilica. The order followed the monastic rule of Saint Augustine and was confirmed in 1213 by Pope Innocent.

The order rapidly spread, and by the end of the 13th century already had almost 100 houses. The brothers ran large hospitals where they took care of the sick – and also of orphans, who could be left anonymously on the institutions' doorsteps. The order gave food and possibly also shelter to the poor or passing pilgrims. It also allowed female members, who similarly to the brothers participated in the hospitals' activities.

The first Scandinavian house of the order of the Holy Spirit came into existence in 1451 when a hospital in Aalborg, already founded in 1431, was incorporated into the order. Other previously existing hospitals joined the order and new houses were founded: Nakskov, Copenhagen, Faaborg, Malmö, and Randers in Denmark, while the hospital of Saint George in Söderköping, Sweden, was incorporated as late as around 1500. There is no information about other Scandinavian hospitals joining

Illustration 2.8 The hospital in Aalborg was founded in 1431 by the wealthy Lady Maren Hemmingsdatter but burned down only three years later. The new hospital that replaced it was incorporated into the order of the Holy Spirit in 1451. The buildings are still standing and are among the oldest medieval houses preserved in Scandinavia. Its charitable function has continued, and today the hospital is a retirement home with a governing board that represents both ecclesiastical and lay administration, including the bishop and the mayor of Aalborg.

Photo Liberaler Humanist 2018. This file is licensed under the Creative Commons Attribution-Share Alike 3.0 Unported license.

the order, although similar kinds of hospitals, often named after Saint George or the Holy Spirit, had also existed in other places since the 13th century. This tradition remained after the Reformation; for example a house of the Holy Spirit still existed in Turku in the 16th century. However, there is no indication that this house would ever have officially belonged to the order of the Holy Spirit.

Embarking Upon the Monastic Lifestyle and the Choice of the Right Order

Becoming a monk, friar, or nun was an important, lifelong decision that was not to be taken lightly. The monasteries receiving novices might have asked the newcomers their reasons for entering the monastic lifestyle, but there are no surviving records that testify to their answers. However, there are other medieval sources that can shed light on the reasons behind the choice to take such an important step: religious motivations, family reasons, a desire to study, or to gain a better social status.

Most medieval monks, friars, and nuns entered the monastic lifestyle voluntarily because of their religious conviction and desire to serve God and the Church, but there might have been other religious motives for taking the monastic vows as well. We have numerous medieval testimonies from people who, in a moment of despair because of illness or life-threatening danger, swore to God or certain saints that if they survived they would spend the rest of their lives in a monastery. Sometimes, parents made such vows to the Church on behalf of their children if they were in great danger. Such vows were taken very seriously, and according to canon law, only the pope – and in certain cases also the local bishop – could liberate a person from such a promise and commute it to other kinds of pious acts.

Nevertheless, some Scandinavians also had other motives for joining a monastic order, which were not religious in nature. One such person was Priest Laurentius Johannis, who wanted to study but had no means to do so. He had therefore made an agreement with the Johannites in Eskilstuna that if they would support his studies, he would join the order. After having studied seven years at the cost of the Johannites, however, Laurentius came to the conclusion that the monastic life was not for him and asked in 1499 for a papal favour so that he could leave the Johannites and serve as parish priest. The papal administration granted him such a permit but expected him to compensate the Johannites all the costs they had incurred through supporting his studies. Other monastic orders, especially the Dominicans, also had their own schools and could offer possibilities to study, so Laurentius was probably the only Scandinavian to enter monastic life for educational reasons. Entering a monastery for learning must have offered a good opportunity for bright young men with lower social status and less economic means to study and thereby to advance socially.

In certain situations, monks and nuns had not entered monastic vocation voluntarily; rather, they had been pressed to do so by their parents or relatives. Often, the motivation behind such an act was to limit the amount of the children dividing the parental inheritance. Girls might have been subject to such a decision more often than boys, but there is no information available regarding the number of children forced to the monastic life. Swedish Nanne Kerling's parents had brought him to the Cistercian abbey of Varnhem when he was in his early teens, whence he escaped after some months because he did not like the monastic lifestyle. But his brother brought Nanne back to another Cistercian monastery, the Alvastra abbey. Unlike many others, Nanne did not have to stay in the monastery: the abbot allowed him to return to secular life because he never fulfilled the year of noviciate. Despite this, Nanne's sister later began a juridical process against him, claiming that he had no right to inheritance because he was a monk – thus confirming that in his case delimiting the number of heirs was a factor. Sometimes, a person had been sent to a monastery for other reasons; ecclesiastics with uncomfortable political opinions, for example, could be sentenced to stay enclosed within a monastery, almost as a prison. This happened in the early 13th century to Valdemar Knudsen, who was bishop of Schleswig and later Hamburg-Bremen, but constantly conspired to become king of Denmark.

The number of unwilling monks or nuns was, however, probably relatively small compared to those who entered the monastic lifestyle and stayed there voluntarily. Since the commitment to a monastic order and monastery was lifelong, the choice of the right order was crucial. Medieval sources do not give us direct information about the choices made, but they can provide some hints. As the case of Laurentius Johannis showed, some chose a monastic vocation because they wanted to study. In these cases, the choice would probably be the Dominican order or the Johannites, who stressed the intellectual side of religious life. Mendicant orders, that is, Dominicans and Franciscans, would have been an obvious choice for those who wanted to preach and spread the Christian faith. On the other hand, those who longed for a good and quiet life would probably prefer the Benedictines or Cistercians, as would those who had more conservative ideas of the monastic lifestyle. The choice of the right order was probably easier in Scandinavia than in the densely populated areas of central Europe where the number of monasteries was higher. In Scandinavia, the best choice was probably the monastery relatively close to one's home, which made it possible to maintain contact with one's parents and friends. Although it was forbidden and considered simony, some monastic orders, like the Benedictines, often expected some monetary compensation when accepting new novices. Such practices excluded novices from poorer social classes.

Monasteries and Medieval Society

Monastic orders and monasteries had various important societal functions, and monasteries had close contacts to the surrounding society, be it urban or rural. Monasteries were typically known for their hospitals and care of the sick, high degree of learned culture, technological innovations, and the cure of souls.

Some monastic orders, such as the Johannites, were founded for curing the sick; in the Middle Ages, this task also spread to other orders. All monastic houses had a hospital where they took care of their own sick, but most monasteries also provided care for Christians who sought medical help. The monasteries often had monks or nuns who had specialised in medicine, and the monastic gardens contained large collections of medical herbs and other necessary plants. Some monastic establishments provided care for anyone, while some were specialised in treating certain illnesses, such as leprosy. Many monasteries also provided care for elderly or disabled people who could no longer live at home alone. In these cases, the people who required caretaking typically made an arrangement with the monastery and paid for their care. Sometimes, they just lived on the land of the monastery, but they often became members of the confraternity of the monks or nuns and also enjoyed the spiritual benefits of monastic life, for example the indulgences conceded to the order.

Learned culture was important for the monastic orders, and some had their own schools. Many medieval monasteries were also known for their *scriptoria*, places where books were produced. Since monks were usually able to read and write, monasteries became cultural centres for the production of manuscripts – for both internal use and for sale. Some of the most beautiful and lavishly decorated medieval manuscripts were produced in monasteries. In addition to book production, monasteries also functioned as libraries that preserved old manuscripts and thereby conserved the classical heritage of the western culture. The monastic libraries did not just keep theological works or law manuscripts, but also most of the medieval copies of secular texts by ancient authors, such as the *Annals* of Tacitus from the 2nd century, have been preserved thanks to monastic libraries. Many of the narrative sources we use today to understand the Scandinavian Middle Ages were written in monasteries, as were the very popular novels and songs about valiant knights.

Monks and friars interacted with the surrounding society; especially the members of the Mendicant orders walked among the local Christians preaching and collecting alms. The monasteries also received donations from people who wanted to be remembered in the prayers of the monks or nuns or to receive their burial place in the church of the monastery. Monasteries also offered consolation for the soul.

The monasteries had several economic ties to the local society. Monasteries were often wealthy landowners and received all they needed from their lands: food, drink, and materials necessary for constructing and renovating the monastic buildings. The monks did not usually run the farms owned by the monastery; instead, they had tenants who took care of the farming and delivered the products as rent to the monastery. This was especially the case with nunneries, because the nuns were not allowed to move outside the monastic walls or interact with laymen. Due to monetary donations, the monasteries often had a supply of cash and they could function as a kind of bank guaranteeing loans for Christians who needed it, or help transfer money to other countries for pilgrims and crusaders. Loans were offered against security in pledges of land, whereby the monasteries became even more closely entangled in the local economy and society.

Many monastic orders were also known for their interest in technology and innovation. The Scandinavian Cistercians were among the first to use water power and construct mills, and some Cistercian abbeys were famous for breeding fine horses. The concentration of manuscript production in the monasteries necessitated large flocks of sheep whose skins could be used for parchment production. As side products, the monasteries got also wool and meat, and they could trade with the surrounding population. Some nunneries are also well-known for beautiful needlework. For example, the Birgittine abbey of Naantali is typically connected to high-quality needlework.

Scandinavian historians have concentrated almost all their research on the monastic orders that brought change – mainly the Cistercians with a new understanding of landscape and agriculture, the mendicants with schools and active preaching in the cities, or the new Scandinavian order of the Birgittines. Historians think in categories of change, and that is probably the reason why so few have studied the largest and oldest of the orders, the Benedictines. These black-clad monks focused on continuing a tradition and had no interest in radical novelties. In the Middle Ages, the Benedictine order probably appealed to individuals with a conservative attitude to life and an interest in solitary studies and contemplation. They left fewer marks in the sources than the more dynamic orders.

3 Tilling the Land – The Local Economy

The Spread of Agriculture

Around 1100, Ælnoth, a Benedictine monk of English origin who settled in Denmark, wrote of a seven-year famine in which 'the mighty and rich became weak, and the weak died'. To feed the population in the Middle Ages was a continuous and often losing struggle against climatic challenges and misfortunes. Viewed from a longer-term perspective, nonetheless, the period between 900 and 1200 was characterised by growth and expansion of villages, cultivated land, and population. All quantitative estimates from the Middle Ages are tentative and imprecise, but food production and the number of people living in Scandinavia may have doubled during these years. The growth was not only caused by a favourable climate but by significant changes in the organisation of agricultural production, resulting in a structure that remained relatively stable from c. 1200 until c. 1800.

The majority of medieval Scandinavians lived in the countryside and got their living from agriculture, supplemented by fishing and some husbandry and horticulture. In the north, summer seasons were too short for agriculture, and the Sámi relied primarily on reindeer hunting and later on reindeer husbandry.

The first medieval centuries in Scandinavia witnessed a significant spread of agriculture. The increased population needed more space to live and larger fields to grow what was needed to supply the population with enough food. Settlement and agriculture spread therefore quickly to new territories. The expansion of arable land had already begun in Denmark and southern Sweden during the Viking Age but continued and spread northwards. Some of Scandinavia's seemingly endless forests had become arable lands by the early 14th century at the latest, and new farmhouses and hamlets were founded.

The expansion of settlement can be observed in place names. For example, many new Danish Viking Age or medieval settlements had endings such as *-thorp*, *-drup*, or *-rup*. They all share the same etymology in the Old Norse word *þorp* (*thorp*), meaning a hamlet or outlying new settlement. The -thorp ending is typically combined with a personal name, such as Svend in *Svendstrup*, and can be connected to the name of the farmer who initiated the settlement. It is difficult to date these hamlets either to the Viking or Middle Ages because we do not know anything about these people. Some others can be connected with certainty to the Middle Ages because they contain clearly Christian elements, such as Munkerup, 'the hamlet of monks'.

It is well attested from place names that there was a Scandinavian Viking Age colonisation of parts of England and Normandy. After perhaps the year 1000, there was a

DOI: 10.4324/9781003095514-5

change, and Scandinavian colonisation turned towards interior territories, the Atlantic isles, and Finland. All along the southern coast of the Baltic, Danish crusaders especially fought and conquered land throughout the 12th and early 13th centuries, but unlike in the territories conquered by German crusaders, the Danish crusaders were not followed by colonists except on some islands in southern Denmark such as Falster and Fehmarn. There was enough land within Scandinavia to put under the plough.

The Scandinavian hamlets were traditionally located a little inland from the coastal area, where the ground was relatively flat, and the sea and rivers allowed easy transportation by water but inhabitants were still protected from direct attack by seaborne enemies. By the end of the Middle Ages, the whole of Denmark, most of the southern parts of Sweden and Norway, and the coasts of Norway, northern Sweden, Iceland, and Finland were permanently inhabited and cultivated. The Scandinavians did not only find new settlements in the nearby areas of the mainland but, especially the Norwegians, in far-away territories: Iceland and Greenland.

The colonisation of Iceland and later Greenland coincided with the Medieval Warm Period, when it was possible to grow grain and also have large herds of sheep, cows, and horses this far north. Houses and stables were normally built with stone walls. One barn in Greenland could house 100 animals, and around 1300 there were maybe 150 farms in the Eastern Settlement, and 90 in the Western. From c. 1200, sheep began to disappear and the arable land diminished, probably because of the cooling climate.

Medieval settlers in Scandinavia, especially those in the north and in Finland, increased the amount of arable land by burn-beating forests: namely, a plot of forest was burned down and the ash turned into fertile soil. That was hard work because the farmers had to fell the trees and clear the soil at least of the largest stumps. The first crop to be cultivated in recently burn-beat land was typically rye, or where the land was not yet smooth enough for grain the farmers could plant turnips. Burn beating made the soil fertile but only for a relatively short period, and after a few years, a new part of the forest had to be burned. It was a low technology system that could function with relatively few workers and independently of neighbours.

Agricultural expansion in Scandinavia took place in two phases. During the first period, c. 700–1100, it depended largely on the particularly favourable climate. Temperatures were pleasantly high: summers warm and dry, and winters more humid. During the second phase, which began in the 12th century and ended at the latest by the arrival of the Black Death around 1350, the climate was no longer as favourable, but new adopted agricultural techniques increased the harvest and made expansion possible. These inventions, in particular spades strengthened with iron, the mouldboard plough, ditching, and the three-field system, made agriculture easier and more profitable.

The introduction of the three-field system was a particularly opportune novelty. The farmers knew that it was good for the fertility of the earth to alternate the crops or grains cultivated in one field. In the early Middle Ages, most farmers used the so-called two-field rotation system, which meant that in one year half of the fields were planted and half laid fallow, and in the following year, the pattern was reversed. Beginning from the 9th century, European farmers developed a new system of three-field rotation. That was adopted in Scandinavia from the 11th century onwards and proved to be very fertile, although the new system did not replace the old one everywhere, with various systems coexisted depending on the location and the soil's fertility. The three-field rotation system in practice meant that the farmers divided their lands into three areas. In the first, they planted either rye in the autumn or barley or oats in the spring; in the second they grew crops like peas, lentils, or beans, and in the third, they left fallow. The three zones were rotated so that each was fallow in its turn, once every three years.

The three-field system was common in southern Scandinavia but was never the only one in use. In many places, the ground was not sufficiently fertile, and it was better to use the two-field system so that the land lay fallow every second year. Other – and less numerous – places were on the contrary so fertile that the fields could be tilled every year, especially if this could be combined with husbandry and extra fertilisation. The three fields were divided into smaller plots of land and then distributed so that all the farms in the village got plots of good soil and of hard and unfertile soil. The amount of land distributed depended on the farm's size. The strips of land could sometimes be up to 10–20 m broad and as long as 600 m. Since it was impossible to separate the land of one farmer from that of another, the fields had to be commonly tilled and harvested.

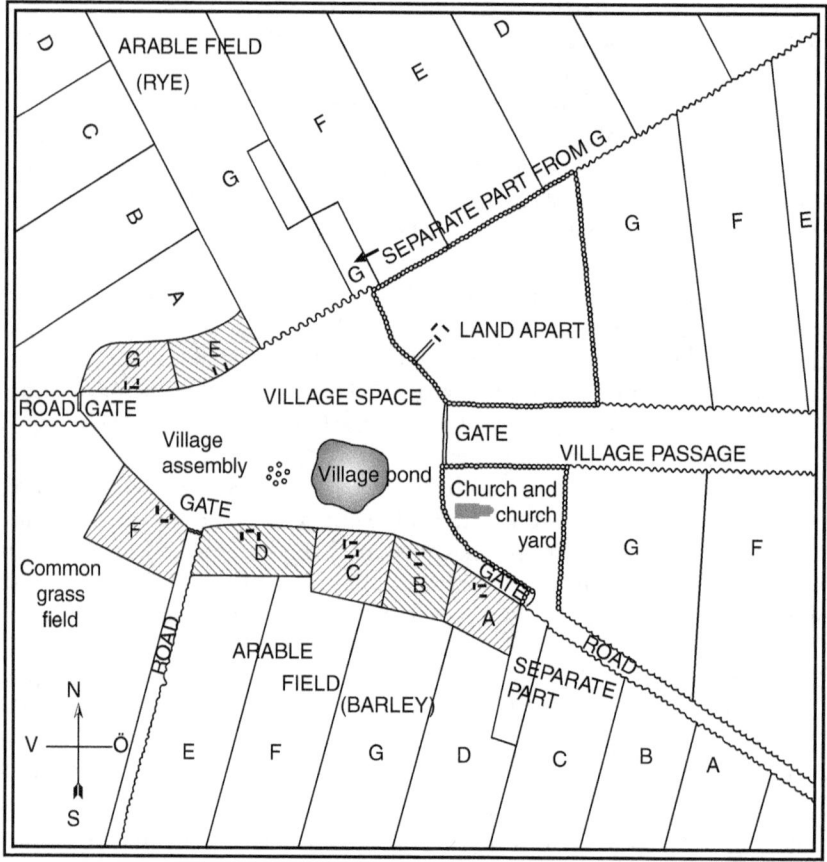

Illustration 3.1 Plan of a typical medieval village in Scandinavia.
By Helle Vogt.

In territories with fertile and flat land, like Denmark or the southern half of Sweden, farms were situated close to each other in small groups, forming a village or a hamlet. In territories with less fertile and mountainous ground like most of Norway, the northern parts of Sweden and Finland, it was more common to have solitary farms located far from each other. The farmers in the solitary farms independently took care of the workload and were responsible for their own needs, while in the densely populated areas, there was a clear division of labour and extensive collaboration between the farms. The land surrounding a village with a greater number of farms could either be organised into individual plots tilled by single farms or in an open field system where each field was subdivided into furlongs, that is smaller units that were not fenced off from each other. To each farm, there belonged a number of furlongs, but since the fields were situated so close to each other they had to be cultivated by all the farms together. In practice, this meant that the peasants had to agree upon when to do the work and what should be done. This contributed to the unity of each village but caused also lots of disagreements.

The wheel plough with iron mouldboard might perhaps already have been known in the Viking Age, but did not become commonly used before the 12th century, and in Sweden apparently much later. It was long and heavy and had to be dragged by several pairs of oxen, but it could also work the heavy clay fields which could not otherwise be cultivated. It turned the mould upside down so that grass and manure were ploughed down into the soil, increasing the fertilising effect considerably. The plough not only turned the grass turf but moved the width of one mouldboard to the side. Over the years, the strips in the fields were moved, forming a typical pattern of ridges and furrows. Ecologically it was a brilliant way of lessening the risk of poor growth. The top of the ridge would be dryer than the bottom of the furrow, and somewhere between the top and bottom, the conditions would be ideal for the grain. Still, it was not a highly intensive system. It has been estimated that most fields during the Middle Ages and much later yielded crops only three or four times the seed.

Population and Family Structure

In the Middle Ages, Scandinavia was less densely populated than the central areas of Europe. The number of inhabitants in different Scandinavian countries is not known for certain, but there exist some estimates of population sizes. For Norway, there is relatively reliable data from around 1330 (thus before the devastating effect of the Black Death) and again from the second half of the 15th century, on which basis the Norwegian population has been estimated at c. 350,000 inhabitants (with variations from 275,000 to 420,000). The estimates for Denmark are much more speculative and include numerous uncertainties, but a broadly accepted estimate for the second half of the 13th century is around one million inhabitants. In Iceland, estimates of the medieval population vary between 50,000 and 100,000. The estimates for Sweden's population are also relatively uncertain but point to 550,000–650,000 inhabitants on the Swedish mainland in the late Middle Ages, and c. 150,000 (and up to 250,000) in Finland.

The medieval family structure in Scandinavia was based on the nuclear family, which in the peasant classes could include both the farm owner's family as well as servants and possible relatives – thus not only the husband, wife, and offspring. It has been estimated that an average medieval Scandinavian household consisted of six or seven persons, which makes the medieval households slightly smaller than the average 10- to 13-member households in the Viking Age. Due to the high child mortality rate, it has been estimated that in a typical family two children survived to adulthood. Additionally, one grandparent might have belonged to the household, since due to the short life expectancy, it was not common for both grandparents to live long enough to see their grandchildren grow.

In addition to the nuclear family, each farm could be the home of other family members, servants, or slaves. Until the 13th century, Scandinavia was a slave society, and it was the norm for all farmers to have slaves, called *trälar*, but there are no reliable estimates of their number. Slaves working in the fields were relatively common in the Viking Age, but slavery become less and less economically viable during the Middle Ages. The slaves, men and women, usually worked on the forms and cultivated land, but some of them could specialise in handicrafts, and some were concubines to the farm owners. The Christianisation of the Scandinavian societies was one of the factors leading to the abolition of slavery after 1200, by which time slaves had also become an economically less profitable labour force. After the 13th century, slavery slowly disappeared from Scandinavia but in different pace from the different Scandinavian countries.

It was always the man who ran the farm and represented it in public – which was very typical of Scandinavian society, in which men had a public role while women were supposed to stay home and take care of the daily errands. It was usually the man who took care of the hard physical work in the fields and forests, and the women of the household. The law gave the wife the task to carry the house keys. The farm buildings could be locked with simple locks but these could hardly prevent anyone from stealing. Thus the carrying of the keys was more a question of status than a practical matter. Gender roles in the Middle Ages were strictly regulated but there was also room for overlapping.

Life in the Countryside

In the rest of Europe, serfdom was common and the land was owned by an aristocratic class, who had received it as a benefice from a ruler in return for obligations of some kind or as personal favour. In contrast, most medieval Scandinavians were independent farmers or tenants cultivating land that belonged either to them, the crown, nobility, or ecclesiastical institutions. In the early period, the noblemen, who in Scandinavia were called the *frälse*, were not royal vassals as was common in Europe but independent landowners who had received from the king an exemption from taxes against obligations to perform military service. The independent farmers owned their lands, and either actually, physically did military service in the royally controlled naval system of the ledung, or paid a yearly tax to the crown but without military obligations.

In the earlier Middle Ages, most farms were hereditary property in the hands of the farmers. The situation changed during the Middle Ages little by little, and by the end of the medieval period, a growing amount of land and property had come into the hands of ecclesiastical institutions, such as monasteries and cathedral chapters, or of rich families that had accumulated wealth. They then further let the land to their tenants. One of the reasons for the diminishing number of independent farmers during the Middle Ages was probably that according to Scandinavian hereditary laws all children had the right to inherit, although not in equally large proportions and the shares varied from one country to the other. Thus the originally large farms tended to become smaller entities which eventually were no longer viable for the needs of a family. Some farm owners had to sell their property, for example if they had committed a crime and had to pay fines, which could easily amount to the value of a small farm. Similarly, farm owners were sometimes forced to sell their farms – after a famine, for example – if they could not pay their debts or the tax for the king or the Church, or if they wished to receive protection from a powerful nobleman.

Although independent farmers were common in all Scandinavian countries, their proportion varied significantly from one to another. For example, the independent farmers owned a little more than 50% of the land in Iceland, while the Church owned c. 45% and the crown only a few per cent. In Sweden (Finland included), the independent farmers owned c. 50% of the land, the nobility and the Church slightly over 20% each, and the crown only a few per cent. In Norway, the Church was the biggest landowner with almost 50%, while independent farmers owned 30% of the land, the nobility 15%, and the crown slightly less than 10%. In Denmark, the division was instead that the Church and the nobility each possessed c. 35–40% of the land and the crown c. 10%. The independent Danish farmers thus owned only c. 15% of the land. The above numbers are just estimates, and there were also regional differences within each country.

The families lived in typical farmhouses that were placed on their own *toft*, the parcel of land with the buildings and marked off with fences. The farmhouses were usually rectangular (sometimes curving) longhouses divided by walls into several rooms with various functions. There were regional differences in the house shapes, but it was common that a byre with cowsheds was placed at one end of the house, while the living room as well as kitchen and eventual storage rooms were at the other end. The houses had only one store, and they were approximately 5–7 m high, while their length could vary significantly – depending on the size and wealth of the farm – from 15 m up to 75 m in the early Middle Ages. In addition to the main house, many larger farms' *toft* could have also other buildings like cooking houses, storage houses, byres, barns, or saunas. On the *toft*, there could also exist smaller huts for additional labourers or artisans, for example pottery makers.

Medieval buildings were usually very dark inside. There could be small windows close to the ceiling and some light could enter from a hole in the roof, from where the smoke was let out because the houses did not have chimneys. Each house had a stove or fireplace in the middle, and the fire gave light to the building and was used for cooking. For lighting, the house tallow candles or lamps were used too. Since most of the farm work took place outside, it was not a great problem that the houses were so poorly illuminated.

Agriculture, Fishing, and Hunting

Barley was traditionally the most common grain in Scandinavia in the Viking Age, as it was also the only type of grain that could be cultivated up in the north, including Iceland. It has been estimated that c. 80% of fields grew barley, while the share of wheat was c. 10%; rye and oats were both cultivated but in much lesser quantities. That changed after the year 1000 with better climate and the new technique of strips and fallow fields, which made it possible to grow rye in autumn without it drowning and rotting during winter. Rye became the most common crop throughout Scandinavia and important for bread baking. Barley continued to be grown and eaten as porridge but its main use was for brewing beer. Oats could grow on poorer soil and were sometimes used in Norway both for porridge and beer, but their main function was as horse fodder. With the huge increase in the number of horses from 1200 onwards, for warfare but especially in agriculture, oats were grown and became important everywhere in Scandinavia. Wheat was also grown but continued throughout the Middle Ages to be an expensive luxury product for delicate white bread.

Because of the poor yield, it was important to collect all the grain when harvesting. That is probably the reason why grain was harvested throughout the Middle Ages with the sickle, and handful-by-handful, and not with the scythe which was known after 1200. The loss of precious food would simply have been too big.

Alongside grain, the medieval Scandinavians grew also hay, which was essential for being able to feed animals all year around. If hay was in shortage many areas also harvested the thin branches from deciduous trees and used that for winter fodder. In certain regions, such as Norrland, linen was also cultivated. It was used mainly for preparing clothing, in particular shirts and underskirts, but from the linen seed, it was also possible to prepare linseed oil. Not all farmland was used for cultivation, but some as pasture lands for animals.

Medieval farmers did not only grow grain and other plants but also ensured the food supply of their families by having animals on their farms. Pigs were the most common domesticated animals in medieval Scandinavia. Archaeological excavations have confirmed that pigs were already domesticated in Scandinavia in the Iron Age, but only on a very small scale compared to the medieval period. In addition to pigs, the farmers had cattle – cows, oxen, and bulls – that were used for milk, cheese, meat, and work. In addition to these large animals, sheep and goats were common in the farmhouses, and their meat and milk formed an important part of the daily diet. Hen and geese were common and also important for their eggs, as were pigeons for their meat, and a few luxury households had peacocks. Some animals like cats and dogs were not meant for food but were important for other purposes. Cats could catch mice, rats, and other small harmful animals, and dogs could offer protection and assist in hunting. Many farms also had horses which were used for riding and transporting things. The horses on typical farms were small, unlike the expensive war horses of the nobility that were imported from abroad or from the 12th century onwards bred systematically on local stud farms run by nobles, kings, or ecclesiastical institutions.

The farmers did not only live on the products of the earth or animals reared on the farm, but their daily diet included berries, nuts, and other edible plants as well as fish and game. Additionally people gathered the eggs of wild birds. Most farms in the villages also had a garden close to the house, called apple gardens or cabbage gardens. Various sorts of apple trees and perhaps other fruit trees were cultivated, spreading from monastic gardens that had contacts with monasteries further south in Europe. Most garden products grew naturally in Scandinavia such as onions, beans, peas, angelica, and hemp. The cabbages had a great advantage that they could survive frost and could be left in the garden until they were needed, and so they were important sources of vitamins during the long Scandinavian winters. There was a special kind of garden for bees, and the production of honey and wax was extremely common in all villages. The gardens were so important that stealing fruit or vegetables from them was as serious a crime as breaking into a house and severely punished.

Illustration 3.2 Milk was a very important part of nutrition everywhere in medieval Scandinavia and would have been processed into butter or cheese to be stored and transported. To churn milk into butter was hard work and a transformation of one element into another, and was therefore considered especially vulnerable to abuse by evil forces. Here a witch is churning, her small demon is vomiting up the milk it has sucked and stolen from the neighbours' cows, and a devil is helping while the head of its tail eagerly licks up the drops of butter. Fourteenth-century wall painting, Söderby-Karl church, Sweden.

Photo © Kurt Villads Jensen, 2022.

Medieval Scandinavians hunted many different animals for various purposes: for their furs, for their meat, or because they were dangerous to domestic animals. The most important fur-bearing animal was the squirrel, followed by ermine. These were hunted mainly in the northern parts of Norway, Sweden, and Finland. The furs were valuable commercial goods sold to southern Europe through the commercial channels of the Hanseatic League, and at least in Finland squirrel furs were used as tax parcels too. The large size animals such as elk, reindeer, deer, and hare were sought for their meat and relatively common. Among beasts of prey, foxes, and wolves were common and hunted all over Scandinavia. Bear was also hunted but much less common. In Iceland and the arctic areas close to water, the inhabitants were also hunting seals, whales, and occasionally even polar bears. Hunting birds were tamed and trained, and hawks from Norway and Sweden exported throughout Europe. White falcons from Greenland could command a fortune in Arab markets around the Mediterranean.

Fishing was an important way to get supplementary nourishment throughout the year. Water was omnipresent in Scandinavia. The fishing on the Atlantic coasts was much more professional and systematic than that for everyday needs; this was done locally, with small boats and inexpensive equipment, and the catch was usually relatively small. Some farmers further north specialised in fishing and made their main living by catching and selling the fish for merchants who traded it on. In Scandinavia, there were no commercial fisheries similar to those in England, Holland, Flanders, or Germany having large boats and able to spend several weeks on their fishing trips. The most important species were cod and coalfish in the western parts of Scandinavia (Iceland, Faroe Islands, Norway, and Jutland), herring in the Baltic Sea (eastern Denmark and Swedish coastline), and also salmon and eels in inland rivers and lakes.

Scandinavian fish were brought to the international market from the 12th century onwards, when the process of urbanisation and monetarisation had begun in full. In northern Scandinavia, it was possible to dry the fish in the wind because the climate was so cold and dry. That treatment was reserved in particular for cod caught up in the north, and the dried fish was known as 'stockfish' because it was hung over a stock for drying. The stockfish market was particularly focussed on Bergen which had become a part of the Hanseatic commercial network from the 13th century, but from the mid-15th century onwards, the northern settlements in Norway also began to profit from producing stockfish, and the production provided a livelihood for several thousand people. Herring in its turn was usually salted, sometimes smoked. Since salt had to be imported from abroad and was expensive, as were the barrels in which the fish were conserved, herring production was in the hands of professionals, typically operating in southern Danish coastal towns. The most important by far was the market in Scania.

Different kinds of fish were caught with different methods. For cod, the fishermen used lines with one or two hooks, while herring was fished with seines and nets. This was usually such cheap equipment that any man could afford to use them. For hunting, farmers used the bow and spear – and from the 13th century onwards also the crossbow. The best hunting season, especially for animals that gained a thicker and sometimes lighter fur, was winter, when it was also easier to move in the wild with the help of the skis. Hunting with a bow and spear was usually an enterprise in which the men of the whole village would participate, especially if the hunting involved chasing game. Sometimes the hunters used dogs for tracking the animals. In addition to the bow and spear, many farmers hunted with different kinds of trap made of wood or from the late Middle Ages onwards also iron, which clamped around the animals' legs.

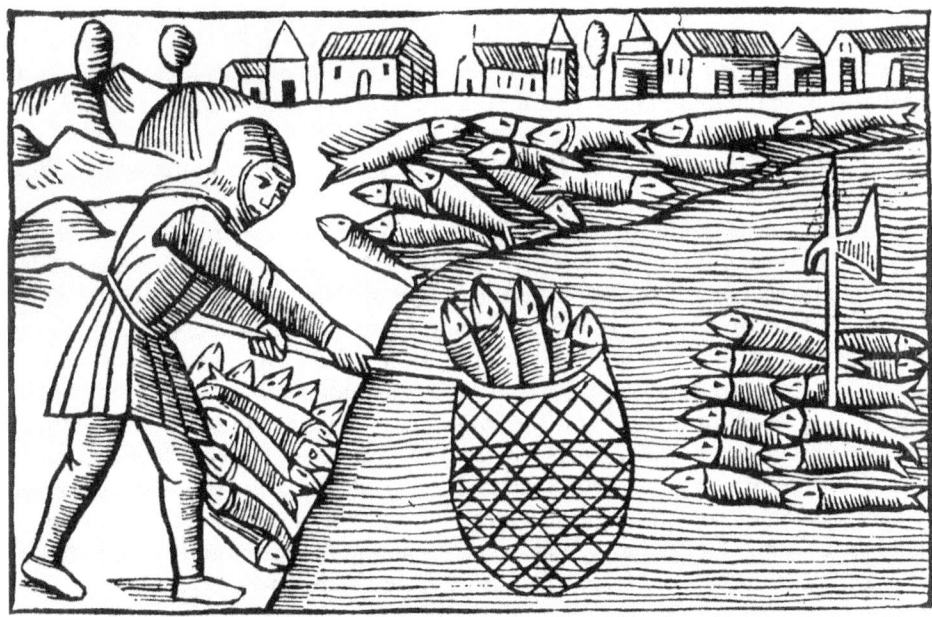

Illustration 3.3 The catch around the big fishing market in Scania was famous from at least the 12th century and throughout the Middle Ages. The herring could be taken up directly by hand, and the fish shoals were allegedly so thick that a spear put into the water would not sink.
Olaus Magnus, *Historia de gentibus septentrionalibus*, Rome 1555. Public domain.

In Scandinavia, the right to hunt normally belonged to the owner of the land, although in many places in Norway and Sweden hunting grounds were commonly owned and anyone could hunt there. Unlike elsewhere in Europe, where hunting was reserved for the landowning rulers and nobility, such reservations in Scandinavia began late. The Danish king was the first to reserve certain geographical areas for his own use in the 13th century, and later on, regulations about the nobility's hunting rights were included in Danish and Swedish legislation.

Life in the countryside revolved very much around the four seasons. Spring was the time to sow and plant, summer was the season of growth, autumn was the time of harvest, and winter for hunting. The daylight was used well, and the long summer days were taken up with working, while dark winter nights were used for work inside but also for storytelling and entertaining. Few could read, but all could tell stories that passed from generation to generation.

The Self-Sufficient Economy and Local Market

Medieval people did not own many things. The houses were relatively poorly furnished. The walls of the longhouses could be decorated with wooden panels or clothes that also gave a little more warmth to the room. Some wealthier houses had wooden floors, but many had earthen floors until the late Middle Ages, usually consisting of hardpacked soil or clay topped off with a layer of straw. The furniture of a farmhouse consisted mainly of benches that were usually placed against the walls. These could function as beds as well as tables. Personal items were usually kept in chests that could be closed with a lock and often kept under the benches. Richer households could also have tables and chairs, and even separate beds for sleeping, but they were not very common in the countryside.

The reason for the small number of possessions was that in countryside all things had to be made at home. The farmers had to be self-sufficient in all necessary items, be it clothes, furniture, tools, boats, or wagons. And the same applied to food. Each farm produced what it needed. The first medieval centuries in Scandinavia can indeed be defined as the period of self-sufficient economy, which meant that there was no need to produce anything more than one required for self-subsistence and taxpaying, and there was little need to acquire anything from others. In self-sufficient societies, there was also no need for money or a monetary economy.

With the growth of population, the founding of towns, and increased trading, it became more common for farmers to begin to specialise their production and sell their surplus to others who in turn produced a surplus in other products. Originally the exchange of goods could be made without exchange of money. This also began to change by the end of the Middle Ages, when even in smaller communities some people had begun to specialise so much that each village would have, for example, a smith who could prepare necessary metal items such as horseshoes and nails.

The local economy and exchange of goods with neighbours could take place without any regulations or limitations, but when farmers increasingly began to need products that could not be produced or exchanged locally, such as salt, spices, or metal products, this required a monetary economy and people specialised in trade. Local trade in the medieval villages was undertaken in different ways depending on the country and region. Each Sunday, when all the locals arrived at their church for Mass, was a market day when they could sell their products and purchase what they needed. In some places, though, local markets could only be arranged much more rarely. The establishment of towns and their trading privileges especially delimited rural trade, since farmers could no longer sell their products locally but to do so had to take them to the nearest town.

Peasants in Scandinavian villages were very different. Some were relatively wealthy and free, others were much more dependent upon local lords. Most lived in regulated villages and had to make decisions together with others and reach a working consensus; others lived on big, isolated farms in the valleys of the Norwegian and Swedish mountains, or on Iceland or some other Atlantic islands. In the medieval understanding of society, however, they were all lumped together in one single category, normally called 'the working people' – *laboratores* – in contrast to those praying and those fighting – *oratores* and *bellatores*. Many preachers described them as a bit naïve and unfit for deep intellectual thought and recommended that sermons not be made too complicated if addressed to ordinary people. They recommended not to present the points of theology that are contradictory or disputed, because that will only make peasants doubt and endanger their souls. This condescending attitude was probably exacerbated by the growth of towns and a more acute sense of difference between urban and rural residents.

On the other hand, intellectuals also had a sharp eye for social injustice and recognised that peasants often lived under very hard conditions. They fought against the 'hard and sharp soil' when breaking new land; they ploughed and spread the seed and saw it grow, only to be destroyed by drought or rain and hail. And if the harvest seemed promising, noblemen began feuding and rode over the fields and tramped everything down, or confiscated it for their horses. There was not much to do about it, except pray.

4 Cultural Tradition and Transition

Romanesque Architecture

People in the Middle Ages looked back to Roman antiquity and constantly tried to imitate the glorious time of the empire in a series of renaissances. The period from early Middle Ages until the mid-12th century is known in the European history of architecture as the Romanesque period, which refers to a style imitating Roman buildings. It was a pan-European style, and Romanesque buildings can be found all around the continent, although sometimes with different designations. In England, the related style is known as Anglo-Saxon and Norman architecture. Romanesque buildings had certain definitive common features: thick walls, small windows, sturdy pillars, round arches, and barrel vaults. The plan of Romanesque buildings was typically symmetrical and regular, with clearly defined forms. The majority of surviving Romanesque buildings are castles, churches, or monasteries but there are also others.

Romanesque features are usually connected to buildings of stone that were constructed all over Europe for centuries not only due to the lack of timber, but also because the Roman buildings of antiquity were built of stone or bricks. Scandinavia, by contrast, had a seemingly unending source of timber in its huge amounts of forest. Thus the great majority of Scandinavian medieval buildings were built of wood. Only the most prestigious buildings such as churches, castles, and palaces were built of stone, and from the 12th century onwards also of brick. Most of the still existing Romanesque-style buildings in Scandinavia are built of stone; wooden buildings have generally disappeared with the exception of Norway's wooden stave churches.

The earliest Scandinavian churches were built in the Romanesque tradition. A good example of a Romanesque church in Scandinavia is the cathedral of Lund. It was finished in the first half of the 12th century, after Lund had been elevated to an archiepiscopal see in 1104. The main altar in the crypt was consecrated in 1123, and in 1145, the chancel's main altar was consecrated. The church itself was finished 100 years later. Other Romanesque cathedrals in Scandinavia were built in Roskilde and Odense in Denmark as well as in Nidaros and Bergen in Norway. The earliest Swedish cathedrals are from the 12th century but they were heavily restructured later, and the Romanesque features have largely disappeared.

Cathedrals, being the central churches of a territory, were usually very complex buildings. All the Romanesque cathedrals in Scandinavia were basilica-type buildings with a higher central nave and lower side aisles and were defined by large, square towers and massive walls, such as the cathedral of Lund. By contrast, the parish churches were much simpler, more modest buildings. A typical Romanesque parish church in

DOI: 10.4324/9781003095514-6

Illustration 4.1 The stave church in Fantoft. Originally built c. 1150 in the parish of Fortun, Norway, and moved to its present location in 1883. It was burned down by an arsonist in 1992. Fantoft church was completely rebuilt and gives a fine impression of how the 12th-century wooden churches in Norway would have looked when they were new.

Photo © Kirsi Salonen 2021.

Scandinavia consisted of three parts: a simple single-aisle nave, a chancel, and an apse. The chancel was typically lower and narrower than the nave and ended in an even smaller round apse. The Romanesque parish churches were usually relatively small: c. 15–20 m long, less than 10 m broad, and c. 5 m high. Nowadays many of them look bigger because a tower was added to the churches later in the Middle Ages.

In Denmark, most Romanesque churches were built of stone, very rarely of brick, and they often replaced earlier wooden churches. There are still around 1,650 Romanesque stone churches left in Denmark, most of them small parish churches in the countryside, such as Høm church south of Ringsted. They were all built in less than a hundred years, an amazing effort and a huge investment in religion. In Sweden and especially in Norway, the majority of churches built in the Romanesque period were made of wood and have not survived to our days, although some examples are still left after almost a thousand years, such as the Norwegian churches of Haltdalen from the 1170s or of Torpo from the 1190s. In Norway, the wooden Romanesque parish churches were built with the so-called stave technique meaning that the building was constructed with standing timber placed on a wooden load-bearing structure, laid on a stone foundation. The idea of using vertical timber originates from the Viking Age palisade constructions that consisted of densely placed planks or earthen pillars, enclosing a square room and carrying the roof of the building. The stave churches are a Norwegian speciality, and more than 1,000 such buildings were built in the country, while the number of Romanesque stone churches from the same period amounts to less than 300.

Good examples of the first Romanesque Benedictine abbeys in Scandinavia are the Selje abbey in Western Norway, which dates to c. 1100, and the Vreta abbey, the first Swedish nunnery, also built around 1100. They are both made of stone, but there are rarer examples of Romanesque brick building such as the church of Saint Bendt in Ringsted, Denmark, which was built as the church of the Benedictine abbey around 1170. Brick was a new building material in Scandinavia. It arrived in Denmark in the 1160s, a little later in Sweden, and in Norway around the 1250s. The earliest brick constructions in Finland date to the 13th century.

The round churches, constructed to a completely circular plan, form a special building type in Scandinavian church architecture of the 12th and early 13th centuries. These two-storied churches with thick walls were sometimes designed so that

Illustration 4.2 Høm church is a typical example of the small Romanesque churches that were built on the Scandinavian countryside during the 12th century. The apse has the original small window that let the sun shine directly on the crucifix on the alter. The tower was added during the later Middle Ages.

Photo © Kirsi Salonen 2022.

they could serve as defence. Round churches architecturally follow the model of the Church of the Holy Sepulchre in Jerusalem, with its round structure over the empty grave of Jesus. Round churches were known before, but this building tradition became much more popular with crusaders returning from the Holy Land to Europe and Scandinavia. In Scandinavia, round churches were built especially in Sweden and Denmark. Good examples of these special constructions are Bromma church close to Stockholm and Bjernede on Zealand, but the island of Bornholm is particularly known for its four round churches, like that in Østerlars, dating probably to the 1160s and dedicated to Saint Lawrence. In Norway, only one round church is known, the Premonstratensian church of Saint Olaf in Tønsberg from the late 12th century. The patron saint himself is buried in the cathedral in Nidaros in a round chapel with measurements exactly the same as the round structure in the Holy Sepulchre church in Jerusalem.

The Romanesque churches of the 12th century in Scandinavia are often compact and solid to look at from outside, a little sinister, and with small windows. This is especially the case in southern Scandinavia with its churches built of grey stone. But they were very carefully constructed so that light entered and illuminated crucifixes and altars, and the church interior shone and glittered. The play of light was enhanced in the Middle Ages by frescos, precious stones that glowed in different colours, or with altarpieces inlaid with mountain crystal. Holes were drilled behind the crystal pieces to allow the rays of the sun through and make them shine brightly.

Viking Age fortifications were dominated by the Trelleborg type from the late 10th century: large, perfectly circular, and geometrically built after the same model and unit of measurement. There were probably seven in Denmark and southern Norway, measuring 120–240 m in diameter. They consisted of huge earthen ramparts with palisades on the top and were in use for only a very short period, of around 20 years. They probably functioned as Harald Bluetooth's military means of conquering all Denmark and forcefully converting the population to Christianity.

Other early fortifications from Scandinavia are poorly understood, but seem to have consisted in ramparts built of earth and with palisades. They were often of the *motte* type, meaning a fortification with a wooden keep situated on a small natural or artificial mound or raised area known as a motte. The keep on top of the hill had a walled courtyard called a bailey that was surrounded by a palisade and sometimes a ditch protecting the area. These constructions were common in England, such as the one in York, but similar fortifications also existed in Scandinavia. Remnants of the mound can be seen for example at the Vosborg castle on the west coast of Denmark. The castle was moved after the low mound and buildings were devastated by a tsunami.

Because of crusades to the Near East and the rapid development of heavier weapons from the 12th century onwards, new ways of building stronger stone castles spread to Europe, and this evolution of military architecture also arrived in Scandinavia. In Denmark, the first known fortifications made of stone date from the 12th century. They were freestanding, tower-like, circular buildings usually surrounded by wooden palisades, rarely by stone walls. Good examples are the early phases of Søborg and Bastrup at Zealand, the latter originally 30 m or perhaps even 50 m high. The earliest Swedish fortifications were a similar kind of round towers. In the following century, these castles were enlarged. Besides the tower castles that were built in easily defensible places without the need for huge wall construction, the Scandinavians also began to build so-called curtain-wall castles from the 12th century onward. The curtain-wall castles were fortifications whereby the castle was surrounded by a wall built between a chain of defensive towers. The earliest Danish curtain-wall castles had a circular shape, like the castle of Bishop Absalon in Copenhagen which dates to the 1160s. In Norway, by contrast, late 12th-century fortifications such as those in Bergen or Nidaros had a more irregular curtain wall around the castle.

There were also a few churches that could be used for defensive purposes. These were two-storied churches or ones with a tower, the upper parts of which were designed for maximum defence, making them difficult to conquer. They could also be used as chapels, perhaps for wealthy families, but the main ecclesiastical venue for the congregation was downstairs. Such buildings were constructed in the 12th century, and they were more common in the islands of Bornholm and Öland as well as in territories around the town of Kalmar. Some Icelandic churches and adjacent farms could also be used for defensive purposes, but only in small-scale local conflicts.

Domestic and functional buildings in Scandinavia were built of timber using one of the four commonly used building techniques: (1) corner timbering, namely using walls of horizontal logs notched together in the corners, (2) stave building, or planking vertically around a frame, (3) planking horizontally around a frame, or (4) the half-timber technique, which used other materials such as brick or plaster inside a timber frame. Corner timbering was particularly well suited to pine buildings and thus common in pine-forest areas such as Sweden. Frame-building and half-timbering were instead common in territories where oak was more plentiful, such as Denmark and some parts of southern Sweden. In Norway, the stave-building technique was particularly prevalent.

The most common Scandinavian farm-house type in Denmark and in some places in Norway was the longhouse, which was built around a frame so that a series of internal posts supported the roof. Longhouses had already been in use for centuries before the Middle Ages and were normally divided internally into different sections for humans and animals. In pine-forest areas like Sweden, Finland, and some parts of Norway, the typical domestic buildings in a farm were different; a farm consisted of a number of independently constructed small timber buildings each of which had a special purpose, such as being a sauna or storehouse. In the countryside, these buildings had only one store and were relatively small in size, but in towns, they could be higher and larger. In Iceland and Greenland, the buildings typically had the form of a longhouse but were partly sunk into the ground and insulated with turf roofs. There are no such houses left intact anymore from the early medieval centuries, but their remnants have frequently been found in archaeological excavations, and the same building tradition continued throughout the Middle Ages.

Romanesque Arts

Art in Scandinavia was multifaceted and inspired by many different cultures. In the Romanesque period between c. 1000 and c. 1200, traditional Viking Age style with its complex geometrical patterns and highly stylised plant and animal figures was still used together with pictures and statues strongly influenced by Byzantine art, by Germanic art from England and Germany, and by the first contacts with France which became much stronger in the following centuries. There were even some imitations of Islamic art in Scandinavia.

The Vikings used elaborate ornamentations on wood, metal work, and runestones, and their artistic carving style, for example on the doors and pillars of wooden churches, continued into the Middle Ages – probably in all Scandinavia, although these have only survived in large numbers in Norway. Today, it is often difficult to discern the different figures writhing and twisting together because they all have the same grey or brown colour. It was easier a thousand years ago when they were painted in various bright colours. Traditional art forms continued to be popular for a longer time outside the churches, especially in secular art and craftsmanship.

The early Romanesque art with its Byzantine and English inspirations is often quite stiff and formal to a modern eye, displaying bright blue backgrounds, with red and golden garments, but being stylised and frozen, depicting unmoving processions towards God. What has survived of these paintings is to be found on the walls of churches.

Some crucifixes from this early period show Christ as the mighty conqueror of death, staring directly outwards at the believer, far from depictions of the suffering Christ in later periods. This is a Christ of the conversion period, fit to convince warrior Vikings, inspired by English art. In the 12th century, however, there emerged a strong influence from France depicting a much more human and suffering Jesus.

Scandinavia's strong connections to the Iberian Peninsula provided other inspirations, some of them Islamic, for its church art. Rygge church in southern Norway is built of square granite stones, red and grey, in a pattern resembling Islamic buildings from Al-Andalus. The inspiration may perhaps have been indirect, with Scandinavians imitating the Christian Mozarabs in Spain who had in turn imitated the Muslims.

The surviving Romanesque wall-paintings in Scandinavia are all preserved in churches, but similar decorations must also have been used in vernacular buildings. The art of wall-painting arrived from abroad and the Scandinavians adopted the system whereby colour was spread onto dry lime plaster, not onto wet as in the Italian fresco style. Romanesque wall-paintings can mainly be found in Denmark, southern Sweden, and Gotland, where the majority of Scandinavian Romanesque stone churches were built. In many places, though, the original wall-paintings are no longer visible but were replaced in the course of the Middle Ages. It is a common misunderstanding that medieval wall-paintings were all whitewashed during the Lutheran Reformation of the early 16th century. Often they were left unharmed until the strong pietistic and rationalistic movements of the 18th century deemed such pictures theologically suspect, irrational, and superstitious with the result that the pictures were covered under white chalk.

Scandinavian Romanesque wall-paintings gained inspiration from Byzantine artistic style. They were usually placed in the apse of the church and depicted Christ seated on a throne as ruler of the world, surrounded by other sacred figures such as the four Evangelists. These settings are known in art history as 'Christ in Majesty', and can be found in many Scandinavian churches, among the most outstanding and oldest examples of which is in the parish church of Vä in Scania, dated to the 1120s. Other common figures were Saint Mary and the Last Judgement.

There are no Romanesque paintings in Norway, Iceland, or Finland. In Sweden, most Romanesque wall-paintings are located on the island of Gotland where they also have a distinct eastern influence, possibly due to artists from Novgorod. The Danish and southern Swedish paintings in their turn have more western characteristics. The earliest surviving Romanesque wall-paintings date to the early 12th century, and the style was in use until the late 13th when it began to mix with Gothic influence.

Illustration 4.3 Christ in majesty, surrounded by the four Evangelist symbols, sitting on the globe and ready to judge the whole world. Vä church in Scania, 1120s.
Photo Yakikaki 2020. This file is licensed under the Creative Commons Attribution-Share Alike 4.0 International license.

The surviving large stone carvings in the Romanesque style are mainly to be found in Scandinavian cathedral churches and towns. Like all over the Latin West, the Scandinavian Romanesque stone carvings are also mainly reliefs and portals, rarely sculptures. Lund was an important centre for stone carving, while Gotland was specialised in the production of baptismal fonts that were exported throughout Scandinavia and even beyond.

The stone portals in Scandinavian Romanesque churches are not as pictorially rich as their equivalents elsewhere in Europe, but there are some very fine examples such as the portal of Ribe cathedral from the late 12th century, known as the Cat's Head portal. Sculptures, like the portals, were also often an integral part of architecture.

The small parish churches were also often decorated with stone carvings, but in a much simpler and small-scale manner. Many had a tympanum over the entrance to the church in granite showing a cross, Christ, or perhaps some saints, and a remarkable number in Western Denmark have a stone somewhere in the outer wall showing a lion. How that should be interpreted is not clear.

The earliest Scandinavian grave monuments in monasteries and cathedrals date to the Romanesque period, and the stone carvings in the tombstones conform to the Romanesque style: the figures are presented from the front and are relatively rigid without individualised features, and rarely with texts. Those that had inscriptions were in Latin, but some were written with Latin letters, some with runes. The earliest preserved tombs with carved tomb stones usually belonged to bishops, abbots, or other high-ranking ecclesiastics, like the tomb of canon Hermann of Schleswig (†1151) in Lund cathedral, from the mid-12th century.

Most Romanesque-style wooden sculptures have disappeared from Scandinavia, but some have survived. All those extant are religious, and most of them are triumph crucifixes or depictions of the Madonna. Large wooden crucifixes were a German invention of the Romanesque period, and the surviving Scandinavian examples iconographically follow the continental style depicting *Christ Triumphant*, that is, a crucified Jesus who is not showing any pain or misery. A fine example of early crucifixes in Scandinavia is one from Åby church in Jutland, created in the second half of the 11th century out of wood and decorated with gold-plated copper plates depicting a Byzantine-style Christ Triumphant.

The sculptures depicting Virgin Mary were also very common and follow the European style. The earliest representations of the Madonna follow the *Sedes Sapientiae* style, in which the Virgin is presented, seated on a throne with the child Jesus on her lap, which is based on a Byzantine prototype. Such sculptures were typical of the 12th and early 13th centuries, while sculptures of the sitting Virgin with a child seated sideways on her lap is a slightly later version of the same motif, representing a more western style. In the late 12th century, other seated saints also began to appear in sculptures.

Norway has proven the most important Scandinavian country when it comes to the quantity and quality of extant wood-carvings, but archaeological evidence shows that this kind of art also existed in the other Nordic countries. Although mainly religious, the wood-carving motifs and techniques in the Middle Ages closely followed the tradition of the Viking Age. Secular objects especially continue the Viking tradition with animal and geometrical decorations, while plant motifs also begin to appear. The most important example of Norwegian wood-carving art is the stave church of Urnes from the second half of the 11th century.

The Church was an important employer of wood carvers and most of the surviving carved wooden objects are from churches, although there are also other more secular items. In Norway, the decades between 1150 and 1200 were an intensive period of church building, with up to 1,000 mainly wooden churches erected. Since these were decorated inside and out with carvings, the latter were in huge demand. Especially important were those around the main doorway, usually situated in the westernmost part of the nave.

Other types of Romanesque items in Scandinavia have also survived because of their strong religious connections. From the Romanesque period, there are a few especially exquisite metal altar fronts from Sweden and Denmark. From Denmark, there survive several so-called golden altars, all dating from the 12th century. Like the Åby cross, the altars also have a wooden frame onto which gold-surfaced carved plates have been fixed. These plates were illuminated in a complicated, extremely poisonous process whereby the gold was fixed to the plate by mixing it with mercury and warming it until the mercury evaporated. Some of the golden altars are still in their original location in the church but some, like those of Lisbjerg and Ølst, are in the collections of the Danish National Museum.

There are yet more objects, such as jewellery, dated to the Romanesque period. Most of them are rings, difficult to date from the style, but some pectoral crosses from episcopal tombs as well as the oldest Scandinavian signet ring, belonging to the Swedish King Canute Ericsson (1167–1196), have been dated with certainty. Another

104   900–1200: Formation

well-known Romanesque piece of jewellery is the Dagmar cross. It is a 4.3 cm high and 2.9 cm broad relic cross made of gold and enamel. It is of Byzantine style, probably dating from the 11th or 12th century and made in the Byzantine Empire. It got its name from the Danish Queen Dagmar in whose tomb it was apparently found, in the church of Ringsted, in the late 17th century.

The Coming of Writing

The Scandinavian secular literature of the first Christian centuries originated from two different traditions. On the one hand, it was closely connected to the Viking Age tradition and the old orally transmitted stories and poems that in the Middle Ages were gradually written down, forming the local literary tradition that went on to outlive the Middle Ages itself. On the other hand, the conversion to Christianity meant the arrival in Scandinavia of the Latin tradition with its religious literature.

In the Viking Age and early Middle Ages, the Scandinavians – apart from the Finns and the Sámi – had a common language, Old Norse, and used runes as their alphabet. Thus the oldest remnants of a written Scandinavian language are runic inscriptions. With the arrival of the Christian faith and the establishment of the Catholic Church, the Scandinavians adopted Latin characters and began to use Latin as an ecclesiastical language side by side with the local languages which eventually developed into the distinct Norwegian, Danish, Swedish, and Icelandic. In addition, the lingua franca of the Hanseatic League, Middle Low German, was used in towns and commercial hubs as the language of commerce. Finnish and Sámi were also used but only as spoken languages.

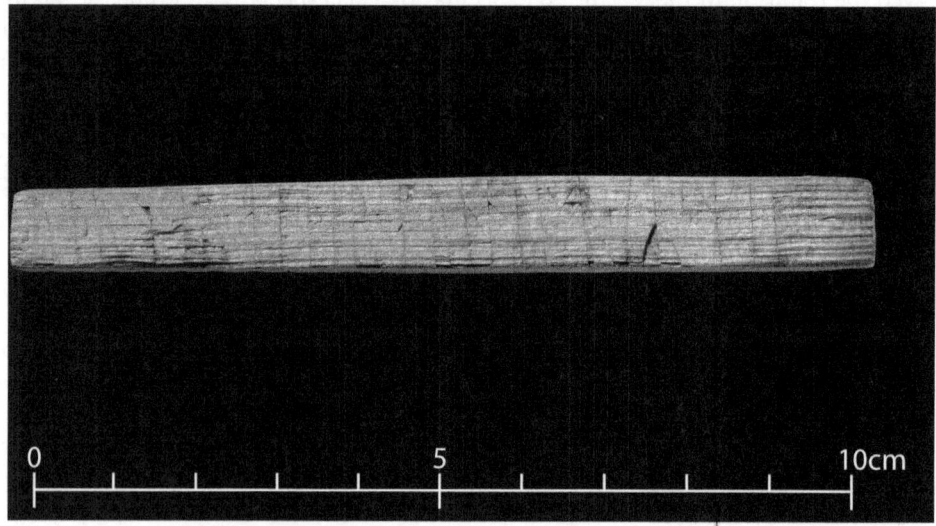

Illustration 4.4   The Runic alphabet was still known and continued to be used for some hundred years in short messages or prayers and amulets and can also sometimes be found on liturgical items. Runes could be used for writing in Latin, but were also common in daily life messages in the local languages, a kind of medieval SMS. Hundreds of small wooden sticks with short messages have been found, as this one from Bergen. It reads *unthu mær ankthær gunnildr kys mik:* 'Love me, Gunhild, I love you. Kiss me'.

Photo Adnan Icagic © Universitetsmuseet i Bergen.

Oral Tradition – Scaldic and Eddic Poetry and Sagas

The early Middle Ages, just like the Viking Period, predominantly relied on oral tradition. The earliest written records preserved in Scandinavia are almost exclusively memorial texts carved on stones in runic letters. These usually commemorate a dead person or an event such as building a bridge or a road. They are short and formulaic. There are, however, other kinds of texts, like the one carved on the so-called Rök runestone from the first half of the 9th century. The Rök stone is the longest known pre-Christian runic text, composed in skilful verse and containing a story of Norse mythology as well as historical references. It is linguistically very complex and difficult to read, and earlier researchers considered that it was all about the Ostrogothic King Theodoric († 526) and the great Scandinavian migrations of late antiquity. In 2020, four Swedish scholars suggested that the inscription recounted the great ecological catastrophe and multi-year winter resulting from enormous volcanic eruptions in 536. No matter how the content should actually be interpreted, this stone's existence testifies to a Scandinavian tradition of storytelling which until the 9th century had been passed on orally. It was only in the later medieval centuries, from the 13th century onwards, that the older oral tradition was collected and written down.

The Viking and early medieval literary tradition consist of the so-called Eddic and Scaldic poems that were written down several centuries after their composition. Most of these poems were preserved in Iceland – thanks to the active tradition of codification on the island in the 12th and 13th centuries – but the same kinds of poems were also to be found in other Scandinavian countries. It is unknown when they were composed.

Eddic poems were composed in Old Norse, in freeform or varying metres, by unknown authors. The poems told of old heroes, mythological issues, and the pagan gods. Two of them are particularly important: *Völuspá* (Sibyl's Prophesy) describes the history of the world from its creation to its end (*Ragnarök*), while *Hávamál* (Words of the High One) didactically recounts the Scandinavian god Odin's teaching of how everyone should behave and how men and women should interact, as well as telling its listeners about runes and magic. Scaldic poetry was much stricter regarding poetic technique and was composed by people specialised in that type of literary genre. Unlike Eddic poetry, most of the Scaldic poems can be attributed to specific authors and thus also dated. The most talented Scaldic poet was Egil Skallagrímsson († c. 990). We know a fair amount about the poet thanks to a saga written about his life (*Egil's Saga*, c. 1230), but it is difficult to gauge the reliability of the stories about him since they were written down more than two centuries after his death.

The sagas form another kind of literary tradition in Scandinavia. They are prose stories about the history of Scandinavia in pre-Christian times. Like the poems, the sagas were originally transmitted orally from one generation to another and later on written down. Most known sagas originate in Iceland and describe the period when the island was colonised, such as the *Íslendingasögur* (sagas about Icelanders). There are also other sagas, like the *Heimskringla* (Orb of the World) which tells the history of the kings of Norway up to 1184. The *Heimskringla* was composed by Snorri Sturluson (1179–1241), who is the best known Icelandic writer. In addition to many other creations, he also composed the *Prose Edda*, which includes numerous heroic tales about Germanic pagan gods and other personages of Norse mythology. Most saga stories take place in the period between 930 and 1030 but were only written down from the end of the 12th century, and sometimes as late as the early 14th. The saga tradition continued in Iceland until the 13th or 14th century, when sagas about the local saints or other heroes were composed.

Scholars have contended for over a century as to how far Edda, Scaldic verses, and sagas actually transmit any knowledge and beliefs about the Norse pagan gods, and how far they are simply products of the 13th century's nostalgic interest in a distant past. Whether to trust or distrust detailed descriptions of individuals living hundreds of years before the saga author is an equally difficult question. One argument for reliable transmission has often been that Scaldic poetry is formulated in such complicated metres that it could not have been changed or invented in the 12th and 13th centuries. That is patently wrong – oral societies have a sensitivity towards language that can often astonish a modern society reliant on writing for communication. Another argument has been that the Edda and sagas contain non-Christian elements and must therefore belong to a period before the Christian conversion. Most of the examples produced to support this argument are actually based on an insufficient knowledge of 11th- to 13th-century Christianity, which was often broader and more inclusive than in later periods. The problem is insoluble; without other and earlier sources, we cannot know anything for certain about Old Norse religion.

The tradition of storytelling and the oral transmission of old stories continued in Scandinavia throughout the Middle Ages and far beyond. In Finland, Sápmi, and Greenland there was an equally strong, living oral tradition, but we do not have any written witnesses from the Middle Ages to its content. Especially with the nationalistic awakening in the 19th century, historians and folklore scholars collected tales and poems from all of Scandinavia and debated their actual age. The creation of the Finnish *Kalevala* belongs to this tradition. Again, they may well contain beliefs and tales from the Middle Ages and even from the pre-Christian period, but it is impossible to date their elements more precisely.

The arrival by the 12th century of the Christian Church and its ecclesiastical administration changed the literary tradition. Ever more stories – old and new – were written down, and new literary genres common in other parts of Europe were introduced to Scandinavia.

Liturgical Literature

The arrival of the Christian faith in Scandinavia also marked the arrival of Latin literacy and literature. The first Latin books were all imported, reaching the Nordic countries together with the missionaries. Local production of liturgical books began only much later. The earliest books or codex-type manuscripts known in Scandinavia are liturgical. In order to carry out his religious functions, a priest needed a number of different liturgical books, and it can be assumed that each parish must have possessed a copy of such works. These indispensable early works include the Missal, the Rituale, the Psalter, and the Breviary as well as certain chant books like the Antiphonale and Graduale.

The Missals were manuscripts that contained the necessary texts for each day of the ecclesiastical year so that the priest could celebrate Mass and carry out other liturgical functions. The Missals also included prayers, scriptural readings, and basic chants. Since they were indispensable to daily activities they became worn out, and most of the early medieval copies have not survived to our day. In the late Middle

Ages, following the development of book printing after c. 1450, the Missals were among the first liturgical books to be mass produced for the use of the Church. The Missal of Schleswig was printed in 1486, and the first printed book for Norway was the Missal for Nidaros, produced in 1519. Alongside the Missal each parish needed a Gradual, a musical manuscript containing the notes and texts of the chants sung in the church during the celebration.

Other common books for use by priests were the Rituale, a collection of texts not included in the Missal that were needed for the celebration of various religious rites. In the 12th century, such texts were for the first time collected in separate volumes called the Rituale, the Sacerdotale, the Manuale, or the Agenda. These collections contained texts and instructions for performing such rites as baptism, marriage, funerals, or anointing of the sick as well as various blessings of persons or religious objects such as candles or palm leaves imported from south. Most of the Rituale was composed for parish priests, but there were also separate collections for monastic use including slightly different texts and rites.

Carrying out the ecclesiastical rituals also necessitated some other books, such as the Psalter that not only contained the texts of the 150 Psalms of David from the Old Testament but also often a calendar, a litany of saints, different devotional texts, and canticles from the Old and New Testaments. Another essential book was the Antiphonary, a musical manuscript containing the chants for the psalms sung during the Divine Office. A Breviary for its part was a liturgical book used every day for praying the canonical hours: Matins, Lauds, Prime, Terce, Sext, Nones, Vespers, and Compline. It thus has more or less the same content as those works known as books of hours, although the latter were usually meant for a broader and not necessarily priestly audience. The name, Breviary, derives from the Latin word *brevis* (short) because it contained an abbreviated or condensed version of the Office. Since all dioceses had their own specific saints, the contents of Psalters, Antiphonaries, and Breviaries from different dioceses varied somewhat.

Contrary to what many imagine, the Bible was not a book owned by each priest and parish in the Middle Ages. In fact, it was extremely rare to have a copy of the entire Holy Bible. Medieval Bibles were in Latin and meant only for the use of priests who could read Latin. Since the priest had to use biblical texts in Mass, however, it was necessary to have certain central texts translated into vernacular languages, including the Scandinavian. Since the Latin rite used for consistency's sake only a limited selection of central texts from Scripture, it was not necessary for parish priests to possess a manuscript of the whole Bible, but it was possible for them to get by with a smaller amount of key texts collected in manuscripts called lectionaries. From Scandinavia, there still remain some early copies of lectionaries or manuscripts containing the text of the Gospels.

Mortality, Illnesses, and Life Expectance

Life expectancy in medieval Scandinavia was between 20 and 25 years. Infant and child mortality rate was relatively high. According to the results of archaeological excavations in various cemeteries, around half of the population died before reaching the age of seven years. After childhood, mortality fell so that a little more than 5 % died after having turned seven but before reaching puberty, less than 5 % in their teens, c. 20 % between the ages of 20 and 40, and c. 20 % between 40 and 60. Only a very small proportion (c. 1 %) of the population lived beyond 60. On average, men had longer life expectancy than women, mostly because giving birth was dangerous not only to the child but also to the mother, and many women died on their childbed. Females were also more vulnerable to infectious diseases since it was usually the task of women to take care of the sick. Males in their turn were typically involved in hunting, wars, and fighting that caused premature death or severe injuries.

The high level of infant mortality resulted from poor hygienic standards causing frequent acute gastroenteritis and epidemics of dangerous intestinal diarrheal diseases like dysentery or typhoid fever. In addition, other childhood epidemic diseases, such as measles, diphtheria, whooping cough, or scarlet fever, occurred at frequent intervals. It is impossible to generate more detailed statistics, but in this respect, there does not seem to have been a great social difference. Children both high and low on the social scale risked an early death. The high infant mortality rate was compensated for by the high reproductive rate. It has been estimated that on average a woman with two adult children might have given birth to six infants.

In the mid-14th century, the Black Death also hit Scandinavia hard, especially Norway, but generally the sparseness of the population and small town sizes helped to prevent the spread of epidemics. At the same time, isolated populations did not develop immunity to many diseases, and an outburst might have severe consequences for them. Generally, many Scandinavian local societies lived at a minimal level of subsistence which made them vulnerable to infections and other ailments, especially in years when the harvest was poor. Our knowledge of medieval disease outbreaks is not terribly good, but the few reliable sources indicate that diseases of deficiency, for example scurvy, were common particularly during winter.

Although European universities had medical faculties, university-trained medical doctors were extremely rare in Scandinavia, even after the founding of Scandinavia's two medieval universities, Uppsala in 1477 and Copenhagen in 1479. However, there were skilled medical practitioners in Scandinavia that were able to cure even more complicated cases. One of them was Icelandic Hrafn Sveinbjarnarson († 1213), a well-known surgeon in command of the principles of medicine as taught at the famous medical school in Salerno. The written sources also mention that many kings or rulers had their own medical doctors to take care of them, like Henrik Harpestreng (c. 1244) who wrote books on herbs and stones in medicine. Some of them had medical training, some were self-taught experts. Most medical experts in Scandinavia, among whom also some women, were skilled in surgery. Archaeological findings can confirm the Scandinavian knowledge of this field. Excavated skeletons from many different cemeteries show signs of healed wounds or broken bones that have been set. Archaeological excavations have also unearthed numerous surgical instruments used by medical experts: knives, blood-letting equipment, needles, forceps, and catheters.

Only a very few people had access to trained doctors or apothecaries who could prepare medicine according to contemporary medical knowledge. Others had to rely on themselves, their family members, or local healers. The latter were normally experts on different herbs or drugs which they prepared from plants and vegetables according to ancient traditions. In Christian times, local healers were sometimes suspicious in the eyes of the Church because of their use of spells or incantations. Medical knowledge was spread in the Middle Ages also through the ecclesiastical institution of monasteries. Each convent usually had someone who was skilled in medicine, and this person not only cured the monks or nuns but also helped others. Monasteries were

Cultural Tradition and Transition 109

Illustration 4.5 Surgery was a well-developed and sophisticated art in the Middle Ages. Hard manual labour with few worker protections or regulations resulted in a high risk for injuries with broken bones, and warfare with its ensuing physical traumas was relatively common, so practical surgery was in high demand. This skull has been trepanned, which is opened to remove from the brain a tumour, coagulated blood, or pieces of bones after a heavy blow to the skull. The patient survived and lived for years after the operation, because the circular hole made by the drill had begun to close. The skull, from around 1500, was found near Pälkäne church, Finland. Now in the National Museum of Finland, Helsinki.

Photo © Kurt Villads Jensen, 2022.

often the only hospitals available and allowed for the care of the sick and the weak. Some monastic institutions were specialised in the care of people afflicted by leprosy, which was also relatively common in Scandinavia.

Medieval medicine did not know of the existence of bacteria or viruses, nor did it include antibiotics or other nowadays very commonly used medicines. However, doctors were aware of infections and that diseases could spread through the air. Therefore they tried, for example, to isolate sick individuals or to cleanse the air with incense. Surgeons were able to treat broken bones and wounds but could do little against diseases like cancer. The most common solution was to amputate a cancerous body member, if possible. In many cases, the best cures offered by the monasteries and similar kinds of hospitals, often in towns and called houses of the Holy Spirit, were based on nourishing food and herbal medication. The monasteries or houses of the Holy Spirit did not only cure severely ill persons but could also function as old people's homes or take care of orphans, the crippled, or the handicapped unable to live in normal society. Sometimes diseases spread within monasteries and caused a significant loss among the monks or nuns, a good example of this happening at Naantali abbey in 1509, when according to the diary of Vadstena abbey, 35 sisters and brothers died in an epidemic of pestilence.

Pestilence, especially the Black Death in the 1350s, was the most feared kind of illness in Europe in the Middle Ages, and in Scandinavia too, new waves of pestilence kept circulating at relatively frequent intervals. Since we have very little written evidence such as the above notice from the Vadstena Diary, it is impossible to know how many waves there were in Scandinavia. However, there were other illnesses, such as tuberculosis, sweating sickness, smallpox, dysentery, typhoid, influenza, and mumps, as well as various gastrointestinal infections, that were much more frequent and thus also in the long run more lethal for the population. Medieval doctors could recognise a variety of diseases – and in many cases even alleviate or cure them – but sometimes could not understand the underlying mechanism. One such disease was scurvy, caused by a lack of vitamin C. Scurvy was relatively common among armies or sailors travelling for long times with poor nutrition. Although the connection between scurvy and lack of vitamin C was not understood, it was known by the end of the 15th century that citrus fruit could cure the illness.

At the end of the 15th century, a new disease was introduced to Europe, and by the end of the Middle Ages had also spread to Scandinavia. This was syphilis, a sexually transmitted infection. It is not known for certain how syphilis arrived in Europe. The traditional explanation is that it was brought from the Americas by the crewmen of Christopher Columbus. In any case, there was an outbreak of the syphilis epidemic in southern Italy in 1494 or 1495. From there the disease spread north via soldiers in the French army, for which reason the illness was also called the French disease. It did not take many years before syphilis had spread to northern Germany and onwards to Scandinavia. There is no information about serious outbreaks of syphilis in Scandinavia before the end of the Middle Ages, but archaeologists have found traces of syphilis in late 15th-century Danish skeletons. The first written sources mentioning syphilis – or *pokker*, as it was called in Scandinavia – are from Denmark and connected to the army of King John in the 1490s. Another source from 1505 mentions that even the King himself had caught it. It is known that the disease spread through close contact in bathing houses and saunas, and therefore some of these establishments were closed later in the 16th century. Many diseases were such that it was possible to cure them with existing medical knowledge or that those affected could recover, with immunity to any new waves. But there were also diseases like syphilis that were incurable until antibiotics were invented in the 20th century.

Special medical knowledge was also needed at the childbed if there were labour complications. In the Middle Ages, there were no professional midwives like nowadays, but experienced women could be called to help when the time of birth approached. Medieval babies were born at home, where the women of the household usually took care of the birth as well as of the newborn baby and mother. As mentioned, most midwives were not professional although medical schools in Europe, especially in Salerno in southern Italy, had a chapter on childbirth in their teaching textbooks. Some women also studied in Salerno.

Many sick people put their faith in the Church and especially certain saints whose help was known to be useful in cases of severe illness. For example, Saint Birgitta of Sweden, herself mother to several children, was particularly keen to help women in labour, and Saint Thomas Aquinas was known to help with stomach and liver problems. In many cases, the saints could not help with advanced illnesses but sometimes they miraculously did and the person was cured.

Some looked for alternative cures not recognised by established authorities. Scandinavian priests warned in sermons against superstitions of all kind, from gathering the ingredients for love potions in the forests at full moon to the idea that girding a man's belt around a pregnant woman could ease childbirth. The borders between the healing power of Christian saints, prayers, and doctors on one hand and superstition on the other were sometimes difficult to draw neatly. The explosion in metal detector investigation from around the year 2000 has led to the finding of very small, thin pieces of lead with inscriptions in runes or Latin letters, beseeching the aid of saints and of elves known from Germanic mythology half a millennium earlier. Such amulets seem to have been much more common than anyone until recently realised.

Food and Drink

What the medieval Scandinavians ate and drank is a very difficult question to answer because of the lack of direct sources. We know what they cultivated, collected, hunted, and fished but what was on their tables every day is still somewhat unknown, as is how often they consumed certain rarer foodstuffs. Apart from scarce written evidence about dishes occasionally served at the tables of the nobility or high-ranking priests, and commercial correspondence mentioning precious wines or spices, the evidence we have of most people's diet and nutrition derives from archaeological excavations that have unearthed animal bones, fish bones, plant remains, and pollen. Such excavations have mainly been made in urban settlements, meaning that the result might not hold good for people living in countryside.

Excavations have revealed what one would expect that the diet consisted primarily of agricultural products. The Scandinavians consumed meat (mainly from oxen, pigs, sheep, and poultry), cereals, eggs, and dairy produce, as well as various vegetables, nuts, fruits, and berries. People living along coastlines or close to lakes and rivers also obviously consumed fish (cod, herring, flatfish). According to the archaeological finds, game was relatively rarely part of the urban diet. Typical medieval beverages were fermented, such as ale, beer, and mead, but water was also a very common drink, and milk was also sometimes drunk. Wine was also known and imported to Scandinavia, but only among wealthier people and typically in towns.

Dishes were spiced with various products of which salt, honey, and herbs of different kinds were the most common. The most used means of preparing meat for longer conservation were drying or smoking, but it could also be pickled in brine or whey. Salt was sometimes used in meat conservation although salting was a much more common treatment for fish, especially herring. Herbs were frequently used and generally available. We know about the use of lovage, dill, parsley, cress, horseradish, mint, marjoram, garlic, and thyme. Mustard and vinegar were also available, as well as hops and bog myrtle which were typically used for flavouring everyday ale. For seasoning food, Scandinavians used also foreign spices, although these were relatively expensive and not always available. Written sources demonstrate that merchants imported cumin, pepper, saffron, ginger, cardamom, grain of paradise, cloves, nutmeg, mace cinnamon, and anise seed. Sugar from sugarcane was a product that arrived in Europe during the crusading period and became more common in Scandinavia only from the 14th century onwards. The traditional sweetener in the Middle Ages was locally made honey.

Barley was the most commonly cultivated cereal, used for brewing ale which even after the Middle Ages remained a very important source of energy. It is a modern myth that all drank beer in the Middle Ages because the water in the towns was polluted and had to be boiled and brewed before drunk. Rye was the second most common cereal in medieval Scandinavia and was typically baked into bread. Oats were normally used for feeding animals, but were additionally cooked as porridge, as were barley and rye. We know less about the daily use of vegetables, which have not left many archaeological remains. But it can be assumed that people grew many different kinds of vegetables at home that were used daily in the seasons when they were available. Different kinds of beet and onion were often used, as was cabbage which could survive in gardens during winters and frost, providing vitamin C when it was most needed. Peas and beans formed a considerable part of the diet across the year because they could be easily dried and conserved. Fruits and berries were also an important part of the diet at the times they were available. In Scandinavia, apples, pears, sour cherries, bullaces, cloudberries, blueberries, sloes, raspberries, blackberries, and strawberries could be found in many places. Fruits like figs, grapes, or oranges were also imported occasionally. They were too expensive for common people but archaeological excavations in urban areas have often unearthed their seeds, surviving to the present day in the medieval latrines. The excavations have also found traces of walnuts imported from the south, but much more common was the hazelnut which in the Middle Ages grew in Scandinavia.

In the far northern areas where agriculture was not possible, a large proportion of the diet consisted of animal meat or fish, and cereals had to be imported over long distances, for example to Greenland or Sápmi. Medieval nutrition consisted very much of what was available, and people ate everything they could capture, cultivate, or collect. Only the Catholic Church put restrictions on the medieval diet. It required Christians to fast on certain days of week, especially Fridays, as well as to observe stricter dietary regulations during Lent, the 40-day fasting period before Easter. During the fast days, one was supposed to abstain from meat, eggs, and dairy produce. Therefore fish was a typical dish for Fridays, for example. In the north, all animals caught from water, including beavers, were considered fish and eaten with a hearty appetite during Lent.

Medieval dishware consisted of pots and jars made of burnt clay that were used for storage and cooking, as well as wooden bowls for serving the food. Most pots and jars in everyday use were produced locally but finer pieces were already being imported from Germany into Scandinavia before the Middle Ages. Wooden mugs or tankards were also part of everyday dishware. Goblets made of glass or metal were known in Scandinavia in the Middle Ages but these were such expensive imported items that only the wealthy could afford them. A wooden spoon and a small knife for cutting bread were the most common pieces of cutlery, and each family member usually had his or her own. Forks, by contrast, were not commonly in use in Scandinavia in the Middle Ages. Wealthier people used silvery plates at their tables and the middle-class pewter, but for others, it was typical to dine off a wooden plate or bread, which was eventually eaten.

Clothing

What medieval Scandinavians wore is a question we can get answers to on the one hand from archaeological excavations and on the other from medieval pictures of men and women. In addition, some legal texts and other normative sources tell us something of the modes of dress. It is also known that the types of clothes used by medieval Scandinavians were not radically different to those in the preceding Viking Age, or after in the early modern era.

In medieval Scandinavia, clothes were generally prepared at home, fabrics usually homemade, and the work done by women. The most common textile for homemade fabrics was sheep wool but vegetal fibres like flax or hemp were also frequently used and grown. Clothes were often dyed with colours from various plants. Only the wealthiest families could afford to buy expensive foreign fabrics like silk or cotton, or higher quality wool imported from Amsterdam, for example. In the winter, clothes made of animal skins were used, in particular in the northern parts of Scandinavia.

Scandinavian fashion did not change much during the first part of the Middle Ages. Women wore long gowns during the whole medieval period. Men wore usually long trousers and long tunics that reached down to the knee. From the late 12th century onwards, male Scandinavian aristocrats began to follow the fashion of southern Europe and use full-length garments, which protected legs so that they could wear long stockings instead of trousers. The use of long garments made the male dress look much like the female, but women's gowns were usually slightly longer to ensure that nobody could see their ankles. Male garments for their part did not normally touch the floor. Common people by contrast wore a short tunic and trousers for most of the Middle Ages.

With fashion also came a criticism of luxury and attempts to reduce the use of expensive clothing. Such a response was generally common in Europe, although examples from Scandinavia are few. In 1283, the Danish king tried to forbid the use of fashionable gowns in two different colours, without much success. Around 1300, a new kind of female dress became popular, with low-cut sleeves so that it was possible to see part of the breasts – so-called 'hell-windows' that tempted men to look and have sinful thoughts. Women with such dresses were depicted in paintings of dancing ladies and were criticised for introducing indecent fashion from decadent Germany into Scandinavia.

In the later Middle Ages, Scandinavian fashion closely followed that of Europe, and from the mid-14th century onwards, it changed remarkably. Men's garments became much shorter and tighter and were buttoned at the front. Better-off men began to use silver buttons to demonstrate their wealth. Archaeological excavations in Sweden have unearthed a complete early 14th-century male costume which consisted of a mantle, a long-tailed hood, a tunic, a hose, a leather belt, and a pair of shoes made of

Illustration 4.6 Shortly after 1350, this young man was killed with heavy blows to the skull and dumped into a moor with a pole hammered through his heart, either to keep the body down to conceal the crime or to prevent his ghost from coming back and haunting his murderers. He was found in 1936 with his clothes unusually well preserved by the acidic water of the moor. The clothes were locally made but followed the latest European fashion at the time. Pictured here is a modern reconstruction.

Photo Toxophilus 2017. This file is licensed under the Creative Commons Attribution-Share Alike 4.0 International license.

Illustration 4.7 Wealthy people dressed in colours, but excessive luxury could be interpreted as a sign of a sinful personality. The young dandy with the hat and very pale complexion and the fool in gold and red are the evil ones mocking Jesus on His way to being crucified. Detail from altarpiece c. 1470, local work, Törnevalla church Sweden, now in the National Historical Museum, Stockholm. Photo © Kurt Villads Jensen 2017.

leather. The 14th century also brought changes to women's clothing: the gowns began to be tighter at the waists and the skirts became wider. The gowns of wealthy women were beautifully embroidered, sometimes with precious threads, made of silver, for example. The gowns of common women were simpler but could also be skilfully decorated and made with dyed fabrics.

Part II
1200–1400
Consolidation and Restructuring

5 Dominion over the Seas

Military Revolution and Expansion into the Baltic

The decades around 1200 were an epoch of revolution, or at least of unprecedentedly rapid development and expansion, in technology as well as science, theology, and moral psychology. In western Europe, the Holy Roman Empire expanded under Frederick I Barbarossa (r. 1152–1190) and Frederick II (r. 1212–1250), at its greatest extent stretching from the Baltic Sea to Sicily and even for a short time including the Crusader Kingdom of Jerusalem. The papacy began a period of steep increase in its power and administrative expansion, especially under the charismatic Pope Innocent III (r. 1198–1216). Constant warfare, closer contact with advanced Muslim cultures, the growing surplus from increasingly well-organised agriculture, and a mild climate spurred innovations and the dissemination of technical knowledge. More effective extraction of natural resources and their semi-industrial processing, alongside huge investments in new energy sources and transportation, supported and accelerated high medieval expansion everywhere, including Scandinavia.

Scandinavian politics of the high Middle Ages were marked by the development of new institutions and understandings of authority, but also by sheer demonstrations of power and often brutal warfare. The technological development of military equipment and means of communication enabled Scandinavian rulers after 1200 to extend their spheres of interest and permanent military engagement much further than earlier.

The 13th century was the period of military conquest, the result of great developments in weaponry. From the last part of the 12th century, engines of war became much larger and more precise in what could best be labelled 'a military revolution'. This is normally a designation used for the transition from the Middle Ages to the Early Modern period in the 16th century, when warfare changed fundamentally because of new weapons – guns and canons – and because of new organisation with very large royally-controlled armies, financed by effective taxation. The feudal armies were, at that point, no longer. The period around 1200 saw, however, a technological and social change that was no less fundamental and decisive for all military enterprises for the rest of the Middle Ages.

Until around 1180, trebuchets hurling stones against fortifications had been manually operated. They could be amazingly big and handle impressively large projectiles if 20–50 people operated them by drawing in ropes at the same time. But they were imprecise because when the operators grew tired, the machines' range shrank. Before 1200, a new generation of trebuchets had emerged. These used counterweight

DOI: 10.4324/9781003095514-8

technology which made them extremely precise. They could also be very large and hurl stones of up to 200 kg at a distance of 400 m or more, or throw firebombs probably consisting of hot glowing iron shavings, using a chain-mail sling to prevent the bomb from setting fire to the trebuchet. Trebuchets were developed elsewhere but soon adapted to warfare in Scandinavia and the Baltic where they were very effective, since most houses were wooden and thatched with straw or reeds. Some of the machines' components were transported with the army, other parts were made on site. To obtain a solid foundation and to increase their range, large ramparts for the trebuchets were constructed at the beginning of each siege, and today they can still be detected and investigated archaeologically on medieval battle sites around the Baltic Sea.

In the same period, the crossbow developed from a light hunting device into a powerful military weapon possessing great impact. Their arrows could penetrate heavy armour, and – in contrast to the long bow – they could be used by troops after very little training. At shorter distances, the crossbow was very precise and became the preferred snipers' weapon. International church councils expressed serious concerns about this new and extremely destructive weapon, repeatedly forbidding its use during the 12th and 13th centuries, 'except against infidels'. These prohibitions had little effect, judging by the huge amount of crossbow arrows found everywhere in Scandinavia, and kings, rulers, cities, and in the later Middle Ages even bishops established contingents of crossbow men for themselves. According to the Danish law of Jutland from 1241, the leader of each ship in the royal conscript navy should be armed with a crossbow; if he was not able to use it himself, he should bring a person who could. In principle, the Danish king could summon a fleet of 1,000 ships each year, and thus at least 1,000 crossbow men.

Much more complex to construct was the *ballista*, a gigantic crossbow machine that shot arrows the size of spears and had a damaging effect if directed toward the centre of enemy troops. Around 1200 King Canute VI of Denmark called in specialists from Germany, probably Saxony, to build these super crossbows during the wars against the Wends in present-day northern Germany. The importance of the weapon is reflected in the awards bestowed on those constructing and operating them. One such ballista master, Ulrik, received huge stretches of lands from the King after the conquest of Estonia in the early 1220s.

The new weapons were immediately adapted to Scandinavian warfare, and the Scandinavian armies were often better equipped than their adversaries which was an important factor in the expansion of the Scandinavian kingdoms.

Naval Revolution

Naval warfare changed after 1200. An important aspect of the development of warfare was how troops could be transported; since Scandinavia was surrounded by water, the development of naval forms of transport was crucially important. The traditional Viking-type longship – the *snekke* – was still the preferred ship of war in the 12th century. In 1996, there was found the wreck of the largest known example to date: a 36-metre-long snekke which could carry perhaps 100 warriors. However, this ship was an absolute exception, most being shorter and smaller. In Norway, there were more of the bigger ships than in Denmark and Sweden because the Norwegians immediately came out into the Atlantic when sailing along the Norwegian coast, while the waters of Denmark and the Baltic were generally much calmer. All Scandinavian snekke were fast and could sail in shallow waters. After 1200, the old, specifically Scandinavian ship-building technique changed and was increasingly displaced by a common northern European one, but the building of traditional longships also continued.

From the second half of the 12th century, the snekkes were supplemented in the North by a new type of ship, the *cog*. The cogs were heavy, slow, and clumsy because they were operated almost exclusively by sail, but they could carry a much bigger load than longships. The cogs' size increased quickly, and soon they could transport up to several hundred soldiers, large amounts of provisions, and above all expensive trained warhorses. The cogs had much higher boards than the snekkes and were difficult to board. Some models included raised platforms or small towers from where crossbow men could shoot at enemy ships.

Fleets for large expeditions consisted of both snekkes and cogs, and they could operate on longer distances than earlier. The different types of medieval ship have become much better understood after the rapid development of maritime archaeology as an academic discipline in the second half of the 20th century. Several longships from the Viking Age and the Middle Ages were found in the Fjord of Roskilde in Denmark in the 1950s. These discoveries showed that the boats were large – one of them, known as *Skuldelev 2*, was 30 m long and had space for a crew of c. 60 soldiers. Through dendrochronology it was possible to date and even physically locate the timber's origin: it had been felled near Dublin in 1042, so the ship must have been built there but ended up in Denmark.

In 1998 a cog-type ship was found in a shallow lagoon in the archipelago outside Stockholm, in a place called Kuggmaren. This is one of several placenames in Sweden with 'kugg'. Etymologically, it can mean an 'elevated place' or a 'small hill', but also 'cog' in medieval Swedish and Norwegian. Some of these coastal placenames probably refer to where cogs could seek shelter or take in provisions, parallel to the many place-names throughout Scandinavia with 'snekke', indicating where ledung ships were kept in boathouses during the winter.

When the so-called *Kuggmaren Cog* was found, it was 1.5 m under the present sea level, corresponding to c. 4.7 m at the time the ship sank in 1215. It was built of timber from western Denmark and held a cargo of barley and oats. These may have been trading goods but another explanation is that they were military provisions, even simply horse fodder. One could argue for the military explanation since Kuggmaren lies en route between Denmark and Estonia, as described in the so-called *Valdemar's Itinerarium*, probably written down around 1230. The *Itinerarium* contains a list of 101 locations on the sailing route running from Udlængen in Danish Blekinge, along the Swedish coastline and via the Åland Islands and Finland, all the way to Tallinn in Estonia. The entire voyage is about 1,000 km, but the *Itinerarium* gives alternative, parallel routes, sometimes depending upon the weather. 'If the wind is favourable, you can sail directly' to some location and would not have to hug the sheltering coast.

The *Itinerarium* demonstrates that seaborne communication between the western and eastern Baltic was regular after 1200 but is clearly not meant to facilitate navigation. It listed fixed points but did not explain how to get from one to the next. Following the route description was possible only for experienced sailors who had travelled it before, and bigger ships or entire fleets were totally dependent upon the assistance of local pilots. Only they knew the changing currents and could find the best, most secure ways through the many islands and rocky capes. Pilots were hired en route and swapped with others when they entered unknown waters. This is one of the reasons why major military expeditions required negotiations with possible allies in local areas, or with hostile neighbours of the enemy. Negotiations often included agreements about establishing contacts with capable, reliable pilots.

If alliances broke down, ships could suddenly be left without anyone to help with their navigation. In 1221, the Danish King Valdemar II sent his representative Gotskalk to take over command in Riga, but Gotskalk made himself so unpopular that nobody would find him a local pilot, 'not even from the merchants' – meaning not even for substantial payment. He had to leave the harbour without one and as consequence lost his course completely due to contrary winds, returning to Denmark only after a long period of erratic sailing. The significance of pilots can also be seen in the old habit of often sparing the crew of a captured enemy ship, while killing the captain and pilot before letting it sail home. This may have been revenge, by leaving enemies in a difficult and dangerous situation, but in any case, it prevented them from efficiently continuing an attack in foreign waters.

The medieval Scandinavian navy usually consisted of both fast, slim ships and big cogs, and these were in use throughout the Middle Ages. Cogs were more expensive to build and perhaps also to maintain, and required larger infrastructures in the form of wharves, arsenals, and harbours. As we will see later, merchant companies could provide an economic basis for this, but war cogs needed large investments provided or organised by central agents, kings, princes, and high-ranking nobles, including bishops. In 1304, the Danish King Eric VI Menved re-organised the registration of free men's income and decreed that for each 10,000 marks of this they should build, maintain, and man a cog, furnishing it with provisions for 16 weeks of expedition. These ships were clearly planned to serve as an offensive force and were most probably not intended to replace the old *ledung* system but to supplement it.

In the second half of the 14th century, centrally employed armies became more effective and reliable, and the ledung in form of the general conscription of materiel and men was replaced by a tax to finance a professional army. The year 1360 was the last when the inhabitants of Denmark had to contribute in kind to ships and provisions, while the system continued in Norway until somewhat later. In Sweden, the general levy seems to have been abandoned at the same time as in Denmark, around 1360. By the time of this shift, the Scandinavian kingdoms had done most of their expansion in the Baltic Sea area.

Expansion in the Baltic

The Scandinavian expansion into the Baltic in the first half of the 13th century was led by the Danish king and his vassals. It began in the western parts of the Baltic Sea and extended gradually all the way to the Finnish Gulf, until coming to a halt in the 1220s. Shortly afterwards, Swedish rulers began an active expansion into Finland and towards Russia. After 1300, the power balance in the Baltic Sea shifted markedly, when the Kingdom of Denmark was pawned to the counts of Holstein, and Sweden gained control over Scania, which had until then belonged to Denmark. The expansion culminated at the end of the 14th century with the formation in Kalmar of a Nordic union, involving all political parties in the entire region but with a central role for the mainly Danish royal dynasty.

The Danish Baltic Empire

The military career of King Valdemar II the Victorious of Denmark (r. 1202–1241) illustrates the art of war of the period, a precarious balancing of long-term preparations, manoeuvring among various possible political alliances, and a few decisive battles. Valdemar's wars are also a prime example of the interconnection of Scandinavia and the rest of western Europe.

Danish expansion took its first steps southwards for reasons bound to Valdemar's background. Valdemar was born in 1170 and became the duke of Schleswig when he was 18 years old, serving under his older brother King Canute VI (r. 1182–1202). The Duchy of Schleswig was an important border area, not only for defending Danish territory but very much also for expanding south and particularly east along the Baltic coastline, with its neighbouring Christian and pagan enemies. Valdemar inherited older conflicts, and his installation as duke created a new one that was severe and long lasting. His appointment as Duke of Schleswig estranged his namesake and grand cousin, Valdemar Knudsen, the bishop of Schleswig who until then had functioned as duke. Not content solely with his ecclesiastical position, in 1192 Valdemar Knudsen invaded Denmark from the north together with Norwegian allies on 35 longships, declaring himself king of Denmark instead of Canute VI. From the south attacked another of his allies, Count Adolf III of Holstein.

A person simultaneously holding the offices of bishop and king was an unheard-of position in medieval Europe. We will never know how legal and theological specialists would have discussed its implications, since Valdemar Knudsen never became king. He lost the battle and was held prisoner in the royal castle of Søborg for the next 14 years. For his part, Count Adolf III managed to escape, but for the next decade, Duke Valdemar constantly sent troops into Holstein on minor operations to weaken him. Duke Valdemar also persuaded and bribed several of Adolf's vassals to switch loyalties and come to him. He promised them lands which Valdemar would in the future conquer from Adolf. Around 1200, he also began a trade blockade and prevented ships from Lübeck trading on the great herring market in Scania – a severe blow to Adolf's income. And eventually, in 1201, Valdemar entered Holstein with a large army and fought Adolf successfully in two major campaigns before withdrawing to Schleswig in November. But it was only a feigned retreat. On Christmas eve, Valdemar suddenly appeared with large contingents outside the walls of Hamburg, to Count Adolf's total surprise. Misled by treacherous scouts he had believed that the Danes would stay home, celebrate Christmas with heavy drinking 'as usual' and be totally harmless, wrote the chronicler Arnold of Lübeck. The Count became Valdemar's prisoner and was only released in return for heavy war reparations and important hostages, who were then kept in custody, some for 20 years. Valdemar had been cautious, only slowly building up his net of alliances and minor victories until the opponent was sufficiently weakened and ripe to be subjugated. It was the strategy that all rulers of the time pursued, with varying degrees of competence and luck.

Valdemar installed a loyal new count of Holstein, his sister's son Albert of Orlamünde, and began to be an important player in northern Europe's power struggles. Two German dynasties – the *Welfs* and the *Staufers* – had for generations striven with each other to be kings of the Germans and emperors of the Holy Roman Empire. Valdemar had now become king and in 1202 began his power play among the Germans by supporting the Welf candidate Otto IV (1175–1218) with large military contingents. He helped with ferrying Otto and his army to England on Danish ships when in 1207 they had to flee a victorious Staufer opponent, and later assisted Otto's military comeback in northern Germany. In 1208, Otto's competitor to the German throne suddenly died, assassinated at night while attending a wedding celebration. The motive may have been private revenge, but Otto seized the political advantage and was for a while the unrivalled king. Valdemar II (for whom a strong German ruler was not optimal) very soon change side and began supporting the young Staufer Frederick II (1194–1250), who in 1211/1212 had already begun to collect political and military supporters in Germany and obtained the patronage of Pope Innocent III. With the young man desperately needing allies, King Valdemar saw a golden opportunity.

On 27 July 1214, and most unusually, Europe's great powers clashed in a huge decisive battle, at Bouvines in Flanders, that changed the continent's political landscape to an extent comparable to the First World War of 1914–1918. King Valdemar II did not participate but nevertheless had an important military function. On one side of the battlefield stood Otto IV in alliance with the English King John Lackland, Count Ferdinand of Flanders, and many great barons. On the other was the French King Philip II Augustus, with some of the mightiest vassals of France. The outcome was a crushing French victory. The English had to surrender their continental possessions, the count of Flanders was imprisoned in the Louvre for 13 years, and Otto lost his powerful allies for the remaining few years of his life.

In this contest, Valdemar had been riding two horses at the same time. His sister Ingeborg had been married to Philip II Augustus in 1193, but the morning after their wedding night the French King had sent her far away from the court, holding her as a prisoner. What had happened that night will never be known, but it resulted in 20 years of diplomatic and ecclesiastical negotiations and threats to persuade Philip II to take back his legally wedded wife. In 1213, the stubborn King suddenly changed his mind, allowing her to return to her position as his queen but on condition that she did not come near him. For Valdemar, who had strongly sided with his sister in the legal battle, this was clearly a concession to ensure that he did not change sides again and support Otto IV. On the other hand, only a few months before the battle at Bouvines, in 1214, Valdemar had married Berengaria of Portugal, the sister of Count Ferdinand of Flanders. In these ways, Valdemar had secured very strong links to whoever emerged victorious after Bouvines – to Philip Augustus through his sister, to Ferdinand through his wife.

Valdemar did not participate directly in the battle of Bouvines, but in 1213 and 1214, he was engaged in several military actions in northern Germany against Otto IV's supporters in Holstein and the surrounding principalities. In this way, he tied up some of Otto's major forces in that area so that they could not support him at Bouvines. In northern Germany, Valdemar burned and demolished castles and strongholds, and several princes were subdued, forced to accept the conditions of the conqueror. The counts of Schwerin, for example, became Valdemar's vassals and had to promise to serve him with 60 knights 'whenever and wherever they are needed'. The one deciding what was needed was obviously Valdemar. The military contingents he could muster seem to have been considerable, and more than one mighty opponent in the years around 1214 simply retreated when faced with his armies.

In 1215, Otto decided to avenge his defeat at Bouvines by attacking Valdemar, who allegedly met him with 60,000 soldiers – one source claims 60,000 soldiers from

Frisia alone but that must simply be an exaggeration. To avoid a great bloodbath, it was decided to settle the matter by an ordeal, in this case a weaponless fight between two men from the Danish side and two from the German. It was not an unknown procedure in western Europe although extremely unusual. Otto was represented by the two best fistfighters in the German Empire, who were however defeated by Valdemar's two Frisians, Brother Gauling and Suen Stærke ('Strong Suen'). Otto withdrew.

The commitment against Otto and his men was also a strong form of support to the young Frederick II, and Valdemar received his reward at the end of 1214 in the form of a 'Golden bull' with Frederick's royal seal in gold. The bull conceded to Valdemar and his successors all rights to all of the land north of the River Elbe. It was an extremely far-reaching concession which Frederick soon regretted and tried to have revoked.

Danish expansion in the Baltic Sea region had acquired influential support when in 1171 Pope Alexander III issued a bull authorising Christian mission to extend into the eastern Baltic. This led to Swedish and Danish expeditions to Finland and Estonia in the 1190s. We know very little of these first expeditions except that they paved the way for the targeted effort that began around 1200. Even a small fleet from Norway had sailed to Estonia in the 1180s.

Holy wars in the eastern Baltic could be defined as wars of defence throughout the 12th century and especially in its second half. The Scandinavians would cast their expeditions as defensive since fleets with pagan soldiers from Saaremaa and Curland had attacked Scandinavia, reaching as far south as Blekinge in 1170. In 1187, Estonians and Karelians sailed up Lake Mälaren all the way to Sigtuna, which was partly burned, and such attacks continued into the early 13th century. At the same time, tiny Christian communities had been established in Finland and probably also Livonia, and any attacks on them by pagan neighbours served as a good justification for a military-religious response.

The first missionaries arrived in Livonia in the 1180s or before, following merchants to the annual summer-markets, and around 1185 Meinhard established himself as missionary bishop along the River Daugava (western Dvina) – the 1,000 km long transport route connecting the Baltic to eastern Europe and central Russia. In 1201, the episcopal see was moved from Ikšķile to the newly founded settlement of Riga at the Daugava's outlet into the Baltic. We do not know the reason for the transfer, but it is possible that ships had become larger, rendering some of them unable to sail up the river, while a mission needed regular communications with the West and regular supplies of religious warriors. Bishop Albert of Riga (r. 1199–1229) established his own knightly military order in 1201, the Sword Brethern, who began the gradual conquest and conversion of Livonia from the south. From the north came the Danish crusaders.

Immediately after he became king in 1202, Valdemar II began to prepare for expeditions to Estonia. During the first in 1206, he succeeded in establishing a Danish fortress stronghold on the island of Saaremaa, but when winter came the troops had to return home and burned it down. In the following years, there were regular expeditions, probably annual, led by Valdemar's nephew Albert of Orlamünde. Valdemar's ambition to conquer Estonia was put on hold for some years while he was militarily engaged in northern Germany in 1213 and 1214. This was unusual after so many years of Baltic expeditions, and even laconically mentioned in one of the Danish annals from 1213: 'There was no crusade this year'. In 1215, after successfully if indirectly intervening at Bouvines, Valdemar returned to his eastern ambitions while preparing to escalate his crusading commitments. He had his son the Young Valdemar elected as co-ruler – a common precaution among western European kings before leaving for crusades, demonstrating the heir's power, and securing his succession if the king did not return. In the same year, the Fourth Lateran Council decided to launch a general crusade to the Middle East. The first participants left western Europe in 1217. Valdemar was represented by several of his great vassals, including Kasimir of Pomerania and Henry of Schwerin. Even Valdemar's illegitimate son Duke Niels of Halland intended to leave to the Middle East but died before his departure.

In 1218, Young Valdemar was solemnly crowned king, to rule together with his father, in Schleswig in the company of '15 bishops, 3 dukes, and 3 counts, and a great number of abbots', as mentioned in contemporary annals. The day chosen for the solemn occasion was 25 June, the feast day of King Valdemar's grandfather, Saint Canute Lavard, who had been a crusader king in the Wendic areas – a good omen. At this occasion, King Valdemar also made agreements with Bishop Albert of Riga for a crusade in the following summer, and Albert continued on from Schleswig to a preaching tour in Germany, to recruit warriors.

In 1219, a Danish fleet allegedly of 1,500 ships sailed all the way to Estonia. The participants gathered and set sail from the traditional crusading harbours in Denmark, the most prominent among them being Vordingborg. The fleet probably followed the old sailing route along the Swedish coast, with its important base on the island of Bornholm. Other parts of the fleet arrived from the Danish dependencies on the southern Baltic coast: Schleswig, Lübeck, Mecklenburg, Rügen, and Pomerania. If we believe the number transmitted by the sources, it must have been the largest fleet that any Scandinavian ruler had mustered to date. If each ship normally carried 20–30 men the entire army consisted of at least 30,000 men, and probably closer to 50,000. An operation so large and so far from the central Danish lands was only possible because of the enormous technological developments around 1200.

The army landed at Tallinn on the northern coast of Estonia and faced with such an overwhelming army the local chieftains and representatives of diverse Estonian groups surrendered, promising to let themselves and their peoples be baptised. It was, however, a ruse to gain time. Three days later, on 15 June 1219, they suddenly attacked the Danish camp from several sides at the same time, killing and advancing rapidly. Theodoric, who had already been appointed bishop over Estonia in anticipation of its successful conquest, was killed in his tent. This was so luxurious that the Estonians were certain it must have been the royal tent, and so they were convinced that they had killed King Valdemar.

Things were looking desperate, with the Danish army pressed upon and retreating, when the troops of Prince Vitslav of Rügen entered the fray. He was one of King Valdemar's major vassals; his pagan grandfather Jarimar had been conquered by Valdemar's father, also called Valdemar, accepting baptism 51 years earlier to the day, on 15 June. Now Vitslav's troops reversed the course of the battle, and the entire Danish army regained its momentum and advanced, killing Estonians in great numbers and accepting the survivors' submission in return for baptism and tribute. The place – and this must have happened after the conquest – was called Tallinn, in Estonian *Taani linna*, the castle of the Danes.

How was this possible? How could an army and a ruler, inspired by whatever religious, political, economic, or other motives, succeed in conquering so far from their homeland? One answer was technological; it would hardly have been possible 50 years or more earlier. Another must have been a degree of cooperation with local forces, welcoming the invaders in anticipation of privileges and advantages for themselves from their new rulers. This element has been totally neglected by researchers until very recently. The conquest of Tallinn has been seen, by Scandinavian as well as by Estonian historians, as a confrontation between two cultures, peoples, and faiths. The reality must have been much more complicated, and political agents had interests and connections across all such conceptual borders. We know this from sources for so many other expeditions in medieval Scandinavia. In fact, it is very hard to imagine that such a large army could have been logistically able to reach Tallinn in a coordinated movement without local connections.

The third explanation, befitting medieval religiosity, is that it was a miracle. When the Danish army was hardest pressed in battle, the heavens opened and the Danish flag with its white cross on a red field fell from the sky. Encouraged by this sign of divine approval, the Danish army launched a counterattack and won. Although this episode is related in all Danish and many Scandinavian school books to the present day, its basis in medieval sources is tenuous and late. With that said, it was a relatively common miracle in the Middle Ages. Crosses were seen in the sky everywhere in the 12th and 13th centuries, and flags fell down before or during decisive battles. In any case, the white cross in the red field also became the symbol on the seal and coat of arms of the medieval town of Tallinn and is still in use.

The conquest of Tallinn marked the beginning of troubled years. The Danish conquest extended further along the coast of the Finnish Gulf and southwards, variously in cooperation or competition with the Swedes. In 1220, King John I Sverkersson of Sweden had already landed in the area with an army, several bishops, and Duke Karl the Deaf. After some negotiations with the Danes, the Swedes started missionising a little further south of the Danish sphere of interest, but the King soon retired to Sweden. A major pagan army attacked the Swedes and burned their fortress, and the ensuing battle claimed the lives both of Duke Karl the Deaf and the bishop of Linköping, the royal chancellor.

The local Estonians fought their new rulers, often with help from the people of Saaremaa. It was a cruel war of violence and terror from both sides. In 1221, a rebellion – or war of liberation, depending upon perspectives – stopped simply because the Estonians became afraid that King Valdemar was returning with his army; all those directly involved in the rising were hanged, with the rest taxed double or triple the previous amount. In a major rebellion in early spring 1223, the Estonians conquered several Danish castles and killed a huge number of Danes. The Danish commander of the county of Järvamaa, Ebbe, was caught, tortured, and cut open, and his heart was taken out while he was still alive. It was cut into pieces, roasted, and eaten by the Estonian fighters to gain his strength. If ever there was one, this was the moment for King Valdemar to come in person and lead a punishing expedition against those who had still not accepted his sovereignty. But before he could do so, the wheel for fortune turned against him in a way he could not possibly have foreseen.

A Traitor: The Black Count Henry of Schwerin

On the night of 6–7 May 1223, the deeply drunk and wounded Valdemar was dragged from his hunting tent on the small island of Lyø in southern Denmark, thrown into a boat waiting on the beach, hastily sailed to Germany, and transported to the stronghold of Dannenberg Castle south of the River Elbe. He had been taken prisoner by his vassal Henry of Schwerin after what must have been a diplomatic meeting to discuss a number of complaints Henry had against his liege lord. King Valdemar had with various pretexts taken land and income from Henry, and from Henry's mother-in-law. Perhaps he had even used Henry's absence on a crusade to the Middle East to seduce or rape Henry's wife, as one contemporary source (but only one) wrote.

Negotiations over the ransom soon began, but they became more complicated than Count Henry had probably imagined. Pope Honorius III intervened with strongly worded letters and threats to excommunicate Henry, since Valdemar had taken up the cross and promised to go on crusade to the Holy Land. He had made his promise in secret, but even so, this placed him under the Church's special protection. He had also done so after encouragement from the Pope, which must mean that Valdemar had been part of Pope Honorius' plans for a large, international crusade to liberate Jerusalem from the Muslims.

Negotiations became even more complicated because Emperor Frederick II intervened and offered to buy Valdemar from Henry. His plan was to let Valdemar free for a promise to raise a large Danish crusading army and to sail it to the Holy Land in summer 1225 on a fleet of 100 ships, consisting of new cogs and traditional longboats – *centum naues cockonibus et sneccis computatis*. Under the offer's terms, Valdemar would stay in the Holy Land for two years and serve the king of Jerusalem; in addition, he would renounce all claims on the lands north of the River Elbe obtained with Frederick's bull in 1214, and his vassals in these areas would transfer their loyalty and vassalage to the Emperor.

Frederick too had promised the pope that he would leave for a crusade in summer 1225, with 1,000 knights and a fleet comprising 100 *calendra* – large Byzantine sailing ships of a type equivalent to the cog – and 50 swift, long Mediterranean type galleys. When Frederick's representative negotiated with Valdemar, they also knew that Frederick was just about to close a deal to marry Princess Yolanda of Jerusalem. If Valdemar were to serve the king of Jerusalem, this would mean that he promised to serve Frederick.

This deal came to nothing, mainly because the Danish barons negotiating and collecting the money for the ransom angrily refused and returned home. They contacted Count Henry instead and bought Valdemar's freedom, for a huge price, but without agreeing that he should leave the country for years. The King returned at the end of 1225 after two and a half years as prisoner. The following year, he began a series of raids and wars to regain territory and take revenge upon Count Henry. The struggle culminated on 2 July 1227 in a great battle at Bornhöved in Holstein, which ended with a crushing defeat for Valdemar who lost an eye and barely escaped alive.

Valdemar's imprisonment illustrates the greatness and the fragility of medieval Scandinavian rulers. He was a king with such military proficiency and resources as to make him one of the obvious leaders for a huge western European crusade to the Holy Land, almost on a level with the Emperor of the Holy Roman Empire. On the other hand, a single vassal in an audacious act of treason could neutralise him for years and stop his Baltic engagement, only a few years after the great conquest of Estonia.

The role of individuals in history is always difficult to estimate, not least in the Middle Ages. Much of existing Danish policy seems to have continued relatively smoothly while Valdemar was in prison. Control over Estonia was upheld through a series of military expeditions by local Danish vassals, even without the king. The government continued to function within Denmark through the royal offices that had been created in the late 12th century, and there was a clearly defined body of political agents that could negotiate with Count Henry and the Emperor. On the other hand, Valdemar's Baltic policy certainly became much less expansive after the defeat at Bornhöved. Instead, in the nearly 25 remaining years of his life, he mainly turned to internal administrative and legal reforms.

Swedish Colonisation and Crusades

In Sweden, Birger Jarl (Birger Duke of the Swedes) opened a series of Swedish campaigns in Finland and towards the border areas with Russian Novgorod, shortly after the Danish expansion in the east had lost momentum in the first half of the 13th century. Earlier connections between present-day Sweden and Finland are well attested but difficult to follow in detail. A crusade and missionary war had been launched in the mid-12th century and was probably followed decade after decade by a slow movement of colonists in search of new lands from Westrobothnia in Sweden, over the waters of the Bothnian Bay, to Ostrobothnia in Finland. This ran parallel to the general expansion of agriculture everywhere in Europe at the time but strengthened by the expansive urges of increasingly powerful kings. They aimed to control trading routes, for example the major one through the Gulf of Finland and the great Russian rivers to eastern Europe, and all the way to the Mediterranean. They also aimed to tax those more remote areas which until then had evaded any centralised control.

Crusading was another important justification for war. On 9 December 1237, the archbishop of Uppsala received a papal bull authorising him to preach a crusade against the Tavastians in Finland, who allegedly had accepted Christianity but relapsed, attacking, mutilating, blinding, and burning Christians as sacrifices to their pagan demons. Birger Jarl led the expedition in 1238, vividly described in the Eric's Chronicle from c. 1320. Stout warriors boarded the ships while wailing women waved goodbye from the beach. They landed and started to conquer Tavastland, a loosely defined and thinly populated area, and the local population was forced to re-convert to Christianity. To ensure future military control, Birger Jarl built Tavastehus (The Castle of Tavastland), a stronghold which around 1300 was moved some 17 km to its present location in Hämeenlinna.

Only a year or two later – the chronology in the sources is confused – Birger Jarl led a new expedition even further to the east with an army consisting of several different peoples: Swedes, Norwegians, Christians from the southern part of Finland, and some of the newly converted Tavastians. They attempted, via the River Neva, to reach Lake Ladoga on the Russian side of the present border between Finland and Russia. Ladoga is Europe's largest freshwater lake, rich in all kinds of natural resources and one of the main gateways to the Russian river system. Birger Jarl built a fortress in the contested frontier area of Ingermanland, where much later Saint Petersburg was founded, but his army was severely defeated by Prince Alexander Nevsky, of the strong city state of Novgorod, in the Battle of Neva in 1240.

During the coming decades, there were minor skirmishes between Swedish troops and smaller contingents from Novgorod, and several papal attempts to raise a crusade against the Orthodox Russians, but the situation only escalated significantly in 1292. In 1300, Marshall Torgel Knutsson led against the Russians an enormous fleet, allegedly of 1,100 ships. The Swedes fought their way up the River Neva, capturing a strong point where they built the Landskrona fortress (not to be confused with the town of Landskrona in Scania, founded around 1400). The large Swedish fleet returned home, leaving a garrison of c. 300 soldiers which were attacked by Russians. After a siege and dire shortage of provisions, the mere 16 surviving Swedes were forced to surrender in 1301.

A large army from Novgorod proceeded far into Tavastland and Finland, returning several times in the coming years. In 1318, it reached as far as the south-western corner of Finland, attacking and plundering Turku, Finland's largest town as well as the episcopal seat for its enormous single diocese. In the end, an agreement was reached to conclude almost a generation of regular warfare. In 1323, the castle of Nöteborg on Lake Ladoga became the meeting place between the prince of Novgorod and representatives of the Swedish king, for the signing of a treaty which for the first time defined the two countries' borders. An important reason for this is revealed by the participation also of two merchants from Gotland, probably representing the Hanseatic League; war was devastating, not least for trade, and should now stop.

The southern part of the new border was fixed and is possible to follow today, but the northern part described a zone more than a rigid line. It consisted in enormous stretches of land – hundreds upon hundreds of kilometres of steppes and very low mountains – thinly populated by hunters and reindeer nomads moving back and forth, following the seasons of the year. The Nöteborg peace stated that Sweden and Novgorod could tax whomever they met, if they met anyone, and the same became the solution for the peace treaty between Norway and Novgorod three years later, in 1326. The longer-term result was that the Sámi population ended up paying tax to three different rulers.

Expansion into the North Atlantic – The Norwegian Dominium

Generations of wars between different dynasties and pretenders to the Norwegian throne ended in 1240, meaning that King Haakon IV Haakonsson (r. 1217–1263) and his successors could concentrate upon expansion into the Atlantic and far up into northern Norway. With one exception, the establishment of a Norwegian dominion over the Atlantic Isles was the result of successful negotiations and not a military conquest, in contrast to the Danish and Swedish extensions of their territory during the 13th century.

The ecclesiastical province of Nidaros was established, independent of Lund, in 1152/53, and its archbishop had ecclesiastical responsibility and the right to consecrate bishops for an enormous area, including Iceland, Greenland, the Orkney Islands, the Sodor islands, the Hebrides, the Isle of Man, Shetland, and the Faroes, together with the far northern arctic part of Norway, and Norway proper. After 1240, this ecclesiastical supremacy was supplemented with a political and economic dominion.

King Haakon was crowned in 1247 by the papal legate, William of Sabina. This happened in Bergen where it rained so much that the ceremony had to be held indoors, without the joyous and solemn processions that would normally have been part of such an occasion. The King had ample time to discuss with Legate William the matter of Iceland, and what should be done. William answered, 'it is not proper that a country does not serve under a king like all other countries in the world do' – a remark that Haakon would certainly have been pleased with. We know of it only from the official royal history, the *Håkon Håkonsson's saga*, but it fits very well with the general European political thinking of the 13th century and may indeed be authentic.

Iceland had not developed a strong centralised power structure with a king or any kind of regent. Perhaps the local magnates, the *goðar*, maintained a precarious power balance by killing each other in bloody multi-generational feuds that prevented any single family from gaining hegemony. Perhaps they cherished the idea of freedom and the memory of the first generations of settlers who had left Norway exactly to escape the suppression of kings. In the beginning of the 13th century, however, this slowly changed. The archbishops of Nidaros appointed bishops loyal to Norway instead of locals to Iceland's two episcopal sees, and ever more Icelandic magnates sought to gain political power at home by gaining a closer attachment to the Norwegian king. In the 1250s, Haakon had control of the majority of offices and could in the end appoint his own representative, an Earl of Iceland. In 1262–1264, Icelanders swore allegiance to King Haakon in return for the promise that they continue to be judged according to their own laws, and that Haakon guarantee regular, necessary ship transport between Iceland and Norway. At last, Icelanders were subjects of a king, mostly as a result of internal strife and competition, and without any direct military coercion.

Greenland was an endlessly larger territory than Iceland but much more sparsely populated. The Norse colonies also submitted to the Norwegian king, in 1261. We know little about why and how, but a guarantee of regular lines of communication back to Norway was probably an important element in the negotiations. Inuit migrations from Canada into Greenland had also begun before 1200 and led to attacks upon the Norse settlement after 1300 – possibly they were already considered a danger around 1260; was the alliance with Norway perhaps also intended to secure military protection?

The islands closer to Scotland were differently organised, richer, and more densely populated, and the possibility of allying with Scotland necessitated a different policy to secure Norwegian control. Ecclesiastically and legally the Faroes and Shetland seem to have been well integrated with Norway. This may reflect close contacts after the great Norse colonisation period in the later Viking Age. The Isle of Man and the Hebrides had a much more flexible and unstable attachment, with a native population, long before the Nordic Vikings came to them. Sometimes, local rulers took the title of king, sometimes the Norwegian king governed indirectly through an earl or directly through a royal governor.

When the Earl of Orkney chose the losing side in the Norwegian civil wars around 1200, royal control of the island became much stronger. A closer connection to Scotland may have seemed attractive to the Orkneyans. In any case, the king of Scotland suggested buying the Hebrides from the Norwegian king and also began raiding and plundering some of the islands in 1262. To prevent this and to ensure the continued control over Orkney, King Haakon equipped a fleet and sailed towards Scotland, but could not provoke the Scots to engage in a sea battle. During Christmas 1263, he died in Kirkwall on Orkney. War did not continue, but King Magnus VI the Law-mender (r. 1263–1280) concluded a peace in Perth with the Scottish King Alexander III in 1266. Scotland's claim to the Isle of Man and the Hebrides was acknowledged, as was Norway's claim to Orkney and Shetland.

The 13th century was a time of expansion not only out in the Atlantic but also to the north in the Scandinavian Peninsula. Around 1250, a church was established

Illustration 5.1 Bishop's crozier and bishop's ring, found in a late 13th-century grave in Gardar, Greenland. The gold ring is relatively simple for a bishop of the time, but the crozier, made of walrus ivory, probably locally on Greenland, is elaborately decorated and on a level with most other croziers of western Europe at the time. The connections to western Europe were still good in the late 13th century, but the Norse settlements in Greenland had begun to be threatened.

Crozier today at the Danish National Museum, Copenhagen. Photo Lennart Larsen 1970–2014. This File Is Licensed Under the Creative Commons Attribution-Share Alike 2.0 Generic license.

in Tromsø, which was still a missionary area with a pagan Sámi population, and in 1307, a fortress and a church were built on the island of Vardøy in the very far north, at the present border between Norway and Russia. Since the Viking Age, these areas had paid tribute or irregular taxes mainly in fur to local chieftains or shifting

Norwegian rulers, but they had now become of interest due to fishing. New fishing villages were founded up and down the coast with churches and local stewards of the bishop or king for collecting revenues.

European demand for fish grew during the 12th and especially the 13th century because of a growing population, and techniques for catching and preserving fish developed. Bigger ships could cross the Atlantic and transport large amount of fish from the north to Nidaros, Bergen, and further south. The hunting of whales became more systematic in this period, as did also the hunting for walrus with its precious ivory. Northern Norway and Iceland were ideal for producing stock fish because the temperatures were so low in fishing season that the cod could dry and be preserved without salting.

The Norwegian dominion – *Norgesveldi* – became firmly established between c. 1240 and the early 14th century. It was a political organisation, built to a large extent upon laws and legal treatises, and surprisingly little upon military conquests, in contrast with the Danish and Swedish empires of the same period. The main reason is that no other big powers had strong interests in the northern Atlantic; Scotland and England both might have, but in this period both were occupied with fighting each other or with internal civil wars.

The Sámi lived in an enormous area, stretching into the Norwegian, Swedish, and Russian political spheres whose rulers had always been attracted by the natural resources of the tundra and forests – and not least by the scope for taxing the Sámi, for which new possibilities arose sometimes in this period. Sources are solely archaeological and meagre but suggest that it may have been in the 13th century that the Sámi domesticated the reindeer and greatly increased the production of meat, fur, and horn. Earlier they had hunted wild reindeer flocks, but now they could control the movements, breeding, and slaughter of large herds.

Killing Kings

It was dark and there was probably terrible weather on the night of Saint Cecilia's Day, 22 November 1286. King Eric V Klipping of Denmark sought shelter in the barn of the miserable little hamlet of Finderup on the empty moors of Jutland. Later in the night, seven men in disguise entered the barn and killed King Eric with 56 stabs to his body. Each man stabbed once for his own part and seven times for the total number of the group, for this was a conspiracy in which all would bear equal guilt – if they were detected.

The murder was the bloody culmination of several years' internal unrest and power struggle between king and nobles, and it was to have dire consequences also for both Norwegian and Swedish kings. Its roots stretch back to the death of King Valdemar II in 1241. He had maintained harmonious relations to the Church and had power enough to keep the nobles under control. He also preserved peaceful cooperation with members of the mighty Hvide family. This did not extend to the reigns of his three succeeding sons. Eric IV Ploughpenny (r. 1241–1250) became unpopular because of his extraordinary taxes levied on each plough, and also began a confrontation with the Church that was to last generations. Bishop Niels Stigsen of Roskilde went into exile at the papal curia in 1245, which was especially problematic for King Eric because the bishop was the chancellor of the realm. Royal administration could function without him, but not well. Eric and his brother Abel were in open war against each other from

1246 onwards. Abel succeeded in mobilising some of the great noble families in Denmark and, as Duke of Schleswig, many of the powerful nobles of Holstein. In 1250, he invited Eric to a meeting in Schleswig to peacefully settle the conflict, but instead, he had his brother killed and dumped in the Schleswig Fjord. Eric IV was soon found by fishermen, his body brought to land and later buried in Ringsted where he became venerated as a saint, albeit without official papal recognition.

Eric had no sons but four daughters. One married the king of Norway and another the king of Sweden, with both husbands meant to have claims to inherit Denmark through their wives. The two other daughters, Agnes and Jutta, entered the Saint Clare monastery in Roskilde. They had done so totally voluntarily, several persons close to the King insisted. Such emphasis indicates the very opposite; the two princesses were put away there, where they were simply meant to remain and pray, for economic and dynastic reasons. But they later took matters into their own hands in a most unforeseen manner.

Abel became king in 1250, solemnly swearing together with 24 co-jurors that he had no part in his brother's death, but many did not believe him. His reign was short – in 1252, he fell in a war against the Frisians, but the year before he had supported rebels against the new Swedish King Valdemar Birgersson (r. 1250–1275, † 1304). Abel's son, also called Valdemar, was very conveniently arrested by the archbishop of Cologne, and so Abel's brother Christopher I (r. 1252–1259) could be elected king

Illustration 5.2 King Eric Ploughpenny was invited to peace negotiations with his brother Abel in 1250, but was killed by Abel's armed men and taken out and dumped into the water of Schleswig Fjord. His body was later found and transferred to the church in Ringsted, where his martyrdom was depicted in wall-paintings from the 1290s.

Photo © Mona Bager Jensen 2004.

before him. Abel's son continued as duke of Schleswig, and the 1252 election marked the beginning of almost a century of regular feuding between the dukes of Schleswig and the kings of Denmark.

During the reign of Christopher and his son Eric V Klipping (r. 1259–1286), the exact relationship of king and nobles was an issue of prime importance and tough negotiations. In the early 1250s, Christopher was able to promulgate an *Abel-Christopherske Forordning* (Statutes of Abel and Christopher) which attempted to regulate the nobles' obligations and fix their status as administrators in royal service rather than equals to the king. If one magnate killed another he should pay compensation not only to the victim's family but also to the king. The magnates are called *decurion* in the Latin version of the statutes, *høffding* in Danish. Decurion is a military title and indicates a dependency upon the king as commander, while høvding (magnate) in old Danish would normally indicate a more independent position.

In 1276, King Eric V Klipping promulgated a law concerning crimes against the king, which were defined broadly. If somebody knew that members of princely houses had married and that this might lead to dangers for the king but did not inform him about it, they should be fined the enormous sum of 100 silver marks. This clause may have been directed specifically against the dukes of Schleswig but could be used to implicate almost anybody the king held a grudge against. Eric V continued to press the nobles and restrict their power in various ways, for example by not involving them in decision-making.

Reaction came. In 1282, King Eric Klipping was forced to sign an agreement, later to be known as the first Danish constitution or the Danish Magna Carta. First of all, King Eric had to promise to convoke 'the parliament which is called hof' once every year; the magnates wanted to be heard again. He had also to promise that no man should be kept prisoner or sentenced to any punishment except after being heard and legally convicted. Additionally, the document confirmed that the king should not build on other men's land without the owner's consent and should not force anybody to work for free on constructing royal buildings or mills, and on royal castles only in case of necessity. A recurrent phrase in the document is that the king should 'follow the laws of King Valdemar' and abolish all (mis)use that had been introduced after the time of King Valdemar. The agreement is clearly the aristocrats' counterattack against all the attempts of kings to enhance royal power for the last 40 years since the time of King Valdemar II. Another counterattack took place four years later, when King Eric was killed in Finderup Barn by unknown assassins. Denmark in the second half of the 13th century was not a safe place for its kings, and internal politics were difficult.

In Sweden, relations between kings and the network of nobles underwent a development which was in many ways parallel to the Danish one. The family group of Folkungar (descendants of Folke) was as mighty in the Swedish context as the Danish Hvide family was in the Danish, and they were actively involved in several rebellions against Swedish kings in the 13th century.

In 1247, King Eric XI Ericsson (r. 1234–1250) defeated a broader coalition of rebels led by the Folkungar in a battle at Sparrsätra, many nobles went into exile in Denmark and Norway, and their leader Holmger Knutsson was caught and executed. His supporters later tried to promote him as a saint but this was suppressed. The rebellion resulted in new royal taxes. When King Eric XI died in 1250 without a male heir, his sister's son Valdemar Birgersson was elected king (r. 1250–1275, † 1304). Valdemar's father was the mighty Birger Jarl, on crusade in Finland at the time. The Folkungar immediately tried to exploit the situation and gathered a new army with support from the Danish King Abel and German mercenaries, but the rebellion was utterly crushed at the Battle of Herrevadsbro in 1251. The victory gave King Valdemar and his father, Birger Jarl, power enough to revise the taxation system and to begin transforming the ledung system from a military into a fiscal entity. In 1279 or 1280, King Valdemar's brother and successor, Magnus III Birgersson (known better as Magnus Ladulås, r. 1275–1290), promulgated a set of laws in the castle of Alsnö that had many similarities to the constitution of Danish King Eric Klipping two years later. The *Ordinance of Alsnö* forbade the magnates to arbitrarily call upon the peasants' 'hospitality', that is to demand shelter and food for men and horses. The extent of the peasants' services thereby became strictly regulated and under royal control. The ordinance also stated that conspiracy against the king was a capital offence. And all who served the king, his brother, the archbishop, or bishops with horse as knights should be free from taxes. The modern interpretation is that with the Ordinance of Alsnö, the lay nobility in the Kingdom of Sweden was established as a privileged class. The aim, however, was also to confirm king's supremacy over the nobles. The Ordinance stated that 'it is just that those who deserve it should have more freedom, and those who serve us better'. They should serve the king with 'help and advice', a standard phrase in Europe for defining the obligations of a vassal to the king. The Ordinance of Alsnö in principle came to regulate the relation between king and aristocrats for a long time to come, but in practice, the aristocrats often had the scope to act independently and sometimes directly against the king.

The Norwegian source material on kings and aristocrats from this period is much richer than the Danish or Swedish, so we know much more about the internal medieval politics in Norway. Two works are of special importance: the *Konungs skuggsjá* (*King's Mirror*) from c. 1250 and the national law-code (*landslag*) of Magnus VI the Law-mender (r. 1263–1280) from 1274. The first is a long guide for a royal prince, in form of a dialogue between father and son. Such King's Mirrors were very common in 12th-century Europe but this is written specifically from a Norwegian point of view. It includes sections on nature and wonders in Norway, Ireland, the Atlantic Isles, and much else of the world. In India, you can find fire-breathing dragons, but they can be tamed and used in warfare. In the sea around Iceland, there are many different species of whales, some of which can be eaten, some not.

More interesting in the King's Mirror, however, are the sections on the king's court and the king's responsibilities. It is the king's obligation to judge fairly, and even to pronounce capital sentences. This is actually an act of love, because it is better for the law-breaker to feel pain for a short moment when executed that to be tortured for his crime for eternity in hell. *Crimen lese majestatis*, high treason against a king, is discussed with lengthy references to King Saul and King David in the Old Testament. One conclusion is that men must always obey their kings no matter what they think about their decisions. The other main conclusion is that kings can lose their right to live only if they are acting against the command of God. The King's Mirror is a strong defence of the king's possession of absolute authority – which he of course should use with justice and fairness and to protect the people.

The king's court is filled with his men, according to King's Mirror. They have different functions and titles and receive different salaries or economic gifts. The text gives an impression of a relatively complex royal administration with a high degree of specialisation and division of responsibilities. It also very much stresses that some men are great in their localities because of their family background and their wealth but are among the lower ones at the king's court. Others are poor or despised in the area they come from but can rise to the highest position at court because of their skills, and because family background counts for nothing in the king's eyes. We gain an impression of a crumbling of the traditional ordering of society and its replacement by the king's firm control.

The discussion in the King's Mirror is not only a utopian dream but reflected actual changes in Norwegian society which become clear from King Magnus the Law-Mender's national law-code (*landslov*) of 1274. Unlike earlier Norwegian laws, this was not a regional law but covered the entire realm of the Norwegian king. It was a ground-breaking act, the first national law in Scandinavia and among the first ones in all of Europe. The law stressed that there can only be one king *ifir noregs vælldi* (over the Norwegian dominion) or over the entirety of Norway including the Faroe Islands, the Hebrides, and Iceland. The law also contained the text of the people's oaths of fidelity to the king. Dukes and barons must swear to support him faithfully with 'deeds and advice' – again a common European formulation. Representatives of the peasants should swear on behalf of the entire population to follow the laws and obey the king. King Magnus and his successors, solemnly promise to adhere to the laws and taxes from the time of Saint Olaf, parallel to the contemporary Danish constitution that claimed to return to the laws of King Valdemar.

In all Scandinavian kingdoms, the latter half of the 13th century was a period of targeted attempts to define royal authority. The kings attempted to ensure for themselves the roles of promulgators of laws and guarantees of justice and to make the office of king hereditary. Strong measures were taken against *crimen lese majestatis*, high treason against the kings, in order to enhance royal authority and reduce the risk of civil wars. In all three countries, the kings attempted to redefine the role of the magnates, changing them from local political agents with strong authority and power to servants within the kings' administration. This they achieved with more or sometimes less success, as the killing of King Eric of Denmark in 1286 illustrates.

Inter-Scandinavian Marriages and Raids

Kings and aristocrats were closely connected throughout Scandinavia. Politics in one country influenced the others, and individuals could often gain help from or flee to one of the other kingdoms. In a very short time, alliances could change and lands be raided.

In 1254 and again in 1258, the Danish and Norwegian kings met with Birger Jarl of Sweden at River Göta, the river marking the traditional border between Norway and the Danish duchy of Halland. King Haakon IV of Norway wanted to take over control of Halland as a pledge for claims he had in Denmark. King Eric IV Ploughpenny of Denmark refused and was supported by Birger Jarl, who probably tried to maintain a balance between his two neighbours, supporting the weakest to prevent the other becoming too strong. Birger Jarl's daughter Rikissa had been married in 1251 to the son of King Haakon IV, and in 1260, his son Valdemar was married to Sofia, sharp-tongued and chess-playing daughter of King Eric IV of Denmark. An important result of the negotiations in the 1250s was in fact that Birger obtained land around the mouth of River Göta, and Sweden thereby access to the coast and the sea in the west. This later became of great economic and military strategic importance.

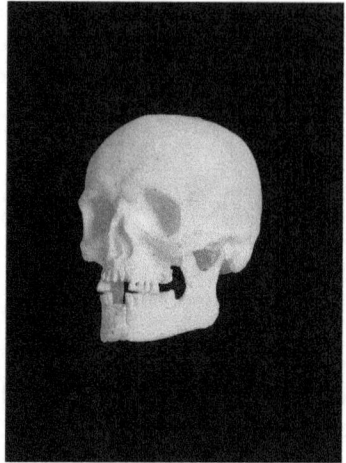

Illustration 5.3 Birger Jarl of Sweden († 1266), crusader, kingmaker, warrior, and diplomat. Medieval chronicles claimed that he founded Stockholm, though modern archaeologists dispute this – the town was already in existence earlier. However, Birger Jarl was strongly influential in directing Swedish perspectives towards the Baltic and in furthering new infrastructure for the rapidly increasing Swedish industry, especially within iron production.

Based on his skull, a reconstruction of the face of Birger Jarl was made in the early 21st century, showing a face full of expression and emotion. It is very different from the 13th-century depiction of him from his burial place in the Varnhem monastery, which is dignified with long and carefully arranged hair and ducal crown.

Reconstruction Oscar Nilsson. Photo skull and reconstruction Medeltidsmuseet, Stockholm. Published with the permission of Medeltidsmuseet. Varnhem sculpture: Photo Axel Forssén, c 1920, Public Domain.

King Eric IV Ploughpenny's two daughters, Agnes and Jutta, who had been put into a nunnery in Roskilde, fled from there in 1271 to Sweden, to their sister Queen Sofia. This was an unfortunate move, since King Valdemar Birgersson was a well-known womaniser and 'came too close' to the very beautiful Jutta, who bore him a child next year. In the eyes of the Church, he was guilty not only of the sin of adultery but also of that of incest, because he had had sex with his wife's sister, and Valdemar had to travel to Rome to seek absolution from the pope. Meanwhile, his brothers rebelled against him with the help of the Danish king, in the form of a large army of mounted knights who defeated Valdemar Birgersson's army in battle in 1275, and he fled to Norway.

Since King Magnus the Law-mender was also married to one of King Eric Ploughpenny's daughters, both the Norwegian and Swedish kings had inheritance claims on land in Denmark through their Danish wives, and tried by raids and political pressure to obtain it, or at least compensation. Things became much worse after the assassination of King Eric Klipping in 1286. In the following year, nine of the King's most trusted men were found guilty of the crime and sentenced to outlawry and confiscation of all possessions, including Marshal Stig Andersen of the mighty Hvide family. Those outlawed had already fled to Norway where they were welcomed by King Haakon V Magnussen (r. 1299–1319). In the following years, Marshal Stig and his accomplices raided Danish waters together with King Haakon, burned down royal castles, and even established a fortress on an island near the town of Århus, where they struck false coins to make money and de-stabilise the Danish economy.

After heavy losses on both sides, the war between Denmark and Norway ended with a peace agreement in 1295. By that time, some of King Eric's murderers had been caught and executed publicly, and cruelly, and the Danish king was occupied with a major new conflict with the archbishop of Lund, who was closely related to the most important outlaws. Modern historians have claimed that those convicted were actually not the guilty ones, because they did not gain from the killing of a king. In reality, we do not know. There may have been connections and conflicts of which we are unaware today, prompting a group of the highest nobles to this 'crime against the majesty'. In any case, the events illustrate how interwoven Scandinavian politics was around 1300, and how closely connected kings and nobles were across borders. King Haakon of Norway helped a group of outlawed, probable regicides, which may explain why the Italian poet Dante in his Divine Comedy (c. 1320) claimed that on the day of Judgement King Haakon will be condemned for his misdeeds.

Models for Governance

According to the earlier presented model of division of state formation process into four periods, the years between c. 1200 and c. 1450 formed the period of administrative states. This definition fits well to the political development and state formation in the Scandinavian kingdoms. While the three Scandinavian kingdoms were formed between 900 and 1200, the period from c. 1200 to 1400 was marked by an increased concentration of power in the hands of the institutions of kingship, although not necessarily in those of individual kings. Some rulers became immensely powerful while otherwise lost everything, in Scandinavia as in western Europe more broadly. The period was also central for the professionalisation and growth of state administration and bureaucratisation. Internationally, the papacy took the lead, and the issuing of papal letters grew exponentially under Pope Innocent III (r. 1198–1216) and his successors. In the papacy's footsteps, France, England, and the Holy Roman Empire created bureaucratic offices, chancelleries, new laws, and accountancy procedures, and Scandinavian rulers followed their example.

State administration in the Scandinavian countries was in principle the same as everywhere else, although there were some differences according to the time and place. Scandinavian state administration and its development reflect contemporary European discussions on the legitimacy of power and tried to balance hierarchy with inclusion. Administrative hierarchy was particularly manifested in the way that rulers described their authority as given from above, delegated by God. This gave them authority to act and govern above others, at the hierarchy's summit. At the same time, a ruler could not govern alone but had to include his supporters in the administration. State administration through the ruler's supporters also took place hierarchically. His closest collaborators and most powerful adherents were immediately below him in the hierarchy, while the positions at the lower local level were reserved for less powerful supporters. This hierarchical model of state administration was similar in the Scandinavian countries, running top to bottom from the king, the council of the realm, and the regional administration to the local administration.

Scandinavian ideas about kingship drew heavily on Old Testament descriptions of the king as the Lord's anointed and the instrument of the Lord. Danish King Niels was the first we know to state that he ruled as *rex Dei gratia* (king by the grace of God) in letters from the period of his rulership (1104–1134). The first Swedish example was that of King Canute Ericsson who styled himself 'king by the grace of God' in a series of letters beginning 1167, the first Norwegian King to do so was Magnus Erlingsson in his privilege to the Norwegian Church 1163–1177. The *Dei gratia* formula had already been used by bishops in Scandinavia before and was clearly intended by the kings to stress the sacral nature of kingship. It was soon also used by Scandinavian queens, dukes, and counts.

Coronation and primogeniture, the practice that the king's eldest son inherited the throne, were also combined in the 12th century. This happened in Norway in 1163–1164, when Magnus Erlingsson was crowned and had a law passed on royal succession, and in Denmark in 1170, when King Valdemar I had his young son and heir crowned, and the magnates swear loyalty to him. The first Swedish king to be crowned was Eric Knutson in 1210 (r. 1208–1216), but primogeniture was not introduced as a general rule in Sweden in the Middle Ages.

Coronation, primogeniture, and the title of *Dei gratia* were means to lift kingship to a higher level and separate the king from others, but in practice were balanced by the kings' need to include allies. Before the introduction of primogeniture, all sons of the king had possessed equally strong rights to succession, and therefore the 11th and 12th centuries were characterised by wars for royal power between close family members. The latter allied with strong magnates, and the many so-called civil wars can also be understood as wars between various networks, each with their own kingly candidate. Sometimes, the conflicts reflected older regional differences whereby some wanted a king from Jutland, others from Funen, others again from Götaland, Svealand, and so on.

Even when kings pressed hard for primogeniture, however, before battles they could appeal to magnates as all being their equals and comrades, fighting for the same cause. Sometimes, the kings would call a general meeting of the realm with representatives from a very broad swathe of society, to gain support for important decisions. This happened at royal coronations, but also for example when King Valdemar II promulgated the important law of Jutland in 1241.

Power relations between the ruler and the nobility were not always easy, especially in the earlier medieval centuries when royal power was less defined and secure. Scandinavian kings strove for better control over the nobility and the big ecclesiastical landowners; one means was via open confrontation, another the more subtle building up of an administration dependent more upon the king than local circles. By the 13th century, Scandinavian kings had noticed that the second route was more advantageous, and they began to assemble around them a group of close collaborators. This was done by creating new administrative positions. These officials had titles such as marshals, seneschals, or drosts. Some already existed in the 12th century, but most were institutionalised only in the following century.

The formal counterweight to the king's power was the group of *meliores regni* (The best men of the realm) which developed into the more formal council of the realm including both lay magnates and bishops. In the 12th century, these best men were a loosely defined and small group of the most powerful individuals and representatives of the big families, appointed by the king. They met when the king summoned them to discuss political matters, for example wars outside the kingdom, new taxes, or to constitute a high court for cases that had been appealed to the king or involving the high nobility.

The councils of the realm became a more formal administrative body during the 13th–14th centuries. Such a body is mentioned for the first time in Denmark in 1320, in King Christopher's coronation constitution, and in Norway around the same time as the designation of the group governing during Magnus Ericsson's minority. In Sweden, the title council of the realm was used already in the late 13th century, but became formally defined in Magnus Ericsson's national law-code (*landslag*) from c. 1350. The law stipulated that the king had to appoint as members of the council the archbishop, as many bishops as he wanted, and a maximum of 12 knights. No foreigners, only Swedes, could be appointed. In practice, the number of knights was often greater than 12, and royal favourites from outside Sweden did sometimes become Council members. As in Sweden, the councils of the realm in Denmark and Norway also had strong ecclesiastical representation, but we know of no limitation to the number of members; in practice, they normally seem to have been had around 30–40.

The councils were to govern the country together with the king but could act alone in periods of interregnum or if the king was a minor and still too young to take decisions. The kings sometimes tried to restrict the power of the councils by simply not summoning them, or by not appointing new members when old ones died.

After 1397, during the Kalmar Union, there was only one union king, but the three councils of the realms in Denmark, Norway, and Sweden continued to exist as separate units and were responsible for their respective countries, often in exemplary cooperation. They were at the height of their power when they were able to depose the Union King Eric of Pomerania in 1439–1442, and during the troubled times from 1450 until the Lutheran Reformation the Swedish council of the realm in practice governed Sweden alone for long periods, together with a regent, but without the union king having any influence whatsoever.

Daily royal administration in the Scandinavian countries was run by officials living at the court of the king and travelling around with him, or sometimes dwelling in their own manors somewhere in the country. The top offices were the highest military commander, responsible also for taxation and financing, and the chancellor, responsible for keeping archives and correctly formulating official charters and laws. The Danish chancellor was normally the bishop of Roskilde, the Swedish one the bishop of Strängnäs, and in Norway from 1314 it was the provost of Saint Mary's church in Oslo.

Everyday administration of the realm was in the hands of the king's men, who had sworn him an oath of personal loyalty. From c. 1200 at the latest, the king's men consisted of two groups. One consisted of the elite warriors of the royal guard, who lived with the king and functioned as bodyguards but also living demonstrations of how brutal royal power could be, if necessary. The other and larger group included men stationed around the country to ensure control and the paying of tax. Some ran the royal farms, some controlled castles, and some were royal representatives in the towns. They were essential for overseeing administration at the local level. These individuals made royal power work in practice, often without any direct contact with the king. They could for example be judges, or experts in local law, following customary traditions which ensured that the laws promulgated by kings were followed. They could also be local bailiffs practically executing the orders of the king's men.

The 13th century was a period when European kings began to be more interested in administration, especially in administering their property and income. One of the results was the registering of the regular royal income, which can be understood as another means to strengthen royal control. The Danish *King Valdemar's Cadastre*, from around 1231, is a very early example of the registering of royal incomes even in a European perspective. County by county, it lists what the king can demand of income in kind or services, and island by island what the king can hunt there. It contains numerous other fiscal information, although it has only been partially preserved. Such a register is a novelty for Scandinavia and we do not know its background. However, King Valdemar II, the ruler behind the registration, may have gotten the idea from his brother-in-law, King Afonso II of Portugal, who had begun to register his income in exactly in the same way in the 1220s. The registers of the Portuguese and Danish kings were the first systematic accounts of royal income since the Doomsday Book in England in 1085 but became an administrative praxis soon adopted by other rulers all over Europe. From Norway and Sweden, similar royal accounts have been preserved only from the end of the Middle Ages, but such registers probably existed earlier. A testimony of such a practice can indeed be found in the saga of King Sverre. According to this, King Sverre had ordered a registration of all he had acquired on the Orkney Islands after one of his successful wars in 1195; and the Norwegian *Hirdskråa* from the same period instituted the royal chancellor's keeping a register of all goods that the king bought or acquired in other ways.

Alongside the registration of royal income there grew up the administration, preservation, and registration of important documents, requiring a system for keeping them safely and in good order – that is, the creation of an archive. Royal documentation from earlier times has largely disappeared due to fires and other calamities. One of the reasons for the archival losses was that the royal archives followed the king on his unending travels around the realm. One can almost say that the royal archive was kept in the saddle bags. From the 13th century onwards, as administration grew the archives became more organised and professional, and important documents began to be stored centrally in royal strongholds. That practice continued throughout and beyond the Middle Ages.

The administrative hierarchy was in principle the same in Denmark, Norway, and Sweden, but in Iceland, Greenland, and Gotland, the situation was different. The latter had all coped without kings until the second half of the 13th century. The situation in Greenland is not well known, and the local leaders of the two settlements in the east and west may have held very great power. In Iceland and Gotland, decisions were taken at common meetings by a group of magnates who in principle were equals. Authority was less centralised and less permanently rooted in institutions, for good and ill. The less economic surplus was channelled towards the centre, instead of staying at the local level. On the other hand, the exercise of power had many different and competing centres. If the economy was good, as on Gotland, the society thrived and, for example, invested massively in church-building and trade. If the economy was more fragile, as in Iceland, it could lead to endless feuds and petty wars that lasted for generations.

Legal Development

The 13th and 14th centuries were a period of the writing down of laws, and of rulers attempting to gain control over them, as the lawgivers and guarantors of correct legal procedures. The laws promulgated in this period remained in force for hundreds of years after the Middle Ages and have had a significant influence on the content and understanding of modern laws in Scandinavia.

The Middle Ages, especially from the 12th century onwards, was a time of fundamental changes in the field of law in Europe, and Scandinavia closely followed this trend. This need for change was driven by two important developments in the high Middle Ages: the birth of the universities and thereby of the study of laws and the birth of kingdoms requiring legislation that would apply to everyone.

The first universities were established during the 12th century, and especially from the beginning of the 13th century onwards they gave an important jolt to the development of jurisprudence. Law – Roman law and canon law – was one of the topics taught and studied at the universities, of which the University of Bologna was the most famous. From the 14th century onwards, the University of Prague was also a highly recognised venue for scholars wanting to receive higher education in the field of law.

As a consequence of the teaching of law at universities, its teachers soon realised that older legal regulations were often contradictory, especially regarding ecclesiastical norms; moreover, it was difficult to gain an overview of the norms because they were not collected together but had to be sought from disparate sources. Therefore, legal scholars began to gather the regulations from different places and compile them into general legal collections. One of these was the compilation of canon law regulations created by Gratian in the mid-12th century, known as the *Decretum*.

University teaching also brought to legal scholarship the urge to systematise, order, understand, and explain the content and meaning of the law regulations so that a single common understanding of law in West Europe would become possible. This was important not only regarding canon law but also Roman law, which formed the basis of legal practices in many European countries. It led to the scholarly legal commentary and explanation of the two most important law collections of the Middle Ages: *Corpus Iuris Canonici* (the Corpus of canon law) for ecclesiastical legislation and *Corpus Iuris Civilis* (the Corpus of civil law) for Roman civil legislation.

Alongside the scientific development of law in the 12th and 13th centuries, numerous states began to emerge in Europe, causing a further great need for legal regulations. With the new states came the development of stronger centralised power in the hands of the rulers, who also began to be considered the ultimate judges and to whom it was possible to appeal against a local court or judge's unsatisfying sentence. With the birth of more clearly defined kingdoms, it became important to treat all citizens equally when it came to crimes and punishments. Earlier legislation and applications of local legal customs could vary widely between different parts of a country, and the idea behind a strong royal power was to unify both the law and legal practices, or process, inside the realm. The unifying of legal process was a novelty of the 12th and especially 13th centuries. The Catholic Church had made a decision in 1215 at the Fourth Lateran Council to abolish arbitrary sentences and sentences based on trial by ordeal. Trial by ordeal was an old judicial practice for determining the accused's guilt or innocence by subjecting them to a painful or dangerous experience, such as trial by fire or water. In the trial by water, the accused was submerged in water three times and considered innocent if they sank, and guilty if they floated, while in the trial of fire, the accused had to carry a glowing hot iron for a certain time or number of steps, and if their injuries were healed after a defined time, they were considered innocent. There were also several other ways to carry out the trial by ordeal. The idea behind these trials, also called the 'judgement of God', was that God would help the accused if the person was innocent and perform a miracle on his or her behalf.

To replace the trial of ordeal, the Church developed a sophisticated judicial system based on summoning the accused person before a judge and giving them the opportunity to prove their innocence. The ecclesiastical courts acted according to a clearly defined procedure, interrogating witnesses and using written evidence when trying to establish the accused's guilt or non-guilt. The new legal principle of fair trial was soon also adapted by the civil courts, and the rulers were keen to support its use because it increased the influence of courts and thereby the royal power as the ultimate judge in the realm. The new procedure also diminished the old culture of revenge and feuds between families or clans, setting the royal power above theirs.

Lastly, the secular laws were important for defining the boundaries between ecclesiastical and civil jurisdictions, which had earlier been unclear. At this point, civil jurisdiction applied many principles taken from ecclesiastical law but at the same time set clear borders as to what kinds of cases belonged to the ecclesiastical jurisdiction and what kinds to the civil. In many countries, these negotiations between the Church and State were not easy, causing problems between the civil rulers and ecclesiastical leaders that sometimes lasted for generations.

During the 12th and 13th centuries, many new states emerged in Europe, and their rulers began to stipulate laws for their realms. One of the earliest was *Sachsenspiegel* (the Saxon Mirror), a collection of customary laws compiled in Middle Low German between 1220 and 1235 for the territory of the German Empire. Similarly, King Alfonso X the Wise (r. 1252–1284) stipulated a law-code for the Kingdom of Castile and Leon in the 1250s, called the *Siete Partidas* (the Seven Part Code).

From Oral to Written, from Provincial to National Laws

Scandinavian rulers had close contacts with other European rulers, and news of legislative novelties in other countries also reached the Scandinavian countries relatively quickly, leading even in the north to the same kind of developments. When we look at Scandinavia, we can see an early phase with regional norms based on oral tradition, which developed into written regional legislation and finally into national legislation. The changes between the phases happened in all Scandinavian countries but at different times.

Medieval Norway was divided into four regions: Gulating in the west and south, Frostating in the north, Eidsivating in the centre and east, and Borgarting in the south-east (including also parts of the present-day western Swedish coastline). Later sources indicate that each of these four regions had its own legal customs or regional laws, but not all of these have survived in their full form to the present day. The law of Gulating is considered the oldest of Norwegian provincial laws, because Snorri Sturluson attributes it in his *Heimskringla* to King Haakon I the Good (r. 933–961), although this information is not necessarily true, and its first written versions are from the 12th century. There is less preserved information about the law of Frostating. Snorri Sturluson attributes also this law to King Haakon I, but he is apparently wrong. Legal scholars date the law as being a little younger than the law of Gulating, with it taking longer to be written down. The law of Frostating was also officially recognised for use in the regional assembly, but we do not know when this happened. There is even less information about the laws of Eidsivarting and Borgating. It has been surmised that these regions must also have had their own laws, but no written evidence for them now exists. In the period of regional laws, the two central Norwegian towns, Nidaros and Bergen, followed their own town laws, which are called *Bjarkøyretten* and date to the 12th/13th centuries. Each of the regional and town laws included a section called *Kristenrett* (Christian law), which consisted of regulations relating to the Christian religion and local church. The *Kristenrett* did not replace the canon law regulations but it defined the border between civil and ecclesiastical jurisdiction. The Christian law sections in different regional laws were not totally identical but reflect regional variation. Traditionally, the creation of the *Kristenrett* is attributed to the Saint King Olaf Haraldsson, but without concrete evidence.

The regional laws were in use in Norway until the late 13th century, when in 1274 King Magnus VI, the Law-mender ordered the collection of all the old Norwegian laws into a national law-code (*landslov*), valid for the whole Norwegian realm. In a European perspective, this is a very early example of a common law for an entire kingdom. His law did not come into force immediately, but each of the four regions discussed it in their regional assembly and made an official decision to begin applying it alongside regional law. The national law thus came into use during the 1270s. At the same time as King Magnus renewed the national law, he also stipulated a new law for the Norwegian towns. This quite closely followed the principles of the new national law but also had some features from the old town law of Nidaros. The new town law was brought into use from 1276 onwards in at least Bergen, Nidaros, Oslo, and Tønsberg. Just as the regional laws had required a Christian section, so did the new national one. This new Christian law was drafted by Archbishop Jon Raude of Nidaros, and King Magnus VI accepted it in 1277 together with the signing of the so-called Tønsberg Concordat with its far-reaching privileges for the Church. The national law-code of King Magnus VI was in use until 1687 when it was replaced by a new law.

The laws of Iceland are closely connected to the Norwegian ones. Icelanders adopted the Norwegian tradition of a regional assembly, deciding upon the significant matters concerning the region. The Icelandic regional assembly, the *althing* covered

146   1200–1400: *Consolidation and Restructuring*

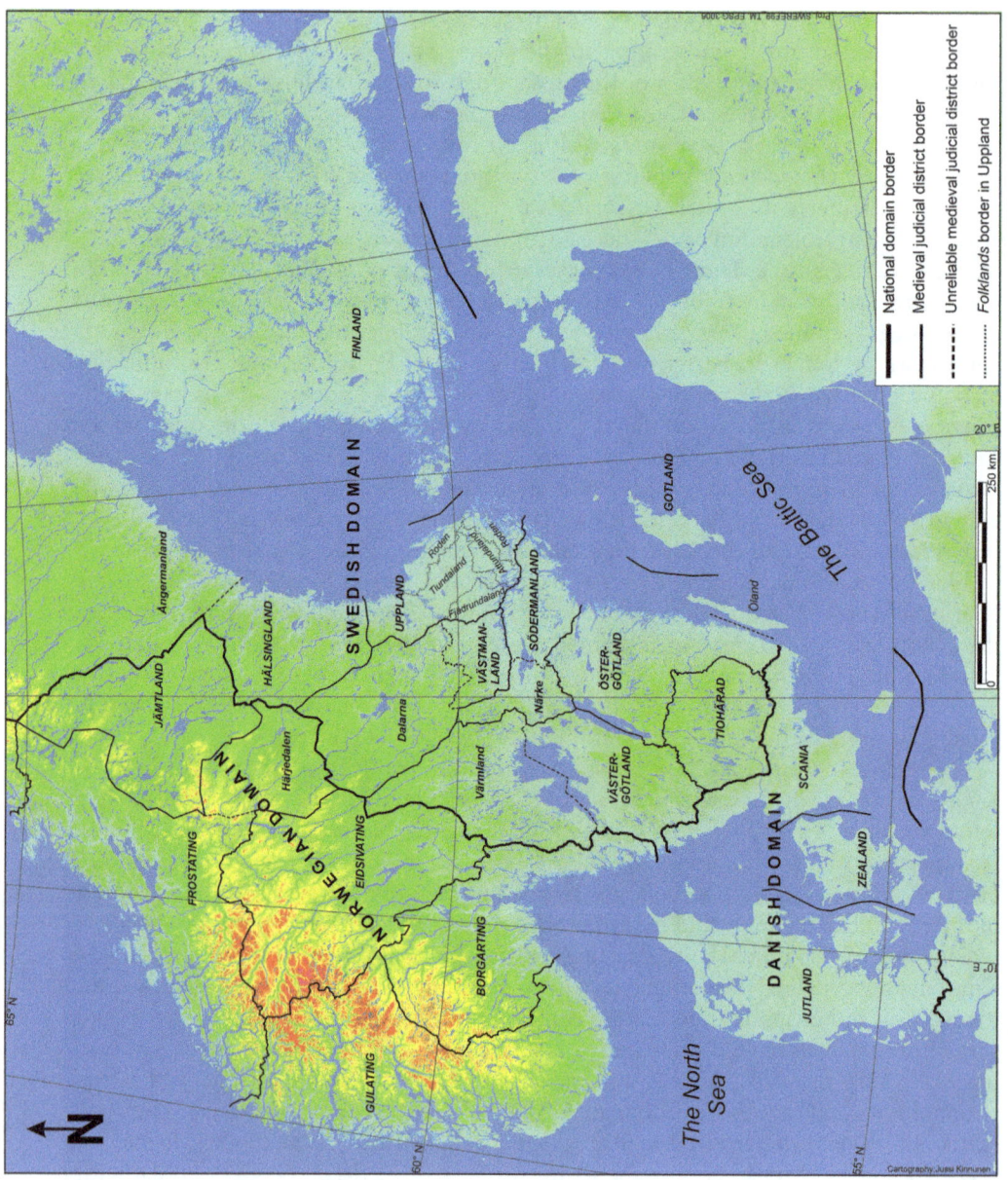

Map 5 The juridical districts in medieval Scandinavia.
Map © Jussi Kinnunen, 2022.

the whole island. It was founded in 930 and assembled outdoors at a place called Þingvellir (Thing fields), around 45 km east of Iceland's present-day capital Reykjavik. In Iceland, the free men gathered at the *althing* and dispensed justice through a law-speaker. There is no contemporary evidence for the early laws in Iceland, but later sagas recount that the first Icelandic law, called the law of Úlfljótr, was based on the law of Gulating. It was compiled by the Icelandic law-speaker Úlfljótr who had been sent to Norway to study law around 927–930. The law would have been valid for the whole island. After Iceland became Christian at the turn of the 10th–11th centuries, the law of Úlfljótr needed to be updated, and a new version of Icelandic law, the *Hafliðaskrá*, was compiled by law-speaker Hafliði Másson in 1117. We have no information about its content, but it is assumed that it functioned as a model for the 13th-century Icelandic laws included in the collection called *Grágás* (Gray Goose Laws). These laws were in use at least until the 1260s when Norwegians took over the island's administration and introduced Norwegian laws.

Medieval Denmark was divided into three regions that had their own regional legislation and assemblies (*ting*) where legal and administrative issues were handled. The Danish regions were Scania (including Halland, Blekinge, and Bornholm) in the east, Zealand (including the islands of Lolland and Falster) in the centre, and Jutland together with the island of Funen in the west.

The earliest known legal texts from Denmark are the Christian laws of Scania and Zealand from the 1170s which had been stipulated by the bishops of Lund and Roskilde. These laws were important because for the first time they regulated the legal borders between the ecclesiastical and secular administrations. The written Christian laws also functioned as models for the secular ones which were codified some decades later. There were additionally some relatively early royal ordinances in which the Danish kings tried to regulate certain important legal issues, such as the *Ordinance on manslaughter* (*Manddrabsforordning*) issued by King Canute VI in 1200 or King Valdemar II the Victorious' post-1215 ordinance for abolishing the use of the trial by ordeal of carrying hot iron. We know that these regulations came into use in Scania, but it has been argued that they might have been intended for the whole Danish realm.

In the 13th century, the Danish legal system still functioned at the regional level, and each region had its own laws. The oldest regional law in Denmark was the law of Scania (*Skånske Lov*) codified between 1202 and 1215, and the regional assembly in Lund accepted it for use in the region. The law of Zealand followed the same pattern as that of Scania. A first version of the law was codified in the 1220s and was amended after 1241. The law of Zealand was supplemented again, around 1248, during the reign of King Eric IV. The third law district of Jutland and Funen was the last to receive such a codified law, promulgated by King Valdemar II in 1241 and known as the law of Jutland (*Jyske Lov*).

Unlike the other Scandinavian countries, Denmark did not get a national law during the Middle Ages but the regional laws were in use until 1683, when the country gained its first national code of law in the reign of King Christian V (r. 1670–1699). It is however necessary to point out that the law of Jutland may have been considered a kind of national law-code, and its regulations were in use in the two other regions alongside their own local legislation.

As in other Scandinavian countries, the king could also grant Danish towns the privilege of using a special town law instead of the regional legislation. There are clear differences among the Danish town laws. On Zealand, they were all relatively short and followed the model of the law of Roskilde. The law of Copenhagen was the only exception. The same pattern was also adapted in towns situated in northern Jutland. The town laws in the southern parts of Jutland show much more German influence and were longer and more detailed, especially concerning criminal legislation. In Scania, the towns usually followed the Norwegian and Swedish traditions.

Medieval Sweden was divided into a number of legally independent regions with their own regional laws, which are divisible into two main groups: the laws of Götaland (for the west and south) and the laws of Svealand (for the east and north). To the Svealand group belonged the laws of the following regions: Uppland, Västmanland, Södermanland, Hälsingland, and Dalarna. Svealand also included the regions of Närke and Värmland but no legal collections from these regions have survived to the present day. To the Götaland group belonged the laws of Västergötland (both the older and newer version of the law), Småland, Östergötland, and the island of Gotland.

It has not been possible to estimate the age of these laws, but the codification of Swedish regional laws has been dated to the 13th and 14th centuries. The oldest of the Swedish regional laws is the older law of Västergötland, of which there are manuscripts from the mid-13th century. A little later is the younger law of Västergötland, the law of Uppland, and the law of Gotland, which were written down in the late 13th century. According to the surviving medieval manuscripts, the other Swedish regional laws seem to be a little later still, dating to the early 14th century. The Swedish regional laws were valid only in the region in question, and only two of them, the laws of Uppland and of Södermanland, were confirmed by the Swedish king. Finland, which was included to the Swedish realm from the mid-12th century onwards, followed the law of Hälsingland and the Kyrkobalk from the law of Uppland.

Regional laws were valid in the countryside, but the Swedish towns could receive from the ruler the privilege of using town law. The Swedish town laws at the time were called *Bjärköarätten*, and it is known that Stockholm already had its town law at the end of the 13th century. Visby on the island of Gotland also had its own town law in the 14th century, but there the German influence was much stronger than on the Swedish mainland.

Sweden received its first nationally valid royal ordinances at the latest in the mid-13th century. These laws, so-called oath swearing laws (*Edsöre*), particularly concerned serious crimes of violence, such as towards women, committed in the house of the victim, or towards people on their way to the regional assembly, court, or church. The name oath swearing comes from the fact that the aristocrats took an oath to the king and promised to defend the general peace in the country. These laws were uniformly valid in all the regions and breaking them made the guilty person an outlaw throughout the Swedish realm.

Due to the derivation of Swedish laws from two different families of law, those of Götaland and of Svealand, the legal culture and punishments for different crimes varied greatly within the Swedish realm. When royal power had become strong enough and the kings could fully control the whole Swedish area, it was possible to begin to unify the jurisdiction. This took place during the reign of King Magnus Ericsson (r. (1319) 1331/1332–1363), who around 1350 promulgated a national law-code (*landslag*). The law was not applied immediately in the whole country but was accepted one-by-one by the regional assemblies and applied gradually, first alongside the regional laws. The first evidence of the use of the new law in Sweden is from 1352 when it was employed in Västmanland and Östergötland, and in the following year, it was

Illustration 5.4 Punishments in medieval Scandinavia could be severe, because they were firmly believed to deter others from committing crimes. Magnus Ericsson's national law-code from c. 1350 is divided into sections according to different crimes. The one on theft opens with a picture of a hanged man and two inscriptions, in Old Swedish: 'Aga bondens barn i tid, då kommer det ej hit' and the other 'Han levde utan aga, därför har han denna plåga' ('Chastise the children of peasants from early on, so they do not end here', and the other, 'He lived without discipline, therefore he ended in this trouble'.)
Ms B68, fol. 141r, Uppsala University Library, manuscript from c. 1450, public domain.

applied in Dalarna, Uppland, and Södermanland. However, the new law's full application was a slow process because documents from the 1430s show that Hälsingland operated still mainly according to the regional law. Magnus Ericsson's law was updated in 1442 by the Union King Christopher of Bavaria (ruled Sweden 1441–1448), but the Swedes never fully accept the new version. In Finland, instead, the law of King Christopher was adopted, and in the 16th century, it was even translated into Finnish.

Magnus Ericsson had a new town law formulated, based on the text of the national law, which towns possessing town privileges could use. The law is usually dated to the 1350s, but it is not totally clear when and where it was applied for the first time. The law was apparently meant in the first place for Stockholm, but was soon also given to other towns; for example in 1365 the Finnish town Ulvila was granted the right to use the 'recently promulgated' town law of Sweden. The medieval town law was in use far into the early modern period, and in 1618 King Gustav II Adolf (r. 1611–1632) confirmed it and let it be printed. The laws of Magnus Ericsson did not include a Christian section, meaning that the national laws were supplemented with the Christian law of the regional law of Uppland.

Issues Regulated by Law

The content of the various Scandinavian laws differed quite a lot between one country and another and also between the countryside and the towns, while the earlier regional laws also differed from the later laws of the entire realms. Moreover, Scandinavian law books differed in their structure. Swedish, Norwegian, and Icelandic laws are divided internally into various sections (*balk*) dealing with one specific legal question, while the Danish laws proceed paragraph by paragraph from one matter to another. The Scandinavian laws follow the common medieval tradition that the paragraphs are very descriptive and always refer to a specific case or events; for example the law of Jutland contains a paragraph about 'if a man fells a tree in another man's forest' and the Swedish legislation has a paragraph about 'if a man throws a stone over a house and hits someone'. This form of presenting regulations is called casuistic, proceeding by concrete cases.

Because of the great differences between the various Scandinavian laws, it would be too big a task to give a detailed analysis of their content. Therefore, the description here takes into account only the most significant features that Scandinavian laws had in common.

One of the important points was the power relation between the ruler and the people. What were the obligations and privileges of the ruler and how could he use his power? The laws also clearly defined the punishments for those who did not obey the ruler. In all Scandinavian countries, the relationship between ecclesiastical and civil jurisdiction was also to some extent defined. In many European countries, these matters were not included in the civil legislation, but a separate ecclesiastical code of law was promulgated and used together with the civil law.

Another important issue defined in all Scandinavian laws was the right to property and especially questions of inheritance. Inheritance issues are sometimes intertwined with the marital because in Scandinavian thinking, marriage was a transaction of property between one family and another: the bride brought property to her new family from her old one, in the form of the dowry, and the groom donated some property to his wife in the form of the morning gift. Since most of the Scandinavian population with anything to leave to their children belonged to the category of small landowners, it was very important to define the right to property in law. Additionally, Scandinavian laws had stipulations about the marriage itself and the gifts the spouses were supposed to exchange.

Since Scandinavian society was largely agricultural, the laws contain sections defining life in the countryside: how and where houses should be built, and who had to take care of the common roads, mills, or bridges. The town laws in particular also pronounced on other professions, and on commerce. This did not concern only selling or buying but also when, where, and to whom people could sell. In Sweden, for example, the right to arrange markets for buying and selling goods was typically given to the towns, and people from the countryside had to travel to a town to sell what they had produced and buy what they needed. A market was allowed to take place in each parish only once a year, on the day of the feast of the patron saint of the parish church. The town laws, for their part, contained detailed regulations about commerce, the use of right measurements, and honest trade.

Scandinavian laws contained also paragraphs concerning the use of justice: when and where the assembly (*thing*) would meet for dispensing justice, who could act as judge, who was supposed to participate, and how the process of accusation and defence was to take place. These regulations varied significantly from one country to another, and in the towns, the legal system functioned much more regularly than in the sparsely populated countryside. In addition to laying down juridical procedure, Scandinavian laws contained a considerable number of regulations regarding what constituted a crime. They varied also in this respect from each other, but the main principles were the same. Scandinavian laws are classed as crimes homicide (distinguishing between murder, manslaughter, and accidental killing, and punishing the first two more severely), violence, theft, cheating, and disturbing others, as well as false accusations or defamation. All accused of such crimes were summoned to the thing and they had to successfully defend themselves to avoid punishment.

The punishments described in the various Scandinavian laws also differed very much, but all recognised the five most important punishments for those found guilty of a crime or offence. The most severe punishment was death, which usually took place by hanging or decapitation. The death penalty was typically reserved in many laws for murderers and heretics but also for those found repeatedly guilty of the same crime, such as stealing. In certain cases, as when the accused was found guilty of sodomy or arson, the death penalty also could be executed by burning or burial alive. Although this sounds horrible to modern people, in the Middle Ages burying alive was considered a 'mild' form of the death penalty, and according to some Swedish laws, women were typically buried alive instead of being hanged because it was not morally proper to leave a female body hanging in the open.

Corporal punishments were very common in the Middle Age. Scandinavian laws included whipping or cutting off parts of the body but varied quite widely in this respect. The Swedish national law stipulated corporal punishment especially for thieves. In normal cases of theft – that is if the thief had not stolen something of excessive value or mutilated the victim – the punishment for the first crime was whipping, or as it was defined in the law the thief was sentenced to the 'loss of skin'. Whipping caused permanent scars, and it was a custom that men and women seeking employment had to show their backs as proof that they had not been punished for stealing. For the second infraction, the punishment was cutting off one ear and for the third the remaining second ear. The fourth sentence was that of death. The thieves were also expelled from towns according to Swedish town law. The town law of Danish Ribe, which followed the German legal tradition, was known to be one of the harshest when it came to corporal punishments, and for example including punishments such as hacking off the hand of a thief.

However, the most common punishments meted out by medieval Scandinavian courts were monetary fines. In many Scandinavian laws, the fine for a smaller crime was three marks, while 40 marks were the fine for a severe crime – a very large sum of money, equivalent to the price of a small farm. The fines were paid to the authorities (king or region) but in some places, as in Sweden, the victim received one third. Despite the fact that the fine was always denominated in marks, it was also possible to pay with other kinds of goods such as foodstuffs. In addition to the fines, the Scandinavian courts often decided that the guilty person had to compensate the victim or their family for the damage – be it economic, physical, or loss of life. In these cases, the amount of compensation depended on the damage. If a person had been killed, the compensation was bigger than in the case of a permanent physical injury or theft.

In the particularly severe crimes, such as murder or lese-majestic, the Scandinavian laws could punish the guilty person with outlawry, which meant that the property of the condemned was confiscated by the king and if anyone caught him (this punishment was reserved only for male criminals) he could be killed without consequences. In practice, this meant that such a person could not be in contact with anyone, and the only solution was often to flee the country. In the times of the regional laws, the outlawry was valid only in the region where the punishment was given, but later throughout the whole realm. The town laws also prescribed the punishment of expulsion from the town, which was typically used in cases of recidivism.

Legal Practice

The medieval Scandinavian thing was more than a modern court of law. In addition to the court sessions, in which a person was judged guilty or not guilty in a criminal case, the medieval Scandinavian things were also legislative bodies and took care of a number of administrative matters such as confirming borders between two farms or regions, or approving economic transactions. Until the establishment of hereditary kingship, the regional things also confirmed the election of a king before the region would recognise his royal authority. From the 13th century onwards, as a consequence of the growing royal power, the political significance of the things began to diminish and the issues handled by them became of a more and more juridical nature.

All the Scandinavian countries were divided into regions that followed the same law. All regions had their own courts. In Norway, these were called *lagting*, in Denmark and Sweden *landsting*, and in Iceland *alting*. In Denmark, there were three *landsting*: in Scania with Lund as its place of assembly, in Zealand with Ringsted, and in Jutland and Funen with Viborg. Each of the regions was further divided into smaller districts called *herred*, amounting to around 200 for the whole Danish realm. The local assemblies took place in *herredsting*. Norway was divided into four *lagting*: Frostating in northern Norway with Logtun in Frosta as the place of assembly, Gulating in the south and west with Gulet, Eidsivating in the middle and eastern parts of Norway, with first Åker in Vang and later Eidsvoll as the places of assembly, and Borgarting in south-eastern area with Borg. The Norwegian law regions were divided into smaller regional entities, called *fylke*. Sweden was divided into *landsting*, which lacked one central place of assembly as in Norway or Denmark: Tiohärad in the south, Västergötland (including Värmland) in the west, Östergötland in the south-east, the island of Gotland, Närke and Västermanland in central Sweden, Södermanland and Uppland on the eastern coast, Dalarna in the north-east, and Hälsingland in north, while Finnish territory was divided into the two law regions of northern and southern Finland, with River Aura as the border. The smaller law regions in Sweden were called *härad* except for northern Sweden, where the word *hundare* was used instead. In Iceland, the main assembly meant for the inhabitants of the whole island was called *althing* and gathered in Þingvellir. In addition to the general assembly, Iceland was divided into four smaller, local law districts that held court sessions every spring.

Regional things and local district things usually differed in the importance of issues brought before them. The regional things were reserved for deciding upon important general issues such as accepting new laws or confirming the election of a new king. With the establishment of the more centralised royal power in the different nation states and the promulgation of national laws in Sweden and Norway, the main judge of the regional thing became a position to which the king appointed a suitable person. In Denmark, he was called *landsdommer* (land judge), in Sweden *lagman*, and in Norway *lagmann* (law man). The position was usually given to a person who was member of the aristocracy, and the appointment did not require any law studies. At the district level, the appointment of judges varied. The Danish *herredsting* were usually preceded by the local bailiff, whose powers increased towards the end of the Middle Ages. In Sweden, instead, the *häradsting* were preceded by an appointed district judge called *häradsdomare*. In Iceland, the local chieftains took care of dispensing justice both in the *althing* and in the local things.

Each town with town privileges had its own courts that functioned more regularly than the infrequent regional assemblies. The hierarchy of the local and regional thing made it possible that a person who was not content with the decision of the local judge could appeal to the regional thing, and ultimately it was possible appeal to the king himself, who as the ultimate judge could have the last word in the case. The use of the ruler as the last resort in a legal case became more common during the later Middle Ages, when the role of the king was strengthened by the national codes of law. During the earlier Middle Ages, by contrast, families had much stronger positions and the uses of violence and vendetta were much more common especially in cases of homicide. There were attempts to replace such practices by the court system during the 12th and especially 13th centuries.

In Sweden and Denmark, all free men could participate in the decision-making at the things, while in Norway and Iceland this right belonged to certain elected representatives. Women, slaves, or children could be present but they had no right to participate in voting or decisions. The thing was predominantly a male place, although women were allowed to participate and even give testimony if necessary. However, women could not function as legal actors at the thing. Scandinavian laws stipulated that men should represent women in most legal cases before the courts – husbands for married women, fathers or guardians for unmarried women, and sons for their widowed mothers. Therefore, legal transactions such as buying or selling are typically described as transactions made by men even if the issue concerned female property. However, this should not be understood to mean that women had no say in matters regarding their property. Many recent studies have demonstrated that although women could not legally sell or buy, they usually played an important role behind such transactions.

1319 – The Year That Everything Changed

It was generally a dull, quiet year for Europe in 1319: the usual fighting between English and Scotsmen, some rebellion and plundering in different countries, but nothing major. The papacy had moved to Avignon and the Teutonic knights to Prussia some ten years earlier, and the Hundred Years war was not to begin for another 20. But in Scandinavia in exactly that year the political situation changed fundamentally. All three kingdoms gained new rulers, the great power of Denmark went bankrupt, and Sweden and Norway were united in a promising but problematic union. A widely-spun political net connected all of their political agents in this time of change, and at its centre sat three women, all called Ingeborg.

The oldest of them was Queen Ingeborg of Denmark, born in the late 1270s, daughter of the Swedish King Magnus Ladulås. Ingeborg Magnusdotter was married to King Eric VI Menved of Denmark in 1296, and in the following 20 years, she bore him perhaps as many as 14 children, all of them dying very shortly after birth, except the last. He was a son and thus a possible heir, but his mother dropped him by mistake from a wagon, the small prince cracked his skull on a stone, and died. Ingeborg entered a monastery and died a year later, in 1319, as did King Eric Menved. The couple had no direct heir, which complicated matters very much.

The second Ingeborg was born in 1297. She was the daughter of the Norwegian King Eric II Magnusson the Priesthater († 1299). In 1312, the young Ingeborg Ericsdotter married Valdemar Magnusson, the Swedish Duke of Finland and brother of the Swedish King Birger and Queen Ingeborg Magnusdotter of Denmark. Ingeborg Ericsdotter died in 1357 after a very active youthful political career in concert with her cousin, the third of the Ingeborgs.

The third Ingeborg was born in 1301. She was the daughter of the Norwegian King Haakon Magnusson, brother to Eric the Priesthater. Her mother was Eufemia of Rügen, one of the Danish border principalities often in open opposition to the Danish king. In 1312 Ingeborg Haakonsdotter was married at the young age of 11 to the Swedish Duke of Södermanland Eric Magnusson, another brother to King Birger of Sweden and the Danish Queen Ingeborg Magnusdotter. She died in 1361 after a relatively long and certainly eventful life.

When the Norwegian Ingeborg Haakonsdotter was just one year old, her father – who had only daughters but no sons – made a very important addition to the Norwegian law of inheritance, stipulating that the throne could also be inherited through the female line. The decision meant that a son of the king's daughter was now nearest in line to the throne than a brother or male cousin of the deceased king. This became decisive to Scandinavian politics for almost the next 50 years, when in 1316 the 15-year-young Ingeborg Haakonsdotter gave birth to the little Magnus Ericsson.

Sweden and Denmark were kingdoms divided against themselves. In Sweden, King Birger Magnussen had been imprisoned by his two brothers in September 1306. He was only released two years later after hard negotiations and in return for humiliating concessions (the so-called *Håtunaleken,* after the royal manor in Håtuna), having to cede control of much of Sweden to Duke Eric and Duke Valdemar. His revenge came and was worth waiting for. Only nine years later, King Birger invited the two brothers to a magnificent banquet at Nyköping castle, on 10 December 1317. After an opulent dinner, Eric and Valdemar were thrown into the castle's dungeon and soon realised what had been prepared for them. They made their testaments and waited, and died slowly of hunger.

King Birger's plan to get rid of his brothers and gain control over Sweden backfired. The reaction was rebellion, and he had to flee to Denmark and seek refuge with King Eric Menved, his brother-in-law. His attempts to raise an army and reconquer Sweden came to nothing. He could not return to his native Sweden, and when he died in 1321 he was laid to rest in the Danish royal burial church of Saint Bendt's in Ringsted, next to his sister and brother-in-law.

In Denmark, King Eric Menved had begun his long reign (r. 1286–1319) by securing his position the hard way: having a group of the highest nobles convicted and outlawed for the murder of his father, and arresting the archbishop of Lund as a possible accomplice. He was successful in these matters, expanding politically in the eastern Baltic and militarily in the western through a series of wars in northern Germany. War was a precarious balancing act at that time. It had become so professionalised that it required effective but expensive mercenaries. When things went well, the conquest or tribute from one of the rich Hansa-towns could cover everything and even yield a respectable surplus. When things went wrong, the ruler had to raise money through loans against solid security. After 1311, King Eric began to lose, trying to finance one defeat after the other with money from the counts of Holstein, pawned against more and more of Denmark. His brother Christopher pretended to cooperate but secretly worked against him to position himself as the next king, because Eric had no sons. When Eric died in 1319 Christopher was ready to succeed him, but at that time almost all of Denmark was pawned away and under the control of the Holstein counts.

Meanwhile, Norwegian Ingeborg Haakonsdotter and Swedish Ingeborg Ericsdotter had been busy. Even before they received the news that their two husbands had been starved to death in Nyköping, in early 1318, they had made a political alliance with Christopher and the arrested Archbishop Esger of Lund. The alliance was directed both against King Eric of Denmark and King Birger of Sweden. Their aim was to pave the way for Ingeborg Haakonsdotter's new-born son Magnus Ericsson. Within the alliance, they engaged one of the great warlords of the time, Knud Porse from Halland, the border area common to all three kingdoms. Ingeborg could make use of his brutal talent for effective killing in warfare, and perhaps the 17-year-old widow was also fascinated by him on a more personal level.

Knud Porse was successful in the wars, and Ingeborg Haakonsdotter realised that she had strong supporters in Danish Scania. A truce was made in late 1318. When two of the kings died and the third went into exile the following year, the small Magnus Ericsson had his momentum. He became king of Norway in May because of his grandfather's lucky change of the heritage law. Two months later he was elected king of Sweden by the council of the realm after Birger had fled to Denmark. Due to his minority, Ingeborg Haakonsdotter became regent and negotiated with the councils of both countries on his behalf.

In 1321, Ingeborg Haakonsdotter made her next important move to secure Scania. She promised to marry her daughter Eufemia to Count Albert II of Mecklenburg. Both were small children, but Albert's father promised to supply Ingeborg with a cavalry force that would help her to conquer Scania. The connection to the strong principality of Mecklenburg was to be renegotiated and reinforced in different configurations for almost the next century and to become an important element of conflict throughout Scandinavia. But as of now, Ingeborg could begin to muster forces from Holstein and other border areas around Denmark to invade Scania in the early 1320s, again with Knud Porse in a central position. Alliances shifted rapidly in these years, and details are complicated, but in 1327, Knud Porse was officially accorded the title of Duke of Halland and the Danish island of Samsø and became the first person outside the Danish royal family ever to become a duke. With this title, it was now possible for Ingeborg to marry him, what she immediately did. She had been waiting for him ten years, and according to rumours the two had already known each other more closely than they ought to. The marriage was short, however. In 1330, Knud Porse died and Ingeborg was a widow again, but now in control of his Danish possessions.

The inhabitants of Scania had a tradition of rebellion and independence stretching back to the late 12th century, and around 1332 they rebelled in a series of bloody wars against the Holsteinians who held the province in pawn. The archbishop of Lund and representatives of the local nobility elected Magnus Ericsson as their new king and in return gained solid privileges. Magnus was now a man of 15 years, but his mother Ingeborg has almost certainly been involved in plotting his take over of among the richest and strategically most important provinces in Scandinavia, in addition to being king of both Norway and Sweden.

Denmark Pawned and Redeemed

Much of Denmark had been pawned away to Holsteinian counts when King Eric Menved died in 1319, and it became even worse. Count Gerhard III of Holstein – Gerhard the Great in the German tradition, Gerhard the Bald in the Danish – became the kingmaker for almost 20 years. He had had a glorious military career in northern Germany, Sweden, and Denmark, when in 1326, he deposed King Christopher and placed on the Danish throne his 11-year-old nephew, also named Valdemar (III) (c. 1314–1364, king 1326–1329), installed himself as regent, and had his young king-nephew enfeoff him with the rich Duchy of Schleswig. At the same time, an official declaration was issued that the Duchy of Schleswig and the Kingdom of Denmark should never be united so that one person ruled over both. In reality, Gerhard and afterwards his cousin divided Denmark between them, in many places with the support of the local aristocrats. In 1340, Gerhard was killed by a petty nobleman, Niels Ebbesen, and the Young Valdemar IV (c. 1320–1375) began a concerted effort to conquer Denmark. He was the son of King Christopher, and since the 19th century, most Danish historians have interpreted the killing of Count Gerhard and Valdemar's wars as a Danish national rising to liberate the fatherland from German occupation. It is complicated, because Danish songs and writings from the period do sometimes contain strong patriotic statements, while at the same time, the majority of the aristocracy seems to have been totally opportunistic, siding with whomever they believed gave the greatest income and freedom. Moreover, the counts of Holstein were so closely connected to the royal Danish dynasty that they actually could stake a legitimate claim to the throne.

Valdemar had support from the imperial German court where he had been brought up, and he married Helvig of Schleswig as part of a peace agreement with Gerhard's heirs. He was elected king, as Valdemar IV, in 1340 and began a military conquest that lasted for 20 years. It took ten years before he had control over most of Jutland and the Danish isles, and another ten before he conquered Scania in 1360 from the Swedish King Magnus Ericsson. In the following year, Valdemar led a major army against Gotland, conquered the strong and immensely rich town of Visby on 27 July 1361, and subdued the entire island under his rule. After the conquest, Valdemar took the title 'King of the Goths', which the Danish kings with great respect for tradition continued to use until 1972, although Danish rule over Gotland lasted only until 1645. In his time Valdemar was a feared ruler. He was called 'the Wolf' by Saint Birgitta of Sweden, and on Gotland, he was known as 'the Dog', his conquest of Visby compared to King Nebuchadnezzar's destruction of Jerusalem in the Old Testament.

Valdemar financed his many wars through confiscation of church silver, direct plunder, and effective taxation, even of the many small watermills. He would not let the water flow out into the sea without having left him some money, a contemporary source explained. In 1346, he sold the Danish possessions in Estonia to the Teutonic knights for the large sum of 19,000 silver marks, a level that must be considered heavily overpriced. It was a good deal for Valdemar. Estonians had rebelled in large numbers against their Danish lords because of their repressive regime, the Swedish King Magnus was drawing ever nearer with large armies, and Valdemar simply did not have the means to keep Estonia. Unknown to Valdemar, the timing was perfect. Only three years later, the Black Death arrived, killing at least a third of the population, and the income from Estonia diminished dramatically. The connection to Estonia was however not totally broken. On parchment at least, King Valdemar's older brother Otto brought Estonia with him as a donation to the Teutonic order when he entered it in 1346. What happened to Otto afterwards is unknown.

Wars with the Hansa, and among the Scandinavian Kingdoms

King Valdemar IV Atterdag cultivated connections with German principalities and the emperor. He participated in several wars in northern Germany, and right from the beginning of his role as ruler, he relied on German vassals. A great number of German knights followed him to Denmark, fought for him, and gained important positions. The advantage of their collaboration for Valdemar was that they were dependent upon him and had no local family loyalties. Many of the later well-known and influential Danish noble families descend from these knights who came to the country with Valdemar in the early 14th century. Valdemar's policy was not unique. It was the time of the *condottieri*, the travelling warrior knights, and German noble families were also introduced to Sweden in the same period. Valdemar himself lived up to the European noble ideal. In 1347, he left for a pilgrimage to Jerusalem, and later he took the *grande tour* of Europe including visits to the papal curia in Avignon in 1364, during which he discussed crusades and liberation of Cyprus from Muslims.

Valdemar inherited enemies and created new ones among those who felt their old privileges endangered after he had gained control over the two of the most important trading nodes in the entire Baltic Sea area, the Scanian market after 1360 and Visby after 1361. These conquests prompted a coalition against Valdemar consisting of the mighty Hansa merchant organisation, Holstein, the Teutonic order, and Sweden and Norway, with the goal of regaining Scania and Gotland for Sweden. After three months of besieging Helsingborg in 1362, the Hansa fleet had to give up and signed a peace treaty, although nobody had great expectations that this would last.

The Hansa was defeated because Valdemar IV was a great war leader, but also because the coalition was deserted by its ally. The son of King Magnus Ericsson of Sweden, Haakon Magnusson, had been elected king of Norway in 1355, and in 1362, Haakon tried with the help of Swedish aristocrats to replace his father as king of Sweden. Under these circumstances, neither Sweden nor Norway contributed troops to the Hansa expedition – on the contrary. In 1363, Haakon changed sides and married

King Valdemar's 11-year-old daughter Margaret. Soon, however, he came back to support his father against Albert III of Mecklenburg, a claimant to the Swedish throne, who was married to Haakon's aunt, King Magnus Ericsson's sister. Albert had been elected as king by the Swedish council of the realm in 1363/1364 and tried to defend his claim by military means. In 1365, he defeated Haakon and Magnus and imprisoned the latter.

The political situation had changed again, and the Hanseatic cities made a new coalition in 1367 in Cologne with the new king of Sweden, northern German princes, and some Danish aristocrats, and began to attack Danish castles along the Sound of Øresund. Albert of Mecklenburg's troops attacked in Scania, and the Holsteinians invaded up in Jutland. After the Hansa had eventually conquered Helsingborg, Valdemar was forced to accept the peace treatise in Stralsund in 1370. It was a major victory for the Hansa cities which had their trading privileges on Gotland and in Scania fully recognised, as well as gained four of the most important Danish castles along Øresund for 15 years and, not least, a substantial income from a toll on ships passing through Øresund. It was also stipulated that the royal council could not elect any king in Denmark without the consent of the Hansa, to ensure that future kings would also recognise their privileges. It must have been a bitter moment for Valdemar, who spent the years 1368–1371 far away from Denmark at the German imperial court and elsewhere, so all negotiations with the Hansa were done by his most trusted officials, first and foremost Drost Henning Podebusk.

Valdemar died in 1375, one year after King Magnus Ericsson of Sweden. Albert III of Mecklenburg had been the king of Sweden since 1364, and his brother's son Albert IV of Mecklenburg now claimed his right to the Danish throne after his mother, Valdemar's oldest daughter Ingeborg. This came to nothing when Valdemar's younger daughter, Margaret, staged a political coup with the help of Henning Podebusk and crowned her son Olaf, whose father was the Norwegian King Haakon. Olaf was then only five years old, and his mother ruled on his behalf; when King Haakon died in 1380, Margaret became regent of both Denmark and Norway. In principle, she ruled on behalf of her son, but in reality, she took power into her own hands and had no intention of ever passing it on to others.

Olaf died in summer 1387, and soon Margaret succeeded in being elected in Denmark and Norway as 'almighty lady and husband and guardian for the whole kingdom'. It is a unique title, created for the occasion and for the person, and as close as a woman could get in the period to becoming king and ruler. Factions among the Swedish nobility used the opportunity to approach Margaret and offer her the Swedish throne. In summer 1388, Danish and Swedish troops began a war against King Albert III who had strong support in Stockholm and among some nobles. The wars were brutal as usual, as becomes apparent in the will made by Margaret more than 20 years later. She donated a substantial sum to compensate the Swedish women whom her soldiers had raped and abused. No male ruler seems ever to have thought about such things.

In February 1389, Albert lost the Battle of Falkenberg, was captured, and kept prisoner until 1395 when he was released in return for a heavy ransom and bequeathing Margaret Stockholm, the important island of Gotland, and of course the Kingdom of Sweden. She had no other children than Olaf, and after his death in 1387, she adopted her sister's grandson Bugislav and designated him her successor. He assumed the Scandinavian name of Eric of Pomerania. He was elected king of Norway in 1389, and king of Denmark and Sweden in 1396, but Margaret still kept a firm control over all important political decisions. The way was prepared for a magnificent and daring project: the unification of all three Scandinavian countries as one single union.

Margaret's rule was not readily accepted by many of the political powers around the Baltic, and in 1401 some of these suddenly seemed to have found an important propaganda argument against her. A person showed up in the important Hansa-town of Gdansk claiming that he was Olaf, that he had escaped Margaret's attempt to poison her own son, and that in reality he was the heir to the three Scandinavian kingdoms. With the help of the Teutonic order, Margaret succeeded in having the claimant handed over to her, and had him burned for offences against majesty in 1402 after he had confessed that he was from Bohemia and actually called Wolf. He had played a high-stakes game and lost, but in a time without central registers of people and no generally recognised identity papers, it was very difficult to prove that people were not whom they claimed to be, and Margaret was very concerned to procure witnesses who could certify that she had not killed her son. Other pretenders are also known from medieval Scandinavia. A woman from the Orkney Islands claimed to be the daughter of the Norwegian King Eric and was burned in Bergen, but still venerated in the early 14th century as a saint by the local population. Another was Sverre († 1202) from the Faroe Islands who also claimed royal descent and actually succeeded in becoming king of Norway

6 Consolidation of the Church

The Western Church 1200–1400

The 13th and 14th centuries were an important time for the formation of the Catholic Church. It strengthened its position in Europe through bureaucratisation and effective administration, and it struggled to defend and expand its position through numerous crusades. These had begun around 1100 but were strongly intensified after 1200 in the Iberian Peninsula against the Muslims and in the Baltic Sea area against the local non-Christian populations.

The 13th century especially was significant in developing the Roman Catholic doctrine through two important councils: the Fourth Lateran Council in 1215 and the Second Council of Lyon in 1272–1274. They made many important decisions regarding the development of canon law and placed more weight on pastoral care and preaching among Christians. The importance of preaching lay especially in the Church's attempt to eradicate heretical movements such as the Valdesians or Albingensians from southern Europe, and led to the foundation of the two important mendicant orders, the Franciscans and Dominicans.

In the 14th century, the Catholic Church encountered many difficulties. Due to political unrest in central Italy, the papacy allied with the French kings and moved the papal administration to Avignon. Since the Church in exile could not get income from the territory of the Papal States as it had earlier, it needed alternative means to obtain money for the running of the institution. This led to a significant bureaucratisation of the Church during the Avignon papacy. In 1378, Pope Gregory XI decided to move back to Rome. His return was celebrated by many Christians, including the Scandinavian Saint Birgitta of Sweden, but ended unhappily when the Pope suddenly died. The cardinals were not unanimous about his successor, and soon the Church was split into two obediences, French and Roman, which lasted until 1417.

The Danish Church 1200–1400

The Danish Church had established itself by the beginning of the 13th century and had close ties to the Danish ruling elite through the family connections of bishops and the archbishops of Lund. In 1201, the learned and influential Anders Sunesen was appointed Archbishop of Lund and began to guide his church with a firm hand.

The 13th and 14th centuries were marked by internal political unrest in Denmark, in which the Danish Church became deeply involved because of conflicting principles of loyalty and the personal connections of the bishops. They were all highly educated

DOI: 10.4324/9781003095514-9

and competent clerics, but Danish bishops were also appointed because of their political connections. They received large territories from the kings as feudal benefices and had to swear them oaths of obedience. When the political winds changed with the arrival of a new king, the bishops could find themselves in political difficulties.

One of the Danish bishops who ended up in political trouble was Bishop Niels Stigsen of Roskilde († 1249), a member of the Hvide family. He was instrumental in summoning a Danish church council in Odense 1245 which solemnly declared that those attacking the Church would automatically be excommunicated. This was considered a very important decision and repeated in later Danish church councils, but it could also be understood as a direct defence against the royal abuse of power. It probably was. The time of harmony between kings and Church in Denmark ended with the death of King Valdemar II in 1241. King Eric IV Ploughpenny became outraged and deprived Bishop Niels of his lands, driving him into exile in France from where he appealed to the pope and tried to get his position in Denmark back. Despite the papal support, Niels was never allowed to return to his native country, and he died in the monastery of Clairvaux.

The fracas between Bishop Niels and King Eric was only the beginning of a long-troubled period between Church and State in Denmark. The Danish Church and Danish rulers maintained a long-running controversy during the late 13th and early 14th centuries, known in Danish historiography as the 'church struggle', *kirkekampen*. The struggle began with a conflict between Archbishop Jakob Erlandsen and King Christopher I, who did not want to pay back a loan he had taken from the Church. The struggle escalated when the Archbishop wanted changes to the ecclesiastical section in the law of Scania to bring it into unison with the recently updated regulations of canon law. The modification of the ecclesiastical law would have given him more power in many areas which had earlier been defined as belonging to the province of secular legislation. King Christopher disagreed and made local supporters rebel against the Archbishop, who threatened him with an interdict and the closing of churches. The dispute was exacerbated by the formulations from another church council, presided over by the Archbishop in the town of Vejle in 1256. Its decisions opened with the ominous 'as the Danish Church is so much persecuted by tyrants …' and stated directly that if a bishop was imprisoned, attacked, or mutilated and the king was involved, or even may have been involved and able to prevent it but had not, the entire country would automatically fall under interdict, all churches would close, and all ecclesiastical services stop – no baptisms, marriages, or burials. This obviously upset King Christopher, and the conflict escalated in 1259 when Jakob Erlandsen refused to crown Christopher's son as co-regent. The King reacted by imprisoning the Archbishop. The attempted closing of churches did not prove effective because many within the Danish Church sided with the King. In the middle of the struggle, the King died – poisoned during communion by an ally of the Archbishop, the rumours soon claimed. The new King of Denmark, Eric Klipping, resumed the fight after a short break and forced the Archbishop to flee the country. After long negotiations at the papal curia, a compromise seemed to have been reached, and Jakob Erlandsen began his return to Scandinavia. But when he was almost home, he died in 1274 on the island of Rügen, and his bones were brought to Lund where he was buried in the Franciscan church. In the 1970s, a grave in the church was excavated, containing a box with a skeleton that had been dismembered for transport. The skull had a hole from a crossbow bolt; the person had been killed. It was suggested by many scholars that these were the remains of Jakob Erlandsen, killed by King Eric Klipping's men, but it is very unlikely that the murder of an archbishop would have left no traces in the written sources from the time.

The controversies lapsed for a while but when Jens Grand, nephew of Jacob Erlandsen and also a Hvide family member, was elected Archbishop in 1290, the struggle began again, this time against King Eric VI Menved, the son of Eric Klipping who had been murdered a few years earlier, in 1286, probably by members of the Hvide family. Again, the King imprisoned the Archbishop, who escaped from the royal dungeon in dramatic circumstances and went into exile. Jens Grand answered with ecclesiastical punishments and summoned King Eric to a trial at the papal court. The King was defended by Martin Mogensen, with great attention to juridical details and acid sarcasm. Martin was a canon from Ribe, an internationally known linguist and later rector of Paris University. In principle, Jens Grand won the case at the curia, but he lost in practice and could not match the royal power. He had to give up his position and withdraw from Denmark. The third act in the struggle between the Danish Church and the ruler involved King Eric Menved and Archbishop Esger Juul, who had supported the King in his fight against Jens Grand. The situation however changed when Esger became Archbishop and realised that both King Eric as well as his successor King Christopher II did not wish to respect the privileges of the Danish Church, ending up in conflict with the Archbishop.

Although each of these controversies had a particular reason, the main question in these struggles was that of the power relations between the crown and the Danish Church, which by the mid-13th century had become immensely rich and powerful. The struggles were not only fought in Denmark but beyond, with both parties using all possible means to win. They appealed to the popes in Rome and Avignon, made political alliances with each other's enemies, and tried to win over the other in ecclesiastical tribunals. It is also typical that the Danish Church was not acting as a unity, but that only some bishops and monastic orders supported the archbishops. Others sided with the king and continued celebrating masses while they appealed to the pope and complained about the interdict.

The struggles between the Danish kings and archbishops settled down when the election of Valdemar IV Atterdag to the Danish throne in 1340 finally brought an end to the country's internal political fighting. In his oath of election, Valdemar promised to defend the rights of the Church and managed to create good relationships with the bishops and the archbishop of Lund. But Valdemar did not restrict his goodwill to Danish ecclesiastics. He made a pilgrimage to visit Pope Urban V in Avignon in 1364 and received many papal privileges for churches in Denmark. From that time onwards, relations with the Avignon papacy and the Danish Church were very good, and numerous Danish laypeople and ecclesiastics turned to the papacy for different issues they needed to solve.

In Denmark, the archbishops of Lund could finally concentrate on ecclesiastical business, with the political struggles over and the country united behind one king. But a strong king was not necessarily good for the ecclesiastical leaders because it meant less power for the Church.

Archbishop Peder Jensen was worried about this tendency and summoned a provincial council in 1345 to Helsingborg, where the participating bishops, abbots, and other ecclesiastics would have considered how to defend the rights of the Danish Church. The situation was politically highly complicated, because Scania had been taken over by the Swedish King Magnus Ericsson. Lund was now the metropolitan see of Denmark but situated in a Swedish province. Economically and politically Peder Jensen leaned towards supporting Magnus Ericsson which may have been the reason for him to take measures against the Danish King Valdemar IV. This initiative, however, did not gain support and *kirkekampen* did not continue. The defeat of the Archbishop also resulted in the fact that a provincial council, which Peder Jensen had planned to organise every year, was not summoned before 1376.

The reigns of Valdemar IV and his successors are for good reasons often called the period of the State Church because on the important issues it was not the Danish bishops who decided but the king – with the support of the popes in Avignon. Or in the words of a chronicler from Lund, Valdemar IV's times 'tramped on all surviving from the old days, the law of the country and the freedom of the Danish Church'. Valdemar's daughter Queen Margaret I continued her father's policy and did not give much freedom to the ecclesiastical leaders in the political sphere.

At the same time, the Danish Church could not complain too much. Both Valdemar IV and especially Margaret were very generous towards it. They donated money, land, and ecclesiastical paraphernalia to Danish churches and monasteries and encouraged the aristocrats and rich burghers to do the same, making the Danish Church extremely rich.

King Valdemar IV had established close connections to the Avignon papacy, but when the popes returned to Rome in the late 1370s, the Danish Church sided with the Roman popes, and likewise after the French cardinals elected a French antipope to protest against the Roman whom they disliked and distrusted. In this decision, the Danish Church followed the German Empire which also sided with the Roman papacy. Especially after the birth of the Nordic union in Kalmar in 1397, Margaret was an important ally in the north for the Roman popes, who granted her numerous privileges that helped her to gain an even stronger grip upon the churches in the Scandinavian countries.

The 13th and the first decades of the 14th centuries were marked by political struggles in Denmark in which the Danish Church was deeply involved. When the struggles were over, the bishops had more time to dedicate to their bishoprics, but at the same time, the strong King Valdemar managed to limit the bishops' power. These centuries were however a positive period for the Church, which grew in wealth. The new mendicant orders, the Franciscans and the Dominicans, also received their share of the growing wealth and quickly spread throughout the Danish dioceses.

The Norwegian Church 1200–1400

The peaceful, amicable relationship between the Norwegian rulers and the Church was established soon after Sverre's son Haakon III ascended the throne in 1202. However, the first decades of the 13th century were defined by internal wars and unrest, and it was not before the 1230s that the Norwegian ecclesiastical province regained its strength and re-established connections with the various parts of its large territory. The archbishops of Nidaros managed to take under their control all of the islands, and the right to appoint bishops was also returned to Norway. In 1266, when the Kingdom of the Isle of Man and the Hebrides were ceded to Scotland, the Scots tried to push the Norwegian Church out of these territories but the archbishops of Nidaros kept them under his ecclesiastical jurisdiction.

The year 1277 was an important demarcation line in Norwegian ecclesiastical history. King Magnus VI Haakonsson, known also as Magnus 'the Law-mender', and Archibishop Jon Raude ('the Red') made an agreement, called the Tønsberg Concord (*Sættargjerden*) after the place where it was signed. The Tønsberg Concord confirmed several privileges of the clergy, the freedom of the Church to conduct episcopal elections without the interference of rulers, and similar matters that were important for defining the borders between secular and ecclesiastical jurisdiction. With this agreement, the crown also conceded the Archbishop the right to mint coins, to judge in ecclesiastical controversies, and not to pay tax to the crown.

The agreement, which has been said to be the high point of the Norwegian Church in the Middle Ages, was part of King Magnus' project to make a national law-code, but his law book of 1274 did not include an ecclesiastical section nor were the boundaries between the secular and ecclesiastical jurisdiction defined. The Church reacted to this, and the intention of the Tønsberg Concord was to remedy this issue. On paper, the Norwegian Church gained a lot of power and independence from the rulers, but historians have debated how far the content of the agreement was actually respected.

Just three years after the Tønsberg Concord, King Magnus died and the guardians of his only son, 12-year-old Eric II Magnusson, began to reduce the power of the Church and to backtrack on the agreement, including confiscating ecclesiastical property. In the course of the consequent power struggle, Archbishop Jon of Nidaros had to flee the country together with Bishops Anders of Oslo and Torfinn of Hamar. After two years, the situation was settled when King Eric turned 14 and thus came of age. He decided that the crown should respect the agreement, but it was never officially re-promulgated and the Church did not regain its earlier powerful position.

The situation shifted slowly in the bishops' favour in the last years of the 13th century, when Haakon V (r. 1299–1319) inherited the throne after the death of his elder brother Eric. Since Haakon did not have male heirs, he appointed as his heir Magnus Ericsson, the son of his daughter Ingeborg and the Swedish Prince Eric. Since Magnus was still a child, when Haakon died, his mother and a group of trusted men ruled the country on his behalf until he came of age. The group of trusted men also included two bishops, which again increased the influence of the Norwegian Church in political matters.

The first half of the 14th century was a prosperous and influential time for the Norwegian Church. It had become a wealthy institution thanks to numerous donations, and together with the monasteries, it was one of the most important landowners in the country. The Norwegian bishops were learned men with university backgrounds and large international networks, including the papal administration. They brought the Norwegian Church to European standards, and the cathedral chapters began to function like anywhere else in the Christendom. The cult of Saint Olaf became known all over western and also Eastern Europe, and his grave in Nidaros became one of Europe's most famous and visited pilgrim shrines, behind only Jerusalem, Rome, and Santiago.

The archbishops of Nidaros regularly organised provincial councils that made decisions and developed the religious life in the country. The provincial councils were well attended, including by the representatives of the overseas dioceses. It has been estimated that despite the shock of the Black Death and the dramatic subsequent depopulation of Norwegian territory, the Norwegian Church had fairly good control over its entire province until the 1380s. The Black Death was a serious blow to the Norwegian Church. Due to the high mortality, several parishes remained without priests, but the generous donations by local magnates kept church life going. The plague hit perhaps harder the monasteries and convents that were dependent on having several clerics. Some monasteries could not continue to function. The rich Benedictine monastery of Munkeliv in Bergen went into decline and was re-established in the 1420s as a Birgittine monastery.

The relationship between the Norwegian Crown and Church in the 14th century can be defined as relatively good. The Church had a great deal of privileges, it increased in wealth, and the bishops had a good relationship with the rulers, with political influence through automatically being members of the Norwegian council of the realm. Bishops in the other Scandinavian countries were also members of their national councils of the realm. The 14th was the century of big change in Norwegian politics, due to the personal unions, first with Sweden (Magnus Ericsson ruled both countries in 1319–1355 and his son Haakon V in 1362–1364) and then with Denmark. Haakon V was married to Margaret, the daughter of Danish King Valdemar IV Atterdag, and their son Olaf ruled both countries in his minority together with his mother. Margaret took over after his premature death and the Union of the three Scandinavian countries was established in Kalmar in 1397. The union period drew the Norwegian territorial rulers' attention towards the union's core, the Baltic Sea, with the consequence that the earlier important western direction remained relatively neglected.

The change in political interest had its repercussions for the Norwegian Church, which began to lose power in the dioceses situated overseas. Lines of communication also slowly became more difficult to uphold because of climatic changes. At the same time, the papal administration was struggling with the Great Western Schism, during which the Norwegian Church sided with the Roman popes as did all countries in political alliance with the German Empire. The weak papacy meant more independence for the local bishops in their appointment of clerics to various positions as well as in their decision-making.

The 13th century brought new ecclesiastical orders to Norway, when the mendicants began to spread northwards in the 1220s. The Dominicans were the first to erect their convents in Norway. These were founded in the three most important large cities, Bergen, Oslo, and Nidaros. The Franciscans arrived in Norway a bit later, but six convents were founded in the realm: first in Tønsberg, Bergen, Konghelle, Marstrand, and Oslo, and a little later in Nidaros.

The 13th was also the century of the spread of the Christian faith towards the north as Christian fishermen founded their hamlets along the coastline, first as far as Trondenes in the early 13th century. In the following decade, Christian settlement spread further north towards Finnmark. Christians settled in Tromsø c. 1250, and in 1307, Vardøy next to the Russian border was also Christianised. But it is important to remember that the Christian settlements were of Norwegian origin, not Sámi. King Haakon Haakonson (r. 1217–1263) made some efforts to convert the Sámi people to Finnmark but without any permanent results. The Sámi were subject to Christian mission again in the 1380s when a local mystic persuaded Queen Margaret to support this activity among the population in north. This mission likewise does not seem to have been successful.

The Icelandic Church 1200–1400

Iceland remained independent from the political power of Norway until the 1260s, when it was placed under Norwegian rule. The Norwegian Church by contrast already had begun to exert a firmer grasp over the Church in Iceland some decades earlier from the 1230s, when the political situation on the mainland had calmed down after the period of civil wars. The Icelanders had been able to block the reform attempts of Archbishop Eystein of around half a century earlier, but in the 1230s, the active Archbishop Sigurd began to force the Icelanders to accept the Norwegian model.

When both Icelandic episcopal seats were vacant in 1237, Sigurd refused to appoint the local candidates to the positions, instead selecting his own Norwegian appointees as bishops to Skálholt and Hólar. The Icelanders were not happy but were forced to accept the decision because the Norwegian rulers and the popes sided with the Archbishop. The Norwegian Church's firm grasp in Iceland was a welcome novelty for the Norwegian kings who thereby managed to gain a better control over the island. The papal administration was also satisfied when the Icelanders were forced to better follow the ecclesiastical norms and the local bishops could not overrule the papal decisions as they had sometimes earlier done.

The reform of the Icelandic Church continued slowly and sporadically for the following 150 years. Reform was enforced during the reign of King Magnus the Lawmender, who attempted to introduce changes to the island's civil law. The King, with the help of Bishop Árni Þorláksson of Skálholt, managed to get his new Christian law accepted by the *althing* in 1275, and Bishop Árni promised to enforce it in his diocese which was also done. The legal reform of King Magnus did not however proceed as intended because of the internal political fights in Norway after the King's death in 1280, which diminished Norwegian influence in Iceland. Ecclesiastically, this meant that the Christian law of King Magnus was never accepted in the territory of the diocese of Hólar, where Bishop Árni had no influence.

A major reason why the Icelanders were reluctant to accept the new Christian law was that it aimed at abolishing the privately owned churches, and thereby at limiting the decisive say of the local chieftains in ecclesiastical matters. The chieftains did not want to accept this and insisted upon conserving the old practice through their privately owned churches. The issue was settled only at the turn of the 14th century, when the Icelandic Church finally gained power over the local farmers owning the churches. But it took still half a century before the inhabitants of the diocese of Hólar recognised the Church's authority over the land. This happened in 1354, when the active Bishop of Hólar, Auðunn Þorbergsson, managed to convince and coerce the inhabitants of his diocese. Bishop Auðunn is known for his energy in uniting the ecclesiastical practices in his diocese.

In Icelandic ecclesiastical history, the 14th century was the period of consolidation of ecclesiastical administration, which first took place in the diocese of Skálholt, and half a century later in Hólar. The century can also be seen as that of the establishment and growth of episcopal power in the island. Like everywhere else in Western Christendom, the 13th and 14th centuries were ones of economic growth. Iceland was saved in the mid-14th century from the lethal first wave of the Black Death, which did not come until 1402. This meant that the 14th century was a period of tranquillity and prosperity within the Church in Iceland.

The Swedish Church 1200–1400

The Swedish church province of Uppsala was established in 1164. The archbishop of Uppsala as well as the suffragan bishops of Linköping, Skara, Strängnäs, Västerås, and Växjö on the Swedish mainland, and Turku on the eastern shore of the Baltic Sea, were however still administratively subjects of the metropolitan archbishops of Lund.

The Catholic Church made many important decisions which had legal and administrative consequences everywhere in the Christian West. It was typically the task of the archbishops and bishops to communicate these decisions to their subjects, but in the case of important issues, the popes could delegate the job to their trusted men, who were sent out to ensure that ecclesiastical reforms were introduced everywhere. In Sweden, this took place in 1248, during the visit of William of Sabina, Pope Innocent IV's legate in the north. All Swedish ecclesiastical authorities – and also probably many aristocrats including Birger Jarl – were invited to a provincial council held in Skänninge in February 1248.

The purpose of summoning the council was to introduce to the Swedes the content of the recently codified collection of canon law, the so-called *Liber Extra* or Decretals of Gregory IX from 1234. According to the new code, priests were to live in celibacy and the Swedish clerics were to start following suit even though many of them were married. The council of Skänninge also made important decisions about the size and rights of the episcopal retinue when the bishops were travelling around their bishoprics. This was a significant decision because the earlier Swedish bishops had behaved like aristocrats in the service of the country, demanding the right to food and places to sleep. The council of Skänninge also had influence in local legislation, because the new ecclesiastical norms were introduced into local laws in the form of a separate church code governing the relationship between the Swedish Church, bishops, priests, dioceses, parishes, and Christians.

The newly introduced code of ecclesiastical law also stipulated the role and obligations of the cathedral chapters and their members. Although cathedral chapters had existed since the early church elsewhere in the Christian West, such institutions did not exist in Sweden, and thus the council of Skänninge decided that it was necessary to establish a cathedral chapter in each Swedish diocese. The role of the chapter was not only to assist the bishop and take care of ecclesiastical celebrations in the cathedral, but its members, the canons and prelates, were also responsible for the election of a new bishop when that was necessary. In some Swedish dioceses, such as Skara and Linköping, there had already been cathedral chapters a couple of decades prior to the council of Skänninge – and Uppsala had gotten one just a year before. The early chapter of Skara had been regular, that is, the members of the chapter were monks and lived together under a monastic rule, the rule of Saint Augustine. After the council, all Swedish cathedral chapters became secular, which is to say the canons were not members of any order but received their income from a benefice connected to their position in the cathedral.

Another important event in Swedish church history took place in 1273, when the archiepiscopal seat was transferred – together with the location of the cathedral – from (Old) Uppsala to Östra Aros (= Eastern Aros), that is to the site of present-day Uppsala. The reasons for the transfer were many: the old cathedral in (Old) Uppsala had burned and been badly damaged, the old location had no more administrative or commercial importance, and the new place could be directly connected to the murder site of the Swedish national saint, Saint Eric. The process of transferring the archiepiscopal seat had begun in the 1250s. The Swedish archbishop had received a papal permit for the transfer in 1258, but it took 15 years before it could take place. At the time of the transfer in 1273, the building of the new cathedral had begun, but it took over 150 years before the work was finished. It was a major project which also included levelling off a large mound, with the building erected on an artificial plateau. Easier locations could have been found, but this one was probably chosen so that the high altar could be exactly on the spot where Saint Eric had been murdered.

The new archiepiscopal seat in Uppsala underlined the role and the significance of the Swedish aristocratic family of the Folkungs. In the 1220s, the descendants of the saintly King Eric ascended the throne and finally replaced the earlier royal dynasty of the Sverkers. The direct descendants of Eric ruled for some decades, after which the power ended in the hands of one of his indirect descendants, that of the Bjelbo family, also known as the Folkungs. The significance of the Folkungs began in the 1250s with the rule of Birger Jarl, whose son Valdemar was elected as king of Sweden. The family not only produced many jarls and bishops but also placed many daughters in important positions such as abbesses of central nunneries. Due to the connection to the saintly King Eric, the Folkung family actively supported his cult – which also strengthened the position of the family in the country and within the Church.

The support of the Church was important for the ruling class, and therefore the aristocratic families tried to get their sons into the Swedish episcopal seats. This was important because Swedish bishops automatically belonged to the council of the realm and were often advisors and close collaborators of the kings. In decision-making, blood seemed to be more important than the unity of the Church, since Swedish bishops often followed very different political lines in their decisions.

One of the main issues causing differences between the bishops was the relationship of the Swedish Church province to the archbishops of Lund. Those Swedish families with close relations to the Danish royal family were not as keen to strive for the independence of the Swedish Church, while those bishops whose families were enemies of the Danish aristocracy were more active in this cause. The conflict between the archbishops of Lund and Uppsala escalated for the first time in 1290, when Archbishop Jens Grand of Lund excommunicated the provost of Uppsala and suspended the whole cathedral chapter because it had turned directly to the pope in a juridical issue which the Archbishop would have liked to handle. The archbishops of Lund considered themselves as the superiors of the Swedish church province because they had handed the *pallium* over to the archbishops of Uppsala and thereby claimed their right over Uppsala's seat. The last Archbishop of Uppsala to receive the *pallium* from his colleague in Lund was Olof Björnsson in 1315, and that happened only by force. The Archbishop Elect had decided to travel to the pope in Avignon and receive his appointment there but the secular ruler in Sweden, in alliance with the archbishop of Lund, stopped him on his way to France and forced him to receive the *pallium* in Lund instead. After that incident, all Swedish medieval archbishops received their *pallium* – and powers – directly from the pope.

From the international point of view, Sweden became integrated with Western Christendom and the papacy during the 13th century: Sweden became an independent ecclesiastical province, or almost so, papal legislation was enforced in the country, and the ecclesiastical administration became more professional. In this, Sweden followed the development of the rest of the Christian West. When the papacy ended up in collision with the German Empire at the turn of the 14th century and the popes moved to Avignon where the French kings offered their support, Sweden adapted to the situation and began turning to the Avignon popes in necessary ecclesiastical matters. At the same time, the Swedes – especially Saint Birgitta of Sweden – were supporting the idea of the papacy's return to Rome. When this took place in the late 1370s, with the consequent split of the Church into the supporters of the Roman popes and French antipopes, the Swedish Church sided with the Romans.

Saint Birgitta had a strong influence also on Swedish royal and church politics, and especially so upon King Magnus Ericsson. Advised by Birgitta and with the support of the popes, King Magnus decided to leave on crusade against the schismatic Russians. The campaign ended in a military catastrophe, with the King in trouble. Magnus had antagonised the ecclesiastical authorities in his country by promulgating a national law-code around 1350 which omitted legislation on the relationship of the Church and the State. The Swedish bishops worked strongly against the King, and he was dismissed and replaced by King Albert of Mecklenburg in 1364. This led to a civil war in which the Swedish bishops played a central role. The civil war ended in 1389 when Danish troops defeated King Albert, and the Danish and Norwegian Queen Margaret also ruled over Sweden.

While the 12th century was known for the spread of the Cistercian order in Sweden, the 13th was the century of the mendicant orders. Both Dominicans and Franciscans arrived in Sweden relatively soon after the foundation of their orders and quickly expanded across the country. In the 1230s and 1240s, the first convents were founded in Swedish towns: Dominican convents in Sigtuna, Skara, Skänninge, Västerås, and Turku, and Franciscan convents in Arboga, Enköping, Skara, Söderköping, and Uppsala. The late 14th and early 15th centuries, by contrast, were the period of the spread of the monastic order of Saint Birgitta of Sweden. Birgitta, proclaimed a saint in the Basilica of Saint Peter in Rome in 1391, had established her own monastic order, officially known as the order of the Most Holy Saviour but usually called the Birgittine order. The order was recognised by Pope Urban V in 1370, and the first monastery founded in the late 14th century in Vadstena from where it spread to the Baltic Sea region and elsewhere during the 15th century.

The Finnish Church 1200–1400

The history of the Catholic Church in Finland is tightly related to Sweden which conquered Finland in the course of the 12th century. Alongside the civil administration, the Swedes also brought ecclesiastical administration to the newly conquered territory. Until the 13th century, Finland was a missionary territory entrusted to the 'bishop of Finns', but the developments in that century made Finnish territory a part of the Christian West. An important figure in this development was Bishop Thomas. During his episcopacy (c. 1220–1245), ecclesiastical administration and parish structure began to take form, and he received a permit to build a new ecclesiastical centre with a proper cathedral in Koroinen, not far from the Finnish ecclesiastical centre in Turku.

The 13th century was extremely important in the formation of the Church in Finland. It is not known exactly when the missionary territory of Finland was established as the diocese of Turku but this must have happened shortly after the mid-13th century, since from 1270, we possess a document which mentions Catillus, Bishop of Turku. All his predecessors of whom we know from historical sources, the suspicious bishops Henry, Rodulfus, and Folkvinus as well as Thomas, Bero, and Ragvaldus, had the title of 'bishop of Finns'. With the establishment of the diocese of Turku, the Finnish territory was also officially recognised. The new diocese was entrusted to the archbishops of Uppsala and became part of the Swedish ecclesiastical province. The first seat of the diocese of Turku in Koroinen turned out to be an unsuitable place, and around 1300, a new cathedral was built on the site of the present cathedral of Turku. Alongside with the cathedral, the ecclesiastical administration moved from Koroinen to the centre of the newly founded town.

Another important step for Finnish ecclesiastical administration was taken in the late 13th century when a cathedral chapter was created in Turku. According to canon law, a bishop should not rule alone but be assisted by a cathedral chapter, which also had the task of electing a new bishop when the old had died or was transferred. Pope Innocent IV had stipulated in 1250 that in the Swedish ecclesiastical province a chapter was full when it consisted of five canons. Originally the chapter of Turku consisted only of four canons, but by the second quarter of the 14th century, it had reached the required number.

The Dominican order had sent the first friars to Finland in 1249. It has been assumed that the Dominicans were working in close connection with the local bishop because the liturgy of the Turku diocese followed the Dominican. When the ecclesiastical centre moved to Turku, the Dominicans had also begun to build their convent close to the town centre, and from 1292 onwards, the sources no longer address them as Dominicans in Finland but as Dominicans in Turku. We do not know where the friars lodged until then, but the convent dedicated to Saint Olaf dates to the first half of the 14th century.

During the 13th century, the Church spread in Finnish territory towards the east and inland. There had already been peaceful missions to these territories earlier, but during the 13th century, the Swedish state began to take a firmer grasp of Finnish territory and organised two larger military campaigns to win these regions to the Swedish crown. Since the campaigns had a religious aspect, both of them are known in the historical accounts as crusades. The first, known as the second crusade to Finland, took place around 1250 and was directed at the inhabitants of the Tavastland region, with perhaps the Swedish leader Birger Jarl as its commander. The second crusade to Finland finally brought the western Finnish territory into the Swedish dominion. The third crusade to Finland was made in 1293 towards Vyborg, Karelia, and the Novgorodians governing the territory. This crusade led to the inclusion of large parts of eastern Finland in the Swedish dominion and the Catholic Church. Resultantly, the Christian religion had spread to most of Finland's permanently inhabited areas.

The borders of the diocese of Turku were defined during the 14th century relative to the Russians or Orthodox Christians in the east as well as to the Swedes and Sámi people in the north. The peace treaty of Nöteborg in 1323 defined the eastern border between Sweden and Novgorod, and that became the eastern border of the Turku diocese. The border in the north was, by contrast, relatively undefined, and most parts of Lapland belonged to the archbishop's diocese of Uppsala. There is no sign of mission from the Finnish territory to Lapland or to the Sámi, who maintained their original spiritual practices based mainly on animism.

Saints

In the medieval Christian world, there was a special place in Christians' hearts for a myriad of saints, men and women, whom Christians had attributed with sanctity and who were venerated. They were believed to have risen directly to heaven and therefore be able to intercede between Christians and God, and they were prayed to and called upon to help Christians in many different ways and places.

In the period of the early Church, until the 10th century, it was the task of the local bishops to oversee the veneration of persons considered holy in the territory of their dioceses. There were no clearly regulated procedures or requirements as to who could be considered a saint. Typically, Christians began to consider their deceased fellow Christians as such if they had lived a particularly exemplary Christian life or had incurred martyrdom because of their Christian faith. Usually, these persons had performed post-mortem miracles: saving someone from death or healing a sick person who had prayed to them. Local veneration often quickly developed into a cult, which was encouraged by local ecclesiastical leaders because the spread of knowledge of the cult and the saint brought pilgrims and money to the place where the saintly person was buried. The saint was also considered the special protector of the monastery or church where she or he was buried. It gave great prestige to the place and could also be used in political negotiations with local magnates, for example over income and right to land.

In the Middle Ages, there were a number of local saints – or saint candidates – who had their own cult, encouraged and supported by the local bishop. Until 1234, when Pope Gregory IX promulgated the canon law collection *Liber Extra*, canon law did not regulate who could be considered as a saint and who not. The promulgation of the *Liber Extra* change this principle: from then onwards, only the pope could decide the sanctity of a person. The new regulations also defined clearly what was required of the person the pope decided to proclaim a saint and what kind of process was needed.

The process of proclaiming a saint is called canonisation, the being included in the canon or 'official list' of saints. From 1234 onwards, the canonisation process began in the home diocese of the saint candidate, that is, where the person was buried and where some kind of local cult had already usually developed around the person. The local bishop had then to support the local cult and authorise the start of the local process. The first step was to compose an official biography – in Latin, a *vita* – of the saint candidate. The vita was a specific literary genre of the Middle Ages. It briefly told the life story of the saint candidate and stressed the events supporting the sainthood: an exemplary lifestyle, important things done for the local ecclesiastical or monastic community, or martyrdom. The papal approval for sanctity usually required that a certain number of miracles had to have taken place through the saint candidate – performing such miracles was considered as a strong testimony of his or her sanctity because God often performed miracles through the saints. In order to prove that such miracles had taken place, the local ecclesiastical authorities supporting the canonisation process collected testimonies of Christians who had profited from the miracles. These collections were eventually presented together with the *vita* to the pope, who could then decide upon the sanctity of the person. The papal decision was typically made in two phases. After the preliminary inquiries and presentation of the first proofs to the pope, he could allow the remains of the saint candidate to be translated from his or her burial place to a more eminent site, for example a shrine on an altar. After that, the local authorities had to gather additional evidence of the person's sanctity before the pope could officially canonise them. When a person had received official papal canonisation, his or her name was added to the official list of saints and he or she received an official saint's day.

There are only a few Scandinavian saints who have officially been proclaimed saints by the popes: Canute the King of Denmark in 1101, Canute Lavard in 1170, and Saint Birgitta of Sweden in 1391. The reason for so few officially canonised Scandinavian saints is that most of the cults of Scandinavian saints were established before the obligatory requirement of papal authorisation in 1234. Thus, there was no need for a papal canonisation. The cults of most of the Scandinavian saints, such as Saint Vilhelm of Æbelholt or Saint Eskil, remained relatively local, while some saints, such as Saint Olaf of Norway, became recognised and widely venerated internationally.

The medieval community of saints consisted of different types of saints. Many central biblical figures, such as the Apostles, the Evangelists, or the Archangels, were automatically counted as saints. In addition, there were those considered saints because of other important qualities. The early saints from late Antiquity, such as Saint Lucy or Saint Lawrence, had typically encountered a violent death because of their Christian faith and they were classified as martyrs. Martyrdom was a typical way to become saint especially in periods when Christendom was spreading to new territories. There were many Scandinavian missionary saints who encountered martyrdom while spreading the Christian faith, such as Saint Henry of Finland and Saints Botvid, David, and Eskil in Sweden, who were all murdered while missionising. Very often, we know very little in actuality about these early missionaries and their cult. Saint Villads must have been active in northern Jutland, where a couple of churches were dedicated to him and a well near one of them was believed to have healing power, but nothing else is known.

Sainthood through martyrdom was an honour for some medieval clerics. There are stories of missionaries actively seeking martyrdom. Sometimes, they did not become martyrs despite their attempts, as was the case for Kjeld of Viborg, an Augustinian canon and later Danish saint. He wrote to the pope for a permit to leave to missionise in the Wendish territory, where he hoped that he would achieve martyrdom. The pope granted him the permit but suggested to stay in his diocese and take care of his tasks as the dean of the local cathedral church. After his death, Kjeld became venerated as a saint in Viborg – not because of martyrdom but because of the exemplary Christian life and services done for the local church.

Another category of saint was that of the confessors, that is, saints who did not belong to the categories of martyrs, apostles, or Evangelists but who had conducted an exemplary life, such as the famous Dominican scholar and theologian Saint Thomas Aquinas. In Scandinavia, such saints typically date to the period when monasteries and other important ecclesiastical centres were formed. Saint Þorlákur Þórhallsson (1133–1193), the patron saint of Iceland, who was officially canonised by Pope John Paul II in 1984, is a good example of such a saint. He was of Icelandic origin, and after years of studies abroad, he returned to his native island in 1165, founded a monastery of Canons Regular in Þykkivaibær, and dedicated his life to contemplation and prayer. In 1178, he was appointed Bishop of Skálholt, and after his death, his earthly remains were translated to the cathedral of Skálholt where his cult grew in importance. Additionally, there was a group of women venerated as saints because of their virginity or dedication of their lives to God, such as Saint Catherine of Siena or Birgitta of Sweden.

A special category are the royal saints, who were considered saints because of the favours they did for Christianity by converting their subjects to Christendom or by bringing the Christian faith to new territories. In the widespread enthusiasm after the First Crusade's conquest of Jerusalem in 1099, several new crusading saints were created in Western Europe, and several older saints had their life stories re-written to turn them into some sort of proto-crusader. The most famous example is Santiago de Compostela, who in the 1120s was changed from a very peaceful pilgrim saint into Santiago Matamoros, the Muslim killer. Similarly in Scandinavia, a new vita was written for Saint Olaf of Norway who was now described as having fought in Syria against Muslims. Canute Lavard of Denmark was canonised in 1170 for many reasons including that he had fought wars of conversion against the Wends in northern Germany in the 1120s. King Eric of Sweden, the third royal patron saint in Scandinavia, had led a crusade to Finland around 1150 and converted the Finns.

Most Scandinavian saints were never officially proclaimed saints by the popes because their cults date to the times when such a procedure was not necessary. There are also Scandinavian saint candidates whose official canonisation processes began in the 15th century, but who never became officially proclaimed saints because the Reformation interrupted the process: Dominican Sister Ingrid Elovsdotter of Skänninge, Bishop Nils Hermansson of Linköping, Bishop Brynolf Algotsson of Skara, Bishop Hemming of Turku, and the daughter of Saint Birgitta of Sweden, Saint Catherine of Vadstena. Their canonisation processes proceeded during the second half of the 15th century. In 1484, Pope Innocent VIII officially accepted the cult of Catherine and in the mid-1490s the cult of Hemming was confirmed by Pope Alexander VI. It was the first step towards canonisation, but the next was never taken.

Most of the records collected by the locals for the interrupted canonisation processes have been lost, and we do not know much about the attempts. The processes were usually slow and required a considerable amount of money. If we take as an example the interrupted canonisation process of Hemming of Turku, the first attempts at his canonisation had already begun in the first decades of the 15th century, some 60 years after his death. At that time, the diocese of Turku began the recording of miracles that had happened after the invocation of Hemming. Although the cult of Hemming was initially local, it was apparently targeted at a larger audience since his miracles were also collected in Stockholm where he had begun his ecclesiastical career before his transferral to Turku. By the end of the 15th century, the diocese of Turku had recorded a sufficient amount of miracles so that Pope Alexander VI could make the cult official in the last years of the 1490s.

The papal approval of the cult of Saint Hemming meant in practice that an official translation feast could be organised in Turku cathedral. There are no contemporary sources describing the translation feast, but it took place around 15 years after the Pope had allowed the cult, in mid-June 1514. We know from the court books of Stockholm that the Swedish Archbishop Jakob Ulvsson, accompanied by Bishops Mats Gregersson of Strängnäs and Otto Olafsson of Västerås, was present at the festivities and returned from Turku with a relic of Bishop Hemming. The relic was carried in procession through the town and deposited in the parish church of Stockholm.

Saints also had other important roles in medieval society. According to the Catholic Church, saints had the special ability to mediate God's goodwill towards Christians through various miracles: resurrecting dead persons, healing from various illnesses or impairment, helping in dangerous situations such as child birth or other kinds of accidents, punishment miracles, liberating from danger, imprisonment, and many others. The most common miracles, resurrection and healing, are familiar from the New Testament and miracles performed by Jesus, but the medieval miracles concerned many areas of human life. Certain saints were better at helping in certain kinds of situations than others. For example, Saint Lucy, whose eyes were blinded, was particularly effective against eye sicknesses, Saint Anthony was strong against plague, and Saint Birgitta as a mother of eight children was often called upon to help when children were in danger or when a birth was difficult.

Resurrecting a dead person was a relatively typical miracle in the extant miracle collections of the Scandinavian saints. The miracle collection of Saint Birgitta mentions eight such cases, while her daughter Catherine's collection includes 13 resurrection miracles. Often there was the element of drowning or accident in which a person had been badly injured and seemed dead, and after the relatives or persons present had invoked the saint, they returned to life.

There were a great number of different healing miracles. In some cases, the issue was a permanent injury or illness, such as being blind or deaf, while other times a person had been liberated from a chronic headache. The spectrum of different illnesses is also huge, and it is often not possible to diagnose these according to modern medical knowledge.

Punishment miracles are miracles that a saint performed upon someone who had doubted the saint's sanctity. In the miracle collection of Saint Birgitta, more than 10% of miracles belong to this category, but other saints also wrought such miracles. One well-known punishment miracle was performed by Saint Henry of Finland, upon a Swedish priest who had claimed to his Finnish colleague that Henry was not a saint. On the following morning, the Swedish priest woke up with a terrible headache, which did not pass until he invoked Saint Henry and asked him to relieve the pain. Another was a man harvesting a field near Odense in Denmark on a Sunday. His arm using the sickle suddenly became lame and dried up. When he prayed to Saint Canute of Odense and promised never again to work on a Sunday, his arm grew back and was totally healed.

Saints could also perform other kinds of miracles, of which saving a boat from a storm or people from a shipwreck are the most common. Medieval Christians typically invoked God or saints in a moment of despair, as Martin Luther did in 1505 during a storm while he was travelling. Unlike many Christians who promised to make a pilgrimage to the shrine of the saint who had helped or saved them, Luther made a vow to join a monastic order if he survived. Such vows were taken very seriously and breaking them was considered a grave sin. It was possible to commute such a vow only by appealing either to the local bishop, if it was a question of a vow to visit a local shrine, or to the pope if a vow to join a monastic order or visit one of the three major shrines in Jerusalem, Rome, or Santiago de Compostela.

Sometimes saints also procured miracles that were not directed only to an individual Christian but to a larger group of believers. Saint Catherine of Vadstena performed such a miracle in Rome when the River Tiber was flooding and threatening the houses of Roman inhabitants. They asked for help from Catherine who told the waters to recede – which they did and the houses survived.

Each saint was different from the others, and their individual representations in churches – frescos, sculptures, and other pictures – allowed Christians to easily distinguish which was depicted. Each saint had their individual attributes that is an object or particular colour that made their recognition easy. The objects were usually related to the saint's life or miracles; for example, a female saint with a wheel could be identified as Saint Catherine of Alexandria, whom Emperor Maxentius condemned to death on a spiked breaking wheel. Saint Lawrence was always shown holding the grill on which he was placed and slowly roasted.

The Scandinavian saints also had their own clearly identifiable attributes. Saint Botvid, the patron saint of Södermanland in Sweden is depicted with an axe in one hand and a fish in the other, while Saint Eskil, another saint of Södermanland, is depicted with three stones in his hand since he was stoned to death by the Swedish pagan King Blot-Sweyn. Saint Sigfrid, who was a missionary in Småland and Västergötland, is depicted with a basket in his hand in which can be seen three small heads, the heads of his three nephews who were killed during his mission. Saint Henry of Finland is depicted trampling at his feet a man with a bleeding scalp because according to his legend, his killer put the Bishop's mitre upon his own head as a triumph, but when he tried to remove it, his hair stuck to it. The three Scandinavian royal saints, Olaf of Norway, Canute of Denmark, and Eric of Sweden, all carry a crown and the royal insignia, in addition to which each of them has their own personal features. Eric is often depicted without beard and can have a sword or a sceptre in his hand. Olaf is typically depicted with a beard and an axe in his hand, and sometimes he tramples at his feet a dragon with a head identical to the saint's head, while the Danish king may have an additional dagger, lance, or arrow in his hand. A book is a common attribute for many saints, for example Saint Kjeld of Viborg and Saint Birgitta of Sweden, whose attributes also sometimes include a pen or pilgrim's staff.

Although the majority of medieval people were illiterate, they were trained in reading pictures. They had no problems in identifying the saints, as they knew the stories behind the attributes. Unlike modern people, medieval people would never for example mix up the attributes of the Evangelists: an eagle for John, winged lion for Mark, man or angel for Matthew, and bull for Luke. Additionally, the most known attributes of the 12 Apostles and the stories behind them were crystal clear to everyone. For example, Saint Peter, who received the keys of the heavens from Jesus, is depicted with a key in his hand, while Saint Paul who was beheaded carries a sword, and Saint James the Great is depicted with scallop shells and a pilgrim's hat.

Relics

Relics were holy items which played an important role in the medieval exercise of religion, but they were of very different kinds. Most desired were the physical remains of saints, that is their bodies or body parts such as bones. Another kind was a contact relic, which is to say saints' personal effects or items that had been in contact with them, such as the table on which Saint Birgitta died, still kept in the house of the Birgittine order in Rome. Contact relics also include the famous items connected to Jesus such as the Shroud of Turin and the Veil of Veronica, or to the Virgin Mary, such as Mary's milk.

Relics were important and necessary items in the Middle Ages. They protected their holders against evil and had healing powers. Those on display at various monasteries or churches attracted pilgrims and consequently money. Due to their popularity, relics became, especially during the high Middle Ages, the subjects of huge commercial activity. Pious individuals wanted to purchase protection for themselves and their families, and when the nobility began to build private churches and chapels for their castles, they wanted to have relics. The dioceses were also in constant need of relics because whenever a new church or altar was consecrated, a piece of a relic had to be put in the altar.

Churches could stress their importance by exposing their large relic collections to attract pilgrims to the sites. Many European monasteries and cathedrals displayed their own local saint's relics, as the cathedral of Odense did with the relics of Saint Canute the King, the cathedral of Uppsala with Saint Eric, and the cathedral of Nidaros with Saint Olaf. The churches sometimes also exchanged relics to enhance the attraction of their collections. Such activity is recounted in the letter of the Bishop of Turku, Magnus Nicolai on 1 July 1493 to the Norwegian Archbishop of Nidaros, Gaute Ivarsson. Bishop Magnus wrote that the Turku cathedral would like to receive a piece of a relic of Saint Olaf and suggested that Nidaros could in exchange receive a piece of Saint Henry.

Many cathedrals had large collections of the relics of various saints. Most Scandinavian relics were destroyed during the Reformation, but the medieval relic lists from different churches still tell us about the numerous examples in different churches. For example, the relic inventory of the cathedral of Stavanger, dedicated to the English saint, Saint Swithun, lists well over 100 relics. None of them have survived to the present, but the relic collection of the cathedral of Turku was hidden away in a hole in the church wall. It was found only in 1911 and still includes around 100 different relics.

Medieval letters sometimes include passages related to the purchase of relics and indeed their falsification. Rome had an unending supply of relics because of the numerous catacombs and saints related to the Eternal City, and Cologne, home of the relics of Saint Ursula and the 11,000 virgins, gave scope for a large-scale relic business. Relics were sold officially and unofficially, and some were forgeries. For example, the relic collection of Turku cathedral includes a piece of bone that was recently identified as a bone of a seal.

We also have ample testimony of a more official relic trade. In autumn 1519, Andreas Jacobi, the parish priest of the church of Saint Olaf in Helsingør, requested a papal licence to bring relics home from Cologne. A year later the priest's brother Michael Nicolai from the house of the order of Holy Spirit in Aalborg made an identical petition to the pope explaining that he wanted to take home a relic of the 11,000 virgins. Both petitioners had honest intentions to acquire relics to their churches and therefore turned to the pope with their requests. However, there were also less honest people like the Benedictine Brother Gregorius Turonis from the diocese of Odense, who had agreed with his prior that he would bring back home a relic of Saint Anthony. Since Gregorius had accepted money for the relic, he was guilty of simony and needed a papal absolution, which he received in autumn 1450.

Pilgrimage

Pilgrimages are visits to a holy place, typically to the shrine of a saint. Probably every Christian in the Middle Ages made pilgrimages, although it was not an obligatory part of Christian life. Any church, monastery, or shrine could be a target for a pilgrimage, and pilgrimages could be made to faraway or nearby localities, or somewhere in between. The choice of a pilgrimage goal depended first on the devotion of the pilgrim to a specific saint, but other matters such as time, money, or obligations could also be a factor. Three shrines – Jerusalem, Rome, and Santiago de Compostela – were particularly important in the Middle Ages and are known as the major shrines of Latin Christendom.

Jerusalem and the surrounding territories in the Holy Land with a multitude of sites connected to the life of Jesus and the Apostles attracted many pilgrims in the Middle Ages, especially after the Christian army had conquered Jerusalem from the Muslims in 1099. Although the Holy Land and Jerusalem are situated thousands of kilometres from Scandinavia, hundreds if not thousands of Scandinavians travelled there. Not only did Scandinavian soldiers participate in the crusades to the Holy Land, but numerous Scandinavian pilgrims travelled to Jerusalem, like Saint Birgitta of Sweden or Bishop Magnus Tavast of Turku.

Rome with its tombs of Saints Peter and Paul as well as the administrative centre of the Catholic Church was another obvious choice for pious pilgrims. Rome became an especially attractive destination for pilgrims during the Holy Years or Jubilees, when the popes granted large indulgences to all pilgrims visiting the Eternal City. Especially in the late Middle Ages when the popes had returned to Rome after the Avignon period and the Great Western Schism, Rome became the target of many Scandinavian pilgrims. Many of them arrived there during the jubilees that were celebrated in 1300, 1350, 1390, 1400, 1425, 1450, 1475, 1500, and 1525. The 1350 jubilee was particularly popular, but also lethal for many pilgrims because of the plague epidemic in the town. Among the many who lost their lives because of the plague in Rome were Canon Thidemannus Ulfhardi from Turku cathedral and Hermannus Hartlevi, parish priest of Finnström in the Åland Islands.

Sometimes a pilgrimage to Rome was combined with taking care of certain issues at the papal curia. The bishops and especially archbishops visited the papal curia regularly, because taking care of business in their dioceses required regular visits to the pope. The papal source material includes testimony of numerous visits by Scandinavian prelates to the papal curia. The Archbishops of Uppsala Jacob Ulvsson and Gustav Trolle were personally in the curia, on the occasion of their appointment to the archiepiscopal see, as were many bishops: Olavus Magni of Turku in 1450, Birger Månsson of Västerås in 1463, and Peder Månsson of Västerås in 1523, for example. Additionally, numerous clerics visited the papal curia during the Middle Ages to secure their appointments to a certain ecclesiastical position or to beg pardon for a severe sin they had committed. One of these was Brother Johannes Petri from the Dominican convent of Västerås, who arrived in Rome in the early 1500 and was guilty of accidentally killing a man while he had still been a member of the Dominican convent of Nidaros.

Scandinavian rulers paid diplomatic visits not only to the papal curia for religious reasons but also the popes as secular rulers of the Papal States. These visits, such as that of King Christian I of Denmark in 1466, often combined political courtesy and pilgrimage. King Christian's visit in Rome was not very successful since the Roman sources criticised the King for bringing Pope Paul II (r. 1464–1472) unworthy gifts – the Danish King arrived in Rome with only one barrel of dried fish from Iceland. A disappointed notary wrote in the copybook of the Sacra Romana Rota that when King Christian left Rome on 27 April 1466, no festivities took place and the Rota had a normal court day, although the arrivals or departures of kings were usually celebrated in the curia with a holiday. Since rulers could not visit the popes regularly, many had a permanent representative in Rome, such as Hemming Gadh who represented Swedish regents and took care of matters important to Sweden.

The Birgittine house in Rome was also a meeting point for Scandinavians who came to Rome. There they could get advice on how to advance their issues at the papal curia. The house also offered shelter for pilgrims, but it could not host all Scandinavian visitors. The representatives of the Danish kings in particular were not always very welcome there, but according to the guestbook stayed at the hospice of the German Santa Maria dell'Anima church.

The third major Christian shrine was Santiago de Compostela in northern Spain, where the shrine of Saint James was located. Saint James was a particularly important saint in the Middle Ages. There were churches dedicated to him all over the Christian West, and these formed a still extant network of pilgrimage sites, the so-called *cammino di Santiago*. Even one church in faraway Finland, the church of Renko, belonged to this network, and medieval sources inform us of foreign pilgrims there. The pilgrim badge from Santiago de Compostela was the scallop shell that the pilgrims sewed on their clothes and were buried with. In southern Scandinavia can be found one of the largest concentration of these shells in medieval graves, so Compostela must have been a very popular pilgrimage site for Scandinavians.

Despite the importance of these three major shrines, pilgrimages to local ones were more common in the Middle Ages since it was easier to take a day off for a pilgrimage to a shrine in the vicinity than to leave on a long journey to a faraway place. Travelling far away also required economic means, and it was not always possible to leave one's family for a longer period. We have no medieval sources telling us about local pilgrimages to the churches of the neighbouring parishes or close-by monasteries, but these must have been extremely numerous. By contrast, there is little more information about pilgrimages to the most important Scandinavian shrines such as Nidaros or Vadstena.

Nidaros with its tomb of Saint Olaf was one of the most important medieval Scandinavian pilgrimage sites and very well known internationally. Especially in the late Middle Ages, when Saint Olaf had become popular outside Scandinavia, numerous pilgrims visited the rich Norwegian archiepiscopal town. Another important Scandinavian pilgrimage site was Vadstena, where Saint Birgitta had commanded the building of the first Birgittine monastery and where the remains of the saint herself as well as of her daughter Catherine were buried. Saint Birgitta's miracle collection recounts numerous pilgrims to her shrine – by people either hoping for a miracle or wanting to thank her for a miracle performed. Her miracle collections tell of people travelling to Vadstena from far away, not only from the Swedish mainland.

Most pilgrims visited a shrine to thank a saint for a miracle, or in hope of one. One example is that of Ragnhild, wife of a farmer in the commune of Rinna in Östergötland, who for a long time had suffered from strong headaches. She states that a certain Magnus Grito from Viby commune had advised her to turn for help to Bishop Nils Hermansson since the Bishop had aided Magnus with his problems. Bishop Nils indeed helped Ranghild to recover from the headache and her testimony was written down among the miracles procured by the Bishop.

Some pilgrims had yet other reasons for making a pilgrimage. According to canon law, a person who had committed a grave sin, such as killing someone, could be sent on pilgrimage as punishment. Killers were often sentenced to make a pilgrimage to the parish church of their victim and to pray there for the soul of the deceased person. Scandinavian murderers could be sent on a penitential pilgrimage to all the cathedral churches in their home countries, or in some cases even further away, to the shrine of Saint Olaf in Nidaros, for example. Those who had stolen from churches were sometimes also sent on a penitential pilgrimage. For example, Kanutus Molle, a priest from the diocese of Turku, had continued in his priestly tasks although he had been deposed from his priestly office because of theft. This was a major offence against the ecclesiastical authorities and the purity of sacraments, and thus he had been sent on a long penitential pilgrimage: to the Holy Sepulchre, Santiago de Compostela, and the Cave of Saint Mary Magdalene in Provence, after which he came to Rome in 1495 and petitioned for absolution from the pope.

An important reason for leaving on pilgrimages was indulgences, which helped the Christians to shorten their time in Purgatory. Pilgrimages to a certain site at a certain time – for example, Rome during the Jubilees or consecration of a newly built church – could grant the pilgrim large numbers of indulgences. Additionally, a visit to a close-by church on the day of its patron saint and giving a generous donation to the church's building fund (*fabrica*) could give pilgrims a considerable quantity. The idea of collecting indulgences in different ways – including by buying them – became particularly popular by the end of the 15th century, and many parish priests turned to the pope to receive a papal indulgence for their church in order to increase the number of pilgrims and thereby the church's income.

There were also other personal reasons for taking up such a journey, such as curiosity to see new places. Pilgrimages could not however be used as an excuse to leave one's family and enjoy life elsewhere, since a person could not leave for pilgrimage without the permission of his or her spouse. This was a practical regulation, because the absence of a pilgrim should not endanger the family or its income for an undefined period. The regulation had a rationale, because it was dangerous to leave on a long pilgrimage. The risk of becoming sick or of dying was constant, but so was that of encountering robbers. Medieval sources are full of stories about pilgrims who were robbed or who never returned home from their journey. It was also common for pilgrims to make a will before undertaking a longer journey.

Saint Birgitta of Sweden

The best known Scandinavian medieval saint is Saint Birgitta of Sweden. She was born to an upper class family in the parish of Finsta in Uppland 1303. Her father Birger Persson was the governor and lawspeaker of the Uppland region and her mother, Ingeborg Bengtsdotter, was a member of the influential Swedish family of Folkunga. Birgitta was married at the age of 14 to Ulf Gudmarsson, who also belonged to the Swedish aristocracy. Birgitta acted as a lady maid for the Swedish Queen Blanche of Namur, spouse of King Magnus IV of Sweden.

Birgitta and Ulf had eight children. In 1341, the very religious couple left for a pilgrimage to Santiago de Compostela. After Ulf's death in 1344, Birgitta decided to dedicate her life to God. She joined the community of Franciscans but began to develop an idea of her own religious community in Vadstena. In order to promote her conception of a new monastic order, the order of the Most Holy Saviour, and to visit Rome in the jubilee year of 1350, Birgitta left on a pilgrimage with her daughter Catherine and some others. She travelled via Avignon, where she tried to persuade the pope to return to Rome and to accept the rule of her order. She did not succeed in these attempts but arrived in Rome which she chose as her permanent residence. She left the Eternal City only for a pilgrimage to Jerusalem in 1373 but returned there the same year, where she died on 23 July.

She was originally buried in the church of San Lorenzo in Panisperna, but her earthly remains were brought back to Vadstena, where the first monastery of her order was to be built. Despite the pope's original refusal to accept her monastic rule, she had further developed the idea of her monastic order and kept sending precise instructions to Vadstena on how to proceed with building the monastery. Her order later obtained papal approval, and Birgitta was canonised by Pope Boniface IX in 1391. She was the first woman ever proclaimed a saint in Saint Peter's Basilica in Rome.

Like her sainthood, her monastic rule was contested, if eventually accepted by the Council of Constance in 1415, because the idea of a double monastery where monks and nuns lived together, even if physically separated, was not tolerated universally. Some theologians were also critical of the orthodoxy of her revelations: the visions that Birgitta had had since her childhood and which became more frequent after the death of her husband. In these visions, she heard and saw Jesus or Virgin Mary talking to her, telling her what she should do and how she should advise other people. The revelations were written down by Birgitta's confessors and in the Middle Ages it existed both in Swedish and Latin versions.

Crusades

Crusades were the largest military enterprise of medieval Western Europe. They began almost a millennium ago with the conquest of Jerusalem in 1099 and lasted for over 500 years. The first crusades were directed at the Holy Land, but the concept was soon also adapted to wars against Muslims in the Iberian Peninsula and against non-Christian populations around the Baltic Sea.

The idea of the crusades was born during the Church council organised in Clermont, France, in 1095. Pope Urban II gave a speech in which he stated that the Christian population of the Holy Land was suffering under Muslim rule and exhorted all to participate in a military campaign to liberate Jerusalem and the Holy Land. For those who decided to join, or 'take the cross', the Pope promised indulgences that would wash away all committed sins. The Pope's speech created a mass movement among Europeans, and hundreds of thousands of men took the cross and decided to participate in the liberation of Jerusalem. French, German, and English armies were the largest and took leading positions in the first crusade, but there were participants from all European countries, including Danes and Icelanders. One of these was Prince Sweyn of Denmark who never reached the Holy Land but was killed on the way in Anatolia in 1097.

The first crusade, resulting the liberation of Jerusalem in 1099 and the foundation of the Crusader States in the territory of the Holy Land, was only one in the long chain of crusades that continued throughout the 12th, 13th, and 14th centuries. Participation in these military campaigns was popular not only because of the indulgences but also because it gave a certain prestige to the person leaving for crusade.

Illustration 6.1 Saint Birgitta, pointing to a book in her hand. Next to her is the missionary Saint Sigfrid with the three heads of his nephews in a basket. Altar from 15th century, Möja church, Sweden, now in the National Historical Museum, Stockholm.
Photo © Anna-Stina Hägglund 2020.

Numerous Scandinavians from all of its countries participated in the later crusades to the Holy Land. We know relatively little about the participants but the names of some of the more famous ones, such as rulers, are known. One well-known Scandinavian crusader was the Norwegian King Sigurd I Magnusson († 1130), who even received a nickname *Jorsalafare* (Jerusalem traveller) because of his participation. In English, he is known as Sigurd the Crusader.

Participation in crusades became popular, and early in the 12th century, the idea expanded to fighting the Muslims in the Iberian Peninsula. The Iberian crusades are known as the *Reconquista*, and they ended as late as in 1492 when the last Muslim stronghold in Granada was conquered. Some Scandinavians also took place in the *Reconquista*; narrative sources relate their presence in the conquest of Lisbon in 1147, the Battle of Silves in 1189, and on other occasions.

From 1108 and especially from the mid-12th century onwards, the crusading idea also spread north, and in the mid-12th century, the Cistercian Abbot Bernard of Clairvaux promised crusade indulgences for those who took the cross and fought against the non-Christian Slavic populations on the eastern side of the River Elbe. Soon the crusading ideology expanded to Scandinavia, and crusades were directed further north and east: to Finland, to the Baltic regions, and to territories in northern Poland and Germany south of the Baltic Sea.

The Scandinavian crusades were mainly undertaken by Danes and Swedes, but Norwegians also participated occasionally. We can see two broad theatres for Scandinavian crusades that developed at the same time, in the mid-12th century: Swedes went on crusades to present-day Finnish territory, while Danes fought in the Wendic territories close to the Bay of Wismar and from around 1200 further east, in the territory of present-day Estonia. This division of labour was not absolute, since we know that Swedes participated in battles in Estonia and that Danes for their part had strongholds in southern Finland. But it seems that there was some kind of coordination between the two countries so that they did not compete with each other.

The Danish crusades around the Baltic Sea are relatively well documented and studied, and they are closely related to rising royal power in Denmark. Participating in a crusade was an important way for the Danish kings to establish their power, and therefore many Danish kings and princes eagerly took the cross. When the Danes had Christianised the Wendish territories by the end of the 12th century, in cooperation and sometimes competition with German allies, they began to make military expeditions further east, to the island of Saaremaa and the northern shore of present-day Estonia. In 1219, the Danish crusading army led by King Valdemar II the Victorious and Archbishop Anders Sunesen of Lund defeated the Estonian troops, and the Danes gained a stronghold in northern Estonia where they built a Danish castle, in Estonian 'taani linna', nowadays Tallinn. The Danes kept northern Estonia under their rule until 1346, when King Valdemar IV sold the territories to the Teutonic order.

The Swedes made three major crusades to Finland. The first is only known from later sources. It was led by the Swedish king and later Saint Eric and directed in the 1150s at the southwestern coastline. In Finnish historiography, it is traditionally claimed that the Finns were converted to Christianity as a result of the first crusade to Finland. However, there are no contemporary sources or reliable evidence concerning such a big military campaign. The second Swedish crusade took place around a century later and its target was the historical province of Tavastland. The third Swedish crusade took place in 1293, and its target was the pagan Karelians.

There is one important question regarding the Scandinavian crusades that scholars have debated back and forth, namely whether or not can they be regarded as crusades.

Some scholars are of the opinion that they were not religious wars but simply political conquests in the tradition of the Viking raids, namely frequent military attacks by coastal fleets against neighbouring territories, the *ledung*. However, other scholars have shown that the papal approval for the Nordic military campaigns, the indulgences granted for participants, and the timing and coordination of the campaigns with contemporary crusades made by others mean that they can be considered real crusades.

7 Economic Growth and Fall – Urbanisation and Agrarian Crisis

Urbanisation

Europe experienced rapid economic and social development between c. 1000 and c. 1300 due to a favourable climate. The increase in agricultural production meant an increase in population, and for the first time, since the Roman period, greater numbers of farmers could produce a surplus they could sell to others. Trade and craft supplemented agricultural work in the countryside, and people began to move to towns that developed at an increasing pace from the 11th century onwards. Urbanisation took place first in central western Europe, but spread gradually over the whole continent in the course of the following centuries. Towns did not only offer work and accommodation for a growing population but became commercial hubs, as well as centres of royal and ecclesiastical administration. Due to the high concentration of wealthy inhabitants, towns also became centres of literacy and culture.

In Scandinavia, urbanisation took place relatively late compared to other parts of Europe. Despite the first signs of towns from already in the 8th century onwards, urbanisation in the full meaning of the word first really began gaining pace in Denmark, Norway, and Sweden from the 12th or 13th century onwards. By then, the countries had reached a sufficient level of population and food production surplus needed for the founding and functioning of towns. Finland followed a century later, while the first Icelandic towns can be dated to the post medieval period.

Urbanisation in Scandinavia took place in three phases, which overlapped with each other and varied from one region to another: the formation of economic centres, the founding of administrative centres (royal and ecclesiastical), and finally the growth of fully developed towns with privileges and various forms of self-governance. The medieval sources do not always distinguish clearly between these types. The words that mean town (*by, stad, urbs, civitas*) have been used differently by different authors and in different kinds of sources. In the early period, *civitas* seems mainly to have been used for cathedral towns but was employed much more generally from the 13th century onwards.

In the first phase of urbanisation, certain places along the main trading routes became more popular and were more convenient than others. These places began to attract more inhabitants and became eventually commercial hubs. A good example of such hubs is Hedeby/Schleswig between present-day Germany and Denmark. In Sweden, a similar commercial hub was formed in Birka on Lake Mälaren and in Norway Skíringssal in the Oslofjord. Hedeby and Birka especially were already relatively large urban communities in the 10th century. From the 11th century onwards, urban development reached a new stage with the arrival of Christianity and ecclesiastical administration located where there was commerce and people, for example in Ribe and Århus in Denmark. At the same time, the incipient centralisation of royal power in the three Scandinavian kingdoms had an effect upon urbanisation. Rulers preferred places that could be easily defended but were also administratively central. Thus, towns were no more simply commercial centres along main trading routes but gained political and legal-administrative functions. From the 13th century at the latest, the functions and status of towns were more clearly defined because each had to receive a royal privilege and town laws allowing it to function as a legal entity and individually take care of internal matters. New towns were founded in several places. By the high Middle Ages, towns had also become places where craftsmen had their specialised workshops and could sell their products.

The number of Scandinavian towns increased steadily from the 10th century onwards. In addition to the Viking Age commercial hubs in Hedeby, Ribe, Birka, and Skíringssal, we know that Århus was founded in the 10th century together with Lund, Odense, Viborg, and Roskilde in Denmark, as well as Sigtuna in Sweden and Nidaros in Norway. All these towns were episcopal sees with cathedrals, and fundamental for ecclesiastical administration. The number of towns grew quickly, especially in the 13th century, but ceased after the Black Death. By 1500, there were c. 100 towns in Denmark and c. 40 in Sweden (including Finland) but only 15 in Norway. Many of these towns were so small – with less than a thousand inhabitants – that it is somewhat doubtful whether they should be called towns, but they had received royal town privileges and were thus officially recognised as such. Examples of such small towns were Maribo in Denmark and Naantali in Finland, which had received town privileges only because a Birgittine monastery had been founded there. Only a couple of hundred inhabitants probably lived in such places. Around 40 Scandinavian towns can be defined as medium to large towns with 1,000–4,000 inhabitants, and these include many ecclesiastical centres such as Ribe, Århus, Odense, Roskilde, Lund, Linköping, and Uppsala but also others like Vyborg on the border with Russia, Tønsberg in Norway, or Gävle in Sweden. The number of towns with over 4,000 inhabitants was very small and included Bergen in Norway, Flensburg, Copenhagen, and Malmö in Denmark, Kalmar, Visby, and Stockholm in Sweden, and perhaps even Turku in the present-day Finland. No Scandinavian town reached the 10,000 inhabitant figure sometimes considered as the upper defining limit of a large town at the European scale. Bergen was the biggest Scandinavian town with over 7,000 inhabitants, and its importance was stressed by its close contacts with the Hanseatic League. Stockholm was the largest Swedish town and Copenhagen the biggest Danish one, both with slightly fewer inhabitants than Bergen. Settlements in Iceland and Greenland were so sparsely populated that it is difficult to talk of towns. Even Gardar with its cathedral and the bishop of Greenland was rather a group of farms than a town.

There were different types of towns in Scandinavia: cathedral towns, monastic, commercial, and administrative. By the late Middle Ages, most towns had more than one of these functions. What was common to them was that the rulers had granted them privileges, allowing them to administer the town independently and to use a specifically tailored code of law. The Danish and Swedish towns with privileges were relatively independent from the crown, and the burghers could freely elect the governing body, the town council led by the mayor. The highest officials were usually elected amongst the most influential and wealthy burghers. The king would appoint his own representative, a bailiff, to secure royal rights in the towns, but they were in practice often appointed from among the burghers and would not normally interfere with the town's self-governance. In Norway, by contrast, towns were independent administrative units but it was the task of the king to appoint the members of the town council as well as an administrator, who would lead the council. In addition to the highest administrative body, the Scandinavian towns had other officials such as firefighters, night watchmen, harbour officers, scribes, notaries, and others. They too were usually elected from among the burghers. The town councils could independently decide on town matters, and they were also responsible for administering justice. The members of the town council met regularly in the town hall and discussed all current issues.

Towns on the Coast

Access to water and commercial routes was important for the development of Scandinavian towns. Before 1200, much cargo from Western Europe and England went over land to Schleswig or Lübeck and from there further into the Baltic. After 1200, many more ships sailed all the way north of Jutland, through the Danish straits and into the Baltic. Transport by boat may have taken longer but it saved a lot of time when the cargo did not have to be loaded and reloaded several times, and a lot of money because merchants avoided paying the many customs fees that had to be covered while travelling along land roads. Not all were willing to spend the extra time at sea, and therefore those merchants who took the longer route got a special name *Ummelandsfarer*, 'around the land traveller'.

All the merchant ships sailing to the Baltic Sea had to pass through the Øresund. Land on both sides belonged to the Danish ruler, and Øresund could be controlled at its most narrow place, with Helsingør on one side and Helsingborg on the other. The Danish ruler could thus control the most important entrance to the Baltic Sea, which caused a lot of controversies during the Middle Ages, especially between the Hanseatic League and the Danish rulers. In 1429, King Eric of Pomerania for the first time introduced a toll on each ship passing through the sound. It became one of the largest income sources for the union kings and later the Danish kings until 1857.

Sailing along the Scandinavian coast required harbour towns at regular intervals so that the ships could bring on fresh water and other supplies. This led to the founding of several smaller coastal towns from the late 12th century onwards. After c. 1350, however, some of these towns lost importance because new and bigger ships could sail directly over the open waters to their destination and did not need to visit ports on the way. Kalundborg and Vordingborg in Denmark had been founded a couple of hundred years earlier as castles – *borg* – to control the water ways, but now began a slow economic and administrative decline. Visby on Gotland also stagnated and grew poorer because ships now sailed directly from Scandinavia to the big cities in Livonia and Prussia. Visby probably also suffered a loss of men and money from the Danish conquest in 1361.

Urban Environment

The life in towns differed very much from the one in the countryside because of the towns' various functions and because of a much denser population that required different kinds of buildings. The houses in Scandinavian towns varied in size and construction material depending on their function. The majority of town houses in Scandinavia were built of wood, which was readily on hand almost everywhere in the north. But from the 13th, and especially the 14th century onwards, stone and brick were also used as construction materials. Stone and brick were particularly used for administrative or ecclesiastical buildings, but wealthy burghers also began to build their town houses with these materials, thus also diminishing the danger of fire. Very few medieval wooden buildings have survived intact to our days to leave us a solid visual testimony of their appearance, but archaeological excavations have unearthed a lot of wooden house structures that enable hypotheses about them and the districts they created. Written Norwegian sources contain additional information about the housing system because they give names for several different kinds of house, such as living house, kitchen house, and storehouse, as well as other household buildings such as byre, stable, and barn. In towns, the different buildings of a single household were built within a fenced area that separated those of one household from another. Each household had thus a private fenced courtyard surrounded by buildings with different functions. In these courtyards or adjacent fields, the burghers could cultivate vegetables and herbs needed for cooking. In the courtyards, there were also places for domestic animals, especially hens and pigs.

Unlike in the countryside, in the towns where there was lack of space, many buildings had several stories. In particular, burgher houses often had a workshop at the street level, and the living spaces on the one above. Archaeological finds do not allow us to know the number of stories medieval houses had for certain, but wooden two-storey houses were probably the most common. With that said, there were higher buildings. For example, the stone houses built according to the model of the Hanseatic towns surviving in the medieval centre of Visby, on the island of Gotland, bear witness to houses with several stories. However, Visby was a particularly wealthy commercial town, and thus might not be the best example of what buildings in an average Scandinavian town looked like. Another good example of a medieval town environment is preserved in Bergen, Norway. The old quarter of Bergen, the Bryggen – although the buildings now visible are only from the 18th century – has a medieval origin and still gives us an impression of how the medieval town might have looked, with wooden two-storey buildings and inner courts.

In Central Europe, most medieval towns were surrounded by walls that connected watch towers from where it was possible to defend the town. A good example of this on the Baltic Sea is Tallinn. In Scandinavia, however, town walls made of stone were much rarer. Because of legal, administrative, and commercial needs, it was important that the town area was clearly separated from the surrounding countryside, but this did not always require the existence of walls. Many Scandinavian towns were surrounded by a moat, or the town territory was separated by natural border, as per towns situated by the seashore or along a river. Many small towns, like the monastic ones of Maribo in Denmark or Naantali in Finland, did not have walls because there was no particular need to defend the town from enemies. For the royal centres, good defence was more important, and therefore Copenhagen, for example, was surrounded by a moat, while in Stockholm, the old town was situated on an island that could be easily defended. In some other towns, with a royal castle, like Turku or Bergen, the castle itself was circled by walls and thus easily defendable, but the town did not have massive town walls or defensive tower structure. Fortification of Scandinavian towns became more common during the later parts of the Middle Ages, when

Illustration 7.1 The storage and trading houses of the medieval Hanseatic League along the water front at Bryggen in Bergen. The wooden houses are not medieval but reflect the architecture and the layout of the original structures relatively precisely. Excavations in the area have yielded a huge range of material illustrating many aspects of everyday life.
Photo Yair Haklai 2010. This file is licensed under the Creative Commons Attribution-Share Alike 3.0.

political conflicts were on the rise and the royal centres had to be more secure. For example, Danish sources describe how the inhabitants of Kolding decided to fortify the town after a rebellion in the year 1313.

In principle, the plan of a medieval town was relatively simple. There was at least one church in the town as well as at least one administrative building, both usually situated close to the main market place. These formed the core of the town. In the town centre, there were usually also the houses of the most wealthy burghers as well as the wealthiest guild houses. Less wealthy burghers had their houses a little further from the centre, and the poorest town dwellers had their houses the farthest away, close to the town limits. Most medieval towns grew during the course of the Middle Ages, and thus the town area became larger and larger. Sometimes, this meant that the town walls or moat had to be built again in another place. A town's street plan, especially in its outer circles, could also change many times.

Most medieval Scandinavian towns had more churches that shaped the town structure with their towers and stone or brick walls. Episcopal towns had cathedrals that were usually larger and more centrally placed than the other churches. In addition to the cathedral or the central parish church of each town, several other churches could be situated within the walls. Most medieval Scandinavian towns had a Dominican or Franciscan convent, sometimes both, and many towns were divided into several parishes. Especially in the episcopal towns, there were also buildings in the centre belonging to the bishop as well as to the highest clerics, the prelates and canons. Some religious societies or guilds could also have their own houses in the town centre. Centrally sited monastic houses could be very fine. For example, in the old town of Stockholm, the cellars of the Dominican convent still exist beneath the more modern houses. We know nothing for certain about the Dominican convent, but late 15th-century texts reveal that this must have had at least two stories. This becomes evident from a medieval document which relates the story of Brother Benedictus Magnus, who together with three other friars had entered the room of their superior, Guardian Birger, with the intention of beating or even killing him. The Guardian grew scared and to escape the men he leaped from his window. Since it is said that he died of the fall, the Guardian's room must have been higher up than street level.

It has been debated whether some of the old cathedral towns were laid out to form a cross, with the cathedral in the centre and divided into four quarters by two main roads, with four churches in total at the roads' ends. If so, they would at a small scale be imitating the structure of medieval Jerusalem. Lund and Schleswig do actually conform to this model but this may also be coincidental and not planned.

Everyday life in a town centred around the town centre, where the market place was situated. All who came to the town to sell their products or to buy something had to head to the market place. The wealthy burghers and craftsmen in their turn did not operate in the market place but had their own shops where they could sell the products. Each town that had access to water also had a harbour area, where the warehouses of the burghers were typically located because transport via water routes was so much easier than by land.

Towns were not only appealing and tempting but also suspicious and dangerous. Towns could provide freedom: they constituted a separate juridical unit, different from the surrounding countryside, and unfree peasants could gain personal freedom by moving into the towns. After a specific time, normally a year and a day, the lord of the manor no longer had any claim upon them. 'Town air makes free' was the short and precise formulation in German sources. Economically, towns often offered better possibilities than the countryside for energetic young persons, but the price could be high. Back home they had had a network of family and friends to help them if their situation became dire; until they had established a new network in the towns, they were less protected against bad fortune.

The towns also contained beauty, and on a much more sophisticated level than could be experienced in the countryside: the amazing shining and glittering altarpieces and religious statues in the big churches, the wall paintings with their pang-colours and lighting-like neon when new, the big, regular processions with relics, and singing from large professionally trained groups of monks and priests, the theatre plays performed by the many guilds in town, the music from organs in the cathedrals. The newest architecture and the latest fashion in clothing came first to the towns. They had much to offer to anyone with a taste for aesthetics. The many public sermons by skilled preachers and great orators gave food for thought and consolation for the soul, and afterwards the towns could offer a large selection of both local and imported beers that one could never find in the countryside.

The status of women in towns has been much discussed by researchers, and it seems to have changed over time and perhaps between different Scandinavian towns. Women could not take part in the governance of the town or become members of town councils, but they often had access to the meetings of the councils and could follow the political decision-making better than they could in the countryside. Women could own property and make contracts concerning trade and employment of workers to a much larger extent than in the countryside; they could be members of some guilds, and inheritance laws favoured women in towns much more than outside the towns.

In spite of all the possibilities they offered, towns also had a sinister reputation for being sinful and dangerous. There was too much drinking, gambling, and fighting in the streets, preachers warned in their sermons. Many Scandinavian town laws specified that one should leave one's weapons when entering the town, or at least, that it was strictly forbidden to ride into town with one's crossbow loaded.

Much of the fighting and disturbances was ascribed to the town proletariats, the poor people who were uncivilised and had not learned how to behave. Much was also ascribed to wealth and to too much money floating around and corrupting virtues into vices. Luxury was a sin and closely connected to towns, and the use of coins was dangerous. It could lead to greed and to money creating money in the form of interest, which was a sin according to the Church. The natural economy in the countryside, with its exchange of goods, was considered much better for the soul.

Prostitution was a particular phenomenon of towns and was accepted by town councils, probably out of simple necessity. There was a constant surplus of young, unmarried men in the towns, living there or passing through while travelling, and it was considered necessary to let them have some outlet for their natural urges. The town councils could quote Saint Augustine, from around 400, that 'if you take away the prostitutes, the world will end in chaos because of lust'. A smaller evil must sometimes be accepted to avoid a bigger evil, Augustine argued.

The offers from prostitutes were a danger to any man coming from the countryside and seem to have been one of the first things to meet him in town. In the Nordic languages, prostitutes were often called 'women of the gates', probably because they were waiting for clients just inside the town gate. The town councils tried to regulate prostitution and concentrate it within certain places or houses, and strictly forbid prostitutes from walking around in ostentatious luxury with expensive clothes and jewellery. Some women had apparently made a fortune from prostitution, but for most it was the last and most desperate way of simply surviving deep poverty.

Towns changed the mind, making it measure and quantify. Medieval towns were based on measuring and standardising much more than was the life in the countryside. Weight and length were clearly defined for things produced and traded in the town, and town halls held the standard measures that all others should conform strictly to: the one pound weight, the inch and foot measure stock, the bushel. From the late 13th century, many towns also began to have big clocks that divided the day and night into totally even units, no matter when the sun rose or set. It also meant that work began to become a commodity that could be measured in hours and ended at a specific time in the evening. Work was not, as in the countryside, simply participating in the continuous production of enough food to survive.

The towns measured because it was practical and necessary to secure stability and fair trading, but possibly also because it was deeply rooted in Christian thinking: the city of the heavenly Jerusalem is described in the Book of Revelation, and it is measured in detail by the angels. To measure is to make a town good. The contrast in the Bible was the city of evil, the 'great whore of Babylon'. Medieval towns on earth represented both of these biblical models.

Trade in Towns: Local and International

In the Middle Ages, towns were the commercial hubs and trade outside the towns was either totally forbidden or very limited to everyday local products. Trade in the towns began to be regulated in Scandinavia when stronger centralised kingdoms started to emerge, and the rulers needed to begin controlling trade especially its income. This was done by granting town privileges to certain places. When a town had received such privileges from the king, it could began to apply town law instead of the law regulating rural areas, and the town laws contained strict stipulations about trade in the towns.

In earlier medieval centuries, in the times of regional legislation, the central Scandinavian market towns could be given the right to use early town laws called the Bjarkey laws. The oldest of these laws regulating trade in towns are known from Norway (Nidaros and Bergen), but they were in use in Swedish and Danish towns as well. With the arrival of national legislation – in 1274 in Norway and in the 1350s in Sweden – towns could receive the equivalent national town laws, making all towns in a single realm more directly comparable. Denmark was an exception in never receiving a national legislation. Therefore, Danish town laws differed more significantly from each other than elsewhere. Town laws regulated trade and stipulated punishments for those who committed crimes within them. Crimes included commercial cheating by using false coins or weights, stealing, violence, and manslaughter. Town laws also regulated buildings in the town, the duties of citizens, and trading times.

Medieval towns had a two-fold significance for trade. On the one hand, they were the commercial hubs of local trade, and on the other, they were the centres of international trading. The role of medieval towns as local commercial hubs was based on the privileging of local trade to them, and the towns' citizens held a monopoly on the purchase and sale of products in the town and in adjacent territories. Since trading was allowed in the countryside only on the local market day, which usually coincided with the day of the patron saint of the local church, farmers had to bring their products to the town if they wanted to sell them. It was also only in towns that they could buy products which they could not make themselves.

The towns were not only the centres of local trade but international import and export additionally had to pass through them. This was a way for the rulers to ensure that all foreign merchants paid taxes and custom duties on the products in which they traded. This practice was in particular directed towards the merchants of the Hanseatic League, so that they could not freely trade at will but only in places controlled by the local authorities. Towns were also places where local artisans could exercise their profession, and craftsmanship in towns was strictly regulated. Not everyone was allowed to start a workshop but the towns regulated the number of professionals through the activity of the different professional guilds.

The Monetary Economy

The monetary economy possessing minted coins whose value was based on the quantity of precious metals – typically gold and silver, later also copper – developed in

Lydia (nowadays the western parts of Turkey) between 650 and 600 BC. From there, the idea of minted coins as means of payment spread quickly to all developed states. In antiquity, Roman coins were used everywhere in the Roman Empire. In the aftermath of the fall of the Roman Empire, the monetary economy declined for centuries, but the emerging European kingdoms began to mint their own money at the latest from the 9th century onwards.

The basic monetary unit within the Holy Roman Empire was the *mark*, corresponding to the value of approximately 234 g silver, while the basic coin was called a *penny*. The Scandinavian kingdoms assumed the same system. The basic monetary unit in Scandinavia was the *penning*, and its value varied slightly in different countries and at different times. In Sweden, for example, 192 *pennings* were worth of one mark, while in Norway the value of a penning was 1/240th of a mark (later 1/480th), in western Denmark 1/288th of a mark and in eastern Denmark, similar to the Swedish system, 1/192th of a mark. Coins worth one mark were not minted in Scandinavia in the Middle Ages, but the usual value of a coin was one penning. From the 1360s onwards, with a growing monetary economy, there was an increased need for more valuable coins. Therefore, coins called *örtug/ørtog* were minted, especially in Sweden. The other bigger coins, *aurar*, were minted only from the 1520s onwards, and the first marks date from an even later period.

The earliest coins minted in Scandinavia are from the Viking Ages. Due to the close connections to Viking Age England, they followed the English tradition and typically depict the symbols of the ruler and of Christianity. One of these early examples is the cross-coin of King Harald Bluetooth from around 980. It was very thin and weighed only 1/3 of a gram. The first pennies issued in Norway and Sweden also date from around the year 1000: King Olaf Tryggvason (r. 995–1000) had the first Norwegian coin minted, and the first Swedish coin was minted during the rule of King Olof Skötkonung (r. c. 995–1022). Minting of coins continued both in Denmark and Norway throughout the Middle Ages, but there are no signs of minting in Sweden between the 1030s and the 1180s. The first Scandinavian pennies were struck on both sides, but from the 12th century onwards, bracteates became more common: bracteates were pennies struck on one side only, the coin being so thin that the symbol struck on one side was clearly visible as an emboss on the other.

In many places in Europe, kings, regional rulers, and bishops could all mint their own coins. In Scandinavia, by contrast, the right to mint was reserved to kings, although coins were minted in different places with royal authorisation. On some rare occasions, the kings also delegated the right to Scandinavian archbishops. Many Scandinavian towns had the right to make coins but this was by royal privilege. All of which meant that the art of coining was in the hands of the kings. Nationally coordinated coining was usually good for the national economy because in good times, with the quality of coins regulated centrally, it could keep inflation down. In some other countries like Germany, where several actors had the authority to mint, the quality of coins varied significantly and could cause inflation if one authority used baser metals. There was also another advantage to centrally coordinated and controlled minting. If the ruler could control the monetary market and demand that only his own coins be acceptable payment, minting also could become a means of state income and inflation control. When all coins were regularly taken out of circulation, melted down, and replaced by new coins with a little less silver content, the ruler could control the national economy and gain a significant profit. Even if the value of the new coins was even only a few percentages less, this was still a substantial source of income for the king when it happened at the level of the entire kingdom. This right could be overexploited, leading to inflation and lack of confidence in the value of the coins, as happened in the decades around 1300 in all Scandinavian countries.

In the Middle Ages, the Scandinavian economy was still very small and there was little use for money, and thus also for minting. The shortage of local coins was not a problem because all foreign coins could be used. In fact, many coins arrived in Scandinavia through foreign merchants, and most of surviving known coins from the period before 1100 are of foreign origin. They have been found in hoards of various sizes indicating that they were not meant for daily use but stored away for times of trouble. In recent years, however, the use of metal detectors has led to many discoveries of single coins in Denmark, Norway, and Finland – although not in Sweden, where the use of metal detectors is forbidden. From the 11th and 12th centuries onwards, the amount of locally minted coins began to increase, and they are also more often found in archaeological excavations. Some of the recently detected coins are found on the sites of known medieval marketplaces, which can be interpreted as meaning that coins were used in Scandinavia for trading right from the beginning of the Middle Ages. The coin finds from the following centuries are more common, and single coins have been typically found in churches, perhaps lost by church goers.

There are only a few written testimonies about the value and use of coins and money in Scandinavia. One of the rare examples is the long legal dispute around 1300 at the papal curia between Archbishop Jens Grand of Lund and King Eric Menved of Denmark, during which the Archbishop complained that the King had constantly debased the coins he issued and created inflation: in the Archbishop's words: 'what earlier could be bought for 3 marks, can now hardly be paid with 25 marks'. The King's answer was that members of the Archbishop's family had kidnapped one of the royal mint masters and forced him to make false coins, and these were the cause of the inflation. When modern numismatists compare these false coins with the King's they have difficulties in finding any difference – they are both equally worthless. This was recognised internationally. When papal collectors were sent to Scandinavia to collect taxes and donations from the churches, they had firm instructions to avoid local coins and were told to prefer precious metal, fur, relics, and any other valuables that could later be sold on the European markets. If they had to accept Scandinavian coins, they should have them changed as soon as possible into some more stable currency.

In addition to the different local coins, many European currencies were in circulation in Scandinavia. Most of them were German – due to the Hanseatic League – but there were also English and French coins. Some of them, especially those rare items from the far east, might have functioned as precious investments or objects. In 1346, King Magnus Ericsson of Sweden had in his treasury 20 Italian Florins and 18 French gold Écu, but no Swedish coins. In 1379, several Hansa towns on the Baltic Sea agreed to standardise the silver content in their different currencies. In 1424, Queen Philippa had the Kalmar Union sign up to this agreement, linking Scandinavian coins to northern German ones, but this did not last long.

Progress and Prosperity: Technological Innovations of the 13th Century

The 12th was the century of a great leap forward in science and technology across Western Europe, Scandinavia included. The generations living after 1200 harvested what former generations had sown in terms of investments and development. The technological development involving more machines meant greater consumption of energy than earlier. For the whole Middle Ages, traditional fossil fuel was the main source of energy: houses were heated with wood and turf, machines sometimes powered by charcoal, and windmills and watermills also helped to meet the need for power.

The big hall of a Viking chieftain around the year 1000 had a central open fire needing more than 25 kg of wood every hour to maintain a temperature of 12°C on a chilly winter day. The amount of work to collect or cut so much wood throughout the year would have been overwhelming. Smaller houses with smaller rooms could be better insulated and more easily made warm. The fact that humans and animals often shared rooms increased the inside temperature. Viking-Age-type buildings did not have a chimney. The smoke from the open fireplaces was let out through holes in the roof, but much of it remained in the room. It cannot have been a healthy atmosphere to live in.

The 12th century saw the invention of the chimney, which from the 13th century began to be used in the buildings of larger institutions as well as in castles and manor houses. The heat from a clay or tile oven was much more concentrated than from an open fireplace, and the chimney made it possible to build houses with much smaller rooms and lower ceilings, without the danger of the house catching on fire. The idea of privacy and private rooms began after 1200 in Western Europe had probably also become common in Scandinavia by that time. This may in some way be connected to the new heating technique and smaller rooms.

Larger buildings made of stone or tiles, such as monasteries and castles, began to include heating systems called hypocausts. The system consisted of a huge construction in the basement of the building with a large fireplace, and above it a thick layer of stones that were warmed up by fire and emitted heat. The hot air the stones produced was let out by channels into the rooms in the building. Hypocausts were also used for heating private saunas and public spas in the new and rapidly growing towns. Sauna culture was common throughout Scandinavia, probably from an early period and certainly throughout the Middle Ages. It was a natural part of personal hygiene.

Wood was cut and collected everywhere for fire and for building, and already before 1200, there were problems with providing enough wood in certain areas, in the Scandinavian context especially in Denmark. Cistercian monasteries in Zealand owned large forests in Halland, several days' journey away, and around Schleswig, it was no longer possible to find sufficient and large enough pieces of timber. This resulted in the import of large quantities of timber from further away in the Baltic or elsewhere from Scandinavia. The growing need for wood made foresting, especially in Sweden, more systematic. Trees were felled during the winter, dragged out on the frozen rivers, and at spring floated down to the new harbour towns on the Baltic coast. Those living in the North Atlantic, on Iceland and Greenland, collected driftwood on the beaches or imported timber from Norway, and possibly also from the far-away Scandinavian station at L'Anse aux Meadows on Canadian Newfoundland.

Wood as fire material was supplemented in the Scandinavian lowlands with turf dug or cut from the moors and then dried. It was suitable for burning but generated a lot of smoke and caused problems for some. One of these was the Johannite brother Laurentius Misener, who in the 1460s complained so much about the heavy turf smoke in the convent of Ribe that he was transferred to the apparently much cleaner convent in Eskilstuna in Sweden. The turf digging technique has been known since the early Iron Age and continued in Scandinavia until the mid-20th century.

A new important provider of energy was mill. The earliest watermills are mentioned in Denmark in the 1130s, but soon afterwards also in other Scandinavian countries. They have probably had horizontal wheels that were easy to construct but not very efficient. The larger mills had vertical wheels either undershot or overshot, meaning the wheels were moved by water running under or over them. These were much larger constructions and probably came to Scandinavia with the arrival of monastic culture in the 12th century, although archaeological finds have shown that there were older mills as well. Five mills mentioned in Tommerup in Scania in 1161 seem to have been royally controlled, as were the three in Schleswig in 1192. Watermills were common in Denmark and Sweden, less so in Norway, and are known in Finland only from the 15th century. Windmills were already used in Scandinavia from the very late 12th century, but mostly in low areas with little water. The big mills were used industrially for driving the hammers working the iron osmonds or the large bellows for the furnaces. They were also used by landowners as a new means of taxing the peasants by demanding that they use mills to have their grain ground. Earlier, this had been done at home by women using simple hand-mills, but these were now often forbidden, confiscated, and destroyed by the landowners' officials – unless a village succeeded in negotiating a special privilege to keep and use their old hand-mills, as the inhabitants in Vä in Scania did in 1250.

Illustration 7.2 Mills revolutionised the energy sector in medieval Scandinavia. Pictured here is an illustration from the mid-16th century with a big watermill and some windmills around Stockholm.
   Olaus Magnus, *Historia de gentibus septentrionalibus*, Rome 1555. *Public domain.*

The Economic Crisis of the 14th Century

The 14th century was the century of economic crisis in Europe and in Scandinavia. The population decreased drastically due to the devastating effect of the Black Death from the 1350s onwards, when the plague struck almost every corner of Europe in several waves. It is, however, difficult to believe that an economic retraction of this size, in many places lasting two centuries, was the consequence of only the plague. Historians have traditionally stressed two internal structural factors that must have deepened and worsened the effect of the plague, and in recent years, the explanations have been substantiated by entirely new source material. The first factor is that of slow changes in the climate, and the second one is the overexploitation of land. Both are longue-durée phenomena and must have already begun a couple of generations before the great plague's arrival. The agricultural crisis was deepened as the decreased population of the towns created opportunities for newcomers. This resulted in increasing emigration from the countryside to the towns, both nationally and internationally.

The Plague

In 1347, the great plague reached Europe. Rumours of great calamities had spread in advance. India was deserted, Syria and Central Asia covered by dead bodies, it was said. Frogs and scorpions rained down from the sky, some had heard. The deadly and highly contagious pandemic originated most probably in Central Asia. It was caused by the bacteria *Yersinia pestis*, and the first symptoms consisted of headache, fever, stiffness of joints, diarrhoea, and nausea. Soon black buboes began to grow in armpits and groins, or if the lungs were infected the sick began to cough blood and had difficulties breathing. In either case, most of the infected died within one or two days.

The Black Death started in the spring and summer of 1347, and people began to die in great numbers in the coastal cities of the Mediterranean. In 1348 the plague reached Paris and most of France, in December Germany and the rich old cultural centres in eastern Europe. In 1349, it came to the rest of Germany, to England, and to faraway Scandinavia. The mortality rate was extraordinary. It has been estimated that in Western Europe 30–60% of the population died, but the regional variations were great and survived knowledge very sporadic.

The pestilence made its entry into Scandinavia in a ship which arrived in Bergen from England in 1349. The crew began to unload its cargo but died before this was finished. As soon as the goods from the ship reached the town, the local population began to die. According to contemporary Icelandic sources, two-thirds of those living in Bergen died. In the same year, the plague was recorded in Denmark, and after 1350, everywhere in Scandinavia – with the exception of Iceland from which we have no indication of the plague until 1402. There is no news about plague in Finland around the 1350s either.

Norway was hard hit by the Black Death and its recurrent epidemics throughout the rest of the Middle Ages, experiencing a demographic decline which was steep during the first hundred years after 1349 but still continuous until after 1500. The population decrease meant that there were not enough inhabitants for all rural areas, with the result that landowners' rents from farms dropped. According to the land register of Archbishop Aslak Bolt of Nidaros from 1430, the archiepiscopal see owed almost 3,000 farms in Norway but could expect a rental income that was 25% lower than before the plague. Church tithes in 1400 in most of the parishes around Oslo were only half of what they had been, in certain areas only a third. Everywhere farms were abandoned. It has been estimated that in Norway some 23–24,000 farms were in operation in the early 16th century, versus as many as 70,000 for the period before the Black Death. This means that almost two farms out of three were abandoned during the later Middle Ages.

The effect of the plague was inevitable and omnipresent. After couple of decades, it was noticed that entire villages had disappeared and could no longer be located. They belonged to the administrative memory of big organisations but had neither inhabitants nor houses, and yielded no income. In 1370, the bishop of Roskilde had a new register of landed income compiled, simply to get a clearer impression of the extent of the economic crisis. Time and again, the new register drew comparisons with the earlier one from 1290 and complained of the loss. The net result was the same for all ecclesiastical institutions from which we have sources. In general, they lost perhaps 60% or more of their income during the crisis that began with the Black Death.

Iceland was not hit by the plague until 1402–1404, but at that point perhaps as much as 60% of the population died, including all priests in the diocese of Hólar and half or more of the monks and nuns in the few Icelandic monasteries. Almost exactly half of all the 177 parishes in Iceland were left without a parish priest – they had all been buried in less than two years. Fresh epidemics came several times during the 15th century, and a large one was recorded in the 1490s.

It is impossible to estimate with any certainty the mortality rate in Scandinavia, except that it must have been terrifyingly high. Narrative sources mention that from one-third to five-sixths of Scandinavians died, and some of them added a small verse: 'The blind death made the heavens rich, and plundered the earth.' The verse was written in Latin, and if one counts the numerical value of the significant letters in the verse, it adds up to 1350, the year of the plague. For a few cities, we have registers of burials of important and wealthy individuals. In Ribe, on the Danish west coast, there had usually been 1.5 burials per year, but in 1350, the number rose to 17. In four other large cities, the yearly burial average used to be 4.3, but rose in 1350 to 32. The island of Gotland fared worst – at least among the places about which we have any information. From 1340 to 1349, an average 10.7 per year were buried in the churches of Visby, mostly from the town itself. In 1350, no less than 153 burials were registered.

In September 1349, King Magnus Ericsson of Sweden and Norway issued a letter with instructions on how to react to the fast spread of the plague. Half of the population in Norway had already died, he stated, and the mortality was hastily spreading towards Sweden: ... *är ey swa mykit folk aather, at ty gither til jorda kommit, som fraan stielper* (<there> is not enough people left so that they can ensure the burial of those who suddenly fall down). The King had agreed with bishops and the council of the realm to take immediate strong action. The letter ordered that all people throughout Sweden, ecclesiastics and lay, old and young, women and men, should each Friday come barefoot to their parish church, hear mass, and pray to the Virgin Mary to appease her Son and alleviate the burden of the plague upon the believers. They should all confess their sins and be ready to meet their maker. Furthermore, each individual should donate to the Church according to their means, and church wardens should distribute the donations to those who had become destitute as a result. All Christians should fast on water and bread. Accepting reality, King Magnus added that those who

Illustration 7.3 Danse macabre. The skeletons have risen from their graves and dance together with the living to remind us that we shall all die. The motif became especially popular after the Black Death in the mid-14th century. Pictured here is an image by the artist Bernt Notke († 1509). The painting was originally 30 m long, but only c. 7.5 m exist today. It is in the church of Saint Nicholas in Tallinn, but Bernt Notke also worked in Scandinavia, e.g., in Århus and in Stockholm. Art Museum of Estonia, Tallinn. Public domain.

would not do so should at least abstain from fish and fast only on beer and bread. In addition, all should financially contribute to a common fund that the King, with the consent of ecclesiastical authorities, could use as he found most efficient to honour God and His Mother.

The memory of the great plague lasted a long time and was later used even when dating letters: 'X years after the Great Pestilence'. Later, the epidemic returned at irregular intervals, never as deadly as the first time, with greater regional variations, but sometimes widespread enough to be registered in all Scandinavian kingdoms: in around 1360, 1370, 1400, 1420, 1452, 1464, 1483–1484, and onwards, in fact, into the 18th century.

In Western Europe in general, the Black Death was followed by widespread pogroms against Jews who were accused of having caused it by poisoning the wells and springs in a great conspiracy against Christendom. Sometimes, they were suspected of having corrupted Christians as their accomplices, and several thousand Jews were burned. One such case is also known from Scandinavia.

In 1350, the town council of Visby had detected an alleged conspiracy against Christianity. At Easter, the council had arrested nine traitors. One was Tidericus (Didrik), a church organist who before being executed had publicly confessed – without being tortured, the council stressed – to poisoning all the wells in Stockholm, other big cities in Sweden, and all over Sweden together with his accomplices. Some of them had later been apprehended by the town council and 'fittingly destroyed'. When the organist began to burn on the stake, he said that he had concocted a mixture which, if he had lived only one more year, would have killed each and every person on Gotland except his accomplices; also that he had a secret society with many members present at the execution. These were disguised as rich merchants travelling around everywhere and were 'signed with Greek or Hebrew letters', whatever that means – a kind of secret tattoo? At the end, the organist shouted, 'I know no more to say, but the whole of Christianity is poisoned by Jews and by us evil ones'.

The town council enquired further into the matter and found two members of the secret society who were priests and had poisoned a maniple, the liturgical band around the left arm of the celebrating priest used during divine service. They had celebrated mass during Pentecost in the local church of Saint Olaf, and all the members of the congregation who had kissed the maniple had died three or four days later, along with all who had visited them. When these evil priests were brought to the fire, one predicted that Christianity was lost unless God intervened, because the secret society had members among priests and ecclesiastics everywhere.

Tidericus and the case from Gotland was investigated further by the Hansa organisation in Lübeck and Rostock, and it was claimed that Tidericus had been commissioned by two wealthy German Jews, one of whom was living in Lübeck. The Jews had provided him with the poison and means to travel to several of the large trading cities along the Baltic coast and perform this terrible deed. In any case, the reaction of the town council of Visby shows that Scandinavia was closely connected to Western Europe and shared the fears and beliefs of the other Latin Christian countries. There were most probably similar cases elsewhere in Scandinavia in which Jews or other people were blamed for the plague and burned, but they have left no traces in the scattered source material.

The Climate Change

Scattered written statements in medieval sources indicate that from the first decade of the 14th century, summers in Scandinavia became colder and rainier. It rained day after day, season after season. The harvest rotted on the fields, and the few straws that could be harvested were infected by mildew. Those who ate it had nervous diseases and uncontrollable spasms – the terrible ailment known as the Saint Vitus' Dance. There were larger epidemics of the disease in the 1370s, for example, corresponding directly with the particular cold periods of the decade.

That the climate had already changed shortly after 1300 has been supported with investigations of oxygen isotopes in Arctic ice glaciers, but they can provide only a very general picture and are not detailed. Recently a huge series of measurements of tree rings in buildings – hundreds of thousands, mainly from Western Europe – have been combined and show without a doubt that the climate had changed and economic crises begun at least a generation before the arrival of the Black Death.

The evidence from Iceland indicates that the coldest medieval period occurred between c. 1150 and c. 1400, while the period beginning from 1450 and lasting until c. 1700 was not particularly cold. The effect of that climatic shift can also be seen in the recovery of the economy from the late 14th century onwards, then lasting beyond the end of the Middle Ages.

The Agricultural Crisis

Since climate change is always slow and difficult for individuals to detect, we must assume that it was only gradually realised in the Middle Ages that the earlier organisation of agriculture was no longer adequate and had to be changed or discarded. The second structural factor contributing to the economic instability in the 14th century occurred, indeed, within agriculture, a result of an increased population and the subsequent expansion of arable land, which meant that it was necessary to begin cultivating areas that could only sustain agriculture under optimal circumstances. After some time, this land became overexploited and less fertile and could no longer yield sufficient crops. This explanation is substantiated both by written sources and archaeological finds showing those farms eventually abandoned were primarily those on marginal land. In some areas in Norway, the viability of farming was often connected to the altitude of the farm. Above a certain altitude, agriculture became very unstable, and the farms in the highlands were the first to be given up. Climate and fertility were better and more stable in the lowlands. Along the coastline, a higher proportion of villages survived, probably because agriculture could be supplemented by rich fishing. Additionally, Norwegian peasants were encouraged, even forced by law, to supplement grain production with husbandry, which could satisfy a growing demand for meat during the 15th century, and also contribute manure to fertilise the land under plough.

The combination of plague and structural problems in food production meant that land became cheaper and labour more expensive. In Scandinavia, this led to a major re-organising of agricultural production. In some areas, less labour-intensive meat production became more common at the expense of growing grain. Big landowners began the systematic breeding of cattle for export, especially from mid and western Denmark to the markets of northern Germany. The increase in this trade can be followed in the toll registers of Danish towns, such as Ribe and Schleswig. It began only a few years after the Black Death, when we suddenly find oxen listed among the transport or war horses that had traditionally been the great export animals. Soon, the horse trade declined and oxen took over almost completely. The export trade virtually exploded from the mid-15th century, and 13,000 oxen passed through Schleswig alone in 1485.

The first 100 years after the Black Death also had the social effect of causing polarisation within the nobility. Many of the middling or low-ranking nobles had to give up their free status. They had no longer sufficient income to keep horses and weapon and provide the military service that had secured them exemption from taxes, and as a consequence they lost their noble status and became peasants and taxpayers. Those with enough capital profited and could buy out their less fortunate neighbours, and large lay landowners became even large and accumulated very large estates, mainly in the form of subservient peasant farms.

Before the Black Death, big estates were run with one or more large farms having a *bryde,* a bailiff, and a large group of labourers living on the central farm but with no or very little land for themselves. After the plague, the big farms were parcelled out into lots of smaller farms, and the former labourers became tenant peasants. It is much debated when this change took place, since sources are ambiguous. The process may have already begun earlier in the 13th century. It may also be connected to the abandonment of slavery which happened in Denmark around 1250 and in Sweden around 1335. The Christian laws prohibiting slavery have traditionally been seen as a reason for the abandonment of slavery, but these cannot have been the only reason. It is evident that it had become more profitable to till the land with subservient tenant farmers, responsible for producing enough to feed themselves, than with slaves whom the landowner had to feed.

The Lack of Labour

With a scarcity of labour after 1350, many individuals sought to improve their personal status and income by offering their services to the neighbouring landowner or by moving to the towns. The landowners tried to keep them on their own land by force, by paying them better, or by threatening that they would otherwise be totally superfluous. Estonia had been bought from the Danish King Valdemar IV by the Teutonic order only three years before the plague came, and Estonian peasants began moving to Tallinn in large groups when the shortage of labour made it very attractive economically. The Teutonic order threatened that if they did not return to the countryside, it would begin importing workers from Finland and even from Denmark.

The threats were probably not totally baseless. There was a huge, steady seasonal migration across the Baltic in all directions of people working in fishing, forest, or agriculture. It was probably a very old phenomenon but is only well attested in written sources from the 14th century onwards. Many from Finland frequently crossed the bay to Tallinn and Estonia, and the Teutonic order could probably have persuaded many of them to settle permanently.

Increased mobility in Scandinavia became possible because of increased demand for labourers in sectors that were becoming more industrialised, and connections over longer distances using bigger and better ships. The half century before 1400 was a period of great economic and social changes because of the sudden and drastic demographic shifts. The consequences for the future differed much from region to region. Norway's agricultural system was weakened for centuries to come while Denmark and parts of Sweden recovered demographically after a couple of generations, with new economic growth following.

8 Cultural Universalism

Gothic Architecture

The period beginning from the late 12th century is known in the history of architecture and arts as the Gothic. It was an architectural style that developed from the Romanesque architecture in northern France around the mid-12th century. Gothic architecture is often defined as the style with pointed arches, although this is too narrow a definition. The Gothic style was much lighter than the Romanesque because new building techniques which developed during the second half of the 12th century and after allowed the construction of much lighter walls and larger windows, often decorated with stained glass windows. Many narrow high towers as well as sophisticated structures supporting the lighter walls are also typical features of the Gothic style.

The Gothic style had its origin in the reconstruction work of the Saint-Denis abbey, close to Paris, in the 1140s. From France, the style quickly spread over the whole of Western Christianity. Although most remaining examples of Gothic architecture are churches or abbeys, the Gothic style was also applied to secular buildings such as castles, palaces, town halls, universities, and guildhalls. The Gothic style developed during the 14th century towards what is called the flamboyant style, which was characterised by towers and spires rising to great heights and richly decorated ribs and vaults. The walls also became thinner and windows larger, which required more supporting constructions. The lighter structures made the interiors of Gothic buildings more elaborate, and churches were typically equipped with a chain of side chapels, all decoratively vaulted. In Scandinavia, the Gothic style became dominant from the late 12th century onwards and it remained in use far after the end of the Middle Ages. It was applied to churches, castles, and palaces as well as to vernacular buildings.

From c. 1200 onwards, brick began to replace stone as the dominant building material in Scandinavia. The very first brick churches were built in Denmark in the 1160s, and a bit later in Sweden, Norway, and Finland. In Denmark, brick became quickly the dominant building material for churches. In Sweden, brick churches were also in the majority, except for in Götaland and Gotland where stone prevailed. In Norway, stone and wood were the most common building materials, but brick was also used especially in the eastern parts of the realm and the two main cities, Nidaros and Bergen. A good example of Danish Gothic brick churches is the cathedral of Roskilde built between 1170 and 1220 according to a French model. Similarly, the cathedral of Uppsala in Sweden was designed by a French architect working in Uppsala in the last decades of the 13th century. Entrusting the designing of ecclesiastical buildings to French masters of Gothic was typical in Scandinavian countries, except for Norway where English influence was strong. Good examples of English-style Gothic are the cathedrals of Nidaros (built between 1180 and 1320) and Stavanger (last quarter of the 13th century). French influence began to diminish during the 13th century and was replaced by German architecture.

Illustration 8.1 Stavanger cathedral. The older Romanesque church burned in 1272, and the new cathedral was built in Gothic style and probably finished already shortly after 1300. It was inspired by northern English church architecture; pictured here is the square choir to the east, with large windows and flanked by two towers.

Photo Vitold Muratov 2019. This file is licensed under the Creative Commons Attribution-Share Alike 4.0 International license.

Like the above-mentioned cathedrals, most Scandinavian cathedrals and abbey churches were built in the form of basilicas according to the French tradition. This meant that the church had a high central nave with lower side aisles on both sides. Alongside the basilica-form churches, there were also hall churches built according to German tradition. A hall church differed from a basilica in that the central nave and the side aisles were of the same height. The mendicants, who attempted to follow the principle of poverty, particularly preferred the more modest hall churches. An early example of such a church is the Dominican church of Saint Mary in Sigtuna, built in the 1230s/1240s. The Birgittines also used the hall church model in Vadstena and Maribo from the decades around 1400.

The 13th century was still a period of active church building, but after that only a few churches were erected. Small Danish parish churches were mainly built before 1200, and thus they are mainly of Romanesque style. The slightly later conversion of Norway, Iceland, Sweden, and especially Finland meant that proportionally more parish churches in these countries are built according to Gothic stylistic principles. Since the parish churches were often small, they never reached the full Gothic form as did the multi-aisled basilicas but remained architecturally rather modest.

Although the building of new parish churches decreased in the course of the 14th century, Gothic style is very much present in Scandinavia. After the economic decline caused by the Black Death had been overcome, many parishes wanted to redecorate the interiors of their churches, and in the course of the 14th century, several earlier churches received new vaulting and wall paintings that stylistically followed Gothic principles. The traditional wooden ceiling was replaced by new brick vaults that not only changed the style but also functioned as an effective fire protection. If the timber construction of the roof began to burn, the vaults prevented the ceiling from breaking and the fire from consuming the entire church interior.

Gothic architectural style was also applied to secular buildings such as palaces and castles. The centuries from 1200 on were period of growing royal power, and thus the building of castles and centralised administrative buildings also began to intensify. In Denmark, the early 13th-century royal castles, like Nyborg on Funen or Hammershus on the island of Bornholm, were relatively regularly shaped curtain wall buildings, with small towers at the corners. The 13th century was also a period of castle building in Sweden, and castles like that in Stockholm were built elsewhere, such as in Nyköping or Borgholm. The same kind of castle architecture was also applied in Finland, where the castles of Turku, Hämeenlinna, and Vyborg were built in the course of the 13th century. In Norway, the same kind of castles were constructed in Båhus and Akershus.

The earliest Scandinavian castles were made for defensive purposes, and the quarters for lodging were usually small and hardly comfortable. The 13th century brought a change in this respect. One of the early examples of the new trend was the palace of King Haakon Haakonsson in Bergen, built around 1250. Like the earlier castles, it was surrounded by towered curtain walls for defensive purposes but was built primarily for royal residence, and therefore, the defensive buildings were supplemented with two large halls meant for show and living. One of them, the *Håkonshallen*, still exists. The building is stylistically early Gothic and has a clear English influence, and it was later complemented with more private lodgings and a chapel.

Developing siege technology also changed the defensive buildings. One example of such changes is the arrival of protecting towers that were built on town or castle walls

Illustration 8.2 Håkonshallen, the Hall that King Haakon of Norway had made in the mid-13th century, as part of the Bergen fortification but also for official occasions. Its entire upper floor consists of the great banquet hall, measuring 33 × 13 m and 17 m high from the floor to the top of the ceiling. It was taken into use for the first time on 11 September 1261 for the wedding of the King's son Magnus. It burned already in 1266 but was soon restored in the early Gothic style and with inspiration from contemporary English architecture.

Photo Petr Šmerkl, Wikipedia. This file is licensed under the Creative Commons Attribution-Share Alike 3.0 Unported license.

from the 14th century onwards in Scandinavia. The earliest examples already date from the late 13th century, such as the town wall of Visby in Gotland built in the 1280s. Other good examples of similar castles are Kalmar in Sweden (modernised in the last quarter of the 13th century), Vordingborg and Kalundborg in Denmark, and Tønsberghus in Norway (mid-14th century). Many castles of this period were made of brick.

Other kinds of vernacular buildings also followed the new style, and the founding of towns meant an increasing need for urban buildings. From 1200 onwards, wealthy burghers adopted the Gothic building style and the construction of stone houses multiplied in Scandinavian towns. Brick was used in secular buildings only very rarely, and the known examples are royal or episcopal residences, such as the episcopal palaces in Koroinen and Kuusisto in Finland dating to the late 13th century.

The increasing influence of the Hanseatic League on Scandinavian towns in particular facilitated the adaptation of Gothic style for public buildings such as town halls and guild houses. Unlike the churches that were rebuilt several times, most medieval secular buildings have not survived to the present due to fires and other calamities. Those that still remain typically date to the last medieval centuries.

In the countryside, the building traditions of the 13th and 14th centuries did not differ significantly from those of earlier centuries. Independent wooden houses, often in longhouse style, were built in the countryside throughout the Middle Ages.

Gothic Arts

The Gothic style which developed from architecture was soon applied to arts, since many artistic traditions such as stone carvings on portals or pillars were closely connected to architecture. The Gothic style spread quickly over Europe, and Scandinavian countries, alongside the rest of the Europe, adopted the new style from the early 13th century onwards. The Gothic was dominant for the rest of the Middle Ages.

The Gothic style was applied to all of the different arts: from paintings, sculptures, carvings, and stained glass to manuscripts and various objects of art. If Romanesque art was mainly in use for ecclesiastical buildings or items, Gothic also spread to secular art, but for the whole medieval period, the Church was still the most important artistic patron. Other patrons of art were the upper classes, as earlier, but now also included the bourgeois class that had accumulated wealth after the rapid development of towns and trade from the 12th century onwards. Wealthy trade guilds and other institutions promoted the new artistic style, which appealed to the sense of beauty with splendid colours and beautiful forms. Gothic art appealed to the emotions and senses, with figures expressing feelings of love and longing, and clad in multi-layered clothes that curved and followed the shape of the body. The stiff and formal style of Romanesque art was replaced with what we today would consider much more human and natural depictions of individuals. Christ the conqueror over death became the compassionate saviour of mankind, and the veneration of his loving mother Mary exploded.

Gothic style can be seen in paintings from c. 1200 onwards, first in France and England and a little later in Germany and Scandinavia. The Gothic painting style was applied to four different kinds of arts: frescos, panel paintings, stained glass, and illuminated manuscripts.

Since numerous churches and monasteries were built in the Gothic period, most surviving Gothic paintings are frescos on the church walls. Many of them followed the style of the *Biblia pauperum*, illustrated Bibles in which the picture, not the text, was at the centre. The idea of these works was to visualise the typological correspondence between stories in the Old and New Testaments, so that each group of images depicted one event from the Gospels, and this central picture had by its side two smaller pictures depicting the corresponding event in the Old Testament. The

Illustration 8.3 Biblia Pauperum, the late medieval collection of woodcuts of biblical scenes with short explanations, came in many different editions. It was used as a model for decorating churches everywhere in western Europe, including in Scandinavia. Pictured here is a page with Jesus rising from the grave and with the two Old Testament typological prefiguration of the resurrection: Samson removing the town gates of Gaza just as Jesus had opened the gates to the land of death, and Jonas raising out of the mouth of the whale-fish just as Jesus had risen from the grave.

Public domain.

term *Biblia pauperum* means 'Bible of the poor', but since books were expensive they were not meant for the poor. The tradition of *Biblia pauperum* began in southern Germany in the 13th century, and they became very popular in Germany and Scandinavia especially after the invention of book printing in the mid-15th century. The tradition of painting scenes in the style of the *Biblia pauperum* upon church walls was particularly common in Scandinavia, and several such pictures have survived in Denmark and Sweden. This tradition continued until the 16th century through artists like the Elmelunde Master in Denmark. Another popular motif in Gothic art was the Virgin Mary because Marian devotion grew immensely in importance during the Gothic period.

A new kind of artistic decoration style emerged after 1200, hand in hand with the Gothic building style whose large windows brought more light into buildings: stained glass windows. Stained glass windows were produced using glass coloured with the help of metallic salts resulting in red, yellow, blue, and other colours of glass. Pieces of coloured glass were then joined together with the help of strips of lead so that they formed patterns and figures. These pictures could then be further decorated with painted details. At their best, the stained glass windows were fantastic pieces of art and could depict even complex figures. One particular example of stained glass windows was the so-called rose window usually positioned over the church entrances in the western wall. They were round multi-coloured windows that had a complex design

Illustration 8.4 The late medieval pictorial programmes in Scandinavian churches often closely followed the international models in the Biblia Pauperum, as Jonas in the whale-fish here in Söderby-Karls church, Sweden, demonstrates. The wall paintings are from the very late 15th century; characteristic for the period is the *horror vacui,* the fear of empty spaces, meaning that all space must be filled with colour and pictures or patterns. The green and bright red were also very common towards the end of the Middle Ages.

Photo © Kurt Villads Jensen, 2022.

resembling a multi-petalled rose. A fine Scandinavian example of this can be found in the cathedral of Nidaros, although the present one is not the original but a restored version of the medieval one. Although stained glass windows were relatively common in medieval churches, there are not many pieces left because glass is very fragile and breaks easily. For example, in Sweden, there are around 150 medieval stained glass windows left in churches, the majority on the island of Gotland. They are all from the period between 1200 and 1400, after which the manufacturing of stained glass windows on the island ceased. There are, however, later medieval windows preserved in the Swedish mainland. The pictures in the stained glass windows became ever more complex during the Middle Ages. While the 13th-century windows were relatively simple and less painted, the later windows are much more complex and colourful with plenty of hand painted details.

With the spread of literacy and accumulation of wealth among the Scandinavian nobility and bourgeoisie, the demand for illustrated manuscripts began to increase during the second half of the 13th century. These manuscripts were illuminated according to the newest Gothic artistic trends. The first illuminated manuscripts could be luxury versions of Bibles donated to the rulers, but other works such as Psalters could also be finely illuminated. From the late 13th century onwards, the demand and production of prayer books for laypeople became an increasing business for the scribal workshops. Some of the books of hours were beautifully illustrated with gold and silver, but less expensive copies were also made for those who could not afford to pay for a lavish copy. The manuscript illuminations were often relatively small in size, either with decorative initials or miniatures. Pictures taking a whole page existed but they were included only in the finest manuscripts.

Since the Gothic style originated from the new architectural style in churches, the first Gothic features in art can be found in monumental sculptures on church walls, in particular church facades. Gothic-style stone sculptures are typical around church doors, not only in tympana, the semi-circular or triangular decorations above the entrance but also around the entrances where rows or figures of saints were sculpted. The motifs on monumental stone sculptures followed the same trend as in paintings: typological side-by-side presentations of events from the Old and New Testaments were common, as well as images of Virgin Mary.

The period from c. 1200 onwards was the period of building new churches and monasteries. Since building was expensive, it usually required gifts from generous donors who in exchange would receive their last resting place in the churches. The tombs of the donors, typically belonging to royal families or upper nobility, became a new industry for stone carvers and, in fewer cases, for metalworkers. The tombstones in churches and monasteries were usually richly decorated according to the Gothic style: long human figures surrounded by pointed Gothic arches. The sculpted figures on the tombs did not represent the deceased person, but the latter's identity can be revealed by the heraldic weapons that became common from the 13th century onwards.

While stone sculptures were typically part of the architectural details of the buildings, the Gothic period also produced a large number of wooden sculptures, painted with bright colours that were intended for decorating the interiors. In churches, wooden decorations can be classified into two separate groups: altar fronts (antemensals) and sculptures.

The earlier tradition of carved antemensals, sometimes covered and embellished with metal blades, continued from previous centuries, but during the Gothic period,

Illustration 8.5 Stained glass windows had probably been common in Scandinavian churches, but few have survived to the present day; almost all of those that have survived are on the island of Gotland. Pictured here is the Ascension of Christ, first half of 13th century, Dalhem church.

Photo Wolfgang Sauber 2007. This file is licensed under the Creative Commons Attribution-Share Alike 3.0 Unported, 2.5 Generic, 2.0 Generic and 1.0 Generic license.

the decorations began to have more and more Gothic-style forms. The antemensal tradition was particularly common in Norway, where wood carving technique was continuously in use and reached a very high level.

Due to the vivid Marian cult of the high Middle Ages, the sculptures representing Virgin Mary were the most common among wooden sculptures, together with crucifixes. In the Gothic period, sculptures of the Madonna developed iconographically so that they often presented a standing Virgin Mary with the child Jesus in her arm. Madonna also became the personification of the ideal woman, and Gothic sculptures typically depicted the Virgin Mary as a graceful and beautiful figure full of maternal love.

The increasing popularity of local saints in Scandinavia from the late 12th century onwards meant that a great number of wooden sculptures depicting the local saints were produced during the following centuries. Among the most popular indigenous Scandinavian saints were Olaf, Birgitta, Canute the King, and Eric. At the same time, their iconography also developed. For example, statues of Saint Olaf survive from the first half of the 13th century onwards. The earliest type represents him seated on a throne, with a beard and crown and wearing a mantle and tunic. In his left hand, he holds the orb and a sceptre or an axe in his right, and very often he is trampling upon a devil or a dragon with a face resembling his own face.

There was some local production of wooden sculptures but most Scandinavian sculptures were purchased and imported from northern Germany or Flanders, especially from the second half of the 14th century onwards. This means that there was a strong German stylistic influence in art, especially in Denmark and Sweden. In Norway, the close contacts with England continued during the Gothic period, and the English influence on Norwegian art can clearly be seen. The local wood carving tradition in Norway entered a period of decline after the Black Death due to decreasing demand and loss of many skilled wood carvers. This can be seen both in the decreasing number of surviving items and the quality of the products.

The Gothic style was also applied to other objects of art whose production continued throughout the Middle Ages. Due to increasing number of towns, a wealthier urban upper class emerged that had money to commission pieces of art, either for themselves or for the churches.

From the 13th century onwards, small carvings became popular, made of ivory and intended mainly for a lay and often female market, both demand and production of which increased. Most of them were of French origin and imported into Scandinavia. They were normally made of African elephant ivory, and sometimes of walrus tusk from Greenland which became an important export item from Scandinavia during the Middle Ages. These objects were usually devotional items often depicting the Virgin Mary, but they could also be practical objects such as mirror cases, combs, or book covers. A small minority were lavishly decorated with jewels or enamelled metalwork. Such luxury items, however, are extremely rare in the Scandinavian context.

A special group of sacred items was imported from Limoges in France where Benedictine monks during the 12th century developed a technique to create enamels in deep, glowing colours that continued to be extremely popular until around 1370 when the town was utterly destroyed. Limoges works were used for relic shrines, incense burners, plates with biblical scenes, portable altars, and above all for crucifixes.

Very common are the so-called pilgrimage badges: small objects of lead or other cheap metals that could be purchased in the vicinity of pilgrimage shrines, not only the central shrines like Rome or Santiago de Compostela but also more local pilgrimage sites such as Vadstena in Sweden or Nidaros in Norway. Pilgrimage badges have been found in numerous Scandinavian urban excavations as well as in cemeteries and give evidence of Scandinavian people travelling and visiting various pilgrimage sites. Pilgrimages became increasingly popular exactly in the period when Gothic art style was dominant.

212   *1200–1400: Consolidation and Restructuring*

Illustration 8.6 Crucifix using Limoges technique, 13th century. From Nävelsjö church in Sweden, today at the National Historical Museum, Stockholm.
Photo © Pia Bengtsson Melin, 2022.

Literature

After c. 1200 literacy began to spread, numerous different types of books came into use besides the standard liturgical works introduced in the previous chapter on literature. Literary tradition was also adapted in other fields of culture than within the Church, and rapidly growing administrative procedures required ever more personnel

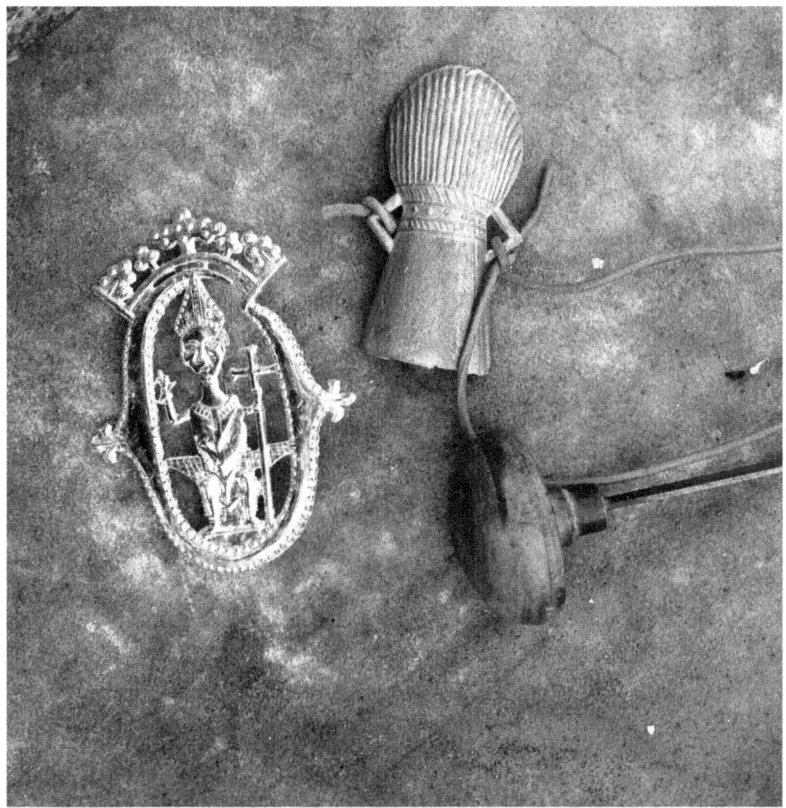

Illustration 8.7 Pilgrim badge from the grave of Saint Thomas Becket in Canterbury. He had been killed by the men of King Henry II of England in 1171 and became a very popular saint, in Scandinavia as well as England. He was a symbol of the liberty of the Church, and gave hope that religious piety was, in the end, stronger than political violence. The badge here, with a depiction of Thomas Becket and the ampulla for consecrated water and a tiny drop of his blood, are modern replicas, as bright and fine as the medieval ones were when they were new.

Photo Afjeffs0, 2017. This file is licensed under the Creative Commons Attribution-Share Alike 4.0 International license.

skilled in writing. Important juridical decisions were written down in charters, and institutions copied their documentation into cartularies in order to preserve the memory of the documents' contents. *Scandinavian towns began to have a specialised town scribe to ensure that all official decisions were formally correct.* The emerging nation states as well as the expanding Catholic Church were spreading all over Western Europe and began to keep registers and write down important matters.

Legal culture too began to lay more weigh upon written evidence. This happened first in southern and central Europe, but very soon the idea of a literate society spread to Scandinavia. A huge legal development took place in the 13th century, not only within ecclesiastical legislation and canon law, but also within civil law. Following the example of Spain and Germany, the first Norwegian national code of law, that of Magnus the Law-mender, was codified in 1274, and the Swedish national law was issued around 1350. The Danes never developed a law for the whole kingdom in the Middle Ages, but each Danish region obtained their own royal legislation in the course of the 13th century. The codification of laws resulted in a huge body of writing and literature in Scandinavia: law books were copied and courts began to write down their decisions. Since the civil legislation was issued for local purposes, they were at least from the 14th century onwards mainly written in the vernacular, as were the court books and legal documentation – although there was variation between the three Scandinavian kingdoms.

In addition to the administrative and ecclesiastical literature, numerous other kinds of literary genres were invented and reinvented in the high Middle Ages. Historical works, chronicles, and annals were retelling the Scandinavian past, while courtly literature entertained the higher classes and scientific works were composed for scholarly use.

History writing in the Middle Ages was inspired by traditions from Antiquity. It served to teach proper conduct via the exemplary deeds of the forefathers and to give authority and legitimacy to individuals and institutions. Specifically medieval, in contrast to the Classical tradition, was the use of history writing to illustrate God's plan with His creation: providential history writing. Leaned ecclesiastics such as Saint Gregory of Tours († 594?) and the English Bede the Venerable († 735) engaged in history writing. They shared the same Christian background, and their works of history began with the biblical story of Creation. The earliest forms of history writing were so-called chronologies, in which the most important events were noted down in chronological order. In the Middle Ages, alongside the birth of the various European nation states, historical works became more popular and widespread. Another genre of historical literature, chronicles, described the history of one institution such as a monastery or town. A slightly less elaborate form of medieval history writing was the composing of annals – short notices of what had happened in certain years.

History writing was also known as a literary genre in Scandinavia, and in the 12th century, the Scandinavians took examples of it from which they created their own versions. Chapter 4 about literature presented the historical sagas composed in Iceland and Norway, but there were also Scandinavian historians writing in Latin. The most famous of them today is the Danish theologian and learned author Saxo Grammaticus, who around 1200 composed, under the auspices of the Archbishop Absalon of Lund, an ambitious historical work called *Gesta Danorum* (Deeds of the Danes). *Gesta Danorum* is a huge and patriotic work that consists of 16 books and approximately 195,000 words in a learned, archaicising Latin very different from the Latin of most of his contemporaries. Its main goal is to describe the history of Denmark as a close parallel to the history of the Roman empire, stretching from Russia to the River Rhine and to the north as far as Ultima Thule, probably meaning Iceland. It is focused upon Denmark but includes important information about the history of other Scandinavian countries as well as Estonia and Latvia, and the still pagan areas of northern Germany. The work begins in prehistory and reaches as far as Saxo's own times. The first nine books are legendary, and very much a construction of Saxo's with no sources that we know of today. It is interesting not only for being heroic and mirroring the Roman empire, but also by including the pagan past and mentioning Nordic mythology. Saxo's work is unique because historical works prior to the 12th century typically began with the Christianisation of the country and totally ignored the non-Christian past. The last seven books of *Gesta Danorum* are about Danish medieval history within the living memory of Saxo's time and describe the Danish crusades in the Baltic Sea area as well as the Danish domestic political fights. *Gesta Danorum* with its erudite Latin is an excellent example of knowledge and scholarship in Scandinavia in the Middle Ages. In its composition and scope it parallels the contemporary *Heimskringla* of Snorri Sturluson.

Crusades gave space for another medieval genre of literary works, namely chronicles describing the heroic acts of crusaders. One of the best known of them was Robert the Monk's *Historia hierosolymitana* (History of Jerusalem), which describes the events of the First Crusade and the conquest of Jerusalem in 1099, and which probably also circulated in Scandinavia. Other crusades were neatly recorded in Chronicles such as that of Henry of Livonia describing the early 13th-century Baltic Crusades, in which the Scandinavians active in the territory of Estonia and Latvia are occasionally mentioned. A Scandinavian description of local crusades is the *Historia de profectione Danorum in Hierosolymam* (History of the Danes' Travel to Jerusalem) from the 1190s. It describes the journey to Jerusalem of a Danish-Norwegian group of crusaders, who travelled to the Holy Land to participate in the Third Crusade (1189–1192) and liberate Jerusalem. They actually came too late; King Richard the Lionheart had concluded a truce with Sultan Saladin and fighting had stopped. The *Historia de profectione* was probably written as an apology and explanation of why this group did not participate in the war, in contrast to other Scandinavians who had excelled and been noted internationally for their strength and bravery.

Annals, chronicles, and diaries were other examples of flourishing history writing in Scandinavia. Annals were historical records in which the scribes of a monastery or town wrote down the most important events year by year in a chronological order. The tradition of annals derives from the Roman times, but annals became more and more common during the Middle Ages, including in Scandinavia. Good examples of the Scandinavian tradition of annals are the *Annales Ryenses*, composed in the Danish Cistercian monastery of Ryd in the 13th century, and its contemporary *Dansk-svensk årbok* or *Chronologia vetus*, describing the events between the years 916–1263 and written by a member of the Dominican order. It was begun in Denmark, later transferred to a Dominican house in Sweden, and is the first example of the annal in Sweden. The cathedral of Lund seems to have been a very early centre for annal writing from around 1130, within the first generation after its establishment. Scandinavian annals were copied from each other and sometimes exist in several versions with only minor differences, and many incorporated themes and information from larger historical works, for example Saxo's. Many were translated from Latin into the local vernacular.

Chronicles also recorded historically important events in a chronological order. The entries in chronicles, be they written by the monks of a monastery or a royal historian, are always composed from the point of view of the author and, unlike most annals that contain relatively short and neutral entries, the description of events in chronicles can be longer and more elaborated, but the borderline between the two genres is not precise. Some medieval Scandinavian chronicles had a political message, as in the Eric Chronicle, written in Swedish by an unknown author describing events related to Duke Eric of Södermanland between 1320 and 1335. Another similar kind of work, called a diary instead of chronicle, is *Diarium Vadstenense*, the chronicle of the Birgittine abbey of Vadstena. It was composed by the monks of the Vadstena abbey and it contains notes of events concerning the abbey from the years 1336–1545.

The high Middle Ages was a period of passionate love, beautiful ladies, and heroic knights, at least if one believes the secular literature was born in the very late 12th century and became immensely popular in the course of the following one. In the Middle Ages, literature became a much broader concept and included several new kinds of genres, such as the crusade histories mentioned above, but also fiction about itinerant knights in quest for valiant deeds and a famous lord to serve. This trend was connected to the activities of the travelling troubadours, like the French *Trouvéres* or German *Minnesingers*, entertaining people with their stories and songs.

Most of the worldly literature used in Scandinavia had a foreign origin, like the *Roman de la Rose* originating in France or the courtly or chivalrous literature that described the ideals of honour and personal glory of brave knights. This literature was part of the courtly culture that spread to Scandinavian royal and noble circles. In the higher, multilingual circles, these stories were read and spread in their original languages, but they were also translated into the vernacular and sometimes even adapted to local circumstances for the local population. A good example of these is the *Eufemiavisorna*, three medieval romances translated into medieval Swedish in the beginning of the 14th century. They were commissioned by Queen Eufemia of Norway († 1312) and sent to the Swedish court, and they became very popular both in Sweden and Norway. Another widespread translation was made from French into Norwegian in the 1260s of several *Chansons de geste*, knightly tales including the Story of Charlemagne, the Story of Ogier the Dane, the Song of Roland, and other accounts of heroic deeds. Several of them were re-translated into Icelandic, Swedish, and later Danish, and they also inspired the writing of new sagas about the prehistoric deeds of Scandinavians. These translations from French introduced common European stereotypes to the Scandinavians, for example by presenting Muslims in Spain as horned half-monsters scaring the horses of the brave Christian fighters.

The 13th and 14th centuries were also the period of the spread of the universities and thereby scientific literature. This included works within the disciplines taught in the universities: theology, medicine, philosophy, linguistics, mathematics, and law. They were formulated in such genres as *summae* or tractates that intended to give a comprehensive and full explanation of a theme, and in commentaries on a more limited subject. The tractates were works dealing in a formal and systematic way with one subject, such as marriage or sin, while the commentaries were works that explained or commented upon specific works, often in theology or canon or civil law. The most disseminated medieval commentaries dealt with the Bible or parts of it. The learned literature was part of scholasticism, the critical method developed in the schools during the 12th century that fundamentally revolutionised science and learning.

Learned literature arrived in Scandinavia in the first place through men studying at foreign universities, where the most important theological and philosophical authors belonged to the common curriculum. One of the greatest authorities was Peter Lombard († 1160) whose introduction to science and theology – *Libri quatuor sententiarum* or Four Books on the Sentences – became a standard textbook for centuries and one of the most quoted books of the Middle Ages after the Bible. From the early 13th century, there began a long discussion about whether or not to study the works of the classical philosopher Aristotle. He was not Christian, and several of his positions were condemned, but in the end, he became another fundamental authority in all university teaching. The students spread this knowledge having returned home with the works of the curriculum.

The 13th and 14th centuries were the centuries of growing individual religiosity and stress upon the care of souls by priests, which resulted in an increase in the quantity and spread of pastoral literature. The liturgical books presented in Chapter 4 continued to be used and produced as earlier, but new kinds of religious literature also emerged.

A good example of the religious literature of the 13th century is the manual meant for parish priests. The manuals concentrated on the care of souls and instructed the priests how they should interrogate their parishioners who came for confession and how they should behave during the sacrament of confession. The priestly manuals were often composed by members of the mendicant orders, such as the early 15th-century *Summa theological moralis* written by Antoninus of Florence, an Italian Dominican friar who was appointed archbishop of Florence and proclaimed a saint. His work spread quickly over the Latin West, especially after it had been printed in 1477, and inspired many similar works in different languages. The Danish *Syndespeglet* (Mirror of sin) from the 15th century is a typical example, listing the same sins as Antoninus but in a much shorter form and with clear, precise instructions to the priest.

Another very typical medieval literary genre was that of the saints' lives (*vitae*). The life stories of saintly persons together with their miracles had been collected and written down from the early Christian centuries but in the 13th century, the genre gained a new direction with the spread of the Golden Legend (*Legenda aurea*). This collection of saints' lives and miracles was compiled by Jacobus de Varagine, an Italian chronicler and archbishop of Genoa, around 1250. Jacobus' work collected the hagiographies of over 150 saints and spread quickly over the whole Latin West, testament to which is over 1,000 still preserved medieval manuscripts or early printings, in several languages. The Golden Legend greatly influenced later hagiographic texts, including those composed in Scandinavia.

By 1200 the cult of a number of local saints had begun to flourish in the Scandinavian dioceses, and the local ecclesiastics compiled saints' legends that followed the foreign examples and style. There were local saints' legends in all Scandinavian dioceses, although not all of them have survived. For example, the late 13th-century legend of the Finnish martyr Bishop Henry did survive but the one for the 14th-century Bishop of Turku, Hemming, has disappeared. The most important Swedish saints' lives include that of Saint Eric from the late 13th century and of Saint Birgitta from the late 14th, while the most famous Norwegian vita, that of Saint Olaf, has survived in several different versions, of which the oldest dates to the 11th century. The best known Danish saints' lives are those of Saint Canute the King from around 1100 and Saint Canute Lavard from the 1170s. The miracles of the Icelandic Saint Þorlákur, who was officially canonised as late as in 1984, were instead included in one of the Icelandic sagas, the *Þorláks saga helga* (the Saga of Saint Þorlákur). The locally composed saints' lives closely follow the foreign examples but also contain interesting local details. Some of them are written in highly sophisticated and eloquent Latin, testifying to the high Latin standards of the Nordic countries. One such example is the office written for Saint Birgitta by Bishop Nils Hermansson of Linköping in the 1370s, known as *Rosa rorans bonitatem* – 'Oh ye rose that drizzle goodness'.

Books of hours were usually nicely illuminated devotional books that became very popular from the 13th century onwards. These small-format books were meant for lay people's private use and contained the Calendar of ecclesiastical feasts, extracts from the Four Gospels, the Mass readings for major feasts, the Little Office of the

Blessed Virgin Mary, the 15 Psalms of Degrees, the seven Penitential Psalms, a Litany of Saints, an Office for the Dead, and the Hours of the Cross. The books of hours originated from the Breviary and were originally in Latin, but in the course of the later Middle Ages, they were translated into several different vernaculars: French, English, German, Dutch, and Danish, for example. Some manuscripts or early printings included a mix of languages so that some parts were in Latin and some in the vernacular.

Education and Learning

Only a very small minority of medieval people had some kind of education, not to mention academic one. Many of those who had the possibility to study strove for an ecclesiastical career in which the ability to read and write as well as knowledge of Latin was necessary. The Church took care of the clerical education in the cathedral schools that had probably existed right from the foundation of the cathedrals in Scandinavia, although we have no secure sources for the earliest period. Monastic orders, especially the Dominicans, had their own schools in the convents. From the early 14th century, laymen could also receive education in the towns where the town councils could establish schools. Unlike the cathedral schools, these schools had a more practical curriculum intended for burghers' sons who needed the skills of reading, writing, and arithmetic. Education in these schools was meant only for boys. Additionally, there was the practical way to learn a profession: an apprenticeship in a master's workshop. Those, who aimed at higher education, had to study at the foreign universities. They were typically men in clerical career but also some laymen have studied abroad.

Local Education

Most Scandinavian men and women lived their lives in the countryside and learned the usual household tasks at home from their parents, neighbours, or relatives. The lack of formal training was not a problem, since most professions did not require special knowledge or skills. Since medieval legislation stipulated that certain professions could be practised only in towns, such as those of skilled craftsmen like goldsmiths, that is where people with a specific professional education typically lived, except for blacksmiths who were also needed in the country.

The training to become a craftsman took place through years of practical learning. Young men interested in craftsmanship could become apprentices at a master's workshop and learn the profession by following the master and being instructed by him. After a certain period of apprenticeship, a skilled man could become a journeyman. Promotion to journeyman meant that they were considered skilled enough to earn their living by working in any workshop. Most journeymen made their career serving in someone else's workshop, since only a limited number of them could become a master and run their own workshop. It was the local guild of the same branch of masters who decided whom to allow to become a master. The masters had to pass an exam and have enough capital to start their own business. People living on craftsmanship had an internal hierarchy. At the top were goldsmiths. Bakers came in second place, followed by smiths, shoemakers, and tailors, which all required particular skills. At the lower lever of the hierarchy were the tinkers, chandlers, ropers, and coopers.

The path to clerical education usually began at one's home parish where the parish priest kept an eye out for skilled young men. The parish priest needed assistance during the celebration of Mass, and he involved intelligent boys as choral boys. The service at the local church was often the first step for a boy towards ecclesiastical education and eventually an ecclesiastical career. Then the boys could continue their clerical education at the cathedral schools. According to canon law, each cathedral was responsible for educating future priests for the needs of the whole diocese. In most Scandinavian dioceses, the cathedral schools would have been the only place where young men could get a clerical education. In the cathedral schools, the schoolboys were taught in the seven liberal arts, the *trivium* comprising grammar, logic, and rhetoric and *quadrivium* comprising arithmetic, geometry, music, and astronomy, but they would also train in the practical sides of the clerical tasks such as liturgy. After finishing cathedral school, the schoolboys were able to read, write, and sing in the right way. They had also learned Latin, the liturgy, and the sacraments, and they had a basic understanding of Christian theology and ecclesiastical norms. Additionally, they could count and were able to determine important dates through astronomical knowledge.

The education in the cathedral schools was sufficient to obtain priestly orders and being able to act as a parish priest. That was also the level of education which the majority of medieval priests received. However, the Church also had need for particularly intelligent and able men who could function in the highest ecclesiastical offices. From the high Middle Ages onwards, almost all men striving for higher ecclesiastical positions did not limit their ecclesiastical education to the cathedral school but educated themselves further in universities abroad. The university education was, however, not possible for everyone because it was not cheap to go abroad for several years. The cathedral chapters could grant intelligent students a kind of study support called *bursa* (a wallet) or they could have other forms of study support. In 1253, Jacob Erlandsen – at that time Bishop of Roskilde but later Archbishop of Lund – established a foundation that enabled the cathedral of Roskilde to permanently have two canons studying at Paris University. The donation in land that financed these stipends later became part of the estate of Copenhagen University and continued as such until modern times.

University Education

The founding of the universities began in the late 12th century, and it was a European phenomenon. Numerous factors contributed to the necessity of higher learning: urbanisation, the rise of the papacy and European national states, and frequent contacts – if not always peaceful – with the learned Islamic world and the learned tradition of Antiquity. The Catholic Church and its various institutions – the cathedral schools as well as various schools of the monastic orders, especially the Dominican *studia* – were at the forefront of teaching and education because it was important for the Church to raise learned men for its service. The idea of a place of universal study began to develop as certain central schools attracted ever more students and famous teachers, and from further away, even from abroad.

In the course of the 13th century, the schools intended for larger groups than just local students obtained the name *studium generale*. Apart from their internationality, the *studium generale* offered their students guaranteed education in at least one of the three so-called higher faculties (theology, law, and medicine) by several teachers who had reached at least the level of *magister*. There were no formal requirements for founding a *studium generale* until the 13th century, but from then on the founding of a higher education institution was considered to require a permit from either the pope or the local ruler. The first university founded by the pope was in Toulouse (1229), while Naples was the first one that received an official permit from the emperor (1224). The older institutions, like Paris or Bologna, did not need such a confirmation but could receive one for the sake or certainty, as Paris did in 1291.

By the end of the 15th century, the term university (*universitas*) had been established as the name of the institutions of higher education, although originally the term meant the community of students and teachers, not the institution itself. The two most famous universities in the Middle Ages were Paris and Bologna. Bologna became the main attraction of students interested in law, both civil (that is, Roman law) and canon laws, while Paris was the best place to study philosophy and theology. During the Middle Ages, the juridical status of the universities, its students, and its teachers also evolved, for example in universities that followed the so-called Bologna model the students formed their own corporation or collegium, as did the teachers or masters. In the Paris model, by contrast, each teacher and his students formed separate groups and the students received their juridical status through their teachers.

These two different models also had their consequences for who could teach in the universities. Like in all other medieval institutions, such as the courts, the institutes of higher education also tended to make their regulations uniform. The Catholic Church – which had an interest in controlling the quality of theological teaching – took therefore an active role. At the Third Lateran Council celebrated in Rome in 1179, it was decided that all qualified persons should have the possibility to teach at the institutions of higher education and that the licence to teach (*licentia docendi*) should be given for free and be valid universally. The licence to teach had its roots in the cathedral schools, where the school master could grant teaching licences for qualified students – but the licence was valid only in the territory of the diocese in question. The idea behind the universal teaching licences was important for the medieval universities, because they offered teaching for all students no matter where they were originally from, and the teachers were therefore allowed to move from one university to another without problems.

The universal teaching licence was important because in the course of the Middle Ages, several universities were founded in different parts of Europe and at different times. The number of institutes of higher education grew from the three 13th-century universities (Bologna, Oxford, and Paris) to around 70 by the end of the 15th century (including Copenhagen and Uppsala in Scandinavia). The founding of universities, or elevating local schools to the level of *studia generalia*, took place at different paces in different territories. In France, Italy, and the Iberian Peninsula, universities were quite frequently founded from the early years until the end of the Middle Ages. The two English universities of Cambridge and Oxford are both among the oldest, but they remained the only ones on the island until three were founded in Scotland in the 15th century. The first university in the German Empire was founded as late as in 1348 in Prague, after which several German towns got their own universities.

The universities of Uppsala and Copenhagen were both founded after the rulers of their respective countries had obtained a licence from the pope. In the second half of the 15th century, Sweden and Denmark were officially joined in the Kalmar Union but in practice the Swedish nobility did not recognise the Danish king, which led to controversies between the two countries. Apart from the union wars, the controversies could also be seen as competition, and the founding of a university was one such fields of competition. The idea of having a Scandinavian university had already existed in the early years of the 15th century, since the founding of several universities in the Baltic Sea area also encouraged the Scandinavians to strive for a national institution of higher education instead of sending students abroad.

The first traces of such an initiative date to 1417, and two years later, the Union King Eric of Pomerania received a papal permit to found a university in one of the towns in his realm. This early permit did not, however, lead to the foundation of such an institution. The idea was taken up in Sweden in the 1430s by the active Archbishop of Uppsala, Nils Ragvaldsson, but this time too the plans did not lead to a foundation. The idea came up again in the 1470s, after the Swedish Regent Sten Sture the Elder had beaten the Danish troops in the Battle of Brunkeberg, close to the centre of Stockholm, in 1471. After the victory, the Swedish council of the realm wanted to strengthen the level of higher education in Sweden and decided to found a *studium generale* in the country. It was important for the Swedes to act quickly and to get a papal confirmation for their idea before the Danes. The Swedes turned without delay to Pope Sixtus IV and received a papal bull confirming the foundation of a university in Uppsala, next to the archiepiscopal seat. The Swedes did not waste time in the foundation process: the papal confirmation was dated on 27 February 1477, the university received privileges from the council of the realm on 2 June, and teaching had already started by the autumn. The Danes got their first university, the University of Copenhagen, two years later. King Christian I had already tried to obtain a papal permit for a Danish university in 1474 when he visited the papal curia, but his request did not bear fruit. It was his wife, Queen Dorothea, who in the following year visited the papal curia and among other things received the papal permit. But it took some time before the Danes got the practicalities for foundation sorted out, and the university was only inaugurated in June 1479.

Although the Scandinavian universities were intended to replace the need to study abroad, Uppsala and Copenhagen never reached such a high status as to replace the need for further education at foreign universities. However, the local universities served a number of young men who would never had been able to go abroad for study. Sometimes, the local universities served as a starting point for Scandinavians. For example, Johannes Werth, a student born in the diocese of Turku, inscribed at the University of Leipzig in 1483, had taken the degree of bachelor (*baccalaureus*) in Uppsala and continued his studies at the masters level at the German university. This shortened the time needed at the foreign universities – and greatly diminished costs of study. Johannes Werth was not the only Swedish student who followed that path, but numerous other students did the same.

After a student had received the title of master in the arts or philosophy faculty, he was allowed to study in the so-called higher faculties of theology, law, or medicine. The students in the higher faculties had to begin their studies from the start and receive first the title of bachelor, which in the case of the Faculty of Medicine in the University of Paris took four years, and then that of master, which took another six. In the law faculty, a student could receive the title of bachelor after six years of study, while the title of doctor of laws required 12 years. The theological faculty was the most regarded, and in Paris alone receiving the title of bachelor in theology required

16 years. In other universities not as highly ranked as Paris, it was possible to complete studies a little faster.

Scandinavian University Students

Although the number of Scandinavian university students was small compared to the number of university students from other European regions, Scandinavian young men were striving for higher education from the earliest centuries of the universities' existence. But where did the Scandinavian students go for this? In the 12th century, there was very little choice in places to study: Bologna, Oxford, and Paris. Already by the 13th century, the number of universities was multiplying, and in the following centuries continued to increase.

The first choice of Scandinavian students was the University of Paris, which until the mid-14th century was the unquestionable centre of knowledge, especially in theology, the primary object of interest for men striving for high ecclesiastical positions. Scandinavian ecclesiastics attended the University of Paris from the 12th century onwards, in the 13th the links became even tighter because of the close contacts with the Dominicans who had their own schools in the same city. Several Scandinavian bishops received their education in Paris, where they became acquainted with other men who achieved high ecclesiastical positions all over Christendom. One of the early Paris students was Archbishop Absalon of Lund, who arrived there in the mid-12th century. His successor to the archiepiscopal, see Anders Sunesen, also studied theology in Paris and law in Bologna in addition to which he visited the University of Oxford. Anders Sunesen wrote a long treatise on theology in the form of a hexaemeron (in seven parts parallel to the seven days of creation) and in fluent hexameters. The aim was to provide students who needed to learn Latin and obtain a theological grounding with a proper Christian text so they did not have to read classical pagan authors. Anders Sunesen studied together with the later Pope Innocent III, becoming part of a strong European network of former Paris students who ended up in the very top positions within the Church.

Paris and Bologna remained the most frequented universities until the mid-14th century, when the German Empire gained its first ones. The oldest of the universities in the German Empire was that of Prague, founded by Emperor Charles IV in 1348. Very soon thereafter many other German towns got their own: Vienna, Erfurt, Heidelberg, and Cologne in the 14th century, and many more in the course of the 15th. Scandinavian students headed in particular for Prague, when the attraction of the University of Paris had slowly diminished because of the disturbances of the Hundred Years' War between France and England (1337–1453), which decreased the number of students from the British Isles. Another blow to the status of the University of Paris was the Great Western Schism (1389–1417) which divided western Christendom into two camps: those supporting the Roman pope and those the French 'antipope'.

The Scandinavian countries were the supporters of the Roman papacy as were the Germans, and therefore, Scandinavian students chose Prague over Paris as their study place. The flow of Scandinavian students to Paris did not, however, cease totally. For example, many students from Finnish territory still headed to Paris, where the ecclesiastical leaders of the diocese of Turku had used to study. Due to declining numbers of English and German students, some Scandinavian students rose to important positions at the University. The later Bishop of Turku, Olavus Magni, was appointed as rector of the University, although only for a short period of three months from December 1435 to March 1436. He was not the only one, but several Scandinavian students before him had held the same position: Hemming in 1312, Peter 1326, and in 1344 Nicholaus Drukken. Johannes Nicholai de Dacia was elected rector in the terrible year of 1348 when the plague reached Paris, and teachers and students died like flies. In 1366 the canon of Lund and Roskilde Macharius Magnussen took over the honourable position.

The University of Prague became the alma mater for numerous Scandinavian students from the late 14th century onwards. Although the University was officially founded only in 1348, since the 13th century there had been a highly qualified school in the town, which had also attracted students from outside Bohemia. The University of Prague originally had all four faculties (artistical/philosophical, theological, medical, and juridical), but the juridical faculty was separated into its own institution in 1372. The juridical faculty originally gave teaching only in civil law, but very soon – especially after the outbreak of the schism – the University of Prague became well known of its high-quality teaching in canon law as well. Studying in Prague was much more effective than in Paris. In Prague, it was possible to reach the degree of *baccalaureus* after only one year's study, and intelligent and diligent students could get the title of *magister* after three years. This was a remarkable difference from the University of Paris, where one was expected to study for seven years.

In the course of the 15th century, the possibilities for study increased notably after the University of Prague split into two, when teachers and students opposed to the reforming ideas of Jan Hus and left Prague to found a new university at Leipzig in 1409. Among those students heading for Leipzig were numerous Scandinavians. At the same time, many other German towns gained their own universities, and Scandinavians began to study in those close to the Baltic Sea. Rostock (founded in 1419) and Greifswald (founded in 1456) became increasingly popular among Scandinavian students in the second half of the 15th century because the Scandinavian countries had always had close contacts with the northern parts of Germany through the Hanseatic League. The level of teaching at the smaller newer German universities was perhaps not as high as in the old prestigious places, but the education was sufficient for the needs of the Scandinavian students.

The preserved student lists of the various universities include the names of hundreds of Scandinavian students who subscribed to various lectures or passed an examination. The student lists from different universities are not, however, preserved entirely, and different universities had different principles in recording the events. Some recorded those who were registered, some the names of those who passed their exams, others the names of those who had borrowed books – and others yet recorded some or all of these.

Most Scandinavian students did not aim at studies in the higher faculties of theology, medicine, or law but participated in teaching in the arts or philosophy faculty. Many Scandinavians never finished their studies because of the high costs of university studies and because the lowest university degree of bachelor was enough for most of them. It was almost a rule that medieval Scandinavian bishops had a university degree, and some of them had even continued their studies further in the theological faculty. Since over a decade's absence from one's diocese was very seldom possible, only a handful of Scandinavians acquired the highest university degree of doctor of theology. The same was the case with law studies. For men in high ecclesiastical positions, a good knowledge of canon law was mandatory, and therefore, Scandinavians studied law in Prague and Bologna as well as in the Roman universities, but only a few of them advanced to the degree of doctor of laws. There is even less evidence preserved about Scandinavians studying in the medical faculties.

The Dominican order, which appreciated education and theological knowledge, gave its members the possibility of studying in Paris where it had its own collegiums. There its members could stay for free and follow the teaching for many years without worrying about the costs of study. Medieval sources mention several Dominicans who became doctors of theology. One of them was Frater Algot, prior of the Dominican convent in Skara, who had received his title in the first half of the 14th century. His decree is mentioned in the acts of the canonisation process for Saint Birgitta of Vadstena. Another Dominican doctor of theology was Frater Nicolaus Johannis from the convent of Lund, who received his title in the second half of the 15th century.

Some Scandinavians chose the academic career and we meet them as teachers at different universities. For example, the Danish Thuo de Vibergia was a known teacher of theology in the University of Erfurt, while another Dane, Kanutus de Arusia, was teaching law in the same university, both during the second half of the 15th century. Another Scandinavian scholar who made a fine university career was Bero Magni. He was born in Lödöse, Sweden, and studied in Vienna in the 1430s. In 1465 he received a permanent position as canon in the cathedral of Vienna and was granted the licence to teach theology and the subsequent degree of doctor of theology.

Student Life

Many medieval universities students and teachers were organised into corporations called nations. In Paris, the students and teachers were divided into four such territorial corporations. Three of them were French – the French (*natio gallicana*), the Picard (*natio picardorum*), and the Norman (*natio normannorum*) – and the fourth was meant for those originating outside French territory. Since the majority of foreign students in Paris were originally from England, the fourth nation was at first called the English nation (*natio anglicana*), but since from the 14th century onwards, the majority of them came from other countries, the name was changed to the German nation (*natio germanica*). In other medieval universities, there was also a similar kind of division into nations according to the student's home region. The few Scandinavians students did not have their own nation in the Middle Ages but were usually admitted to the German. There is no information about nations in the medieval Scandinavian universities.

The main function of the nations was to supervise teaching and the make sure that the members obeyed the statutes of the nation and university. Thereby, the nations controlled the members, and in case of misconduct acted as the punitive body. The nations were also responsible for organising parties and various official celebrations. The nations had houses where some of the members could lodge and eat. The nations additionally employed a *procurator*, who supervised the activity of the nation, and a *receptor*, responsible for the economy. These persons were elected among its members for a limited period.

There is not much information about the life of students in the university towns. We have some details about the size of their *bursa*, that is, the amount of money they had as a form of study support. These numbers show that some students were significantly better off than others. Despite studying being difficult in the Middle Ages, the students had free time as well and they enjoyed life together with their study companions, as we can read from some survived letters, the Scandinavian students have sent home. It was typical that most events in student life took place in the nations, which meant that the students could probably also communicate with their friends in their own language instead of all the time using Latin, which was the official language of teaching.

The statutes of the universities or their nations strongly condemned any kind of violent behaviour or excessive drinking of alcohol. It is perhaps not wrong to conclude that these sins were mentioned in the statutes exactly because they were relatively common among the students. We have also some other sources, like petitions of absolution and dispensation to the pope by students who had ended up in trouble while at foreign universities. Two separate petitions from the 1490s give us an unusual glimpse of students' recreational activities as well as show with whom they spent their free time.

Johannes Johannis, a cleric from the Norwegian diocese of Nidaros, explained on 30 December 1493 that while he and his study companions in the university of Rostock, northern Germany had been dining together, a certain Petrus Olavi, cleric from the diocese of Skara in Sweden, had come and insulted him, after which Johannes had hit and injured Petrus. After that another student, Johannes Elavi from the diocese of Stavanger in Norway, whom Petrus had beaten up earlier, took his knife and fatally wounded him. Johannes Johannis asked for and received a declaration of innocence, which allowed him to continue in the ecclesiastical career he was striving for. Almost a year later, Johannes Elavi asked for and was granted a papal absolution and dispensation from the crime and sin of killing, which allowed him to receive priestly orders despite the incident.

As the above sad story testified, students' time at a foreign university allowed them to acquire other assets, such as an international network of friendship, which could last for decades. It is usually not possible to know with whom the medieval Scandinavian students bonded, but there are sources that give us glimpses of these networks.

Archbishop Absalon of Lund was one of the early Scandinavian scholars at the University of Paris, where he studied theology probably in the 1140s and 1150s. One of his study companions was a young Frenchman with the name Vilhelm, who was canon at the church of Sainte-Geneviève-du-Mont. Vilhelm was a fervent supporter of the strict monastic life and ended up in the 1160s in collision with his superiors. When Absalon at the same time needed a good man to reform the monastery of Saint Thomas at Eskilsø in Denmark, Vilhelm had nothing against being invited to Denmark by his friend. Vilhelm successfully reformed the monastery and later transferred it to Æbelholt. He remained in Denmark and acted as the abbot of the monastery until his death, after which numerous miracles took place at his grave and Pope Honorius III canonised him at the request of Absalon's nephew and successor, Archbishop Anders Sunesen of Lund in 1224. We do not know whether Vilhelm was the mentor of Archbishop Anders Sunesen, who spent years in the universities of Paris, but it is known that Anders sent his brother Peder Sunesen – who followed Absalon onto the episcopal seat of Roskilde – to study in Paris. At the same time, as Anders and possibly also Peder were studying in Paris, one of their fellow students was Ugolino di Conti, who later became known as Pope Gregory IX. His collection of canon law regulations included a couple of letters from Anders Sunesen, who had asked the Pope's opinion on legal issues in the province of Lund. It cannot be proven but is possible that Anders Sunesen had written to the Pope encouraged by their common university background, possibly even friendship.

Another Scandinavian example of university networking is that of Petrus de Abo, a Dominican friar who originated in the diocese of Turku and made a career in the service of the Avignon popes as a papal confessor in the 1330s and 1340s. We know no details of his studies but he must have studied theology, perhaps also canon law, in one of the *studium generale* run by the Dominicans, most likely in Paris but perhaps also in Bologna. Later correspondence shows that he became a close friend of a Norwegian Dominican, Jon Hallordsson, from the convent of Bergen, who studied in both Paris and Bologna and later became bishop of Skálholt in Iceland. Their correspondence shows that they also had a third study comrade, Haakon Erlingsson, who after his studies became the bishop of Bergen in Norway. Their correspondence bears witness to the fact that the friendship between the three men also continued after their university days

Part III
1400–c. 1550
Power in Crises

9 Rise and Fall of the Kalmar Union

The Scandinavian Union – The Apogee of Scandinavian Power, or a Colossus with Clay Feet?

On 17 June 1397, Eric of Pomerania, a mere 15-year-old, was solemnly crowned ruler of three Scandinavian kingdoms: Denmark, Norway, and Sweden. The coronation festivities took place during a meeting in the Swedish town of Kalmar, and the day was chosen with consideration. It was the Sunday of the Holy Trinity, to mark that three kingdoms were now brought together as a unity under one single ruler, but with individual representation in the form of separate councils of the realm for each. The day was chosen for a good omen, but the future of the Kalmar Union was to be troubled.

The mastermind behind the Union's creation was Queen Margaret who had become ruler of the three countries, in principle on behalf first of her deceased son Olaf and then on behalf of her adopted son Eric of Pomerania. In practice, she continued to reign and have the decisive word until her death in 1412.

During the Kalmar meeting or maybe shortly afterwards, two documents were issued by Queen Margaret and the members of the councils of the realm of the three kingdoms. One was the so-called *Crowning document*, the other was later labelled the *Union document*. The Crowning document is large, elaborately written on parchment, and with 67 hanging seals. It confirms that Eric had been crowned as ruler of all three Scandinavian countries. The Union document is written on paper with only 17 witnesses and is much simpler to look at. It had only ten seals, imprinted into the paper and therefore looks much less authoritative than the parchment charter with hanging seals. The exact status of these two documents has been much debated by modern historians.

The content of the Union document is much more interesting than that of the Crowning document. The Union document is an attempt to regulate the relation between the three kingdoms in detail. It is the first document, which attempted to regulate the question of the common rulership and stated that the Union would also continue to have one common ruler after Eric of Pomerania. The document further stipulated that the ruler should always consult members of all the three council of the realms, and not rely on the advice of the councillors from only one country. Secondly, the document pronounced on the internal relations between the three kingdoms. Each should continue its traditional systems of administration and trade, but the inhabitants of one country could freely trade with those of the others. The document also stated on the topic of legal consequences that those declared outlaws in one of the countries should be considered outlawed throughout the whole Union. Thirdly, the document considered the foreign policy of the Union. It stipulated that an attack on one of the countries should be considered as attack on all, and all should together defend the union. Additionally, negotiations and agreements with foreign powers should be made for the entire Union, not for single countries.

The solemn Crowning document, by contrast, is very vague when it comes to how the relations between the three kingdoms should be regulated. Basically, it leaves much to be decided by the ruler alone and gives less weight to the councils of the realms and to the aristocracy. The Union document, on the other hand, stipulates a long list of paragraphs to ensure the involvement of the highest aristocracy from all three kingdoms in all decision-making. The Swedish historian Erik Lönnroth suggested in 1934 that the two documents reflected two different political theories and political programmes, the *regimen regale* and the *regimen politicum*. The first is built on the idea that authority comes from above, from the ruler. *Regimen politicum*, in contrast, operates with the idea of authority from below, from the people, which in this context was the high aristocracy. The first aimed at a strong king for the entire Union, the second at a kind of aristocratic republic.

Lönnroth's interpretation has been criticised by later historians for being too schematic and sharp. Nevertheless, Lönnroth's explanation of two concepts of authority fits well with general discussions within western European philosophy and social science in the 14th century, and the history of the Kalmar Union for more than the next century indeed became a constant struggle between strong rulers and aristocrats who acted as rulers in their own right, especially in Sweden. The two documents reflect the unsolved situation. They are actually mutually exclusive, but both are part of the founding of the union.

The Union document from 1397 had ordained that 'the three kingdoms shall never again be separated from each other, if God so will'. God did not. It was officially dissolved in 1523 but its countdown began with a bloodbath on the main square of Stockholm in 1520. But before that it had been a troubled time with many large wars in which Sweden especially aimed at gaining a semi-independent status. Antagonism between different parties within the Union ramped up after the middle of the 15th century, but right from the beginning mighty opponents also hovered outside the Union and were suspicious of the concentration of power in the hands of the union ruler. These were enemies not easily fought off. Strong weapons were necessary, one such being an unusually far-reaching papal privilege to Queen Margaret to support her against her enemies, but without specifying who these actually were.

Licence to Crusade – Even Against Christians

On 29 March 1401, the Roman Pope Boniface IX issued a very unusual bull to the three archbishops of the Kalmar Union: of Lund, Uppsala, and Nidaros. With the apostolic authority bestowed upon him, the Pontiff commanded the archbishops to preach a crusade in the kingdoms of Scandinavia, in the neighbouring areas, and on the isles in the north, against the enemies of Queen Margaret – be they pagans or Christians!

Such a formulation is unique in the history of the Catholic Church, but when put in the larger context of the history of western Europe it begins to make sense. The bull was issued in the time of the Great Western Schism, when two popes – one in

Rome and the other in Avignon – were fighting against each other. The Hundred Year's war between England and France, and many other armed conflicts between Christian rulers, had made wars between two Roman Catholic armies an almost everyday business. In addition to internal fights, the Christians also fought against the religious enemies in the east. One of the most significant expeditions of the time was the crusade Battle of Nicopolis in 1396, where the Ottoman army destroyed the huge joint European army. There were crusades everywhere, also involving powers which considered themselves – and their adversaries – absolutely and undisputedly Christian. Since the religious rationale was important to the armies and soldiers, those who declared a war had always been very cautious to declare their opponent heretical and deviant Christians, because that gave the war the status of a crusade and ensured the participants the blessing of the ecclesiastical authorities. That the ruler of the Scandinavian Union gained unrestrained papal permission to crusade against Christians was in that context a remarkable and exceptional concession.

Margaret obtained the bull as a recognition of the longstanding and solid support the Danish rulers had provided the papacy, Pope Boniface explained. He even granted her a special seal she could use in her private correspondence with him – a kind of red phone to the pope. Margaret got her special treatment because of heavy lobbying. She had lavished lawyers and money upon the Roman curia, critics complained at home in Scandinavia.

Margaret had turned to the Roman Pope in 1400 and complained about all the enemies attacking the Scandinavian Union: burning, plundering, killing, and raping. The Union had an enormous coastline which it could impossibly defend without support, and therefore she had applied for authorisation to crusade. Unfortunately for us today, she did not specify who these attackers actually were. There were several possibilities, and to list them gives a snapshot of the complicated political situation of the Scandinavian Union immediately after its foundation.

One possibility was that of the Sámi people in the north. Immediately after her victory over King Albert of Sweden in 1389, Margaret initiated a mission to the Sámi in northern Sweden and Norway. She had been approached by a Sámi woman, also named Margarete, who had informed her about the state of the Sámi and the possibility of converting them. Queen Margaret's mission seems to have been intended to be a peaceful one, in contrast to most relations with Sámi in the period. Sámi were believed to provide the northern Scandinavian link between Greenland, Asia, and ultimately Jerusalem. Geographers believed that these areas were all connected by land, or via the ice over the frozen northern ocean. Sámi peoples were reported to have attacked and burned down several places in northern Norway in the 14th century even as far south as Nidaros, and during Margaret's reign, they were blamed for laying waste to the Christian colonies in Greenland. Later, in 1457, the Union King Christian I complained that his lands were attacked by hundreds of thousands of Sámi. This does not make sense and probably reflects that Christian Scandinavians did not distinguish between Sámi, Karelians, and other peoples in the north. The area was very sparsely populated, and to imagine Sámi in their thousands attacking and threatening the Union illustrates how little was actually known of the areas in the distant north.

Another enemy may have been the Orthodox Christian Russians. Margaret had been brought up by the daughter of Saint Birgitta of Vadstena, who had claimed to have received revelations commanding the Swedish king to convert the Russians to Catholicism. Birgitta in her Revelations called the Russians not only schismatics or heretics, but even outright infidels. In 1348 and 1351 King Magnus Ericsson of Sweden – at Saint Birgitta's instigation – had led crusades against the Russians and approached them with two banners, one showing Christ, the other the sword, so they could choose to convert to Catholicism or fight. King Magnus' initiative was neither a military nor a missionary success. The border area in eastern Finland between the Scandinavian Union and Russia continued to be insecure, with constant raids, plundering, and sometimes bigger expeditions. In 1399 came the Turbot War. Russians sailed to northern Norway and stole enormous stocks of dried turbot and other fish that should have been exported to the towns in the Baltic area. Queen Margaret sent a fleet against them and strengthened her political power in the region, gaining huge booty.

The third possible enemy of Margaret could have been the Hanseatic League, the major economic and political player in northern Europe. It was a relatively loose confederation of the big trading towns along the southern shores of the Baltic. Together they controlled extensive resources and could finance, arm, and man a sizeable fleet of warships. In 1395, the former King of Sweden, Albert, had been released from Margaret's prison, and the Hanseatic League guaranteed Margaret that Albert would pay the agreed ransom three years later. If not, they would hand Stockholm to her. Albert did not pay, and the rich town of Stockholm became Margaret's. Relations with the Hanseatic towns were however strained. They complained about her interpretations of old trading privileges, which were always to their disadvantage, and around 1400, they openly accused her of supporting their enemies and the many pirates who plundered their ships.

The Victual Brethren was Margaret's fourth possible enemy. It was a loosely organised but highly effective and feared group of pirates and freebooters that operated in the Baltic Sea region, mainly against Margaret and the Hanseatic League. They had kept open the lines of communication from Mecklenburg to Stockholm and secured the town with provisions, both during Margaret's siege of it and later while Albert was imprisoned by her. The activities of the Victual Brethren were however much broader, and they contributed to a general destabilisation of the Baltic. In the early 1390s, they established themselves on the strategically important island of Gotland. They were expelled from there in 1398 by the Teutonic knights, but still formed a formidable military force. Margaret may have thought about the Victual Brethren as possible targets for a crusade. However, it is very unclear where she actually stood in relation to them. Rumours circulated widely, probably also as part of deliberate misinformation campaigns both by Margaret and her opponents. In 1396 it was said in the German towns that she had given the small island of Ertholmen outside Bornholm to the Brethren to build a strong castle there, and that she had equipped a fleet of 1,000 men to sail east against the Russians, together with a fleet of 1,000 men of the Victual Brethren. In the same year, however, Margaret actually sent messengers to Swedish towns asking them to equip ships and contribute to her war against the Victual Brethren. If there was any alliance or even mutual understanding between Margaret and the pirates, it was fragile, and it would have been a great advantage for Margaret to have had the scope to launch a crusade against them, if needs be.

An even more formidable and much better established possible enemy was the Teutonic order. In 1398, the Grand Master Konrad von Jungingen equipped a fleet of peace ships that expelled the Victual Brethren from Gotland and held it in mortgage from King Albert. Margaret immediately intervened and demanded the island as a consequence of the peace agreement of 1395 with Albert, but the Grand Master again and again postponed any decision. The matter should be settled directly between Margaret and Albert, he answered; everything else would be infringing upon his honour. And in any case, he demanded compensation for the many expenditures he had had in conquering the island and cleansing it of the Victual Brethren. Communication was slow, envoys from the order did not come to Margaret because they had gone on summer crusade in Lithuania, and nothing really happened. Had the Grand Master perhaps planned to expand the order's sphere of interest further westwards and take over Gotland permanently? In any case, Margaret lost patience and tried to take the island militarily in 1404, without success, but she pressed the Teutonic order to negotiate and finally gained control over Gotland in 1408 after negotiations and compensation of 8,000 marks – a huge sum, but much less than the Grand Master had demanded from the beginning. The idea of a crusade against a military crusading order perhaps seems bizarre, but was not impossible. The Teutonic order had lost their main raison d'être in 1386 when pagan Lithuania united with Poland and officially adopted Christianity. There were no more pagan states in the Baltic to launch crusades against, and the order was increasingly being criticised for counter-productive behaviour. They had not been able to convert the pagans but scared them away from Christianity by sheer brutality. They continued to fight, now against Poland-Lithuania, but for political more than religious motives. In such circumstances it was not impossible that Margaret could have used her crusading bull to drum up allies in a war against the Teutonic knights.

One further enemy that Margaret may have had in mind was remarkably silent in these years, namely the counts of Holstein. The counts controlled half of the Dutchy of Schleswig by the Danish border and had traditionally been fighting the ruling dynasty in Denmark since the 13th century. Margaret had pacified them with alliances and enfeoffments before going to war in Sweden, so relations were peaceful in those years when Margaret was corresponding with the pope about crusading. This situation was soon to change, but around 1400 there was no indication that the Holsteinians could be the target for a crusade.

The Kalmar Union had many external enemies, and Pope Boniface IX's crusading bull for Margaret was so generally formulated that it could have been used against one or all of them. However, it also had an important internal function. Margaret's right to rule was based on a combination of inheritance, an election which had been staged, an invitation to invade, and sheer military power. One way of making all the areas and peoples of the Scandinavian Union work together and accept a common ruler was to have a common enemy and even better, a common crusade.

The Early Union in International Politics

The official ruler of the Kalmar Union was Margaret's sister's grandson Bugislav of Pomerania who took the Nordic name of Eric (1382–1459, r. 1397–1439). In reality, Margaret did not hand power to him but continued to pull the strings until her death in 1412. A splendid example is her letter from winter 1405 to Eric, who had been sent to Norway. Margaret instructed the 23-year-old King about how to rule and to behave, even in the smallest details. He should treat the Norwegians well and make allies. He should serve them the German beer that had been ferried up to him by somebody called Staffan. If any Norwegian, man or woman, offered him anything to eat, he should accept it gratefully so as not to offend anybody. In all complicated matters, Eric should claim that Margaret was soon coming to Norway and he could make no decision before she was there, and in any case delay things as much as he could. If he really had to issue any privileges, Margaret instructed him to do it on paper with printed seals and never on parchment with hanging seals, because the latter were juridically more binding.

Eric was important to the international policy of alliances. A treaty between the Kalmar Union and England was sealed with his marriage to Philippa of England in 1406, while the planned marriage of Eric's sister to the brother of Philippa, King Henry V of England was never realised. Members of the royal councils in the Union blocked this because it could potentially have given the English ruler a claim upon the Kalmar Union if Eric and Philippa had no children. The alliance with England never resulted in common military expeditions, but it secured the Union peace on the western front along with advantageous trading circumstances, and it confirmed the status of the Kalmar Union as a major player in the north.

The relationships between important political parties within the three kingdoms were relatively good in the first half of the 15th century. They all knew each other. The high-ranking aristocratic families had members in Norway, Sweden, and Denmark. One of the most influential was Axel Pedersen Thott († c 1446), a member of the Danish council of the realm, and whose nine sons gained central positions in the Union: as marshal and drost in Denmark and Sweden, as regent in Sweden, as governor of Finland, as commander of Gotland, and much else. But the Thott family is also a good example of how the alliances could change. Axel Pedersen Thott served the Union rulers, but his granddaughter Ingeborg sided with her husband, the Swedish regent and anti-unionist Sten Sture the Elder. In addition to family alliances that bound the three kingdoms together, another binding element between the high-ranking administrators was that of university friendships. Bishops, who were automatically members of the councils of the realm, had usually received their university educations in northern Germany or central-eastern Europe, and often knew each other from the studies. They could freely move from one episcopal see to another throughout the Kalmar Union in their ascent of the ecclesiastical career ladder.

Schleswig-Holstein had become a problem, mainly because of Queen Margaret's expansive policy after the creation of the Union. She had tried to gain control over the most important castles in Schleswig-Holstein, sometimes by imposing herself as protector of the small children and widows of important fief-holders. The result had been open war against the counts of Holstein, and Margaret was actually in the middle of invading Schleswig when she died of the plague on her battleship in the Fjord of Flensburg in 1412. Eric of Pomerania continued the war, now with additional legal arguments. The constitution of 1326, which stated that Schleswig could never become part of the Kingdom of Denmark, was questioned by Eric's lawyers. One argument was that the knights of Schleswig and Holstein had lost the right to independence by starting a war against Queen Margaret. Another important argument was that the inhabitants of Schleswig actually spoke Danish and therefore should have been part of Denmark. This is an early example of the idea that people, land, and language form a national unity. Eric brought the case to the court of Emperor Sigismund and explained that Denmark had never had fiefs but only provinces. Schleswig could therefore not be an inheritable, independent fief, but must necessarily always have been under the royal jurisdiction. The Emperor agreed and passed judgement in 1424 in the favour of King Eric, but in practice, wars continued.

Eric brought the case of Schleswig to the Emperor during a magnificent *grande tour* through Europe in 1423–1425, which gained Eric connections at the highest international levels. He met with the Holy Roman emperor, the Greek emperor, and the representative of the Ottoman sultan. The great humanist cardinal, Enea Silvio Piccolomini, later Pope Pius II (r. 1458–1464), described Eric as an unusually handsome man, who could jump into the saddle of his horse without using the stirrups and who moved the hearts of the high-ranking ladies to long for his love, even that of the empress. In Bohemia, he studied the latest military strategies in the wars against the Hussite heretics, and he continued as a pilgrim to Jerusalem, incognito for fear of the Ottomans, and was dubbed Knight of the Holy Sepulchre. He was received everywhere with pomp and prestige and supported lavishly with huge loans which were never paid back.

By the end of Eric's reign, the status of the three kingdoms in the Union was becoming less and less balanced. Except from a period at the beginning of his reign, Eric did not seem to have visited Norway, and members of the Norwegian council of the realm did not visit Eric's court, or did so only very seldom. The Swedish councillors by contrast systematically nurtured connections with Eric and regularly came to meetings with him in Sweden or in Denmark. The Union document had stipulated that castles and high administrative positions should not be given to individuals from another country of the Union but only to locals, but Eric neglected this. There was a steady influx of Danes, Swedes, and Germans into Norway, and many Danes into Sweden. Eric's argument was that this did not matter since all were members of the same Union now, but it could be and was used in propaganda against him.

The marriage between Eric and Philippa was childless, and Eric attempted to designate his cousin Bugislav IX of Pomerania as his successor, while beginning to enfeoff members of his Pomeranian family with castles in Denmark. Eric had great plans for Bugislav. In 1423 he had gotten far with negotiations for a marriage between Bugislav and Jadwiga, the daughter and sole heir of King Wladyslaw II of Poland-Lithuania-Hungary, who was in his mid-70s. Had the marriage materialised and Bugislav succeeded both Eric and Wladyslaw, it would have resulted in a union from the farthest northern tip of Norway to the Black Sea. However, in the same year, Wladyslaw married a princess 57 years younger than him who soon provided him with two male heirs, and Eric's grandiose plan came to nothing.

In the early 1430s, the Scandinavian Union began to seriously crack. The independent *Dalkarler* ('Men of the Dalarna mountains'), the people of the mid-Swedish mountains of Bergslagen with its rapidly expanding iron production, gathered around the petty nobleman Engelbrekt Engelbrektsen and in 1434 rebelled against King Eric and one of his bailiffs. The Swedish high nobility hesitated a little but soon joined the rebellion which also attracted huge groups of peasants. It spread to large parts of Sweden and eastern parts of Denmark and was neutralised only with difficulty. In the end, the rebellion died out when a Swedish nobleman killed Engelbrekt in what may have been a private dispute; thereafter the Swedish high nobles took control over the movement, fought the peasants, and burned their leaders.

Was this rebellion the Swedish peoples rising against their Danish oppressors, as historians understood it in the 19th century and as new research has claimed in the 2010s? Hardly. It was the first manifestation of discontent over the Danish union king. The Engelbrekt Rebellion was followed by large uprisings among peasants and the lower nobility in Denmark, in the west as well as in Jutland. These began in 1438 and were with difficulty quenched only in 1441 by Eric's successor. The reason for the discontent and the need to get rid of Eric may have been economic. The Holsteinian nobility had invested heavily in iron production in Bergslagen, and the iron was shipped from a few Swedish ports, especially Stockholm. Eric's wars with Schleswig and Holstein threatened these investments, and his attempts to block the Hanseatic League from trading with the Kalmar Union because of its support of Holstein severely damaged the iron trade through the Baltic. The wars were expensive and financed by ever heavier taxation which may also explain the peasant uprising in Denmark against Eric.

The peasant uprisings in Scandinavia were part of a general European movement that had to be taken seriously by the aristocracy and kings. Peasants had become an unpleasant nuisance in the eyes of the rulers in Europe as well as in Scandinavia. In the mid-15th century, the heretic Hussites in Bohemia fought emperors and kings and amongst themselves in *cotidiana bella,* 'the daily wars', regularly interrupted by much larger scale ones. These were unusually bloody and involved all layers of society, without any of those involved ever gaining a decisive victory. It may perhaps be compared to the trench warfare of the First World War, except that the Hussite wars lasted for much longer. The peasants – in reality, often well off free peasants and local lower nobility – fought with new firearms and new strategies, including for example wagon fortresses. These were forerunners of a more fundamental shift in medieval warfare that began in the 1460s, from the use of aristocratic knightly armies to infantry controlled by princes – larger, more expensive, but more effective.

After the great rebellions, King Eric took up residence in the stronghold of Visby on Gotland where he could muster his fleet and whatever economic means he could. But he was now alone. In 1439–1441, the councils of the three kingdoms renounced their loyalty to him and thereby deposed him as king. Among their many accusations was that he had provoked the peasants into rebelling to the detriment of the aristocracy, that he had brought the treasures of the realms with him to Gotland, and that he had broken the agreements in the Union document. Eric held his position in Visby until 1449 when he moved to his home town in Pomerania, where he spent the last ten years of his life. Modern historians often claim that he lived as a pirate on Gotland and plundered indiscriminately; it is rather the case that he did not accept his dethronement and actively fought to re-gain military control and his position as king.

Eric's nephew Christopher of Bavaria was chosen to succeed him by the councils of the realm of the three kingdoms in 1440–1442. Before ascending the throne he had to sign a constitution that severely limited his power. Eric's failure as ruler had strengthened the aristocracy, which had demonstrated that it had the power to elect and depose kings, and it had no intention of letting that power go. However, if the cooperation between the king and the councils were to work, the concentration of power would be formidable. Christopher accepted the conditions.

Coronation ceremonies were old traditions, including in Scandinavia, but it is only for the 15th century and later that we know more details of their performance. Christopher of Bavaria was crowned in Lund cathedral in 1438. He took the unusual title of *archirex,* 'archking', to show that he ruled several kingdoms and was positioned somewhere between the emperor and ordinary kings. Christopher was led into the choir of Lund cathedral by four high-ranking princes, one each carrying the royal sword, the crown, the sceptre, and the orb. He was seated on a throne and surrounded by nobles, their wives, and the clerics of the cathedral. The archbishop sang the first hymn, and Christopher read a passage from the Bible. The archbishop and five bishops anointed and crowned Christopher and blessed him, and he read aloud the coronation oath with his hand on the Bible, promising to rule with justice and protect the Church. The same coronation ceremony was probably later used in the cathedrals of Nidaros in Norway and Uppsala in Sweden.

Christopher however died suddenly and unexpectedly in 1448. Eric was still in Gotland, interested in staging a comeback as king, and the three councils of the realm were in disagreement about what to do. In 1448 the Danish council elected as their ruler Christian I (r. 1448–1481) from the small principality of Oldenburg. He was only very remotely related to the royal dynasties in Scandinavia, but was willing to marry Christopher's young widow, Dorothea of Brandenburg (c. 1430–1495), with the huge estates she had received as a morning gift thereby remaining with the crown. The Norwegian councillors followed their Danish colleagues in 1450, while the majority of the Swedish council elected as their new ruler the Regent and Marshal Karl Knutson Bonde (1408?–1470) – against a minority that opted for Eric from Gotland. The first severe break within the Kalmar Union had now become apparent.

Modern Scandinavian historians since the 19th century knew that the Kalmar Union did not last. They have tried to explain that fact by arguing for an inbuilt weakness or a structural problem with the union: medieval nationalism and antagonism between Swedes and Danes; uneven production capacities meaning that the centre in Copenhagen exploited the peripherical areas economically; or problems with communication and military control because of the enormous distances from one end of the Kalmar Union to the other. Similar issues did not prevent other contemporary unions from lasting, in spite of recurrent internal political problems. The Polish-Lithuanian Union, for example, was founded in 1386 and was not decisively dismantled until as late as 1792, mainly by Russia. The Castilian-Aragonese Union of 1474/1479 continued to exist and expand, and eventually became the present-day Kingdom of Spain.

The Kalmar Union was a complicated construction for geographical and economic reasons, but it ought not to have been impossible to maintain. It was probably the result of unfortunate coincidences that Sweden left the Union in the early 16th century. It was a long and absolutely not straightforward process; indeed, in 1450 many still believed that the Kalmar Union could still be fully restored.

Conflict and Commerce

The following 30 years saw regular but minor wars between Christian I and parts of the Swedish aristocracy. When the Swedes were winning, Karl Knutson Bonde was put forward as king, in 1448–1457, 1464–1465, and from 1467 until his death in 1470. In between he was in exile in Poland, and Christian ruled the Union until the next war.

With the death of Karl Knutson in 1470 the internal situation within the Kalmar Union seemed to have calmed a little, and Christian I aimed at taking Sweden. He went to Stockholm in 1471 with a Danish army supported by mercenaries from Scotland and northern Germany. Lübeck had been promised wide-ranging trading privileges in return for help in transporting Christian's navy. Lübeck had agreed because this would give it a significant advantage against rapidly increasing competition from the merchants of the Netherlands. However, the expedition turned into a military catastrophe for Christian I. His soldiers were lured from their camp on the small hill of Brunkeberg, just outside Stockholm, and when Christian himself was hit by a bullet which knocked some of his teeth out, and began retreating to the ships, there was general panic. In trying to escape some were trampled, while others fell into the sea and drowned in their heavy armoury. The Swedes in Christian's army were left on the shores and cut down by the inhabitants of Stockholm, with the help of the always eager free peasants of Dalarna. Swedish chronicles explained the victory as a miracle. Blood had begun dripping from the procession crosses among the defenders, attesting to divine assistance. The golden sword of Saint Eric was seen in the blue sky and in later tradition this episode was counted as the first appearance of the Swedish flag. Danish chronicles ascribed the defeat to the Swedes' use of learned magic.

The Battle of Brunkeberg aggravated the schism in Scandinavia between the Kalmar Union and Sweden. Although large circles of the aristocracy in Sweden as well remained interested in preserving the Union, while warfare was limited for the next almost 30 years and negotiations continued, this all had very little practical impact. An example is the agreement in Kalmar 1483 after the death of Christian I in which the Swedish councillors accepted his successor John (1455–1513) as their king, as the Norwegians had done the same year and the Danes two years earlier. The conditions, however, were so severe that John would have become king in name only while the Swedish aristocrats would have continued to make all decisions in practice. The Swedish council of the realm was led by Sten Sture the Elder (c. 1440–1503), who had been elected by the council as regent in 1470 and who had defeated Christian I at Brunkeberg. He did not want to give power to the Danish king but continued to delay any real rapprochement between Sweden and the Union.

External enemies were a constant threat. In the 1480s, the principality of Moscow had expanded and threatened the Union's eastern border in Finland in an attempt to gain access to the Baltic Sea. According to the contemporary understanding of holy war, this would have been a good reason for a crusade, and in 1485 King John had been promised papal support to confirm his right as King of Sweden, if he would lead a crusade against the schismatic Russians. The crusade never took place because King John instead began to negotiate with Grand Prince Ivan of Moscow over a military alliance against Regent Sten Sture. In 1495–1496 the Russians attacked the border castle of Vyborg in eastern Finland, advanced far into the country, and kept large Swedish armies tied down in Finland. Meanwhile, King John led an army including 6,000 mercenaries of the famous and feared Saxon Guard towards Stockholm. He also conscripted one in every ten peasants into his army, the first step towards a modern general conscription. At the Battle of Rotebro north of Stockholm on 28 September 1497, John's army defeated and destroyed the 30,000 men that had followed Sten Sture. The King could now continue to Stockholm where he was also crowned as king of Sweden.

In the Atlantic, the political and military situation differed greatly from that in the Baltic. Regular connections with Greenland were lost during the 15th century, but not with Iceland or up north along the coast of Norway. Fishing was of ever-increasing importance, as was the growing bulk trade between the Baltic and the Atlantic through the straits of Denmark. Christian I attempted to balance the Netherlands and the Hanseatic League in his bestowing of trading privileges, and in contrast to his predecessors he deliberately tried to exclude England. In 1469–1473, he allied the Kalmar Union with Burgundy and Scotland, and fought several minor naval wars to prevent England from fishing around Iceland. An alliance in 1469 was confirmed by the marriage of Christian I's daughter Margaret to King James III of Scotland, and part of the dowry consisted of the Orkney and Shetland islands, which then came to belong to Scotland, and ecclesiastically too soon after. The presence not of only Scottish merchants in Scandinavia but also of Scottish soldiers and officers became very common for centuries afterwards.

The century-long problematic relationship with the border regions of Schleswig and Holstein at last found a solution which was advantageous to the ruler of the Kalmar Union but also illustrates the complicated juridical status of the Union's political elements. In 1448, the mighty aristocracy of Schleswig and Holstein had pressed Christian I to confirm the agreement from 1326 that Schleswig should never be a part of Denmark. In 1460 he was in a totally different and much stronger position, having been chosen by the same aristocrats as duke of Schleswig and count of Holstein on the precondition that the two territories should be *up ewig ungedelt* (for ever undivided). Christian's prestige was greatly enhanced when the Holy Roman Emperor Frederick III in 1474 elevated Holstein to a duchy. Christian was now Duke of Holstein and as such vassal of the Emperor, but independent of the Danish council of the realm regarding his income from Holstein. At the same time, he was duke of Schleswig and therefore vassal of the Danish king, actually of himself. This status of being one's own vassal continued with all later kings of Denmark, until 1864.

However, another obstacle remained in the border region. The Frisians on the flat lands facing the North Sea had made almost a tradition of refusing to pay taxes to their overlords, despite their great wealth from large-scale cattle breeding and from working abroad as well-paid mercenaries. In 1500, King John decided to remedy the situation and invaded Friesland with an army of 10,000 solders, mostly the Saxon Guards. Everything went wrong for him. Rain poured down, making the canons useless and impossible to drag in the mud. The tactic of advancing in closed square order with long pikes had been refined internationally since the mid-15th century and proven effective not least against cavalry, but was useless against Frisians. They simply jumped using long poles over the ditches from one dike to the next, moved up and down the flanks and attacked the guards from the sides and behind. King John's defeat was crushing and total. He lost most of his men, a fortune in money owed to the mercenaries, his booty, and his income from tax. He also lost the Danish flag that had fallen from heaven in 1219 at the conquest of Tallinn in Estonia – all to a small peasant population on the fringe of civilisation. Most of all, he lost all the prestige he had just gained by finally becoming king of Sweden and restoring the Kalmar Union.

The result was an immediate rebellion in Sweden, this time with the support of large parts of southern Norway where the aristocrats gathered and demanded a new king. The answer from King John was new and expensive military expeditions into Sweden continuing for the following 15 years, and an economic boycott with the help of the Hanseatic League, which broke the Swedish economy totally and resulted in mass starvation in large parts of Sweden. No battle proved really decisive, however, and in 1515 both sides gathered resources for a final attempt. Money was provided by every means, from taxation and huge international loans to royally approved piracy, and canons were cast in great quantities. The last big confrontation in medieval Scandinavia was brewing, and about to take place in Stockholm.

The Bloodbath and the Shining Light of the Gospel

The Middle Ages were not unaware of the concept of *Realpolitik*, 'the realistic politics', that sometimes necessitated breaking oaths and neglecting fundamental standards for treating enemies. However, from around 1500 it became the norm rather than the exception. A new political science was inspired by Classical Roman and Greek laws and history, and spread rapidly to Scandinavia as well. The example best known today is that of the Florentine Niccolò Machiavelli (1469–1527). He recommended that a prince should quench resistance as fast and violently as possible in order to prevent it from spreading. In the long run, this would be more humane and even more peaceful than the traditional medieval idea of meeting aggression on the same level and avoiding escalating conflicts. To kill more at the beginning would mean killing less at the end, while to make a community and not merely individuals answerable would lead to the community itself reducing rebellion among its members.

The first signs of the new policy can be seen in Scandinavian politics immediately after 1500. Some Norwegian aristocrats had begun gathering armies and mobilising peasants against the Union king and Danes having important administrative posts in Norway. A central figure in this movement was Knut Alvsson († 1502), a Norwegian nobleman with close connections to anti-unionist Swedes. He began as King John's trusted commander of Akershus, the strong royal castle on the Oslo Fjord, but turned against the King and in 1502 gained control over most of southern Norway. King John sent his son Christian against Knut's troops together with Henrik Krummedige (c. 1464–1530), a member of the Norwegian council of the realm. Henrik Krummedige invited Knut Alvsson to negotiations on his ship, during which Knut was killed despite guarantees of safe conduct. Afterwards, King John staged a posthumous trial of Knut Alvsson and had him found guilty of high treason and therefore of having been legally killed. The case provoked scandal and criticism, but well served a practical, cynical political end. Knut Alvsson later became a heroic icon of the national fight against foreign oppressors. The great Norwegian poet Henrik Ibsen (1828–1906) wrote that 'the blow to the head of Knut Alvsson was a blow to the hearth of Norway'.

King John applied the harsh new policy again as soon as 1505. He had negotiated with Svante Nilsson Sture (c. 1460–1512), who had been elected as the new regent of Sweden in 1503. They had decided to meet in Kalmar in summer 1505 and to agree on the conditions for accepting John as King of Sweden, but Svante and other members of the Swedish council of the realm did not show up. After waiting a long time, King John held an official trial for which one of his judges was Bishop of Odense, Jens Andersen – son of a simple shoemaker, exceptionally intelligent with excellent connections to the papal curia, and the mind and training of a high ranking lawyer, in addition of being the author of delicate, moving Latin poems. Svante Nilsson and seven other councillors were sentenced in absentia to death and loss of property because they had been *unhörsam* – rebels 'unwilling to hear and obey'. To stress that this was meant seriously, King John had the mayor and some ten burghers and members of the town council of Vadstena executed in the aristocrats' absence. This was a bloodbath against all traditional rules, but a deliberately chosen policy to re-establish order and respect. It did not work.

The ensuing 15 years were characterised by blockades of Swedish ports and by regular, recurrent warfare. It brought the Swedish economy to its knees, deliberately so to facilitate a large-scale invasion by King Christian II (r. 1513–1523) who had followed his father onto the Danish and Norwegian throne in 1513. Norway did not however fare much better economically. Since he had become viceregent in 1506, Christian had taxed the Norwegian populace as never before. The consequences were regular rebellions, all in vain, and severe poverty. In 1517 the Swedish Regent Sten Sture the Younger eliminated one of his mightiest opponents and unionists, Archbishop Gustav Trolle of Uppsala (1488–1530). Gustav Trolle was deposed as Archbishop by a general council under the firm guidance of Sten Sture. He was kept prisoner and tortured or humiliated, and Sten Sture took over the stronghold of Stäket belonging to the Archbishop. The illegal deposing of the Archbishop gave Christian II a reason to punish the Swedes. His preparations took a long time, but in winter 1519 the Archbishop of Lund excommunicated Sten Sture for violence against an ecclesiastic, and Christian led two large armies into Sweden. In late January 1520, Sten Sture was badly wounded in a battle and after his subsequent death on 3 February Christian could proceed. In the following months, the commanders of one castle after another surrendered to the Union King. But one did not give up the fight; Christina Gyldenstierna (1494–1559), the 26-year-old widow of Sten Sture and mother to six children, took over the military command of Stockholm and was supported by three main port cities along with the whole of Finland. She was a firm negotiator, not opening the gates of Stockholm to Christian before September and only for promises of safe conduct.

When the capital had finally surrendered, the Swedish council of the realm had to accept Christian as not only the elected but also the hereditary king. It was a new position and meant that his descendants would inherit the throne of Sweden without the need for election. Christian was solemnly crowned on 4 November by Archbishop Gustav Trolle, who had been reinstated to his office. The occasion was celebrated by a major banquet at the royal castle in Stockholm on 7 November. In the evening, the gates of the castle were locked, and a trial began against the nobles and burghers present. They were accused of 'evident heresy' for having participated in or allowing the imprisonment and deposition of Archbishop Gustav Trolle. Bishop Jens Beldenak's juridical expertise again proved useful, as did the knowledge of the professor of both laws (Roman law and canon law), Friar Laurentius of the Dominican convent of Västerås, which in 1505 had become a *studium generale*, a university-level college. The accused were found guilty and immediately handed over to the secular authorities, who took care of the punishments in the form of executions on the main town square.

The first two to be beheaded were the bishops of Strängnäs and Skara, and numerous members of the council of the realm and the town council of Stockholm followed. The killing began on 7 November and continued until the end of the following day. 80–100 people died, and blood mixed with the rain ran along the pavements. The dead bodies were piled up and carried away on wagons, and the heads in big barrows, and burned. The corpses of Sten Sture and even of his infant son were exhumed and placed on the pyres. The event is known as the Bloodbath of Stockholm. It was a massive demonstration of power, not the irrational behaviour of a king's deranged mind as some historians claimed in the first half of the 20th century. The entire affair had its own logic. Many offices in the town council were shared by two persons, and in most cases, one was killed and one spared. It was a signal that King Christian II wanted absolute obedience, but also that he wanted the town council to continue functioning so that he had some official body to work with.

Illustration 9.1 King Christian II's siege of Stockholm 1520, showing the attack and bombardment from ships, the peace agreement, and the crowning of Christian as King of Sweden. Below, festivities with tournaments and immediately afterwards the Stockholm Bloodbath are pictured. Swedish nobles and two bishops have been decapitated on the central square, and their heads have been collected in big barrels. The illustration was ordered in the 1520s by Gustav Vasa and was an early example of the new use of printing for propaganda. The picture is known today only from this copy, a copper engraving from 1676.
Royal Library, Copenhagen. Public domain.

Internationally, reactions tended to show some degree of understanding for King Christian. He was married to the sister of Emperor Charles V, and Christian's imperial family-in-law tried to keep him under some control in the following years to avoid major scandals and political problems, but had no sympathy for the noblemen who had rebelled against their legitimate rulers. The papal curia received Christian's explanation that he was totally innocent with no part in the killing of ecclesiastics, but the pope and the cardinals did not believe him. At the same time, the Church did not want to press him too much to confess his guilt or to fulfil the necessary penance because they did not want to risk eventually driving him and his realm into the arms of the schismatic Orthodox Russians, or of the rapidly growing danger to ecclesiastical unity, the new heretic Lutheran movement.

Christian's plan backfired. Rebellion against him began immediately in Sweden, and a young petty noble, Gustav Ericsson Vasa (1496–1560), gained enough followers to take over and become King of Sweden in 1523. He very conveniently adopted Christian's new title of hereditary king, so that his sons could follow him. In Denmark, nobles and over-taxed peasants united and used the cruelty of the Bloodbath of Stockholm to depose Christian, electing his uncle, in 1523, as King Frederick I of

Denmark (r. 1523–1533). The councillors in Norway were more hesitant. They did not accept either Gustav Vasa or Frederick as their king and continued for some years to rule their kingdom without recognising any king. In 1531 Christian, who had been forced into exile, had managed to gather an army from the continent and sailed to southern Norway to re-gain his kingdoms. He was well received at the beginning, but could not take important castles such as Akershus. In 1532, he was promised safe conduct and arrived to Copenhagen to negotiate with Frederick I. As had now almost become a tradition within the family, Frederick broke his promises. Christian spent the remaining 27 years of his life as prisoner in the castle of Sønderborg in southern Jutland.

The changes of 1520–1523 were political and dynastic, but also became closely connected to the introduction of Lutheranism in Scandinavia. Gustav Vasa founded a new dynasty in Sweden in 1523 and found general support. Many of the leaders of the big noble dynasties had lost their heads in the Bloodbath of Stockholm, and their families wanted change and a split from the Kalmar Union. There was apparently also a general weariness of warfare and readiness to accept serious measures to obtain peace. Gustav Vasa confiscated ecclesiastical property and gained a large income for the crown in the future, with nobody trying to stop him.

When Frederick I died in 1533, his 30-year-old son Christian had already worked hard to cleanse his Schleswig duchy of Catholicism and to impose Lutheran priests. Catholic members of the Danish council of the realm, including the bishops, blocked Christian's election as the new king for a year. Meanwhile, Count Christopher of Oldenburg (1504–1566) led an army from Lübeck into Denmark, demanding the imprisoned Christian II back as king, and soon gained support from peasants, from some towns in Denmark, and from Norway. In 1534 Christopher was elected regent on behalf of Christian II in all of eastern Denmark, while King Frederick's son was elected king in Jutland, as Christian III. The civil war – later called 'the count's feud' after Christopher – ended with Christian III's victory in 1536, and his confirmation as the King of Denmark and Norway. As the winner he could now introduce Lutheranism from above throughout Denmark and Norway, and he confiscated all ecclesiastical land.

10 Fall of the Church

The Western Church 1400–1550

The beginning of the 15th century marked a new era for the Catholic Church, with the Great Western Schism. The return of the popes from Avignon to Rome and the sudden death of the returning Pope Urban V had resulted in a schism with two simultaneous conflicting obedience: to the Roman popes and to the French 'antipopes'. These turbulent times gave scope for broader criticism of absolute papal power, and the churches in the various European nation states began to demand more power to decide upon local matters – including important ecclesiastical matters. The attempts to reconcile the two popes led to the summoning of a Council in Pisa in 1409, which failed in its task and instead managed to elect one further pope, creating a third obedience.

The Great Western Schism was over only after the election of Pope Martin V by the Council of Constance in 1417. Martin V was recognised as the new Pontiff by all countries in western Christendom. With him the papacy returned to Rome, and the Eternal City began slowly to flourish and attract ever more pilgrims. The election of Martin to the see of Saint Peter was however a compromise, and the Pope had to give in to many national demands to maintain peace. This led to the period of numerous ecclesiastical councils where the representatives of various countries presented conditions for their support of the papacy. From the papal perspective, this meant decreased influence in all territories and more power for local ecclesiastical authorities, but this was the price the papacy had to pay for keeping western Christendom united.

The increasing independence of the national churches also meant less income for the papacy, and the Church had to find other means to finance its functions, especially the expensive crusading movement and the re-building of the basilica of Saint Peter in Rome, which by the 1450s had become the main church of western Christendom. Aggressive indulgence selling was the answer to the Church's monetary needs and provoked increasing criticism among Christians. The papacy and the Church faced growing criticism because of the lavish lifestyle of the high ecclesiastical persons and the wealth that the Church and monasteries had accumulated during the centuries. Their criticisers meant that that kind of life was very far away from the apostolic lifestyle of Jesus that should be the model for all members of the clergy. Also, the political power of many archbishops, bishops, and abbots was not gladly accepted by secular rulers.

The turning point in the criticism towards the Catholic Church came in the year 1517 when a German theologian and monk, Martin Luther, published his 97 theses criticising the indulgence selling and what he considered the greedy papacy. Luther's protest led to the Reformation movement that in the course of the 1520s and 1530s sundered some national churches from the Catholic Church. The Scandinavian churches alongside the English and northern German were among those that embraced Protestant Christianity.

The Danish Church 1400–1550

The 15th century and the first half of the 16th were positive ones for the Danish Church, although Danish rulers constantly tried to limit its power. The conciliar movement of the first decades of the 15th century was positive for the local ecclesiastical authorities because it increased the national churches' independence of the papacy – and as such limited local rulers' scope for using the papacy for their own political aims. For the Scandinavian Union, the conciliar period brought particular problems because the Swedish Church aimed at independence from the Danish union kings.

Danish bishops were active supporters of the conciliar idea and participated in the reform councils of Constance (1414–1418) and Basel (1431–1449). Peder Lykke, who immediately after participating in the council of Constance was appointed Archbishop of Lund, summoned a provincial council to Copenhagen in 1425 with the intention of renewing the Danish Church in the spirit of Constance. He managed to take measures to strengthen the enforcement of clerical celibacy but otherwise the participants of the provincial council were not very keen to accept big changes. The only important decision made by the bishops was to increase episcopal power over monasteries and their abbots. Peder intended to make the councils into a yearly event, but the bishops were too busy with other matters and no more were summoned during the Middle Ages.

The bishops were indeed busy with political intrigues. Queen Margaret's successor, King Eric of Pomerania, continued the same firm but generous policy towards the Church as Margaret and her father Valdemar IV. This strategy however ended when Eric was sent to exile in 1439 and the Danish council of the realm, with the help of the Church, chose Christopher of Bavaria as the new Union King. Christopher formed a close alliance with the aristocrats and the Church when he needed to fight against rebelling peasants in Jutland, and when the rebellion was over he had to reward his allies. Thus he granted the Church and individual bishops a number of rights that made them richer and more powerful.

The conciliar period ended in 1448, when Pope Eugene IV (r. 1431–1447) signed the so-called Concordat of Vienna with the representatives of various European countries and rulers. With this treaty, the Pope made an end of the conciliar period and regained his power over the Church in the Latin West. For the local rulers and churches this meant decreasing of ecclesiastical power. The newly elected Danish King Christian I had to adapt to the new situation and decided to make the best out of it. He maintained good contacts with the papacy but had to give in on certain questions of ecclesiastical appointment rights. Christian travelled to Rome to meet the Pope, managing to gain some privileges and concessions from Pope Sixtus IV (r. 1471–1484). The most important of these was persuading the Pope to appoint Jens Bostrup to the archiepiscopal see of Lund, which the Pope had previously given to one of his men, Franciscus Gonzaga. The Pope agreed to remove Franciscus from the see – albeit for huge compensation of 40,000 florins – and appoint Jens. Christian was thus successful in the important issues (and in particular because Franciscus never got a penny of the promised payment). But he also received some sharp rebuffs from the members of the curia: he only brought the Pope the gift of a barrel of stockfish (far below the acceptable level of a royal gift to a pope) and was unable to speak Latin (unacceptable in a Renaissance ruler). Later on, King Christian and especially his Queen Dorothea successfully obtained a papal privilege for founding the University of Copenhagen, solemnly opened some years later, in June 1479.

Christian I's successor continued the same strategy of seeking papal support in important matters and keeping the political power of the bishops limited, while, however, not offending them. Danish bishops belonged to the Danish elite and could enjoy a number of special privileges. The kings had also to remember that the archbishop of Lund was the head of the council of the realm, which was responsible for the election of the new king.

From the second half of the 15th century onwards, papal indulgence sellers had spread all over the Christian West and become ever more aggressive in their marketing strategies. In 1517 Martin Luther began to protest against them and many other forms of misconduct within the ecclesiastical administration. Although Luther only intended to reform the Catholic Church, his ideas were so radical that they led to the birth of an independent reformed church. It split off from the papacy, and later obtained the name of the Lutheran Church.

The ideas of Luther arrived quickly in Denmark, since numerous young Danish men were studying at European universities and had learned about the reforming ideas there. In the early 16th century, the Danish Church was an important and wealthy landowner. Some of the wealth belonged to the bishops, some to the monasteries, and some to the parishes, all of these having a lot of tenants and servants working for them.

The ecclesiastical leaders in Denmark wanted to keep their privileged position and power, and until 1513 they had managed to maintain a balance with royal power. However, Christian II, who was elected as King in 1513, sought to considerably diminish the political power of the Danish bishops and at the same time to interfere in ecclesiastical appointments. A good example of Christian's clumsy interference was when five men were appointed successively as archbishops of Lund in 1522 and 1523 – only the last of them, Åge Sparre, was good enough for the King. Since the pope refused to appoint him to the position after all previous appointments, Åge remained in the position without papal authorisation. The good relations between the papacy and Danish kings diminished considerably when Christian II together with his Swedish ally, Archbishop Gustav Trolle of Uppsala, turned Christian's crowning festivities in Stockholm into a bloodbath in November 1520. This led to his expulsion from Sweden, and soon the Danes also rose against him and drove him into exile.

Before leaving the country, however, Christian II had begun a reform movement in the Danish Church. Following the ecclesiastical reform movements in Europe as well as the division of labour between the Renaissance ruler (responsible for politics) and ecclesiastical leaders (responsible for ecclesiastical matters), Christian intended to reform the Danish Church and to add to his own political power. For this purpose, he had supported the Carmelite Monk Poul Helgesen, who had learned in Europe about the new reform movement. Poul Helgesen began to preach in Copenhagen against the corruption within the Church and the need for a proper reform. He was so active and enthusiastic that his preaching led to wider criticism of the Danish bishops, abbots, and monasteries in general. Helgesen was a tragic figure in the sense that with some justification he was accused by conservative Catholics of propagating Lutheran ideas, while at the same time he was highly critical towards many Lutheran ideas and wanted a reformation of Catholicism, not a change to something else. He therefore became highly criticised from both sides. Another very important figure in the reformation movement was one of Poul Helgesen's students, the Johannite Monk Hans Tausen, who had also studied in Wittenberg with Luther. Back in Denmark, he began preaching Luther's ideas and a break with the Catholic Church. He was expelled from the Johannite Order, but after the Reformation taught Hebrew at Copenhagen University, translated the first five books of the Old Testament into Danish, and later became Lutheran bishop of Ribe.

At the same time, Lutheran ideas had arrived in Schleswig and Holstein from Germany. The reforming ideas began to spread in Denmark from the two directions of Copenhagen and southern Jutland. In 1536, this led to the split of the Danish Church from the Roman papacy and to a new, independent Danish Church led by the Danish king.

Alongside political turbulence and criticism towards the Church, the activities of the Danish parishes continued as earlier. Donations to churches and monasteries continued to flow in due to increasing lay piety. This contributed to the building, enlarging, and embellishing of many Danish churches. The discontent towards the Danish Church was more at the political and upper levels than among the Christians at the parish level. New monasteries, such as the Birgittine abbeys of Mariager and Maribo, were founded in the first half of the 15th century, and the 'domestic' Birgittine order was strongly supported by the rulers of the Kalmar Union. The mendicants also spread to smaller towns, and the hospitals run by monasteries were necessary for the well-being of Christians.

The Norwegian Church 1400–1550

The founding of the Kalmar Union turned its political attention from the west to the east and the Baltic Sea and had consequences for the Norwegian Church facing on the west. Although the relationship of the Norwegian Church with the union rulers, Queen Margaret and King Eric of Pomerania, was good and the rulers were generous in their donations to churches and monasteries, the period of the Scandinavian Union meant a decline in the power of the Church of Nidaros. Until around 1380, the archbishops of Nidaros had controlled the episcopal appointments in their province, but by the early 15th century, the Scottish isles had slid toward more independence from the Norwegian Church, and in 1472 the diocese of *Sodoriensis* (including the Isle of Man together with the Hebrides), as well as the Shetland and Orkney islands, were joined to the new province of Saint Andrews in Scotland. This replacement of the Scottish diocese, however, merely confirmed the fact that for some time already the islands' attachment to the province of Nidaros had been only nominal. The Faroe islands as well as Greenland and Iceland, by contrast, remained part of the Norwegian province for the whole Catholic period.

The period of the Kalmar Union also meant the concentration of political power with the union rulers, which meant that Norwegian bishops' political power began to gradually decrease. They still belonged to the Norwegian council of the realm, but the political independence of the council was more limited and many important decisions were made elsewhere. The first decades of the 15th century formed part of the conciliar period in papal administration, which increased the influence of the local ecclesiastics, but the ending of the conciliar period with the election of Pope Martin V and the subsequent increase of ecclesiastical power in the hands of the pontiff meant decreased independence for the local churches, including Norway's. The first decades of the 15th century were not very prosperous times for the Norwegian Church either politically or economically.

Illustration 10.1 Nidaros cathedral was an important pilgrimage site throughout the Middle Ages because of the grave of Saint Olaf and the many miracles that were recorded to have happened here. The saint was buried in a chapel at the eastern end of the cathedral, which is an exact copy, centimetre by centimetre, of the rotunda with Jesus' empty grave at the Church of the Holy Sepulchre in Jerusalem.
Photo © Kurt Villads Jensen, 2014.

The period of Archbishop Aslak Bolt (r. 1428–1450) brought a change to this. He began to actively restore his metropolitan authority and the autonomy of the Norwegian Church. He also managed to bring the finances of the see of Nidaros into balance and to settle the borders with royal power. This was possible from the 1430s onwards because the internal conflict within the Scandinavian Union diminished the union ruler's political powers during the reign of King Eric of Pomerania and his successors. But from the second half of the 15th century onward, the Norwegian Church was more and more controlled by the union rulers. At the same time, the Norwegian Church increased its political power in the country and became an important institution for conserving the national administration within the Scandinavian Union. The archbishops of Nidaros became the heads of the Norwegian council of the realm and thus the key figures in Norwegian politics. The role of ecclesiastical leaders in politics was particularly important because they were usually of Norwegian origins, unlike the administrators appointed by the union rulers who often preferred men with Danish, German, or Swedish background.

Although the political influence of the Norwegian Church remained limited in local politics, the 15th century was a positive period for the Church. Norwegian bishops could guide their dioceses relatively independently, and the period was positive for the ecclesiastical economy thanks to the income from dried fish caught along the Norwegian coastline that enriched the Church's treasury. The 15th was also the last century of independence for the Norwegian church province, because when the Reformation arrived in Scandinavia the union kings who also ruled Norway soon decided to radically diminish the political power as well as possessions of the churches in their realm. King Christian II began the Reformation process in Denmark and Norway, but his successors carried it to the end. It was King Christian III who in 1537 abolished the Norwegian Church by closing down the archiepiscopal see of Nidaros, making it just one episcopal see among others. The king had taken over the Norwegian Church.

As in the case of the Danish Church, the last medieval century was not a bad time for the Norwegian Church. The Norwegian Church continued to expand its influence towards the north, where fishermen had founded new parishes and where Union Queen Margaret had sent missionaries for converting the Sámi peoples. The Church received a large income from fishing alongside the coastline, which together with the pious donations of Christians increased the income of the parishes and monasteries. Like in Denmark, in Norway this income was used for enlarging and embellishing the older churches, as demonstrated by numerous late medieval pieces of church art. Monastic culture flourished, and new monasteries were erected. The Scandinavian monastic order of Saint Birgitta of Sweden also arrived in Norway with the transforming of the Munkeliv abbey in Bergen from a Benedictine abbey into a Birgittine one.

The Icelandic Church 1400–1550

The late Middle Ages from the period of the Kalmar Union until the Reformation is a strange period in Icelandic ecclesiastical life, especially for its administration. With their political interest focused on the Baltic Sea region, union rulers paid little attention to the territories in the Atlantic belonging to the Norwegian realm and Norwegian Church province. This meant that the close connections between Iceland and Nidaros slowly weakened and the island's inhabitants could increasingly begin to take direct care of the ecclesiastical matters in the dioceses of Skálholt and Hólar.

When the archbishops of Nidaros lost close contact and interest in the Church in Iceland, ecclesiastical appointments gradually fell into the hands of the papal curia. This meant that the Norwegian archbishops no longer appointed their own trustees to the Icelandic episcopal sees nor did they supervise the papal appointments. This resulted in a lot of completely nominal episcopal appointments; popes appointed men close to the papal administration to the Icelandic sees, and these had little if any interest in their distant dioceses, in which they never set foot. Nor was papal administration interested in local opinion regarding the appointments. An illustrative example of a wrong episcopal appointment was the case of the former Archbishop of Uppsala, Johannes Gerechini, who abdicated from the see of Uppsala after accusations of various forms of misconduct in 1421 and was later appointed to the see of Skálholt in Iceland. Unlike many of his predecessors, he arrived on the island in 1429 where the locals killed him by stuffing him in a sack and drowning him after growing tired of his misbehaviour.

Although episcopal appointments by outsiders were apparently unwelcome to the Christians on the island, for the latter the late medieval period was one of ecclesiastical liberty. Since foreign bishops did not reside in their dioceses, Icelanders could take care of their ecclesiastical issues independently without having to obey any outsider. Scholars investigating Icelandic ecclesiastical history in the late Middle Ages have concluded that while the Icelanders were happy with their independence, their ecclesiastical administration did not follow the norms of the Church, and neither did the Christians in their daily life. The Icelanders were forced back into line only after the Danish King Christian III introduced the Reformation to Iceland, enforcing it by the mid-16th century.

The Swedish Church 1400–1550

With the ascension to the Swedish throne of Queen Margaret in 1389 and after the establishment of the Kalmar Union in 1397, there was only one ruler for the three Scandinavian countries, and for a while the political life was peaceful. Queen Margaret was the daughter of the Danish King Valdemar IV, and at the age of 10 she was married to the Norwegian King Haakon, in 1363. The young bride was after some time taken to Norway where she was raised by Saint Birgitta's daughter Merete Ulfsdotter, whose husband was in alliance with the Norwegian King. The years under Merete's instruction made the Queen favourable to the Birgittine order, which can be seen in many of her later actions in favour of the Birgittines, including her involvement in the canonisation of the Swedish saint.

Despite the relatively peaceful period after the establishing of the Kalmar Union, the Swedish Church did not wholeheartedly support the common Scandinavian Union. From the point of view of the Swedish Church, a strong ruler was not the best solution because that left less influence for bishops in Scandinavian politics. Swedish bishops opposed Margaret's attempts to give ever power to the royal administration and the ruler's need to collect more money in taxes. The Swedish Church however remained loyal to Queen Margaret until her death in 1412.

The Swedish Church had its controversies not only with the Union Queen but also internally. Unlike bishops in all other European countries, Swedish bishops could not agree upon which obedience – the French, the Roman, or the conciliar – they would support during the Great Western Schism. This led to events in the course of which the Swedish bishops loyal to different popes excommunicated each other. The situation stabilised after some years, when the Council of Constance elected Martin V unanimously as the new Pope in 1417. The Swedish bishops – although not everyone had been present at the important event – accepted the new situation and peace returned to the Swedish Church.

The Council of Constance (1414–1418) was important for the Swedish Church also for another reason: during the Council, the Swedish bishops tried to lobby for the ongoing canonisation processes of a number of Swedish saintly candidates: Bishop Brynolf Algotsson of Skara, the Dominican Nun Ingrid Elovsdotter of Skänninge, Bishop Nils Hermansson of Linköping, and Catherine, the daughter of Saint Birgitta. The Council did not advance their canonisation processes, but the order of Saint Birgitta received the blessing of the Council despite serious concern which had arisen over the idea of a double monastery. The acceptance led to the spread of the Birgittine order in the Baltic Sea region.

After the death of Queen Margaret in 1412, Eric of Pomerania took over the governing of the Kalmar Union. He continued in Margaret's footsteps and increased Danish influence in Sweden, not only in the civil but also in the ecclesiastical administration, by appointing his supporters to important positions. The biggest blow to the Swedish Church in this respect took place in 1408, when the native Dane and former royal Chancellor Johannes Gerechini was appointed to see Uppsala. Archbishop Johannes became extremely unpopular among his Swedish colleagues, not only because of his luxurious life and interest in women but also his mismanagement of the province. His misbehaviour went so far that in 1421 he abdicated after the colleagues in Uppsala had begun a juridical process against him. He was, however, found not guilty, and his career resumed after some time as the bishop of Skálholt in Iceland.

After that episode, the Union King Eric did not want to impose his candidate upon the see of Uppsala, and there was a few years' peace within the Swedish Church under Archbishop Johan Håkansson. The election in 1432 of his successor, Archbishop Olof Larsson, without involving the King was in its turn a mistake by the Swedish Church because the King himself opposed the election strongly and turned to the pope to cancel it. Meanwhile, King Eric's candidate for the seat at Uppsala, Arnold Klemensson, tried to force his way into the archiepiscopal manor house. The use of violence by the Danes, together with discontent towards the King, led to a large military confrontation, the so-called Engelbrekt rebellion against the Union King.

Archbishop Olof Larsson got his position back, but died only a few years afterwards, in 1438, after which Nils Ragvaldsson, the earlier Bishop of Växjö, was elected as the new Swedish Archbishop. His appointment was not confirmed by the pope but by the Council of Basel, which had been summoned by Pope Martin V in 1431 to discuss the Hussite problem in Bohemia, the rise of the Ottoman Empire in the east, as well as the disagreement as to who held the supreme power within the Church: the popes or the Church councils. The decision to seek the Council's confirmation for the election of the Swedish Archbishop clearly shows the interest of the Swedish Church in supporting the conciliar movement, and thereby the larger independence of the national church from the central papal government.

Nils Ragvaldsson died in the same year, 1448, as the last Union King, Christopher of Bavaria, whose ascension to the three Scandinavian thrones the Archbishop had warmly supported. To the see of Uppsala was elected Jöns Bengtsson, member of one of the powerful Swedish aristocratic families of Oxenstierna. Alongside his family, he played an active role in the Swedish fight against the Danish rulers, which resulted in the dissolution of the Kalmar Union and the election of the Swedish nobleman Karl Knutsson Bonde to the Swedish throne. The de facto dissolution of the Scandinavian Union led to bitter fights in Sweden between the supporters of the Union and those of Karl Knutsson, and in 1451 the new Danish King Christian I of Oldenburg declared a war upon the 'rebellious Swedes'. King Karl asked the Archbishop for military help against the Danes but the Archbishop, who had a private army, did not want to help him, which led to a split between the two men. King Karl also needed money for financing the war, and turned to the Church's treasury. This was too much for the Archbishop and he began a rebellion against the Swedish King, who was forced to flee the country. The Archbishop was elected as an interim vice-king before the Union King Christian was in turn elected to the Swedish throne.

Since Swedish bishops were typically members of the leading Swedish aristocratic families and deeply involved in the country's internal politics, the Archbishop was not the only ecclesiastical leader who grasped the sword – according to one of the versions written down about the events – and led an army against his enemies. Other bishops did the same but not all of them were politically on the same side, which ended up with episcopal armies fighting against each other in a civil war. King Christian soon became unpopular in Sweden because of extensive taxation, and the Swedes began to want King Karl back. One of those wishing for this was Archbishop Jöns. He betrayed King Christian, who captured the Archbishop and took him to prison in Copenhagen – an episode that came to the attention of the pope who excommunicated the King. The Archbishop was liberated, returned to Sweden, and elected vice-king but instead of supporting Karl Knutsson he allied with his Danish imprisoner. In the end, both Jöns Bengtsson and King Christian were driven out of Sweden and Karl Knutsson returned to the throne, supporting one of his family members onto the seat of Uppsala.

In 1470, both King Karl and Archbishop Tord Pedersson (Bonde) died, and a more peaceful period in Swedish ecclesiastical history was able to begin under the auspices of Archbishop Jakob Ulfsson, who governed the Swedish Church for 45 years, from 1470 to 1515. Like his predecessors, Jakob Ulfsson was active in politics, and used his influence to strengthen the Church's political and economic power in the country, which led to conflicts with the secular rulers. Swedish history of the last half of the 15th century is marked on the one hand by the power struggle between the ruler and the Church, and on the other by the power struggle between the supporters of the Scandinavian Union kings and those of the Swedish regents. The Archbishop of Uppsala played a central role in these struggles. So did two other prelates in Linköping, Bishop-Elect Hemming Gadh and Provost Hans Brask. Gadh was in alliance with the Swedish rulers, while Brask ended up in conflict with them.

During the reign of Jakob Ulfsson, Swedish nationalism could also be observed in the attempts to canonise the Swedish saint candidates. Although the canonisation processes never reached the desired end, some of them took a step forward in the form of translation celebrations. This was the first official step towards canonisation, and during the solemn celebration the remnants of the saint candidates were translated from their original burial places to a more eminent location. Saint Catherine's translation was celebrated in 1489, while the feast for Brishop Brynolf of Skara took place in 1492, Nun Ingrid of Skänninge in 1507, and Bishop Hemming of Turku in 1514. The Archbishop was also active in the foundation and development of the University of Uppsala, which was to become an important place for the education of Swedish clerics.

When Jakob Ulfsson died after his long career as the leader of the Swedish Church in 1515, Gustav Trolle was chosen as his successor. The new Archbishop soon came to disagreement with the relatively newly elected Swedish Regent Sten Svantesson (Sture), also known as Sten Sture the Younger, who had decided to use archiepiscopal property for his own ends. The Archbishop, whose family was among the supporters of the Kalmar Union, then decided to ally with the recently elected Danish King Christian II, but the Danes did not succeed in invading Sweden. In 1517, this action led to a juridical process in which Sten Sture the Younger accused the Archbishop of treason. Gustav Trolle was found guilty and deposed from the archiepiscopal seat. Since according to canon law only priests could judge a clergyman, the tribunal judging Gustav Trolle consisted of his fellow bishops, who all confirmed the sentence with their episcopal seals – except for Hans Brask, who at that time had been elected to the see of Linköping. According to a contemporary Swedish chronicle, he is claimed to have hidden in the seal wax a small piece of paper in which he would have written that he was forced to seal the document. In Swedish history-writing this is called the *brasklappen* (note of Brask) and has become a concept in itself, meaning the excuse one can use to avoid fulfilling an oath or a promise.

In order to avenge the treatment of his ally the Archbishop, King Christian invaded Sweden in 1520, which meanwhile had been set under interdict by the Danish Archbishop of Lund for the misbehaviour of the Swedish ruler. The Danes had already tried a couple of years before to invade Sweden without result – but this time the Danish troops won. The badly wounded Sten Sture the Younger died and Christian II became the king of Sweden. His coronation was celebrated in Stockholm on 4 November 1520.

The coronation party ended abruptly on 7 November when the gates of the celebration site, the royal castle of Stockholm, were closed. The members of the high Swedish nobility along with the participating bishops had been trapped in the castle when Gustav Trolle, who had been allowed to return to Sweden and resume his archiepiscopacy, stepped forward and began a juridical process against those who had unjustly dismissed him from his seat some years earlier. During the unconventional trial, the opponents of the Archbishop – and those of Christian II – were found guilty of opposing the righteous ecclesiastical leader and thus of heresy. According to the juridical definition of the time, Christians guilty of heresy were to suffer capital punishment, and the coronation party turned into what is known as the Bloodbath of Stockholm. On the days following the juridical process, around 100 aristocrats were executed in the vicinity of the royal castle, among them two anti-unionist bishops: Mats Gregersson of Strängnäs and Vincent Henningsson of Skara. Bishop Hans Brask of Linköping is said to have been saved because of the *brasklappen* – he could thereby show that he had not acted willingly against the Archbishop.

King Gustav ascended the Swedish throne after a rebellion following the events of Stockholm and Archbishop Gustav Trolle was sent to exile. When King Gustav came to the power, he found that the treasury of his country was totally empty after the expensive wars. During the Middle Ages, the Swedish Church had gathered large properties and was extremely rich, and many Scandinavian rulers had used the ecclesiastical property when they had needed money. So did Gustav Vasa, but much more effectively than his predecessors. The new King had also seen what kinds of troubles the participation of high ecclesiastics in politics had caused, and he wanted to make an end of the Church's political power. In these attempts, he seized on the recent ideas proclaimed by Martin Luther, according to which the state should take care of governing and the Church of the care of the souls. In a diet held in Västerås in 1527, King Gustav forced through regulations which led to the appropriation of the 'excessive' property of the Church and removal of political power from the Swedish bishops. When the pope in Rome was not satisfied with the King declaring himself the leader of the Swedish Church province, Gustav cut off all connections to the papal administration and the independent, reformed Swedish Church was born.

Apart from the political developments of the late medieval Swedish Church, the cultural side of Swedish ecclesiastical history followed the pattern of the other Scandinavian countries closely. Parish churches were enlarged and embellished in the central regions, while new stone churches continued to be erected in the more remote areas. In many Swedish parishes, the older churches were vaulted with brick vaults that were decorated with wall paintings. One artist in particular, Albertus Pictor, is well known for his artistic activities. He decorated, for example, the churches of Härkeberga and Täby in the archdiocese of Uppsala. The papal acceptance of the Birgittines, the 'Swedish monastic order', was an important factor of the Swedish 15th-century ecclesiastical history. The first Birgittine abbey was built in Vadstena, but the order spread soon around the Baltic Sea, and even further. In the 1490s, the first Swedish Carthusian monastery was founded in Gripsholm by the Swedish Regent Sten Sture the Elder. Swedish churches and monasteries blossomed in the 15th century and received numerous donations from Christians in the form of money, land, property, and different ecclesiastical utensils.

The Finnish Church 1400–1550

The 15th century was a time of growth for the Catholic Church in Finland. Unlike in the previous centuries, the late medieval bishops of Turku were all native Finns, and traditional Finnish historiography has strongly underlined their independence from the other Swedish bishops. In many ways, this was true, because the bishops of Turku were not so active in the Swedish power struggle between the unionists and the nationalists, but it would be wrong to talk of an independent Finnish Church since the diocese of Turku continued to be part of the Swedish ecclesiastical province. Some Finnish bishops were more active in politics, such as Konrad Bitz (r. 1460–1489) who in the first half of the 1460s got involved in the union wars as a supporter of King Christian I, and received the fief of Raasepori in return. But when the nationalistic side won and Sten Sture the Elder came to power, Bishop Konrad had to pay for his mistake. He was found guilty of treason, had to plea pardon from the Regent and had to turn to the pope for absolution from his sin, since priests should not participate in violent acts. Because of this Konrad Bitz has suffered from a poor posthumous reputation.

The other medieval bishops, by contrast, enjoy a very good reputation in Finnish historiography. Especially loved has been Magnus I Tavast (r. 1412–1450) who during his long episcopacy developed and enriched his diocese in many ways. During his and his successor's times, the cathedral was rebuilt into a modern, gothic church and the cathedral chapter received two new prelatures and a number of new chapels. A large number of stone churches replaced the old wooden churches in different parts of Finland – and modern scholarship has demonstrated that there may have been an episcopal plan behind this intensive building programme in the diocese. Turku diocese also aimed at raising its ecclesiastical significance by beginning the canonisation process of the 14th-century bishop of Turku, Bishop Hemming. The first steps towards his canonisation had already been taken in the first part of the 15th century, but the process only moved forward at the end of the 1490s when Pope Alexander VI allowed his translation feast. The translation did not take place immediately but a great celebration was held in the Turku cathedral in 1514.

During the 15th century, monastic life expanded to the diocese of Turku in a new way. A Franciscan convent was erected in Rauma and a Franciscan *terminus* (not a full-size convent but rather a place where the friars could lodge and preach to people sailing along the coast) on the island of Kökar. The easternmost town in the Swedish realm, Vyborg, hosted both Franciscans and Dominicans who preached in the nearby Karelian region. In 1438 the Swedish council of the realm decided that a Birgittine monastery should be built in Finland. After some years the monastery was constructed, first in Masku but later moved to a better place in Naantali. The erection of more monasteries in just a few decades after such a long hiatus indicates that by this time the parish structure had been fully established, that Christians could also financially support other ecclesiastical institutions, and that there was need for them.

The Reformation in Finland was a part of the Swedish Reformation, during which the Swedish King Gustav Vasa expropriated a great deal of ecclesiastical property and removed high prelates from political power. The events in the diocese of Turku exactly followed the same lines as on the Swedish mainland.

The last medieval century was still a time of expansion for the Catholic Church in the Finnish territory, when the borderline between the Kalmar Union and Russia was also established further in the north, following the expansion of inhabitation to Savonia. The newly inhabited territories were included in the diocese of Turku; new parishes were founded and churches built. In the other Finnish parishes, stone churches replaced the older wooden churches, and many older stone churches were vaulted and decorated with wall paintings.

Church and Everyday Life – Sacraments Signposting the Christian Life

The Catholic Church and religion were involved in the everyday life of medieval people from their birth to their death, and into the afterlife. This section examines the different aspects of medieval life. Although the Church and religion function here as the framework, the section deals with numerous different matters of everyday life, having more or less direct connections to religion.

The seven sacraments of the Catholic Church formed the steady points of a human life from the birth to the grave. Some of them – baptism, confirmation, marriage, and priestly ordination – could be received only once in a lifetime, while a Christian could receive the last unction more times if necessary, and confession and the eucharist belonged to the regular activities of a good Christian.

Birth and Baptism

The sacrament of baptism was the first official step in a Christian's life. Although baptism was given to adults after they had become Christians in the conversion period, in the Middle Ages the sacrament of baptism was usually performed upon infants.

If a newly born child was very weak, he or she received an emergency baptism that could be performed by anyone, but because the baptism could be performed only once, it was very important that it be done correctly. Therefore, all women involved in childbirth had to know how to do it correctly: to say first the name of the child and then the phrase 'I baptise you in the name of the Father, the Son, and the Holy Spirit'. Receiving the sacrament of baptism as quickly as possible was crucially important for weak children because an unbaptised child could not be buried in consecrated ground. Since the ecclesiastical norms did not allow for baptising a stillborn child, it was a custom in difficult situations for the midwives to baptise the child as soon as they saw the head coming out. Thereby they could say that they had baptised a living child who had unfortunately died immediately after birth.

When the birth went smoothly there was no need for emergency baptism, and the child was taken to the parent's parish church for baptism. This usually happened relatively soon after the birth, sometimes on the same day. It was normally the father of the child, the midwife, relatives, and friends who participated in the baptism. The mother of the child could not participate because according to the tradition of the Old Testament, a woman was impure after giving birth and not allowed to enter the Church before six weeks had passed from the birth and the priest had cleaned the mother ritually by prayers.

The rite of baptism originally included several ritual parts: catechetical instructions to the people involved, chrismation, exorcisms, laying on of hands, and recitation of the Creed. By the high Middle Ages, the practice was simplified and the baptism was usually performed by affusion, that is by pouring water on the head of the child, instead of the older total immersion of the person in water. When a child was brought to the church, the parish priest met the baptismal party at the church door. The priest began with inquiring whether the child had been baptized already and wanted to know the baby's sex. After that the priest blessed the child, put salt into its mouth (this was done to represent the reception of wisdom), and exorcised the baby from any demons. After that the priest examined the godparents, who were usually chosen among the friends or close relatives present, in order to find out if they knew the Creed and the two most common prayers, Our Father and Hail Mary. This was important because the Christian education of the child was the responsibility of the godparents.

After these rites at the church door, the group entered the parish church and went to the baptismal font. By the font the priest anointed the naked baby, placed Holy Water on the baby's head and front, and gave him or her a name. One of the godparents then wrapped the baby in a white linen christening gown and took the infant to the altar, where the rest of the baptism ceremony was celebrated. At the altar, the godparents made the profession of faith for the child. When that was over, the party could return to the parent's house and celebrate.

The baptismal water was typically changed once per year, after Maundy Thursday, when the priests according to the ecclesiastical order should bless the Holy Water. Sometimes it is claimed that dirty baptismal water was the cause for high infant mortality in the Middle Ages. The high infant mortality rate because of dirty baptismal water is probably only a myth because ecclesiastical instructions state very clearly that it was the obligation of the parish priest to make sure that the Holy Water was clean. For this purpose, the medieval baptismal fonts were equipped with lids that protected the water from dust and other dirt. But it is true that the water could not remain clean for an entire year because it was used every once in the while.

In Scandinavia, where the parish churches could be located far from the dwellings of parishioners, baptising the child on the day of his or her birth was not very common. Especially in winter with its cold weather it was sensible to wait at least a few days before taking the child out into the cold for a longer time. Cold winters also caused other problems for Scandinavian baptisms: the water in the baptismal font could freeze in the cold churches. The Norwegians tried to solve this problem in the 13th century by asking for a papal permit to use beer instead of water – but Pope Gregory IX firmly replied to the archbishop of Nidaros that doing so was not allowed in any circumstances, and that even suggesting such a thing was very wrong and unorthodox. The learned pontiff gave also a clear explanation for his decision. As he explained, the Bible says that man is saved by water and the Holy Spirit, not by beer and the Holy Spirit.

Adolescence and Confirmation

Childhood ended with puberty. For girls, the age of adulthood was 12 and for boys 14. At that age, they were considered to be adult enough to be responsible for their deeds before the courts of law, as well as to be able to get married. One of the important rites of passage into adulthood was confirmation – or chrismation – during which the confirmand received the blessing of the Holy Spirit. In the Christian tradition, the sacrament of confirmation was a rite that confirmed and completed the act of infant baptism at an age at which the Christian could understand the meaning of the sacrament. Therefore, the required age for the confirmation in the 13th century was changed from seven to 12 years. In Scandinavia, the recommended suitable age for confirmation could not always be respected because it had to be conferred by a bishop, and busy bishops did not sufficiently often visit all the parishes in their frequently very large bishoprics. For example, Swedish sources mention old people who had never received confirmation because no bishop had visited their parishes. It was also possible to receive confirmation in another church than one's own parish church, and it was common that Christians wanting to be confirmed went to any church in their vicinity where the bishop was visiting. It was part of the episcopal visitation to ask if there was someone who wanted to be confirmed and then the bishop conferred the confirmation during the Mass he held in the visited parish.

The sacrament of confirmation was an especially solemn event in a Christian's life because it had to be conferred by a bishop. During the confirmation, the celebrating bishop laid hands on the confirmands and prayed that God would send the Holy Spirit forth upon them. The rite continued with the bishop anointing the sign of a cross on the forehead of each confirmand with Holy Ointment. Then the bishop gave a slight blow to the confirmand's cheek and said the words 'Peace be with you'. After that was repeated a prayer that the Holy Spirit would dwell in the hearts of the confirmands, and the celebration ended with the bishop's blessing. The parents had chosen godparents who laid their hands over the confirmand while the bishop anointed them. After receiving confirmation, the person was a full member of the religious community and could receive the sacrament of eucharist.

Lifelong Practice: Eucharist and Confession

Eucharist or the Holy Communion is a sacrament instituted by Jesus Christ during the Last Supper. It could be received as many times as the Christian wished, but not more than once per day. Apart from priests and men and women in monastic vocation, it was rare to receive the eucharist daily. Medieval men and especially women – who were considered to be more religious than men – were expected to regularly participate in the Mass, during which they could receive the eucharist if they had confessed before. One could not receive the eucharist if burdened by unconfessed sins. The eucharist was part of the liturgy of the Mass, as it still is, and during the sacrament bread and wine were consecrated by the priest on the altar, after which the eucharist was distributed and consumed.

According to medieval Catholic dogma, which was confirmed by the Fourth Lateran Council in 1215, the substances of bread and wine changed and became actually and physically the body and blood of Christ (known as *transubstantiation*), while their appearance remained that of bread and wine. The defining of the dogma of transubstantiation was a difficult issue for the Church. It was an old discussion that had already become vexed 150 years earlier, and doubts and protests against how to understand the dogma continued throughout the Middle Ages, most notably raised by the English reformer John Wyclif. When the Fourth Lateran Council agreed upon the dogma in 1215, the Danish Archbishop Anders Sunesen was also present in the Council.

The idea of transubstantiation might have been clear to educated medieval theologians like Anders Sunesen but it can be doubted how much other Christians really grasped the theological subtleties. The story of the Swedish heretic Botulf told elsewhere in this book, sentenced to death because he refused to receive the eucharist which he considered cannibalism, is a single testimony of the fact that there may have been more Scandinavians who had a wrong understanding of what really happened during the eucharist. However, Christians understood the importance of regular participation in Mass and eucharist, that the piece of wafer they received from the priest was particularly powerful, and could protect against evil. Misuse of the eucharist must have been relatively common since Scandinavian ecclesiastical legislation has stressed that it was not good to spare the wafer and use it as an amulet or protection against the Devil.

Easter was the most important ecclesiastical feast in the Middle Ages, and the period when every Christian was supposed to participate in the Holy Mass and eucharist. Easter was the most common period for Christians to confess their sins because one could receive the eucharist only after having confessed. Since the seal of confession forbade priests under pain of excommunication and dismissal to reveal what they had heard in confession, it is impossible to know how often Christians came to confess and what they told the father confessors. The Fourth Lateran Council in 1215 stipulated that each Christian had to confess to the local parish priest at least once a year. It is plausible that Christians followed this regulation and confessed at least before Easter. Most likely many Christians came more often than that because sins had to be confessed and absolved as soon as possible so that in case of sudden death there would be no danger of ending in Hell for unconfessed sins.

The medieval manuals for confessors stressed that the priests should ensure their parishioners understood the differing gravity of various sins. A lesser sin, called a venial sin, could be atoned for without confession by praying and committing good deeds, and thus there was no danger of ending in Hell in the eventuality of a sudden death. A more severe sin, called mortal sin, by contrast, had to be confessed and absolved as soon as possible to avoid the soul of the sinner ending in damnation. Since the border between a venial and mortal sin was not always clear, it was better to confess than not. The confessors' manuals often list three questions that helped in

Illustration 10.2 Church tabernacle, 14th century, 2.17 m high, in the church of Rimbo, Sweden. The chalice for the wine and the paten for the bread were kept securely under lock and key in a tabernacle when not in use during mass, as were the wafers of the Eucharist that had been consecrated but not eaten because they were now the real and physical flesh of Christ according to the theology of transubstantiation. They needed to be secured against theft and used as amulets or in magic rituals.
Photo © Kurt Villads Jensen 2022.

distinguishing a venial sin from a mortal one: (1) Did the act of sin involve a grave matter? (2) Was the sin committed with full knowledge that it was wrong? (3) Was the sin committed with the full consent of the will? If the answer to all these questions was affirmative, the committed sin was a mortal sin.

The manuals for confessors give a good impression of what happened during confession. The act of confession was not only about telling the priest of the sins committed but was also an act during which the priest could check that his parishioners could recite the Our Father, Hail Mary, and the Creed, and knew the Ten Commandments. It was also an opportunity for the parish priest to learn to know all his parishioners and if necessary to instruct them in various important things.

The sacrament of confession consisted of three parts: contrition of heart, confession, and the penance. For a successful confession all three parts had to be properly fulfilled. For contrition, the sinner had to understand what he or she had done wrong and to genuinely regret it. For confession, the sinner had to truthfully and completely communicate all that they had done. For the penance, the sinner had to fulfil the penance the priest had ordered them to do, be it reciting prayers, giving alms, fasting, or something else.

According to the manuals for the father confessors, the priest should keep his eyes piously down while talking to the penitent, especially with female confessants. The confession should take place in a quiet place but not behind closed doors like in the sacristy, especially with women. The confession began when the sinner contacted the priest and expressed their need to confess, after which the priest should ask them gently to kneel beside him so that he could receive the confession as the vicar of Christ. Then the confessant should make the sign of cross in the name of the Father, the Son, and the Holy Spirit, and ask the priest to listen to their sins and to bless them. After that the confessant recited the general confession:

> In this way, I confess to almighty God, to Blessed Virgin Mary, to all saints and to you, father, all sins that I have committed until this day and for which I beg for mercy and indulgence from God and from you, who are here the vicar of Christ.

This ended the general part of the act of confession, after which the priest had the possibility to inquire about other sins that the confessant might have committed and about the details of the sins so that he could be sure that none of the confessed sins had been mortal. The manuals encourage the priests to inquire about the details but at the same time state very clearly that it was not recommend to ask too detailed questions, especially regarding sins related to sexual acts, because that could lead the priest to temptation or could provide the sinner with ideas of new ways to sin. Although the manuals instruct the priests to inquire about different sins, it is probable that the priests very rarely took these instructions literally. It is likely that most priests just listened to the sins the penitent confessed without further inquiries and kept the sacrament as short as possible. This was sensible, since medieval parishes were usually not very large, and most Scandinavian priests must have known their parishioners relatively well. The confession always ended after the priest had absolved the sinner, ordered the necessary penance, and blessed them. Subsequently, the sinner had to fulfil the penance, after which the absolution was valid and the Christian could continue his or her life without fear of going to Hell – until he or she sinned again.

Adulthood and Marriage

The third sacrament relating to adult life was that of matrimony. Since most Christians got married at some point of their lives, marriage was a common sacrament in the Middle Ages. The ecclesiastical norms laid out clear rules as to who could get married, to whom, and when, and entrusted the parish priest with the task of inquiring about any possible marital impediments for the spouses. According to the regulations of canon law, a couple could not get married if there was such an impediment but had to call it off and find another spouse.

Marital impediments were many. One of the most common was too close blood relations, or consanguinity. According to the norms stipulated by the Fourth Lateran Council in 1215, it was forbidden to marry a person to whom one was related more closely than the fourth degree of consanguinity. The degrees were counted on the basis of how many generations there were between the spouses and their first common ancestor. Consanguinity regulations forbade, for example, marriages between siblings (first degree), cousins (second degree), second cousins (third degree), and third cousins (fourth degree) in the horizontal line as well as any in the direct line, between parents and children (first degree), grandparents and children (second degree), and so on. The regulation might sound strict, but actually amounted to a mitigation of the earlier regulations forbidding marriages up to the seventh degree; the Council also decided that with a papal dispensation a couple could marry despite an impediment of consanguinity, unless it was in the direct line.

Another common marital impediment was affinity, which forbade marriages between spouses too closely connected to each other by a former marriage or a sexual relationship of one of the spouses to a close relative of the other. The earlier regulations here had also set the limitation at the seventh degree of affinity, but the Fourth Lateran Council reduced it to the fourth. The degree of affinity was calculated according to the degree of consanguinity between the relatives in question. Thus, a man could not marry a woman if he had been married to or had had sexual relationship with her sister, cousin, second cousin, or third cousin, for example. This impediment could also be removed by a papal dispensation, as could the so-called impediment of quasi affinity, which referred to same kind of case but where one of the spouses had been engaged to the relative of the other.

Canon law stipulated numerous other marital impediments too. These included the spiritual relationship of the godparents and their closest relatives to the baby they had baptised or confirmed and his or her closest relatives. A man could not marry the daughter of his godfather, for example. This was an important fact in the choice of godparents and often led to the godparents being chosen among the closest kin. Similarly, marriages were forbidden between the members of two households involved in adoption. This impediment was called a legal relationship or legal fraternity. In addition to these relatively common marital impediments, marriage was not allowed if one of the spouses was mentally ill, already married, or had been ordained in the Holy Orders (as a subdeacon, deacon, or presbyter).

To eliminate the possibility of a marital impediment existing between the spouses, the Church required that couples who intended to be married had to contact their parish priest. The priest was supposed to find out if there were possible impediments. This was done through the reading of the banns, that is, announcing on three consecutive Sundays that the couple intended to marry and inviting anyone who knew of an impediment to inform the priest. If nobody came forward, the priest could celebrate the marriage 'in the face of the church'. The medieval wedding ceremony took place outside the church door, but the content was the same as in the modern one: the couple stood in front of the priest, the bride on the left and the groom on the right. The priest asked those present if any knew a reason why they should not be married and

Illustration 10.3 Table of consanguinity from the jurisprudent Cardinal Henry of Segusio's (also known as Hostiensis) *Summa Aurea*. The picture presents the multitude of different kinds of blood relations that impeded the contracting of a marriage. The Fourth Lateran Council in 1215 set the limit for the forbidden relations to 4th degree of consanguinity.

French manuscript, c. 1275.

Photo Cleveland Museum. This file is made available under the Creative Commons CC0 1.0 Universal Public Domain Dedication.

if not, the celebration continued with the couple promising to love, honour, and obey each other, and exchanging wedding rings. After that everybody entered the church for a special Mass.

Before the ceremony the priest had to ensure that both spouses were entering the marriage by their free will; if not, he could not marry them. In the Middle Ages, marriages of people from the upper social strata were rarely love matches but often arranged unions between members of two families wishing to be allied. However, it is important to stress that ecclesiastical legislation was very insistent that nobody should be forced to marry. In fact, canon law states that a forced marriage was not a valid one.

A girl had to be at least 12 years old before she could be married, while the age limit for boys was 14. We do not have exact knowledge of how old Scandinavian brides or grooms usually were but numerous sources, especially related to the nobility, show that girls often married relatively early. Queen Margaret was engaged to King Haakon of Norway, 13 years her senior, at the age of six years and their marriage was celebrated when she was 10. Saint Birgitta of Sweden was 14 when she married her husband Ulf Gudmarsson, who was a few years older. These examples from the members of royal or noble families are, however, not necessarily good examples of the typical age of marriage among the peasant or burgher families.

Not all medieval marriages were celebrated in the church but were nonetheless legally valid, including for the Church. The reason for this was that Christians could not receive the sacrament of matrimony twice, and thus a widow or widower who wanted to re-marry could not celebrate the second marriage in the church. This is remarkable since remarriage was very common in the Middle Ages due to high mortality rates, and women in particular died relatively often, in childbed. It was also common that married couples did not have to be of the same age – or even generation.

An ecclesiastically recognised marriage was also unnecessary in Scandinavia because local civil legislation considered it to be a civil rather than an ecclesiastical matter. Legally speaking, Scandinavian countries differed significantly in this respect from the southern European countries. The medieval Scandinavian laws additionally contain a large number of regulations regarding the marriages; the Swedish law, for example, gives very precise rules for the proposal, the dowry, and the morning gift – which the ecclesiastical legislation was not interested in at all. In the Swedish civil law books, marital regulations are gathered in a special section (*Giftermålsbalken*). Danish laws did not have special sections like the Swedish laws, but they too contain regulations about marriages, but typically in the context of inheritance law. In Norwegian medieval laws, marital matters were included in the inheritance section (*Arvebolk*), because, from the civil legislator's point of view, the two issues often went hand in hand. The dowry was a sum of money or other property that the parents of the bride donated to the newly wedded couple, while the morning gift was a present from the newly wedded husband to his wife on the first morning of their married life.

When the ecclesiastical wedding was over, the party left the church and continued the celebration at the house of the groom to which the bride was solemnly led. The celebration at the house of the groom was known as the 'wedding beer', referring to a big dinner with drinks. Especially in the wealthier households, it was a huge party with many invited guests – and many sources testify how the party sometimes became violent when the participants got drunk and began to quarrel. Sometimes even priests participated in the violence, like the parish priest Michael Nicolai of Högsäter in

Sweden. Together with a number of neighbours, he had been invited to the wedding of the daughter of one of his parishioners, Tord Räv. According to Michael's story those present were in a good mood and somewhat drunk later in the evening. Suddenly a quarrel broke out among the guests, who pulled out their weapons and wounded each other. The priest wanted to go to bed but was trapped between the fighters, asking the host to stop the fight and to avoid a scandal. Tord was unable to do so and the fight escalated. Suddenly the bridegroom attacked one of the guests, layman Bard, with his sword. Michael had meanwhile obtained an axe to defend himself if necessary, and while he was holding it high in the air the bridegroom accidentally hit his head on it and the axe went in deep, resulting in his death a few days later. This sad story certainly does not describe the events of a typical wedding party, but a marriage becoming a funeral was not unusual in the Middle Ages.

When a couple was married, they had to remain together for the rest of their lives because the Church did not recognise the possibility of divorce. The only way to get rid of an unwanted spouse was to be able of demonstrate before the ecclesiastical court that the marriage was not valid and therefore had to be annulled, after which the spouses were free to re-marry. It was possible to request an annulment from the pope if there was question of a forced marriage, or if one of the spouses was mentally ill, too young, or could not marry because he or she was already married or in an ecclesiastical career (as a priest, monk, or nun). A marriage could also be annulled because of an existing marital impediment.

Annulments were not common in the Middle Ages, but neither were they extremely rare. We know of royal marriages being annulled but no such information exists for marriages between common people. One of the most famous medieval attempts to annul a marriage was between King Philip II Augustus of France and his wife, Ingeborg, daughter of the Danish King Valdemar I. Their marriage took place in August 1193 and was supposed to create an alliance between Denmark and France. There were no apparent problems between the spouses during the wedding but something happened during their first night together, because the morning after King Philip was frightened of Ingeborg and sent her away immediately. Afterwards, the King summoned an ecclesiastical council and wanted an annulment based on a falsified family tree showing that the spouses were too closely related. Since affinity was an impediment their marriage was annulled, but Ingeborg and her brother King Canute VI of Denmark appealed to the pope, who cancelled the false annulment. They never lived together again but remained officially wife and husband, although King Philip did reconcile with Ingeborg after 20 years, in 1213.

Before the arrival of Christian laws in Scandinavia, a man could have other women than his wife, together with illegitimate children. Men could even legitimate their children by their concubines so that they had the same inheritance rights as the children by his legitimate wife. This was especially common among the aristocratic and royal families in which men were expected to marry with a woman from the same social class, and thus marriages with a lower status woman were not possible. The arrival of Christian law and the stricter sexual norms of the Catholic Church diminished this practice, and relationships outside marriage became forbidden and criminalised. The Norwegian and Icelandic medieval laws punished both married men and married women equally if they were found guilty of infidelity, while the Swedish and Danish laws typically punished only married women, although the ecclesiastical legislation stipulated that married men who cheated their wives should also be punished.

Most laws allowed the cheated husbands to kill the men with whom their wives had had a relationship.

The stricter legislation around sexuality did not concern only married men or women but also the unmarried. Norwegian and Icelandic laws for example permitted the relatives of an unmarried woman to kill the man who had seduced her. With the arrival of ecclesiastical regulations on priestly celibacy, the idea of chastity became more and more popular. Not only were priests, monks, and nuns supposed to observe celibacy, but many unmarried or married women – like Saint Birgitta of Sweden – also decided to live chastely. Virginity also became increasingly important from the 14th century onwards, whereas earlier Scandinavian society had more greatly appreciated fertility.

Priests, Monks, and Nuns: Ordination

Not all medieval adults were married. Some remained unmarried because they could not find a suitable spouse, and some because they chose an ecclesiastical career and were not allowed to marry. After the ecclesiastical reform movement of the 11th and 12th centuries, named after Pope Gregory VII (r. 1073–1085), monks as well as men in Holy Orders (subdeacons, deacons, and presbyters) could not be married. Nuns in their turn were considered brides of Christ, having to remain faithful to him and observe celibacy. Similarly to the sacrament of matrimony for laypeople, the men and women in the service of the Church also had a sacrament conferred upon them when they chose to follow God. The priestly ordination was one of the seven sacraments of the Catholic Church, and the taking of the monastic vows was also a comparably sacred ceremony.

The sacrament of ordination had to be conferred by the local bishop, and before which the candidates had to pass an examination whereby the bishop ensured that they were capable of serving the Church. The candidates were tested in Latin grammar, reading, and singing, all skills required for successful celebration of ecclesiastical services. Additionally, the candidates had to fulfil a number of other preconditions: they had to be born in wedlock, old enough (18 to receive the order of subdeacon and 25 that of presbyter), and without any physical faults (such as limping, missing fingers, or other physical injuries) that would make them incapable of faultlessly performing the Mass. The candidates should also be considered morally sound, and could not be excommunicated or irregular. The candidates for the highest ecclesiastical order, of priesthood, were asked to have a guarantee of an ecclesiastical benefice for their maintenance.

There were also a number of preconditions for the act ordination itself: only the bishop of the candidate's home diocese could confer ecclesiastical orders – unless the candidate had received a papal dispensation for this, or the local bishop had delegated the task to someone else. The ordination could take place only on certain Saturdays: on the first of Lent, the first after Pentecost, the first after the feast of the Holy Cross, the first after the feast of Saint Lucy, on the Saturday of the middle week of the Lent, and on the Saturday of Holy Week. The candidate should also receive ecclesiastical orders in the right order and only one order could be conferred at a time.

When the candidates had passed the examination and were found suitable for an ecclesiastical career, they could participate in the ordination. The rite occurred within the context of Mass, during which those to be ordained were called forward, made an oath of obedience to the ordaining bishop who laid hands upon each candidate prostrated in front of the altar, and blessed and anointed them with the chrism. After that, the ordained could continue and co-celebrate the Mass, and those who had received the priestly ordination could act independently and confer all sacraments. The rite of monastic vows was equally solemn and took place in the church of the chosen monastery or nunnery, after which the monks or nuns joined the brothers or sisters and began their monastic life with full obligations and rights.

Old Age: Preparations for Death and the Last Unction

Life expectancy in medieval Scandinavia was not very long. Many died as infants, and many relatively young because of hard labour, insufficient nutrition, and various diseases – women were in particular danger of dying during childbirth. Although the majority of people died in what we would nowadays call middle age, some could live a long time, especially those belonging to the upper social strata who obtained enough nourishing food. On the other hand, many of these risked a sudden and violent death in warfare or feuds. Medieval society did not know the system of the old age pension but it was rather the task of the family or the society to take care of the old, sick, and poor. The Church had a particular role in this.

In Scandinavia, especially in the countryside, it was typically the family that took care of the older generation. It was usual that children cared for their parents and possibly also grandparents, with a greater number of generations lived together on a farm. In towns, there was less space for several generations to live under the same roof, but it was typical that children here also took care of the older generations. If someone had no offspring, it was possible to make an agreement with a monastery and move there in return for a testamentary donation. For example, an elderly couple donated a house to the Dominican convent of Turku on condition that the couple could stay in the house until their death, and that the friars would take care of their needs. As in this case, donations to churches or monasteries could be bound to certain services such as the celebration of a daily, weekly, or yearly Mass for the commemoration of the donator and his or her relatives and ancestors.

The practice of making wills came to Scandinavia together with the Catholic Church – until then the inheritance was divided between the heirs according to the local civil legislation. With the introduction of wills, it became customary to donate part of one's property to someone other than the legal heirs. Usually, the recipient was a local church, a monastery, or a nunnery. The earliest preserved Scandinavian wills date to around 1200 and were made by bishops. During the 13th century, the making of a will became more common among the members of aristocracy, including women. With the Black Death, the number of Scandinavian wills increased significantly, and the practice became more popular.

The last will was often written when someone thought that he or she might be in danger of death. Sometimes this took place before a longer journey – for example a pilgrimage to Jerusalem or Rome – but most often wills were composed on the death bed. These had a conventional form and were often written down by a local priest who could read and write. The wills began with a statement that the testator was mentally capable of making decisions and that now when death was approaching, the testator's last will was as follows … Usually the wills began with larger sums donated to the church or monastery in which the testator had decided to be buried. Thereafter came a list of smaller sums or items that the testator wanted to give either to some institutions or to individuals. Because of the strict inheritance regulations of local legislation, a person could not give away his or her whole property in a will but only a certain part of it, including cash and purchased property. Hereditary land or property had to remain in the family.

The last will was usually composed in good time before the last moment arrived – unless a person encountered an unexpected disease or accident. In the Middle Ages, and especially from the early 15th century onwards, it was very important to be prepared to death. There circulated a number of guide books with good advice for preparing a good death called *Ars moriendi* (the Art of Dying). Composed originally in Latin by an unknown author (although often connected to Jean de Gerson, a French scholar, reformer, poet, and chancellor of the University of Paris in the early 15th century), the guide books were soon translated into the vernacular, including Scandinavian languages, and printed.

When the time came, the priest would visit the dying person. The priest received the last confession, absolved the dying of all sins, and gave the last unction. The sacrament of the last unction meant that the priest anointed the dying person with Holy Ointment and prayed for his or her soul. After that, the person could die without the danger of ending in Hell. The last confession and last unction were the last sacraments performed for a person since the funeral, although celebrated by a priest, was not among the sacraments.

In the Middle Ages, people died typically at home and their bodies were prepared for the funeral at home. The corpse was washed and clean clothes were put on. After that, the body was put in a place where family and friends could come to pay their last respects. The room where the body was kept was usually lit with candles, and praying people surrounded the body. This event was called a wake, and its intention was to keep away the bad spirits until the body had been buried in consecrated ground in the churchyard. For the funeral, the relatives and friends of the deceased transported the body to the church in a procession typically led by the parish priest. The body was usually put into a coffin, but poorer people could also be carried to the church on a plank or plate upon which the deceased laid wrapped in a shroud. The burial rite itself took place in the church, where a Mass for the dead was celebrated. During the rite, the priest blessed the corpse and prayed for the dead person. After the Mass, the body was carried out to the cemetery in a procession and buried in consecrated ground. Wealthier persons could be buried in the church. It was usually the deceased themselves who had chosen the burial place. Some aristocratic families began to have family graves in certain churches or monasteries which they had particularly supported.

The Rhythm of Life

Medieval everyday life was divided into different recurring temporal cycles: the day, week, and year. The daily cycle was based on light, beginning when it was light enough for activity and ended when the darkness came. In Scandinavia, the length of the day varied significantly between winter and summer, and the difference was bigger in the northern parts. According to an old tradition, the day was divided into day and night. The day began with the sunrise (c. 6 a.m.), ended with the sunset (c. 6 p.m.), and was divided into 12 hours (Lat. *horae*). The night, in its turn, began with sunset and ended with sunrise. Unlike the day the night was divided into four sections of around three hours (Lat. *vigiliae*).

The original tradition of the day's division had originated from the Mediterranean, where the difference between the length of days and nights was not extremely large in summer or winter, and the length of the hours and vigils remained relatively stable. In Scandinavia, by contrast, the respective length of daylight in summer and winter varied greatly and caused difficulties in following the hours. The hours were especially important for clerics, monks, and nuns because the Church had established a model for the recommended praying hours marked by the ringing of church bells. In the daylight the bells rang for *prime* (at c. 6 a.m. or sunrise), *terce* (c. 9 a.m.), *sext* (noon), *nones* (c. 3 p.m.), and *vespers* (c. 6 p.m. or sunset). At night, the canonical hours included *compline* (before going to bed), *midnight office* (midnight), *vigil* (c. 2 a.m.), *matins* (c. 3 a.m. to dawn), and *lauds* (early morning). Matins, lauds, and vespers were the most important hours for payer, carefully marked in churches and monasteries, but laypeople were not required to participate in them.

Just as with the short winter days and long nights, the long summer days and short nights made it difficult for the Scandinavians to follow the hours. In Nidaros, the night lasted only three and half hours in summer, while at the winter equinox, the daylight hours lasted only from 10 a.m. to 2.30 p.m. It was difficult for priests and monks to celebrate all five daytime offices or five night offices in such a short time. Therefore, the Scandinavian bishops occasionally petitioned for a papal dispensation to celebrate the hours in an unusual way.

A strict daily rhythm was mainly relevant to the ecclesiastics, while laypeople could complete their daily tasks by the rhythm that suited them. The animals had to be fed and the cows milked at regular intervals, but there were no particular regulations for daily life. In the towns, the gates were closed at sunset and opened at sunrise, which regulated the market times. Burghers and craftsmen working in workshops usually did so at times when it was possible to see in the daylight, but during the dark winter months they used candlelight.

Each week had its own rhythm too, based on religion. Since it was written in the Bible that God rested on the seventh day of the Creation, Emperor Constantine decreed in year 321 that a week should consist of seven days, one which was supposed to be kept free from work. In the Jewish tradition, the free day was Saturday, the *Sabbath*. It began at sunset on Friday evening and lasted until the appearance of three stars in the sky on Saturday night. Christians instead celebrated Sunday as the free day. The Church was relatively strict in the keeping of Sunday as the resting day, and throughout the Middle Ages, ecclesiastical courts punished Christians who had fished or done other work on Sundays or major saints' days.

The weekly cycle was visible in medieval life in other ways too. One of these was in the activity of the legal institutions. The ecclesiastical courts in episcopal towns assembled, for example, on Mondays, Wednesdays, and Fridays. Similarly civil courts in towns assembled on certain days, like the town court of Stockholm that had sessions on Mondays, Wednesdays, and Fridays. In towns, markets were held on all working days, and craftsmen worked in their workshops from Monday to Saturday. The weekly cycle was visible also in monasteries, where the liturgical chants differed on different days.

The medieval life moreover repeated a yearly cycle in which midsummer was marked by the summer solstice and midwinter by the winter solstice. These days had been marked in Scandinavia before the Middle Ages and the arrival of the Christian Church. The Christian yearly cycle was based on Christ's life and punctuated by two main events: his birth on Christmas Day (25 December) and his resurrection on Easter Day (Easter is a moving feast, falling on the Sunday following the first full moon after the vernal equinox, between 21 March and 23 April).

According to the Christian reckoning, each new calendar year began at Christmas. The new ecclesiastical year, by contrast, began on the First Advent Sunday, on the fourth Sunday before Christmas Day. There were four Advent Sundays before Christmas. Epiphany, that is the revealing of Christ to the magi, was celebrated on 6 January, 13 days after Christmas Day. Then there was a short break in occasions for the ecclesiastical year before Lent began, six and a half weeks prior to the second great ecclesiastical feast, Easter Day. Easter Sunday, the day of Christ's resurrection, was preceded by Holy Week, including among other special days Maundy Thursday and Good Friday. Fifty days after Easter Day came Pentecost, also known as Whit Sunday, when Christ's followers received the gift of the Holy Spirit. A week after Pentecost there followed Trinity Sunday, marking the Holy Trinity of the Father, the Son, and the Holy Spirit. There were no important recurrent ecclesiastical events in summer and autumn before Advent time arrived again.

In addition to the biblical feasts, the ecclesiastical year was full of feast days commemorating the saints. The four feasts dedicated to Virgin Mary (Purification on 2 February, Annunciation on 25 March, Assumption on 15 August, and Nativity on 8 September) were the most prominent, but the feasts of the Apostles, All Saints (1 November), and Corpus Christi (ten days after Pentecost) were also very important. Some saints were venerated throughout Christendom, while some others were local. For each parish, the high point of the year was the saint's day of the patron saint of the local church. Since the feast attracted a large number of people, including from outside the parish, the ecclesiastical celebrations were often combined with a market in the community. Medieval Scandinavian laws did not normally allow markets outside towns, but the day of the local patron saint was an exception.

Scandinavians soon adopted the Christian yearly cycle, and the local saints were venerated together with the international ones. The saints also began to define the rhythm of working life. For example, Saint Michael's day (Michaelmas) on 29 September was the typical date for servants to change their working place.

The rhythm of agriculture defined that of life in the countryside, and working cycles were taken into account in the calendar of court days. The court systems in different Scandinavian countries varied somewhat and it is impossible to identify a clear rule, but if we take the Swedish court system as an example we can see how the court sessions accommodated the working cycle. According to Swedish law, court sessions in the countryside followed in three cycles, of summer, autumn, and winter sessions. The winter sessions began on 13 January (Saint Canute) and lasted until the start of Lent. Summer sessions lasted from 17 June (Saint Botulf) until 29 July (Saint Olaf), while autumn sessions were held between 29 September (Saint Michael) and the beginning of Advent. Thus, the most busiest farm work periods in spring and autumn were kept free from juridical issues. Moreover, court sessions did not collide with the major ecclesiastical feasts.

11 Economic Expansion – The International Market Economy

The Hanseatic League

The Hanseatic League was the most powerful economic organisation connected to Scandinavia. It was an association of towns and merchants in northern parts of Germany, the Baltic Sea, and the North Sea areas. International trade in northern Europe was largely in the hands of the Hanseatic merchants from the 13th century onwards, but the League increased its influence throughout the Middle Ages. At its summit in the 15th century, the Hanseatic League sought to gain monopolies over maritime trade in the North Sea as well as the Baltic Sea regions and obtained far-reaching privileges from Scandinavian rulers. In the Baltic Sea region, the most important Hanseatic town was Lübeck, the centre of trade between the Hanseatic towns and the important commercial hubs outside the Baltic: Novgorod, London, and Bruges.

The Hanseatic League was mainly an association of German and Baltic towns, but two Scandinavian towns were officially part of it, namely Stockholm and Visby. An equally important Scandinavian Hanseatic town was Bergen in Norway, possessing a Hanseatic *Kontor* (the League's foreign trading post in non-member towns). Other Scandinavian towns with a Hanseatic *Kontor* were Malmö and Falsterbo in Scania, but unlike Bergen, which became a *Kontor* in 1360, the two Danish towns only joined the League in the 15th century. The Hanseatic League also had commercial connections to numerous other Scandinavian towns, including Kalmar, Nyborg, Nyköping, Nidaros, and Turku.

The Hanseatic League began in the late 12th century as a grouping of a few commercial towns and merchants in northern Germany. The very first step towards the creation of the League was probably the treatise of Artlenburg 1161 between Duke Henry the Lion of Saxony and the inhabitants of Gotland, who gained the privilege of trading with towns under Henry's control. The treaty also specified compensations in case of loss of goods and guaranteed the same privileges for Saxon merchants in Gotland. The treaty is known only in a later copy and it is highly disputed how much is original and how much later additions, but it is true to the broad idea upon which the Hanseatic League was built: free but firmly controlled trade.

By the 15th century, the Hanseatic League encompassed almost 200 member or associate towns. The originally loose association of merchants gradually grew into an official organisation, the members of which enjoyed extensive privileges: they could trade in many places without paying customs and duties, received military protection

Illustration 11.1 Lisa von Lübeck, a reconstruction from 2004 of a ship from 1470 of the Carrack type, which replaced the Cog as the big transport ship in the Baltic and the Atlantic.

Photo Henning Axt, 2009. This file is licensed under the Creative Commons Attribution-Share Alike 3.0 Unported license.

and juridical help from the League, and could profit from the League's many political relations and resultant privileges. The Hanseatic League became so economically and politically powerful that it became involved in wars in the Baltic Sea region in the attempt to defend the rights and privileges of its member towns.

The Hanseatic League was also a powerful enemy of the Scandinavian kingdoms, especially Denmark, which led to military confrontations. One of the economically most important conflicts took place in the 1360s when the League waged war against Denmark, which had required that the Hanseatic merchants should pay taxes for products crossing the Danish sounds. The war between the Hanseatic League and Denmark ended in the peace treaty of Stralsund in 1370, in which the League gained profitable economic concessions from Denmark. Another war between Denmark and the Hanseatic League took place in 1426–1435 after the Danish King Eric of Pomerania had introduced a new toll for foreign ships passing through the Øresund. The Hanseatic League won the war and in the peace negotiations in Vordingborg in 1435, the King had to grant it freedom from taxation. The Hanseatic League also contributed to financing warfare between Denmark and Sweden during the Union wars of the late 15th century and was often directly involved in shipping provisions and troops.

The Internationalisation of Commerce: Transnational Commercial Networks and Routes

Through its large international commercial network, the members of the Hanseatic League could easily reach merchants in Italy, England, Portugal, and Novgorod. Thanks to the League, Scandinavian products reached international markets and foreign products arrived in Scandinavia. Scandinavian trade was however not only dependent on the Hanseatic League but had a long tradition far back in the Viking Age.

Most of the trade in the Baltic Sea and the North Sea area was local, but the Scandinavians had since the Viking Age traded much farther afield. Long-distance trade typically involved luxury objects. In the Viking period, Scandinavia was known as the exporter of fur, slaves, and soldiers, and they traded with western Europe mainly via the Rhine River, as well as the Byzantine and Arabic territories in the east via Lake Ladoga and the big Russian rivers down to Constantinople. From the east, the Scandinavians imported high-quality clothes made of fine materials such as silk as well as precious metals like silver, while from western Europe, the Scandinavians bought glass, weapons, pottery, and woollen clothes. In the Viking Age, Hedeby in Schleswig-Holstein was the most important commercial hub for the Danes and Norwegians, while Birka in Lake Mälaren was the Swedish equivalent. Due to a lack of Viking Age sources, it is not known for certain whether the Scandinavian trade was in the hands of Scandinavian or foreign merchants. Investigations of DNA in skeletons from Viking Age Sigtuna indicate that the population was very mixed, with half coming from outside Sweden, from many different places in Europe and the Mediterranean. The samples are few and conclusions cannot be too firmly drawn, but they indicate a high degree of internationalisation at a very early stage. Most Scandinavians participating in trading expeditions were not merchants in the proper sense but probably made their main living from agriculture, only occasionally leaving on a long voyage to sell their products.

The Middle Ages did not bring any drastic change to Viking Age trading routes or products, the most important imported goods being woollen clothes (mainly from Flanders or England), salt, and, in increasing quantities, grain because the short domestic growing season and relatively cold summers could not always provide enough grain for the growing Scandinavian population. Scandinavian export products in their turn were timber, tar, bark, and firewood as well as luxury war horses and other animal products, especially fish. Hops for spicing and preserving beer were one of the most important trading goods both internally and externally. Scandinavian trade continued earlier traditions but from the 10th century onwards at the latest Gotland began to gain a more central role as an important trading hub.

Until c. 1100 European trade had been very limited, while the international trade was only occasional and mainly concerned luxury products. From the 12th century onwards, the political situation in Europe grew relatively stable compared to earlier, and good climatic conditions had increased productivity so that farmers had a surplus they could sell. This led to urbanisation in Europe, which increased the trade significantly. Within economic history, the period between c. 1100 and the Black Death in c. 1350 has been designated as the medieval commercial revolution. It had consequences for Scandinavian trade in two different ways.

First, the German merchants of the Hanseatic League gradually took over long-distance trade in Scandinavia and turned it into a profession requiring capital along with frequent connections to overseas suppliers and buyers. The professionalisation of trade and its concentration in the hands of a small international group of town dwellers increased the towns' importance as commercial hubs and highlighted the need for legal control on trade. The professionalisation of long-distance trade was also important for customers, who knew that professional merchants could secure the supply of certain products almost throughout the year, while greater competition between merchants could be a better guarantee of products' quality.

Second, the growing European market and emerging towns meant that there was suddenly an increasing need for certain products for mass consumption, such as fish, butter, and metal, that earlier were produced only for personal or local use. For most Scandinavians, who could not produce more than what they themselves needed, this development may not have meant much, but for those who could produce a surplus it meant extra source of income. The increase in such products for mass consumption also changed the transportation of goods, since merchants could no longer rely on their earlier large profits from luxury trade. Merchants therefore needed cheaper transport, which promoted bulk-cargo transport by water and larger boats.

The commercial revolution had far-reaching consequences for Scandinavia: fishing grew in importance in Iceland, Norway, and Scania, and iron mining (later also copper and silver mining) intensified in Sweden. In the 15th century, Iceland exported huge quantities of sulphur which could be found naturally and dug out. In Europe, natural sulphur deposits exist only in Sicily, in Poland in small quantities, and in Sweden, or had to come from Asia, so Icelandic sulphur supplied the entire European market. The demand for sulphur increased in particular with the development of weapons using gunpowder, for which sulphur was one of the principal ingredients. We have less information about the butter trade and its consequences for Scandinavian dairy production but there are plenty of examples of the use of butter as means of payment. For example, some Scandinavian students studying at European universities received their study support in the form of butter which they could sell, using the proceeds to cover their educational costs.

Many products were transported by Scandinavians without links to the Hanseatic League. In the 14th–15th centuries, there was a rapidly growing demand for timber and all tree products for constructing buildings, for the transport industry including shipbuilding, and as a source of energy. At the same time, large areas of southern Scandinavia and northern Europe including England and the Netherlands had become deforested since the 11th century. Northern Scandinavia and the Baltic countries therefore became providers of timber. All major Norwegian towns had an important tree export business since the early 13th century, which steadily grew for centuries after. This was mainly in form of large trunks to be processed by the buyers, but from the mid-15th century onwards, Norwegians began to build water-powered sawmills. They could now produce timber in much greater quantity and of many more kinds, and the trade grew. This new combination of industry and trade required substantial investments, which however paid off. Those nobles with sufficient economic means to enter the timber trade became very rich.

The commercial revolution also meant that the commercial network of the Baltic Sea and the North Sea regions became much denser. New towns were founded everywhere in Scandinavia, new areas even in far north and east were populated, and new commercial hubs were born. Professional fishing expanded the commercial networks far out into the North Sea, and many seaside towns grew in importance. One of the

274 1400–c. 1550: Power in Crises

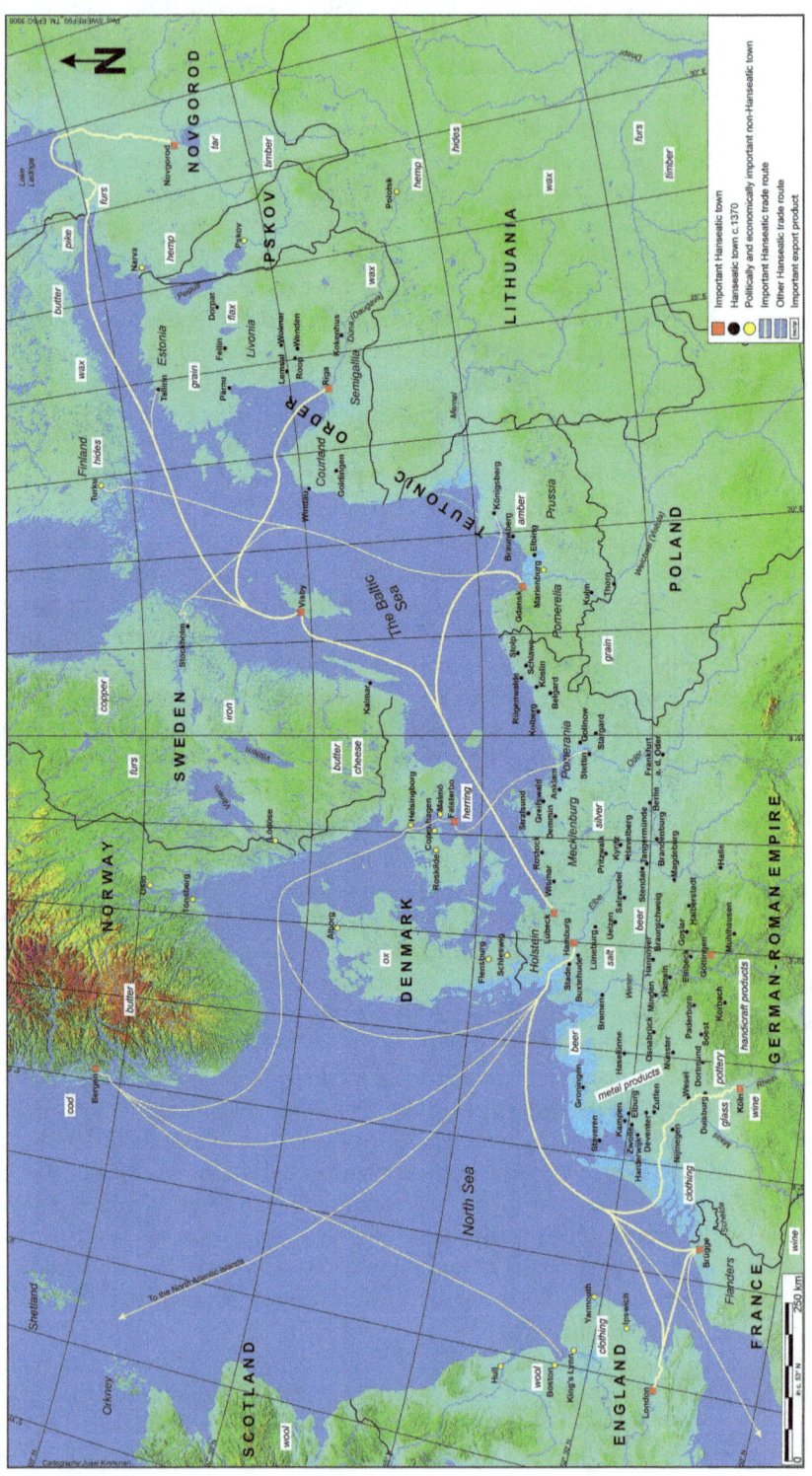

Map 6 Hanseatic cities and trading routes in Scandinavia around 1370.
Map © Jussi Kinnunen, 2022.

most popular trading places for fish was in Scania, which was the great centre of the herring trade and whose annual herring market was of huge economic significance.

Harvesting Lakes and Seas: Professional Fishing in Scandinavia

Fish was an important part of the daily diet everywhere in Scandinavia and western Europe, especially because the dietary requirements of the Catholic Church stated that the consumption of meat was not allowed on certain days like Fridays or in certain fasting periods such as the 40-day season of Lent before Easter. The amount and kind of fish consumed changed over time, according to ecology, technology, and fashion. Until around the year 1000, most fish eaten in north-western Europe was freshwater but with the commercial revolution, growing urban population, and the increasing demand for fish, the consumption and fishing of saltwater varieties grew massively. In Scandinavia, the situation may have been a little different compared to other parts of Europe, and the amount of consumed saltwater fish was probably always relatively high compared to the rest of Europe because of the long coastline. But we do not have any reliable data for the early period, only indications. The most common types of exported fish in Scandinavia were salmon, cod, and herring, but in addition, whales and other types of fish large and small were regularly caught and eaten, such as eels, pikes, and perch. Of the three most commonly traded fish, salmon was a typical freshwater fish, while cod and herring were saltwater.

Salmon was very common, popular fish all over Scandinavia. These hatch in the northern rivers, migrating to live in the ocean and then returning to their home rivers to reproduce. There are a number of Scandinavian rivers already well known in the Middle Ages for their salmon and fishing sites. One of these is the River Kemi in Finland, which is about 500 km long and famous for its abundance of salmons both in the Middle Ages and today. Since fishing in the northern rivers was already strictly regulated in the Middle Ages, it is possible to follow the amount of salmon fishing from then onwards using extant tax registers and accountancy books. In good years, 1,000 barrels of salmon could be caught, packed, and exported from the River Kemi alone during the short summer fishing season. The salmon trade was of such economic value that fishers along the River Kemi as well as other important salmon rivers paid a special 'feast day tax' to the local church authorities so that they could continue fishing on Sundays and feast days when work was normally forbidden. The northern salmon was exported all over Scandinavia, into western Europe, and beyond. In the 15th century, for example, the Teutonic order sailed Scandinavian products including salmon far up the great rivers to central eastern Europe, Bohemia, and Hungary.

The fishing of salmon took place during the early summer months when the salmon were going up the rivers to spawn. At these times, the rivers were full of fish, and they were easy to catch. The fishermen usually caught salmon with small or large nets that were either stretched out between poles in the river or simply by fishing from the land with rods and lures. At other times, salmon was caught by dragging a net between two boats, and sometimes with spears, while written testimonies from Iceland claim that it was possible to divert the water away from some of the rivers, and the salmon could then be plucked by hand. From the mid-12th century at the latest, when salmon had become an important export product, it grew necessary to begin regulating the right to fish. Therefore, rivers were divided into sections in which rulers, institutions like churches or monasteries, and local peasants each had an exclusive right to fish, sometimes on certain days. The division of fishing rights also caused a great deal of legal disputes, highlighting fishing's importance of fishing as a source of income.

Freshwater fishing became very effective in the course of the Middle Ages and seems to have led in some areas to over-exploitation. There were at least attempts to regulate and diminish overfishing in several places in Scandinavia. The typical aim of such regulation was to ensure that rivers were not closed by dams or mills preventing fish from ascending the river. From the 12th century, we have also the first examples of fish farming. This was done by enclosing local river basins, while some farmers dug special basins in the vicinity, and fish fry was then placed into them. Sometimes, fish were also placed in rivers where there were too few.

The Scandinavian laws regulated the building of fish farms in the same way as the mill dams: one could dig dams only on one's own land, and water could not be dammed so as to flood another man's land. In recent decades, scholars have also debated what effect watermills had on fishing. Some have claimed that the damming of water to create mill dams prevented the fish from getting up the rivers. It has also been suggested that if the fish did succeed in ascending, the dams might still have created other problems. For example, water in dams moved more slowly, which meant that silt and sediments could cover the stony river bottom which salmon eggs needed to hatch in sufficient numbers. This interpretation could perhaps explain why salmon seem to have diminished in some Scandinavian rivers while remaining unchanged in others. It is plausible that in those rivers with many mills and regulated courses, especially after 1200, it became more difficult to prevent the decline of salmon populations, while in more isolated rivers with fewer mills large populations of salmon – and other fish – may have survived longer.

Saltwater fishing changed fundamentally in western Europe shortly after the year 1000. The 11th century was a period of rising temperatures which favoured agriculture but was problematic for some fish. The Baltic Sea is the southern limit for cod and herring, and the quantity of cod especially must have steadily reduced after the mid-11th century, making it very scarce in England and further south. This means that the traditional ways of fishing cod and herring could no longer answer to the period's growing demand for fish. The result of the increasing demand and diminishing amount of fish was what could be called a proto-industrialisation of fishing in northern Norway. This term refers to the expansion of the North Sea fishing area from the shorelines out to the high sea, of the swift sale of freshly caught fish, and of the production of stockfish.

To make stockfish, the cod was gutted immediately after it was caught and dried on wooden racks along the coast before it was exported all over Europe. It is possible to prove the change in fish production through archaeological finds, for example from English towns that bought their fish from Norway. While the finds from earlier periods contain always fish-head bones, from the 11th century onwards, more and more fish bones are found without any traces of heads and must have been imported. Another medieval way of preserving fish was to salt it but this was more expensive as salt had to be imported. Most of the salt used in Scandinavia in the Middle Ages came from salt mines, the largest of which were situated in Lüneburg. The industrial production of salt began in the 12th century. Salt production was based upon wells or springs having water with a very high salt concentration. The water was boiled in large iron pans until it had all evaporated, leaving only the salt. Similar salt-producing

Illustration 11.2 Fish could be dried either by hanging them on stocks or by being laid out on the cliffs along the shore. Pictured here is an illustration from the mid-16th century when this procedure of conserving fish was already very old.
Olaus Magnus, Historia de gentibus septentrionalibus, Rome 1555. Public domain.

outfits were established in many places in southern Scandinavia, on islands or along the southern coast of the Baltic, often by Cistercian monasteries. Scandinavian production of salt was probably relatively big, but the demand was so enormous because of the huge quantities of fished herring that most salt used had to be imported. Additionally, the imported salt was usually of a higher quality than the local. Due to the high price of salt, the drying of cod with the stockfish technique was more cost-efficient for fishermen.

With the professionalisation of fishing, fishing territories expanded in the course of the 11th century ever farther from the coastline, and fishermen began to have more permanent settlements on the North Sea islands as well as further up in the north. It was also in these places that the conservation of fish developed. The Lofoten islands in Norway were among the first places to organise the systematic conservation and export of cod and other fish of the cod family, as well as turbot. This happened in the 11th century, and Lofoten was soon followed by other regions along the Norwegian coast. The cod was fished in relatively deep water away from the shore, either with nets or hooks on long lines. From the 14th century, fishing moved further out into the Atlantic, and Iceland became an important centre for preserving and trading fish. At some point, around 1,400 Scandinavians began sailing as far as Greenland for fishing cod, in competition and sometimes cooperation with fishers from other nations. The Portuguese joined the Scandinavian fishing fleets, reaching Newfoundland in their search for dried cod, the bachalau.

The Baltic Sea region was famous for its herrings. Adam of Bremen in the 1070s had told of abundance of herrings that could almost be scooped by hand into the boats, and his impression was confirmed by several 12th-century sources. The richest fishing places were the Øresund, the coast beyond Bohuslän, the Limfjorden in northern Jutland, and the south-western coast of Norway. These were fished at low tide near the coasts, with nets from open, often small, boats.

The caught herrings were prepared in a different way to cod. They were cleaned, salted, packed in barrels, and traded at seasonal fairs. The most important Scandinavian fish market took place in Scania between 24 August and 9 October. The most common place for the fair was between the towns of Skanør and Falsterbo, on the small peninsula of Falsterbro, but other towns in the Øresund region were also involved in the trade. The fair had no stable location but the fishermen every year set up their small trading booths. This meant that in the winter the fairground was almost totally empty, while in the fishing season in August and September, it was filled with representatives of every kind of institution and person. The small peninsula of Falsterbro was divided for the fair into plots, given for example to the big merchants' towns along the Baltic coast which could then build whatever buildings they needed on them, including sometimes chapels with services in their own language. The merchants also had a special bailiff present during the fair whose task was to settle economic disputes between sellers and buyers. In addition, the place was filled with beer sellers, fast food stands, and prostitutes.

The fishing industry and market also gave work to other professionals. Artisans were needed within all areas of ship maintenance and building, but numerous barrel makers also made their living from producing the thousands of fish barrels (sometimes *firkins*, a quarter the size of a barrel) needed for packing salted fish. The fishers also needed people, often women, to process the caught fish: opening and gutting them, and removing the scales. Men were additionally needed to move the heavy loads onto the merchants' ships. On top of this were all the administrative staff to keep accounts and financial officials to change money and even facilitate loans.

After the establishment of the Kalmar Union in 1397, fishing in Scandinavian was to an increasing extent included in the political manoeuvring. The Scandinavian rulers could more actively and powerfully engage in a fishing policy in the North Atlantic and in the Baltic. England had begun intensively fishing around Iceland, but it was slowly excluded from the middle of the 15th century through treatises and threats. In 1484–1490, there were open wars in the waters around Iceland. The Danish fleet was led by Didrik Pinning, who had been the Kalmar Union governor of Iceland around 1480. He was born in Germany, entered the service of the Scandinavian king, and fought as a freebooter against the Hanseatic towns in the Baltic and later against the English in the Atlantic, a not totally uncommon career of the time.

The 15th century saw an increase in the exploitation of maritime resources of all kinds. In the Baltic seal, hunting became more systematised, and buildings for boiling seals and extracting their fat – half the weight of a seal – were common in all coastal cities. The fat was boiled into oil to be used for lighting and medicine. Smaller whales had been caught along the Scandinavian coasts for a very long time. Different kinds of dolphins would get into fjords during their seasonal migrations and could then be herded with noise from small boats into shallow waters where they could be killed with spears. This is mentioned in the oldest surviving written source from the Faroe Islands, a set of paragraphs from 1298, but the method was also known and practised elsewhere in Scandinavia. During the 14th century, the whalers began hunting bigger whales further out into the open waters of the North Atlantic. The whales were caught not only for their meat but also for the oil or fat employed for uses such as lighting. Additionally, the Scandinavians collected oysters along beaches and in shallow fjords, for example from the Limfjorden in northern Jutland, kept them alive and exported them as far as Russia.

Economic Expansion – The International Market Economy 279

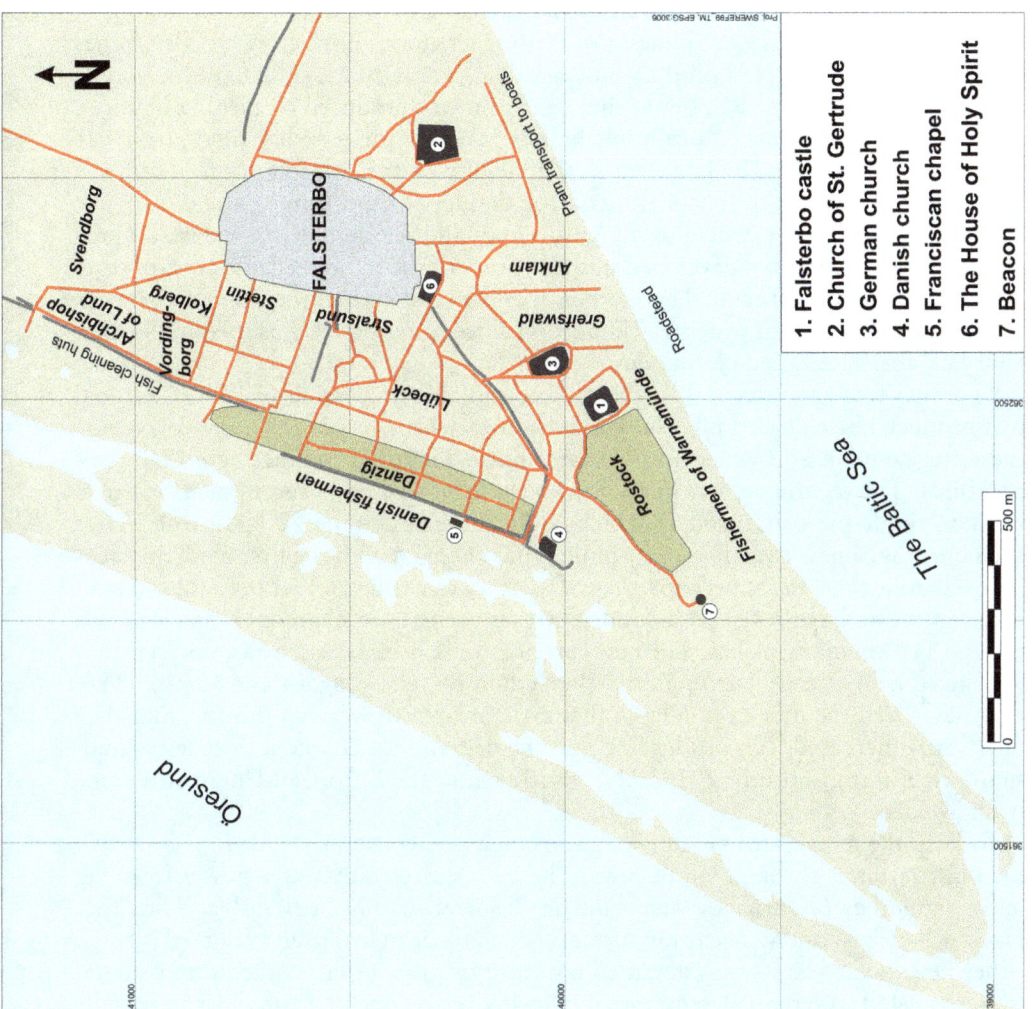

Map 7 The Scania fish market at Falsterbo.
Map © Jussi Kinnunen, 2022.

The Mining Industry

The other industry furthered by the medieval industrial revolution was mining. There had been an increasing demand for metals in Europe since the 9th century. Metal was necessary for agriculture, construction, and not least for weapons, and with the increase of population from the 11th century onwards, the demand for metal grew significantly. Increasing demand resulted in better mining techniques as well as the opening of new mines in different parts of Europe.

Medieval Sweden is especially well known for its mining industry. In the history of Swedish mining, Bergslagen is the most central territory, but there were also mines in many other places. Iron production began in Scandinavia long before the Middle Ages, in the 5th century BC, but at that time iron was produced by melting bog iron found in moors and at the bottom of shallow lakes. In these earlier times, iron was usually extracted from the bog iron in the vicinity of the extraction site. From the 11th century onwards, the production of iron developed significantly, and due to new techniques, it became possible to mine iron in quantities suitable for industrial production. Settlement often developed in the vicinity of the mines because transporting heavy minerals was difficult. Therefore, it was easier to extract the iron and to work it in situ. A proximity to water was important since water power was used in the metallurgical furnaces called bloomeries.

Charcoal was fundamental to the production and processing of iron. Charcoal was produced by charring piles of wood using very little oxygen in order to exclude the water content, and when this was later burned it could produce very high temperatures. The technique was known from the Iron Age and used to melt bog iron in small single-use clay furnaces which could produce around 40 kg of iron. After each burning, a new oven had to be built. That changed with the first blast furnaces in Sweden in the 1190s, perhaps even 10–20 years earlier. Local investigations of lake sediments have revealed a sudden strong increase in charcoal particles from around 1180 in many places. The new furnaces were 3–4 m high and could produce 900 kg of iron at each burning, and they could be reused again and again. These may have been the first examples of that type of oven in western Europe, and they drastically increased iron production and the demand for charcoal. Sweden is unusually rich in iron ores; in 2019, 92% of all iron in the European Union still came from Sweden.

To keep the temperature high enough, oxygen was constantly added to the fire in the blast furnaces through big bellows. These were driven by water power from big mills. Hundreds of furnaces were built in Sweden, mainly in Bergslagen or other places where iron ore was near the surface. When the iron had been extracted it could either be exported as it was (so-called pig iron) or more often worked into osmond iron, re-melted, and refined to cleanse it of its high coal content. Osmond iron was the most normal form of export iron.

Were technological developments in mining invented by locals or were they foreign imports? Most researchers today are of the opinion that locals in Sweden were behind the inventions and experiments necessary to construct the new furnaces, but also that this needed heavy investments by the Swedish aristocracy or from abroad. In the late 14th century, for example, wealthy princes from distant Schleswig held huge investments in Bergslagen. It has been estimated that about a third of all exports from Sweden to Lübeck in 1368 consisted of osmond iron.

Illustration 11.3 Iron production required high heat and constantly working bellows, driven by water power. This technology was already well developed in Sweden in the 13th century and continued to work along the same principles for centuries. Pictured here is an illustration from the mid-16th century.
Olaus Magnus, Historia de gentibus septentrionalibus, Rome 1555. Public domain.

The mining of copper also became extremely important but probably began a little later, in 1235–1245. It fast became very important, especially because there were very few copper mines in Europe besides the Swedish ones. The centre of Swedish copper production was Falun. At the end of the Middle Ages, silver mining began in Sweden and continued into modern times. In Norway, there were experiments with silver mining in the last decades of the 15th century, but it was given up as the mines yielded too little, with too much fighting between German labourers and locals.

Sweden's major mining centres also spurred the development of the necessary trading and transportation infrastructure, which received large new investments as the iron trade exploded in less than two generations. New towns were founded at strategic transport nodes or on the coastline, with large ports that could be accessed by the cog-type ships capable of loading and shipping tonnes upon tonnes of iron directly across the Baltic to Gdansk, Riga, and northern German towns of which Lübeck was by far the largest and most important. On the interior, the new Swedish iron towns for example included Arboga, which linked the streams from Bergslagen with the Lake Mälaren. On the coast, there grew up Söderköping, Nyköping, and Stockholm, all established around 1250.

International Banking and Money Transfer

The growing international trade of the Middle Ages also required financing, as did warfare and the many large ecclesiastical and royal building projects. The Catholic Church, the rulers of European nations or counties, individual traders, or even simple travellers occasionally needed to borrow money from others. Sometimes, people or institutions borrowed money because they were poor and did not have enough income or property, and sometimes simply because they were short of cash at the precise moment. In the early Middle Ages, there were no banks to which one could turn for a loan, but when the European economy began to grow from the 11th and especially from the 12th century onwards, a banking system began to develop at a European level.

Until then, people in need of money had often turned to the Church – or to a rich monastery – which often were in possession of some cash due to collected taxes, inherited property, and other income. A need for a larger sum in cash was very rare until the high Middle Ages, when the great majority of population were producing what they needed, and eventually trading with neighbours for what they could not produce themselves. But there were occasions when someone needed a larger sum of money in cash, and until the economic revolution, the Church was the only institution with money. During the Middle Ages, there were only a few occasions when a person might need a larger amount of money, because in normal economic transactions, one could often pay in other goods than in coins.

One of these occasions was paying fines after a serious crime. According to Scandinavian laws, people guilty of killing someone could save their own lives if the victim's relatives permitted, but on such occasions, the killer had to compensate them with a huge sum of money. We have documentation of several transactions that took place after a murder case, in which the killer gave a farm to the Church as pledge against a large sum of money in cash. One example of such a transaction is a letter issued by Johannes Kalenskæ in Masku in March 1376. He explains that he had made an exchange with the cathedral of Turku, giving the cathedral his part of the island of Arvassalo and receiving from it a farm called Kurittula in Masku, together with 200 marks in Swedish money and other currencies to the value of 50 marks. Johannes writes that a part of the cash went to the local administrator in compensation for his crime. By the same letter, he donated the farm back to the Church for his 'demerits'; he had been sentenced to death and to lose all his property. He does not explain what his demerits were but he was probably guilty of murder, which according to Swedish law had to be punished with death and the loss of property.

The previous example was one in which the Church had functioned as a bank for a private person in need of cash to pay his fines and probably also compensation to his victim – and who was willing afterwards to donate the rest back to the Church, which thereby profited greatly from the transaction. However, the Church was not always as lucky as a creditor. Sometimes, local princes took loans without asking, and sometimes they could not pay them back or had no intention of doing so. To finance his second large crusade against Novgorod, the Swedish King Magnus Ericsson in 1351 took a loan out of all the papal crusading taxes collected in Sweden. When the papacy claimed the money back in 1355, King Magnus could not pay. He had not left for the crusade because of the Black Death but had used the loan for other things. He was excommunicated by the papacy in 1358, but as soon as 1361, his debt was cancelled and he was allowed to take a new one to finance another crusade. He had probably had the intention of paying. This is more uncertain in the case of King Christian I, who in 1455 simply had the chest in Roskilde Cathedral, containing collections to help Cyprus, opened and emptied, placing inside a piece of paper promising that he would pay it all back later. We have no evidence that he ever did.

In both these examples, the Church functioned as creditor for others, but in the course of the Middle Ages, the Catholic Church and the popes in Rome or Avignon also needed a lot of money for running its administration, crusades, and building projects. The Church was in the favourable position of having huge incomes from all over Christendom, in the form of tithes and other payments for the pope. To gather these sums, the Church sent out a number of collectors who had to ensure that the money was sent to the pope. It was however neither sensible nor safe to transport huge amounts of coins from all over Christendom to the papal curia. Therefore, the popes began to use banking houses as middlemen, and when the banking houses had established an extensive network of offices they also served other clients such as merchants. The best known medieval banking house was the house of Fugger, based in Augsburg, Germany, but which also had large offices in Florence and Amsterdam, for example. Other famous bankers were the Medici and the Pazzi, both based in Florence and responsible for the papal economy. The houses functioned so that it was possible to deposit a certain amount of money in one office and withdraw the same amount in another office and country. The banking houses could also give credit to people with enough property to guarantee their ability to repay the loans. Scandinavian merchants, travellers, and even pilgrims also used the services of the international banker houses.

Within the Baltic Sea and the North Sea regions, the Hanseatic League could also act as a banking house because merchants belonging to the League could get credit in one Hanseatic town against their property in another town. They could also deposit money in one town and withdraw it in another. In this way, travelling became safer as merchants did not have to carry large amounts of cash around with them.

Guilds

Active town life consisted of participating in the activities of different associations called guilds. In the Middle Ages, there were different kinds of guilds: professional, religious, and combinations of the two. The religious guilds are also known as confraternities.

Most of the medieval guilds were professional. They were associations of merchants or different artisans, and their aim was to control the activity of the craftsmen or merchants as well as to protect their interests. The earliest guilds were associations of merchants that tried to regulate trading, but the idea of closed societies that protected the rights of a single profession soon spread to practically all key professions in towns, from the most prestigious to the less glorious: goldsmiths, silversmiths, bakers, rope makers, blacksmiths, weavers, carpenters, carvers, masons, and so on. The guilds centrally made all the important decisions concerning the craftsmen and monitored the quality and price of the products in the town. The guilds also limited the number of professionals in different crafts since town regulations stated that only guild members were allowed to practice their respective forms of craftsmanship – or in case of merchants' guilds trade – in the town. Only men were admitted to the craft guilds because women could not officially run businesses in towns – although many wives participated in the business alongside their husbands. On some occasions, widows or daughters of deceased masters could be temporarily allowed into the guilds until a man took over family's professional activities, and by the end of the Middle Ages in some European towns, there were also guilds for professional women, in particular within textile craftsmanship.

Becoming a member of a guild was a long process because the towns and the guilds wanted to restrict the number of professionals, within the towns and especially in the craftsmen's guilds, to make sure that they were truly professionals at their craft. Only those who had successfully passed the master craftsman's exam could open their own workshop and become member of a craft guild, if the other members were favourable. But before taking the master's exam, the person had to have passed a considerable time practicing the profession. There were three steps towards the master's title. A person had first to act as an apprentice in a craftsman's shop, where he could learn the basics of the profession. After that, he could work for a master as a journeyman. The period as trainee and journeyman could be as long as ten years in specialised professions such as goldsmithery, and yet it was not a guarantee that one could become a master. In addition to the required and tested skills, the applicant had to have enough financial means to start his own business. Once a person was accepted as member of a merchants' or craftsmen's guild this was for life, unless they moved to another town or were banned from the guild for cheating or some other irregular behaviour.

Unlike the craft guilds or merchants' guilds, in which the number of members was limited and entry depended upon the other members, the entry to the medieval religious guilds was less regulated. The purpose of the religious guilds was to financially support the religious functions in a church or at a particular altar and to ensure that all the guild members would receive prayers and Masses after their death. Anyone, whether male or female, rich or poor, could join these guilds. Guilds expected new members to make a donation at the moment they were inscribed, but poorer members were exempted, and everyone was able to pay according to their financial means. It was possible to be inscribed into multiple religious guilds in the Middle Ages. We know very little of the activities or regulations of these guilds, whereas the professional guilds and their activities are much better known.

The members of a guild met regularly to discuss their common business and make decisions about the entrance of new members, or product prices, for example. This was the guilds' main function, but they also organised other activities. The guild members gathered together for festivities, which included eating and drinking together. Guild feasts were organised regularly and often coincided with major religious festivities or assemblies where important decisions had to be made. Sometimes, the merchants' guilds organised fine banquets in honour of foreign visitors or to commemorate deceased members, and the urban elite including the highest clergy could be invited. The large, wealthy guilds had their own guild houses in the town centre where members would gather and organise the banquets. One of the most famous still extant guild houses in the Baltic Sea region is that of the young merchants in Tallinn, known as the Blackheads' guild. The smaller guilds by contrast gathered in places like local taverns, and the religious guilds or confraternities in ecclesiastical buildings.

In Scandinavia, the guilds were primarily an urban phenomenon in the Middle Ages, and most of them were concentrated in Denmark. There were guilds in some Swedish and Norwegian towns, in particular in Bergen with the Hanseatic *Kontor*. The earliest Scandinavian guilds were established in Denmark in the 12th century and dedicated to Saint Canute. They were originally merchants' guilds but when Denmark lost its commercial position to the Hanseatic League in the late 13th century, the guilds changed their nature and continued as religious confraternities for the urban elite. They accepted male merchants as members but allowed the wives and daughters to participate in the festivities and other activities.

During the 14th century, guilds for regulating trade as well as craft guilds for the protection of craftsmanship began to develop in many towns. This was a later phenomenon because the earlier town laws had forbidden any kind of associations to regulate trade. The first known craft guild in Scandinavia was that of the tailors and shearers in Ribe, already in existence before 1350. Other artisans that are known to have organised to craft guilds in Scandinavia were shoemakers and smiths, for example. Most of the Scandinavian craft guilds were founded in Danish towns, mainly in Zealand and Scania, but we also have knowledge of guilds in Sweden, from Stockholm, Arboga, and Kalmar. In Bergen, we at least know of the guild of German shoemakers. The known Scandinavian craft guilds were all meant for male members, although women participated in the craftsmen's activities. We know almost nothing about the functioning of the medieval Scandinavian guilds as there are very few surviving medieval sources. There must however have been many more guilds in Scandinavia, both religious and craftsmen's, than those we know about. For example, some Finnish sources contain references to associations in small towns or even villages whose activities clearly correspond to those of guilds in the bigger towns.

12 A Revolution in Communication

Late Gothic Architecture

There were no significant changes in architecture in the late Middle Ages, which continued the tradition of the Gothic style. The only slight difference was that the late medieval Gothic style became more ornate. This style is known in Europe as flamboyant style, and while typical in France and Flanders it did not reach Scandinavia, where the traditional Gothic style was dominant until the Reformation.

Building activities largely ceased after the devastating effect of the Black Death on the population and economy, and recovered only in the course of the 15th century, the major period for renovating and embellishing churches. During the 15th century, towns developed greatly, and the wealthy bourgeoisie began to build solid stone houses in the Gothic style in the town centres.

The 15th century is not known as an important century for new churches, but instead it was a century when numerous older, Romanesque churches were renovated and vaulted with Gothic-style vaults. Additionally, many older churches were enlarged, having become too small when the population had again reached the pre-pestilence level in Denmark and Sweden. Through this process, many small churches gained a new bell tower, and some new side naves and a cross-like form. Some were in blooming merchant towns at the sea like Danish Faaborg, where the church has a very big tower, and some in rich parishes near important cultic sites like Fraugde near Odense which was significantly expanded several times during the 15th century.

The richest and most progressive cathedrals invested in elaborate astronomical clocks, such as Lund already in the late 14th century. Ribe, Stockholm, Uppsala, and Turku installed clocks during the Middle Ages, as did also some of the Dominican convent churches and a few royal castles.

Among the Scandinavian territories Finland was Christianised last, and in Finland, the 15th was the great century of replacing old wooden churches with new stone ones. Finnish stone churches were typically built and vaulted according to the Gothic style, although most of them were very modest in style and size. The cathedral of Turku was also enlarged and raised in height in the 1460s, through this renovation gaining its present Gothic style.

Renovation and embellishment works ceased with the Reformation after the first quarter of the 16th century, when the national churches were created. During this period, the rulers who had declared themselves ecclesiastical leaders confiscated the property of the churches and ruined the ecclesiastical economy for a long time. This caused a long break in ecclesiastical building works in all Scandinavian

DOI: 10.4324/9781003095514-16

Illustration 12.1 Clock, Lund cathedral, mentioned for the first time in 1422. The big astronomical clocks were time machines, constructed to show the time, the date, the saint's name of each day, the day's position in the movable liturgical year of the church, lunar phases, sunrise and sunset, and the position of the day within the zodiac system, for hundreds of years. It struck a bell four times or at least once per hour, and some clocks had small figures that came out when the bell was struck, playing music or blowing trumpets and then disappearing inside the clock again. The four figures in the corner of the upper clock are famous astronomers, one from antiquity, one medieval Spanish king, and two Muslims. The harsh anti-Islamic polemics of medieval Christians did not prevent them from using the superior science of Muslim researchers, also in Scandinavia. The clock was completely restored in 1923 and can now show information for every day until 2123.

Photo Gduendel 2014. This file is licensed under the Creative Commons Attribution 4.0 International license.

countries, but in particular in Sweden where King Gustav I Vasa's confiscations were very effective.

The Scandinavian castles continued the same style of construction as in the previous centuries, but from the 15th century onwards, more attention was paid to the comfort of the lodgings and the public spaces. The Renaissance style, which arrived in Scandinavia relatively late, in the 16th century, stressed comfortable accommodation even more.

New, more effective weapons and especially cannons had their effect upon the construction of 15th-century castles as well. Since round towers were more resistant to cannon fire, castles with round towers and walls were built according to models often copied from the castles of the Teutonic order in the Baltic. A good example of such a building is Saint Olaf's castle in eastern Finland, which was begun in 1475 and completed 20 years later. It was the first castle in the medieval Kingdom of Sweden with circular towers along curtain walls to better withstand cannon fire. Similar castles also often had big towers where defensive cannons could be kept. Such a castle was built in the 1520s in Steinvikholm in Norway. Most of the 15th- and 16th-century castles were built by the crown for administrative or defensive purposes but high ecclesiastical functionaries such as bishops also built their own castles, as did the bishop of Roskilde in the case of the castle of Gjorslev around 1400, likewise imitating closely some of the contemporary fortification architecture of the Teutonic order. During the Reformation, the episcopal castles were confiscated by the crown and either destroyed, as was the case with the episcopal castle in Kuusisto near Turku, or turned into royal ones. Gjorslev was kept by King Christian III for three years before he gave it to one of his men, as a reward for trusted service as international ambassador and rector of Copenhagen University.

Another 15th-century building innovation in Scandinavia was that of fortified manor houses such as Vik's house in Uppland and Glimmingehus in Scania, both constructed around 1500. These were mainly built by the members of the Scandinavian nobility unable to avoid taking part in the 15th- and early 16th-century political controversies. These houses were not only meant for defensive purposes but also functioned as a manifestation of wealth.

Wealthy burghers in the towns also began to build more solid stone houses and warehouses around the market places in town centres. These houses were often built according to the northern German Hanseatic style. They had usually several stories so that at the street level there were the commercial spaces, while the upper stories were used for living. The burghers could also have places for storage in their houses, but often they had separate warehouses. In towns, there were additionally other larger stone buildings such as the town hall and the guild houses of various craftsmen's and religious guilds. The lodgings of the high ecclesiastic functionaries of the cathedrals might also have been made of stone, and sometimes of brick too.

In the countryside, the building style of the 15th and 16th centuries continued the earlier style. The farmers lived in wooden houses, around which were assembled different domestic buildings: barns, saunas, storages, and so on. Usually, the local church was the only stone construction in the countryside.

Late Gothic Arts

The period beginning from c. 1400 until the end of the Middle Ages continued the Gothic tradition in arts. Until the Reformation, the Church was the main patron of arts due to the numerous rebuilding and decoration projects that took place in churches all over Scandinavia after the societies had recovered from the shock and loss of population caused by the Black Death soon after 1350. The later Middle Ages were also a period, when the burghers and nobility wanted to show their wealth and piety by donating to the churches important pieces of art. They also began to have personal collections and became important supporters of arts.

The Gothic legacy is visible in paintings, sculptures, and other forms of art until the Reformation in the 1520s and 1530s. A large part of the surviving art of the period are wall paintings executed in churches that were renovated and modernised in the 15th century. The 15th century introduced in Scandinavia also the Renaissance art, and especially the oil paintings became popular among the wealthy laypeople, who also commissioned expensive jewellery.

From c. 1400 onwards, the majority of pictorial arts produced in Scandinavia were wall paintings made in churches with the lime technique. There was a break of some half a century in the decoration of churches after the devastating effect of the Black Death around 1350. With the population decreasing as dramatically as it did in the second half of the 14th century, it took some time before communities were wealthy enough to continue construction and pictorial work. In Scandinavia, this happened in the course of the 15th century. When the population had grown back to the pre-pestilence level, a need to renovate and enlarge the local churches emerged. Therefore, numerous churches were vaulted in the 15th century with Gothic-style vaults, and after the renovation, the vaults were decorated with Gothic wall paintings. At the same time, the old Romanesque frescos in other churches had become outdated or faded, and they were replaced by new, more modern style wall paintings.

The motifs depicted on church walls followed the tradition of the previous centuries and presented typological events from the Old and New Testaments side by side. At the same time, large pictorial presentations covering every inch of the walls and vaults became more common. A good example of these are the Swedish churches, like those in Härkeberga and Täby, decorated by Albertus Pictor in the second half of the 15th century. Many of his paintings show Jews as grotesque figures with big noses and grinning lips, in accordance with the strong anti-Semitic racial thinking that was becoming common in Germany and the Iberian Peninsula at exactly that time. Another of his illustrations, of Death playing chess with a young nobleman, has become iconic, especially from its use by Swedish filmmaker Ingmar Bergman in his *The Seventh Seal* from 1957.

Apart from the biblical motifs, local saints were often depicted in the churches. The 15th century was the period of growing lay piety and reflective religion, which can be seen in the motifs: Jesus was not any longer depicted as a majestic figure, but rather the new piety stressed the passion of Christ, and the pictorial representations showed him as a suffering and bleeding figure. Additionally, pictures that made people reflect on their life and faith, like the wheel of fortune, became common. Paintings were usually executed by professionals, but sometimes also by local artists which can be seen in the lower quality and more primitive style of the paintings. Such paintings, sometimes called builders' paintings, are particularly common in the southern parts of present-day Finland like in Nousiainen or Ulvila but are also represented in the very strange, almost cartoonlike paintings of stickmen on Danish Funen by the so-called *træskomaler* ('clog painter'), who worked around 1500 and signed his 'art' with a clog. During the Reformation, it was usual in Germany and Switzerland to whitewash the medieval Catholic wall paintings. This happened in Scandinavia as well, but seldom. Surprisingly many paintings were left intact in their places and were only whitewashed during the pietistic movements of the 18th century. Therefore, there are unusually many medieval wall paintings in the Scandinavian churches.

During the last medieval centuries, a new painting style arrived in Scandinavia, namely painting with oil on canvas. The technique began in Renaissance Italy and spread all over Europe in the 15th and 16th centuries. The Netherlands was the centre of oil painting. The earliest oil paintings were stylistically rather Gothic, but the artists soon adopted many Renaissance painting innovations such as the use of perspective. Many late medieval oil paintings were created for religious use, but from the late 15th century onwards, the wealthy classes began to commission small panel paintings from foreign artists. Realistic portraits showing individuality became more and more common.

Painting with oil was, however, not a novelty in Scandinavia; there are some early pieces of art in which oil had been used as fixing agent in painting. Some of these painted items were crucifixes, the earliest of them from as far back as the late 12th century, such as the triumphal crucifix of Alskog on Gotland which may have been imported from German areas. From Norway, there are also preserved beautiful late 13th-century antemensals decorated with oil paintings, showing influences from England. One of these is the antemensal of Kinsarvik in Hordaland, illustrating the crucifixion with evil soldiers torturing Christ and angels in attendance. Thirty-one painted antemensals from c. 1200 to 1350 are known from Norway, which is the largest number in northern Europe. They had certainly been common everywhere in Latin Christianity, but most were replaced by more modern ones in the later Middle Ages or after. Following the Black Death in 1350, many places in Norway no longer had the economic strength to renovate their churches.

The last medieval centuries did not bring any innovations to the art of sculpture, but the Gothic tradition continued in both stone and wooden sculptures. By the end of the Middle Ages, the local production of sculptures diminished and was replaced by works produced in the workshops of northern German masters. The close commercial relations with the Hanseatic League made it possible to also obtain the continental masterpieces for Scandinavian parishes. One of the best examples of sculptures executed by foreign masters is the depiction of Saint George and the dragon in the Storkyrkan of Stockholm produced by the famous German sculptor Bernt Notke and inaugurated in 1489 by its commissioner, the Swedish Regent Sten Sture the Elder. Of more local production were many of the tombstones possessing carved figures or reliefs. Some show the deceased in an official pose, in knightly armour, and surrounded by the family coat of arms. Others showed a skeleton and the worms of decay as a reminder to the spectator that we shall all die.

From the 15th century onwards, there was an increasing demand among the nobility and wealthy burghers for signet rings with coats of arms or house marks. Most of these rings were produced locally, the finest by goldsmiths in towns. The production and demand of expensive jewellery also increased during the late Middle Ages, when the nobility and burghers had accumulated wealth. Most of the fine pieces of jewellery were imported, although there were skilful goldsmiths in Scandinavian towns too.

Due to increasing religious piety among Christians, it became more common for wealthy parishioners to donate expensive items to churches such as chalices, monstrances, or reliquaries. Some of these were produced locally but many were purchased from foreign masters and decorated with expensive materials and precious stones. In Scandinavia, there are only a few such splendid items preserved because most of them were confiscated by the rulers and melted down during the Reformation, as the Lutheran liturgy did not need such items.

Literature – the Printing Revolution

The 15th and early 16th centuries continued the literary traditions of the previous centuries but with two very important changes. One was that the local languages had changed. During the 14th and 15th centuries, the German presence was strong all over Scandinavia and the common language all around the Baltic was German. It significantly and lastingly influenced the Swedish, Danish, and Norwegian languages which in this period adopted some 30–40% of their words and expressions from German. To a modern speaker of these languages, it is not a great challenge to read 15th-century Swedish and so on, but it really is to understand the provincial laws of the 13th century. The languages changed very much in only 100–200 years. The literary production of the 15th and 16th centuries was formulated in the new German-influenced language. In the more western parts, the languages changed less, with Icelandic and Faroese not influenced by German to the same extent. Sámi and Finnish were not written languages in the Middle Ages, so we have no sources to judge the impact of German upon them.

The second innovation of the later Middle Ages was the speed at which written word spread. This accelerated from the last decades of the 15th century onwards, thanks to the recently developed book printing technique typically attributed to the famous German printer, Johannes Gutenberg. The printing technique and the use of paper instead of parchment made book production much quicker and cheaper, and although books were still expensive, it was possible for a larger audience to gain access to literary products. Book printers did not produce books only with scientific or religious content but also other kinds of works targeted at different audiences. One bestseller was indulgence letters, printed in tens of thousands of copies for the papal indulgence sellers, with space left in them to add the name of the recipient, the amount of the indulgence, and the price paid for it. Another bestseller included polemical pamphlets such as Martin Luther's famous theses against the papacy and indulgence sellers, which spread in the last years of the 1510s and caused the splitting of the Catholic Church. Best of all, from an economic point of view, were breviaries and other liturgical books or Latin grammar, indispensable to any serious school system.

Another phenomenon typical of the last medieval centuries was the translation of works into the vernacular, which also gave access to literature for people who had not mastered Latin. Translations into the vernacular began with certain ecclesiastical or devotional literature such as books of hours and all kinds of pious prayer books, but by the turn of the 16th century, numerous other works had also been translated into vernacular – including into the Scandinavian languages.

The increasing scope for acquiring books also meant that the variety of books available became wider. This meant that the late Middle Ages was a period when new kinds of works began to circulate among lay people, not only among the learned clerics.

Bearing witness to this are different kinds of practical works targeted at specific audiences, such as cookbooks, heraldic manuals, or works on the martial arts. Cookbooks hark back to Ancient Greece and Rome but it was in the late Middle Ages in Europe that the genre took off. The first real cookbook in Europe, containing a number of recipes, was called *Du fait de cuisine* ('On cookery'). It was written in French in the 1420s by the master chef Maistre Chiquart Amiczon, who served at the court of Duke Amadeus VIII of Savoy in northern Italy. One of the most popular cookbooks was the old Roman Latin *De re coquinaria* ('On cookery'), copied throughout the Middle Ages and published as a printed edition for the first time in 1483. Since all regions had their own distinctive products and culinary history, certain recipes remained local, and many have not survived to the present day, but several chefs of the different royal courts produced cookbooks bearing witness to the culinary tradition in that territory.

One of the earliest medieval collections of Scandinavian recipes is known in several manuscripts from c. 1300. Two versions are in Danish, one in Icelandic, and one in old German. They contain copies of older recipes dating back to the previous century, some collected by the famous Danish royal doctor, Henrik Harpestreng († 1244). Medieval cookbooks were not meant for simple homes or beginners. They usually contained recipes described in relatively general terms, and only those who knew enough of the art of cooking were able to follow the instructions. The aim was not only to make food that tasted better but also to teach the making of healthy food. Harpestreng gives recipes for a lot of different sauces to go with fresh meat, cured meat, fish, fowls, and game of different kinds. He distinguished between sauces for the lords, with exotic and expensive spices, and sauces for common people using local Scandinavian products like onion and parsley, or honey and mustard seed. Some contain egg, others oil from different kind of nuts, and Harpestreng carefully describes how long the sauces keep and can be used, from 3 to 40 days or longer. He also includes recipes for various meat dishes, for example some ten different ways to prepare hen: old and young, in soup or different sauces, with bacon or spices, in dough and baked as bread, etc.

Another type of practical literature typical in the late Middle Ages related to the martial arts and heraldic. The tradition of books on martial arts is rooted in Ancient Rome, and all surviving manuals and treatises about martial arts from the Middle Ages are either translations of classical works or new manuals from late medieval or even early modern times. The earliest book about martial arts was the Latin *Epitoma rei militaris*, written by Publius Flavius Vegetius Renatus between the 4th and 5th centuries and copied and translated throughout the Middle Ages, but no new practical literature on warfare seems to have been written in Latin Europe, in contrast to Byzantium or the Islamic world.

As the many early or high medieval pictures, textiles, and references in written texts testify, martial arts and warfare were practised continuously from the Roman times but there are no surviving written manuals before the later part of the Middle Ages. The earliest manuscript on the art of fighting dates to c. 1300 and was written in France. In the second part of the 15th century, the number of such manuals increased, and they began to be composed in different languages, including German (*Fechtbücher*, combat manuals), Italian, Spanish, Portuguese, and English. Some of these books found their way to Scandinavia as well, and the Swedish Peder Månsson († 1534) translated Vegetius' *Epitoma rei militaris* into Swedish with the title *Stridskonst och strids-lag*. Peder Månsson's translation is interesting because he was not a military man but a Birgittine monk and priest, heading the Birgittine house in Rome in the first decades of the 16th century. Another important book on warfare that must have been known in Scandinavia was Johannes Bengedans' *Kriegkunst und Kanonen*. Johannes Bengedans worked as the cannon engineer of Union King Christopher of Bavaria around 1450 and is well known for the detailed description of cannons, bombs, and other war machines as well as for his recipes for gunpowder.

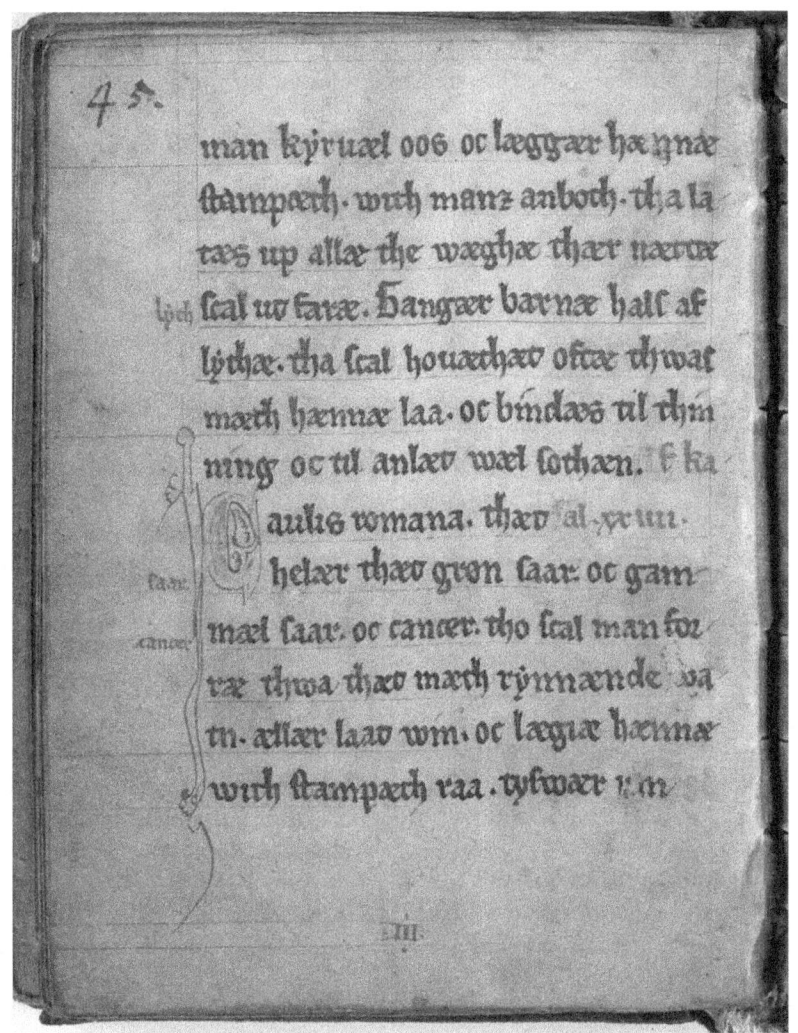

Illustration 12.2 The Danish Doctor Harpestreng wrote in the mid-13th century about medicine and cooking, which for him were closely connected. On this page, he explains how to treat green cabbage (*Kaal*) with water or wine; it can then be used to heal infected wounds ('green wounds') and to treat cancer. It is an effective pain killer, heals bad eyes, assists digestion, and reduces swollen milt. It is even effective against hair loss and becoming bald.
MS NKS 66 oktav, p. 45, Royal Library Copenhagen. Public domain.

His handwritten book is lavishly illustrated with coloured drawings of all kinds of weapons and military equipment, including a diving suit and mask that enabled castle attackers to sneak in unobserved through the water of the moat.

Printing technology and large number of printed books made it possible to get copies of recently published works. The first book to be printed in Denmark was produced in Odense in 1482 by Johann Snell († after 1519), who travelled around the Baltic area with his printing press, trying to establish himself and earn a living. The book was a Latin description of the Turkish siege of Rhodes only two years earlier, in 1480, which had heroically been averted by the order of Hospitallers. The book, written by the Hospitaller Guilielmus Caorsin († 1501), was a great success and immediately published in many other countries besides Scandinavia. Snell also printed a large Breviary for the Odense diocese in 1482. His work was well received, and he was invited by the Swedish archbishop to come to Stockholm where in 1483–1484 he published a *Dialogus creaturarum moralizatus* (A moral dialogue between animals) containing 122 animal fables discussing moral questions with references to the Bible and Aristotle – a very popular genre at the time, and with funny illustrations. Snell also published a Missal for the church province of Uppsala.

A work that may have influenced Scandinavian policy directly was Niccolò Machiavelli's *The Prince* (It. *Il Principe* / Lat. *De Principatibus*), written in Italian in 1517 but only printed in a Latin version in 1532. Niccolò Machiavelli was an Italian diplomat and political theorist who wrote his moral treatise as an instructional guide for young rulers. *The Prince* followed the old tradition of the *mirrors for princes* genre but heralded a new era with more emphasis on strong, harsh princely rule and less on the traditional medieval idea of balance and moderation in warfare. The Danish King Christian II requested that the Danish Carmelite Monk Poul Helgesen translate Machiavelli's *The Prince*, which he apparently never did. Instead, he translated some unknown works of Erasmus of Rotterdam with whom he had studied, and whose more traditional instructions for princes he probably believed more fitting. Translations into the local vernacular were common at the time and probably meant that King Christian II was not able to read Machiavelli in the original. However, his acts during the Bloodbath of Stockholm in 1520 could very well have been inspired by the ideas propagated by Machiavelli, although they backfired. They did not consolidate Christian's rule but led to the dissolution of the Kalmar Union, and Christian's exile and later lifelong imprisonment.

European Renaissance interest in everything Greek must have been well known in Scandinavia but has left only a few sporadic traces. One manuscript from Ryd monastery in Schleswig from 1434 contains a number of Aesop's fables in Greek with commentaries in Latin and German, made by a local monk. In the early 16th century, the knowledge of classical Greek became more widespread among theologians and well-educated nobles. Count Christopher of Oldenburg († 1566), one of the great leaders of the civil war in Denmark three years before the Lutheran Reformation, was known for spending his breaks between mass killings of enemies by peacefully studying Homer's Iliad in the original Greek.

The last medieval centuries were the period of increasing individual religiosity and piety, which is also reflected in the religious literature of the period. The increasing focus on the doctrine of Purgatory and the selling of indulgences show that Christians were worried about their souls after death, and a special kind of manual for dying people was composed for their consolation. These manuals were called *Ars moriendi* ('The Art of Dying'). The genre consisted of Latin texts which gave consolation and advice for Christians on how to 'die well'. The manuals were originally related to the effects of the Black Death in the mid-14th century but they became increasingly popular among the upper class in the course of the 15th. There circulated three separate versions of the *Ars moriendi* guidebooks: a manual called *De arte moriendi* composed by Jean de Gerson, a French theologian and rector of the University of Paris in the late 14th and early 15th century, another called *Tractatus de artis bene moriendi* composed by an anonymous author, and a short version of the *Tractatus*. In addition to these, there also circulated other versions. The guidebooks were printed and translated into several European languages: Latin, German, Low German, Dutch, Italian, Spanish, and English. Gerson's *De arte moriendi* was also translated into Swedish by Ericus Nicolai, Archdeacon of Skara and for a short while rector of the Leipzig University (1518–1520), and it was published in 1514 with the title *Om konsten att dö*.

From the later Middle Ages, there survive a considerable amount of sermons. Preaching was not only one of the most effective medieval ways to spread information but it can also be considered a literary genre in its own right. Sermons differed according to the audience: there were learned sermons to fellow theologians or university colleagues, sermons to kings and rulers stressing their moral obligations towards their subjects and God, and sermons to the 'common people' teaching them to live a decent life without drinking and fighting, and sometimes stressing that they should obey their secular lords and remember to pay taxes. The preachers were also instructed that they should not become too technical in theological discussions when preaching to lay people, because they could not understand the intricacies of theology and should not develop doubts about their faith. Throughout the Middle Ages, the method of composing sermons and their content was amazingly stable, so sermons from the earliest church fathers could be an inspiration a thousand years later. And many medieval sermons could also be reused with few or no alterations after the Lutheran Reformation.

During the late Middle Ages, there circulated several model sermon collections among the clergy. One of the most widely spread was the collection made by Humbert of Romans, a French Dominican friar living in the 13th century. He reached the highest position within the Dominican order as master general but is best known for the material he composed to train Dominican preachers: a collection of model sermons called *De dono timoris* ('On the gift of fear') and a treatise called *De eruditione praedicatorum* ('On teaching of preachers'). He also wrote a manual for preaching the crusades which became very popular in the 15th century in central eastern Europe for use against the Hussites. Humbert's collections also spread outside the Dominican order and were used by parish priests all over the Latin West. Although Humbert of Romans' model sermons were composed in Latin – as with all other similar works by others – the clergy preached in the vernacular. The priests could use the model sermons verbatim and just translate the message into the local language, or they could use some parts of a model sermon and add and remove other parts as they wished.

In addition to preaching from the model sermons, the priests also composed their own, but these have very rarely survived to the present. The largest still extant collection of 15th-century sermons in Scandinavia originates from the Birgittine abbey of Vadstena in Sweden and is now kept in the so-called C-collection in Uppsala University Library. In the Vadstena collections, there are also sermons in medieval Swedish but these are relatively few compared to the amount of Latin sermons. Most of the surviving medieval Scandinavian sermons are from the later Middle Ages, but since the priests had been preaching all the time there must have been a lot of older sermons too – it is only that a very few of them have survived to our days. One example of the older sermons that have survived to our days has a Cistercian provenience, the sermon of Bishop Radulfus of Ribe from the 1170s. Most of the sermon collections circulated

296   1400–c. 1550: Power in Crises

Illustration 12.3 Ars moriendi, the Art of Dying. It was translated into Swedish in 1514 with the subtitle, 'How you can learn to die in a way to secure the blessedness of the soul'.
This file is licensed under the Creative Commons Attribution-Share Alike 4.0 International license.

in the Middle Ages as manuscripts but the most famous ones were printed in the late 15th or early 16th century.

Priests were all able to understand Latin, but due to increasing lay piety, it became necessary to translate some religious texts into the vernacular for those who did not master Latin. In medieval Scandinavia, most such translations were made by clerics or monks, whose identity often remained unknown. Many translations in Sweden can be connected to the Vadstena abbey, like that of the *Sju vise mästare* ('Seven Sages') from the first quarter of the 15th century. It is a very popular collection of stories that circulated widely in Europe about a young prince who was sent away from court because of an evil stepmother and educated by seven wise men. When he returned the stepmother tried to seduce him and afterwards accused him of all manner of wrong things. In the end, he proves to his father the king that he is innocent, and the evil woman is executed. The stories have a Middle Eastern and maybe even Asian background; perhaps they had originally been legends about Buddha.

In most cases, it is not possible to know who among the monks or nuns was responsible for the translations but sometimes the author can be identified. One of these was the Monk Jöns Budde († c. 1493), who lived in the Birgittine abbey of Naantali, in present-day Finland. He has been connected to the authorship of several translations of religious texts into medieval Swedish. His works included the translation of some books of the Bible into Swedish, such as those of Ruth, Esther, and Judith, and the Books of the Maccabees. He also translated religious works such as the Revelations of Saint Mechtild and Saint Birgitta as well as a collection of scholastic literature and other religious stories. Monasteries with large libraries and easy access to all the necessary books were obvious places for translation work.

Jöns Budde was not the only Scandinavian who translated biblical texts. Parts of the Latin Bible, *Vulgata*, were translated into all Nordic languages. Although Bible translations are usually connected to the Reformation, there are Danish and Swedish biblical manuscripts from the years beforehand. For example, Christiern Pedersen translated parts of the New Testament into Danish in 1514. In a preface to his translation of the Book of Homilies, he explains his motivation for the translation and declares that nobody should consider the Gospels to be more sacred in one language than in another. Although several biblical texts were already translated into Scandinavian languages in the Middle Ages, the whole New Testament was translated into Danish only in 1524 and Swedish in 1526, and the entire Old Testament even later, after the Reformation. The earliest Nordic testimonies to Bible translation are however much older, as there are translations of Old Testament texts into Old Norse that have been dated to the mid-14th century. The texts were in use both in Norway and Iceland. A list of the belongings of King Magnus Ericsson, also from around 1350, mentions 'a large volume with the Bible in Swedish', but it is unknown whether it actually contained the entire Bible. The Bible was translated into Finnish only during the Reformation period and into Sámi and Greenlandic long after the Middle Ages.

Medieval Music in Scandinavia

There is relatively little information about music or musical instruments in medieval Scandinavia, but the extant references, for example in the Saga literature, tell of flourishing musical culture after the Viking Age. Similarly, medieval wall paintings depict several different musical instruments which demonstrate that they were known in the Nordic countries – although some representations can be imaginary or symbolic. Since Scandinavia was part of the general European culture, it can be assumed that travelling foreign musical groups have arrived in the North and spread the knowledge of continental music and musical instruments, and that Scandinavian students and soldiers abroad returned home with new music and instruments. We have no evidence as to what kind of instrumental music was played in Scandinavia in the Middle Ages but there is plenty of testimony about songs and chants used in ecclesiastical celebrations, as well as some folk songs and ballads that survived orally to later generations.

Music has been an integral part of the Holy Mass since the earliest church and considered beautiful but dangerous. Music can elevate the spirit to God, and it reflects the harmony of the spheres and the singing of the blessed in heaven, theologians explained. But it could also be so beautiful that it distracted Christians from listening to the word of the Bible and sermons. Illustrations of music in Scandinavian church paintings are normally always positive and spiritual. In a few instances, they depict vanity and moral emptiness, but then only in connection with lay music and dancing.

Certain parts of the Mass, like the Psalms and hymns, were sung by the church choir. At the beginning of the second millennium, the Catholic Church wanted to standardise the ecclesiastical chant, and the Roman style became dominant in the Christian West. The Roman chant style is better known as the Gregorian chant, named after Pope Gregory I (r. 590–604) to whom the chant was erroneously attributed. Gregorian chant is monophonic and it can be performed in three different ways: responsorial, antiphonal, and solo. Responsorial singing means that a soloist sings a series of verses, which is then followed by a response from the choir. Antiphonal singing means that a soloist and a choir sing the verses alternately, while solo means that a soloist is singing alone. In responsorial and antiphonal singing, a choir can sometimes replace the soloist and a congregation the choir, but it was not typical in the medieval Mass that the congregation participated in singing.

The Mass texts changed daily, so there had to be special chants for each day. Since liturgy followed the local calendar of saints, there were differences in the chants between various dioceses or ecclesiastical provinces. From Scandinavia, special chants have survived from Masses related to the local saints, such as Saint Olaf of Norway, Saint Canute Lavard of Denmark, Saint Birgitta of Sweden, and Saint Henry of Finland. Many of these chants have survived to the present in medieval Mass books, some with notes so they can be reconstructed fairly precisely.

The monophonic Gregorian chant was the main type of church music until the late 13th and early 14th centuries, when polyphonic songs began to emerge. Unlike monophonic chant, in which a single melody was sung without harmony or instrumental accompaniment, polyphonic chant consisted of multiple simultaneous melodic lines so that different voices were interwoven. Polyphonic music began first with two different melodies sung at the same time, but it soon developed into chants with several melodies and often also some accompaniment by instruments. Musical development can also be seen in changes in the musical notes, which were a medieval novelty together with musical theory. The idea of musical notation was to make it easier for singers to learn new melodies and also to ensure that a certain melody could be sung in the same way in different places. The later medieval notation is much more complex and rich than the earlier one.

We know almost nothing about musical change in Scandinavia. The only written reference to the arrival of a new singing tradition may be traced to the choral statutes of the cathedral of Uppsala from 1298, which state that singers should receive an extra fee on those occasions when polyphonic chant was performed. This mention is however relatively vague and does not tell us anything concrete about the singing tradition. Nonetheless, the statutes do refer to the use of professional singers in the cathedral, and other cathedrals also had officials assigned to singing called *cantors*. Documents from the first half of the 12th century show that first *cantors* in Scandinavia often had foreign backgrounds. In the later Middle Ages, the cantor taught and led the church choir.

Music belonged to the secular life as well. It was an indispensable part of big celebrations such as weddings and various public festivals, especially market gatherings. In the bigger festivities, the music was usually played by professional musicians, but in smaller parties, local people with musical skills could take care of the performance. Also, foreign professional musicians like troubadours travelled in Scandinavia, but they were usually performing only for larger audience of upper class, not in local fests.

If we have relatively little medieval evidence of church music, there is even less evidence about the secular music, since they were normally not written down in the same way as the ecclesiastical chants. Therefore, the existing information is very sporadic, and often based on much later tradition that is possible to trace to the medieval centuries. There are numerous Scandinavian folksongs and ballads, which apparently have medieval origin but have survived only in oral tradition. The folksongs were typically catching melodies and rhymes that were easy to remember. The earliest known Scandinavian ballads date to the 13th or 14th century and include for example the so-called *Eufemiavisorna* that are early 14th-century Swedish version of the knightly ballads. Also, the Finnish national epos, *Kalevala*, is rhymed and sung, and it can be considered as a kind of medieval folk song, but unlike most folk songs, *Kalevala* belongs to a tradition of telling a long and complicated story, and its dating is very uncertain. Some late medieval popular melodies are known because they were used by Lutheran reformers for new hymns in the church.

Although most of the secular musical pieces cannot be dated with certainty, there are also songs that can be related to specific historical events. For example, the song *Ex te lux oritur, o dulcis Scotia* ('A light rises from you, oh sweet Scotland') is a song composed in honour of the marriage between the Norwegian King Eric Magnusson and his spouse Margaret, daughter of King Alexander III of Scotland. They were married in Bergen in autumn 1281, and thus the song is easy to date to their wedding. The oldest piece of music with notes preserved from Scandinavia is the long liturgy for the canonisation of Canute Lavard in 1170. The oldest lay music is from a manuscript dated c. 1300 with a copy of the law of Scania written with runes. The two lines preserved are also in runes and read *Drømde mik en drøm i nat um silki ok ærlik pæl* ('I dreamed myself a dream this night, about silk and real peals'). The melody for this short piece was used for years as the pause signal on Danish radio.

No instrumental music has survived from the Middle Ages in Scandinavia, and it is not known whether this is because such manuscripts have been destroyed or whether music was just not written down. We have however a few musical instruments used in Scandinavia from the Middle Ages and pictures of many more. Most date from the late Middle Ages, and it cannot be said for certain whether they depict real instruments or whether they are imaginary, but combining the existing information in written sources and from archaeological excavations, it is possible to say something about medieval musical instruments. In the Middle Ages, like nowadays, they can be divided into groups according to how the sound is formed: wind instruments, stringed instruments, and percussion instruments.

Wind instruments can be divided into woodwind and brass. Wooden wind instruments were very common in the Middle Ages because it was possible to produce them at home, while brass instruments such as trumpets were difficult to manufacture and thus more expensive. They were only for the entertainment of the higher social classes or for use in churches. Most of the brass instruments were straight horns, but sources from the second part of the 14th century already depict a curved trumpet. The Scandinavian pictures include only straight horns, typically blown by angels in the churches. Other medieval blown instruments included flutes, most often the end-blown version. Recorders were perhaps the most common musical instruments because they were easy to make from wood or animal bones. Bagpipes were also common.

The most common stringed instrument used in the Middle Ages was the lute, a pear-shaped string instrument and a kind of predecessor to the guitar. Medieval musicians also used other types of stringed instruments such as the mandore, which was very similar to the lute but smaller. The gittern was another typical string instrument, also similar to the lute but played with a quill plectrum. Another kind of string instrument type was the fiddle, which had a lot of different variations in different parts of Europe. Finally, there were zither type of instruments like the psaltery. Other typical stringed instruments included the harp, in particular played by the upper class.

Finally, medieval musicians played a large spectrum of different percussion instruments such as drums of different sizes. At their simplest, these could be round wooden sticks hit together, but there were also drums made of animal skin stretched across a circular wooden frame. Drums were also used as an integral part of the religious ceremonies of the Sámi people.

The organ was integral to late medieval ecclesiastical music. The first organs are known from as early as the 3rd century in Greek and Roman territories, from where they spread towards the north alongside Christianity. Medieval organs were pipe organs that could vary in size significantly. In churches, there were large inbuilt organs, but there also existed smaller portable organs that wandering friars, for example, could take with them when they travelled and preached. Ribe, Lund, and Nidaros all had organs in the decades around 1300, and an organ built in Norway was brought to Iceland in 1329. From Scandinavia, there are preserved two organs, incomplete but with enough intact that it is possible to reconstruct how they were made. Both are from Gotland, one from 1370 and built by an artisan from Germany, the other being from 1430 at the latest.

With the Protestant religious reform movement of the early 16th century, a new understanding of singing in the churches developed. Earlier, the priest and a choir of trained ecclesiastics sang while the congregation listened. Within Lutheranism, the congregation's song became an integrated and important part of religious service. It led to a huge production of new hymns in local languages by Luther and Lutheran theologians, often to melodies known from popular songs. In Scandinavia, the first generation of new Protestant songs were translated into Danish and Swedish from Low German.

The Medieval Legacy

The Middle Ages ended in 1523 in Sweden when Gustav Vasa came to power and founded a new royal dynasty, and in 1536 in Denmark, when King Christian III confiscated Church property and cut all ties to the papacy. It was the end of a long and dynamic period with rapid changes and developments. Most of the institutions fundamental for modern Scandinavian societies were created in the Middle Ages: kings and the idea of centralised administration; Church and the idea of common responsibility for the spiritual and material welfare of other individuals; laws and fixed procedures in courts; writing, education, and universities. The idea of the three kingdoms of Norway, Denmark, and Sweden as coherent and distinct political entities, developed during this time, as likely did a great number of other concepts and attitudes that modern Scandinavians are not necessarily aware of themselves. One example is a fondness for the sea and for sailing, a tradition strongly present in the art and literature of Scandinavia between two oceans.

The importance of the Middle Ages cannot be overestimated. Nevertheless, they cannot in themselves explain the specific formation of modern societies. The welfare state – the social security system, the very low degree of corruption, and the general trust in institutions so characteristic for Scandinavian societies – is also the result of developments and lucky political initiatives that happened after the Middle Ages.

The kings were the winners of the Lutheran Reformation, and also in fact of the division of the Kalmar Union – economically bolstered by ecclesiastical property, winners of wars in both Denmark/Norway and Sweden, and now also heads of churches. The aristocracy had been effectively pacified by the kings, and in Norway, most of the high aristocracy died out for different reasons. Both Gustav Vasa in Sweden and Christian III in Denmark and Norway had more power than they can ever have dreamt about. With these strong new kings and the introduction of Lutheranism – immediately in Denmark and Norway, more gradually in Sweden – the Middle Ages has traditionally been seen by historians as coming to an end, and a new age has begun. To what extent people living at that time shared this opinion is more complicated to answer.

Some theologians sensed a sharp break with a past characterised by a pope and a European Church. The monasteries were closed down, while many parish priests continued in their benefices and delivered sermons with just a few theological and liturgical modifications. Many parishioners continued their traditional way of behaving in church. Rulers and aristocrats stressed their historical legitimacy and dynastic claim to power, stretching back to times immemorial, or at least medieval. Laws and legal courts had been established centuries earlier, while universities and printing had already been in Scandinavia for a couple of generations, and most of this continued to function without interruption. The large majority of people, of high and low status alike, did not know that they no longer lived in the Middle Ages. No sudden change occurred to mark the transition from the Middle Ages to a modern period. That was the later construction of historians.

Sources and Literature

Literature on medieval Scandinavia is overwhelmingly big and published in diverse, Scandinavian languages. A small selection of central works in English is listed here as suggestions for further reading.

Databases

There exist now several large databases collecting references to scientific literature on medieval studies. A comprehensive one which is updated continuously is the *International Medieval Bibliography*. May 2022 it contained c. 20,000 references to 'Scandinavia'. It is easy to make more targeted searches, for example 'Scandinavia' and 'medicine' and 'eleventh to thirteenth century'.

Journals

Several journals publish articles in English about Scandinavia in the Middle Ages. *Medieval Scandinavia*, after 2004 renamed *Viking and Medieval Scandinavia*, contains solely articles about the Middle Ages. This is also the case with the Norwegian online-journal *Collegium Medievale*, publishing in Scandinavian languages but very often also in English. The *Scandinavian Journal of History* covers all periods and contains regularly articles focusing on medieval themes. *Scandinavian Studies* is strong in literature in general and especially on medieval Nordic sagas. The first issue of *Apardjón Journal for Scandinavian Studies* came in 2020 and can potentially develop into a strong academic journal.

Sources

There is a long tradition in all Nordic countries for editing their medieval documents, and the editions are nowadays available online:
Denmark: Diplomatarium Danicum, https://diplomatarium.dk
Finland: Diplomatarium Fennicum, http://df.narc.fi
Iceland: Diplomatarium Islandicum (Íslenzkt fornbréfasafn) 16 vols. Reykjavik: Det Islandske Litterære Selskab (Hið Íslenzka Bókmentafjelag), 1857–1976.
Norway: Diplomatarium Norwegicum, https://www.dokpro.uio.no/dipl_norv/diplom_felt.html
Sweden: Diplomatarium Suecanum, https://riksarkivet.se/diplomatarium-suecanum

Literature

Aavitsland, Kristin B., *Tracing the Jerusalem Code 1: The Holy City Christian Cultures in Medieval Scandinavia (ca. 1100–1536)*. De Gruyter 2020.

Andersen, Kasper H., Jeppe Büchert Netterstrøm, and Lisbeth Imer, eds., *Urban Literacy in the Nordic Middle Ages*. Brepols 2021.

Antonsson, Haki, 'Traditions of Conversion in Medieval Scandinavia: A Synthesis', *Saga Book of the Viking Society for Northern Research* 34 (2010), pp. 25–74.

Bagge, Sverre, *Cross & Scepter. The Rise of the Scandinavian Kingdoms from the Vikings to the Reformation*. Princeton University Press 2014.

Boje Mortensen, Lars and Tuomas M.S. Lehtonen with Alexandra Bergholm, eds., *The Performance of Christian and Pagan Storyworlds: Non-Canonical Chapters of the History of Nordic Medieval Literature*. Brepols 2013.

Bregnsbo, Michael, and Kurt Villads Jensen, *The Rise and Fall of the Danish Empire*. Palgrave Macmillan 2022.

Bysted, Ane, Carsten Selch Jensen, John Lind, and Kurt Villads Jensen, *Jerusalem in the North. Denmark and the Baltic Crusades, 1100–1522*. Brepols 2012.

Christiansen, Eric, *The Northern Crusades. The Baltic and the Catholic Frontier 1100–1525*. University of Minnesota Press 1980.

DuBois, Thomas, *Sanctity in the North: Saints, Lives and Cults in Medieval Scandinavia*. Toronto University Press 2007.

Eriksen, Stefka Georgieva, ed., *Intellectual Culture in Medieval Scandinavia, c. 1100–1350*. Brepols 2016.

Etheridge, Christian, and Michele Campopiano, *Medieval Science in the North: Travelling Wisdom, 1000–1500*. Turnhout: Brepols 2021.

Etting, Vivian, *Queen Margrete (1353–1412) and the Founding of the Nordic Union*. Brill 2004.

Gustafsson, Harald, 'The Forgotten Union', *Scandinavian Journal of History* 42 (2017), pp. 560–582.

Gyönki, Viktória and Andrea Maraschi, eds., *Food Culture in Medieval Scandinavia*. Amsterdam University Press 2022.

Helle, Knut, ed., *The Cambridge History of Scandinavia 1: Prehistory to 1520*. Cambridge University Press 2003.

Huang, Andela Ling and Carsten Jahnke, eds., *Textiles and the Medieval Economy: Production, Trade, and Consumption of Textiles, 8th–16th Centuries*. Oxbow 2015.

Jakobsson, Sverrit, 'Conversion and Cultural Memory in Medieval Iceland', *Church History* 88 (2019), pp. 1–26.

Jensen, Janus Møller, *Denmark and the Crusades, 1400–1650*. Brill 2007.

Jensen, Carsten Selch, Tracey R. Sands, Nils Holger Petersen, Kurt Villads Jensen, and Tuomas M. S. Lehtonen, eds., *Saints and Sainthood around the Baltic Sea. Identity, Literacy, and Communication in the Middle Ages* Medieval Institute Publications 2018.

Karras, Ruth Mazo, *Slavery and Society in Medieval Scandinavia*. Yale University Press 1988.

Line, Philip, *Kingship and State Formation in Sweden 1130–1290*. Brill 2007.

Magnúsdóttir, Auður, Marianne Holdgaard, and Bodil Selmer, eds., *Nordic Inheritance Law Through the Ages: Spaces of Action and Legal Strategies*. Brill 2020.

Mulligan, Amy C., and Else Mundal, eds., *Moving Words in the Nordic Middle Ages: Tracing Literacies, Texts, and Verbal Communities*. Brepols 2019.

Münster-Swendsen, Mia, Thomas Heebøll-Holm, and Sigbjørn Olsen Sønnesyn, eds., *Historical and Intellectual Culture in the Long Twelfth Century: The Scandinavian Connection*. Pontifical Institute of Mediaeval Studies 2016.

Nedkvitne, Arnved, *The Social Consequences of Literacy in Medieval Scandinavia*. Brepols 2004.

Poulsen, Bjørn, et al., eds., *Nordic Elites in Transformation* 1–3Routledge 2019–2021.
Pulsiano, Phillip, and Kirsten Wolf, *Medieval Scandinavia: An Encyclopedia*. Routledge 2017.
Salonen, Kirsi, Kurt Villads Jensen, and Torstein Jørgensen, eds., *Medieval Christianity in the North: New Studies*. Brepols 2013.
Sawyer, Birgit, and Peter Sawyer, *Medieval Scandinavia. From Conversion to Reformation, circa 899–1500*. Minnesota University Press 1993.
Scheel, Roland, *Narrating Law and Laws of Narration in Medieval Scandinavia*. De Gruyter 2020.
Semple, Sarah, Alexandra Sanmark, Frode Iversen, and Natascha Mehler, eds., *Negotiating the North: Meeting-Places in the Middle Ages in the North Sea Zone*. Routledge 2020.
Statens Historiska Museum, ed., *Medieval wooden sculpture in Sweden* 1–5. Kungl. Vitterhetsakademin 1964–1980.
Vogt, Helle, *The Function of Kinship in Medieval Nordic Legislation*. Brill 2010.
Wellendorf, Jonas, *Gods and Humans in Medieval Scandinavia: Retying the Bonds*. Cambridge University Press 2018.
Widgren, Mats, 'Fields and Field Systems in Scandinavia during the Middle Ages', in *Medieval Farming and Technology: The Impact of Agricultural Change in Northwest Europe*, eds Grenville Astill and John Langdon. Brill 1997, pp. 173–192.
Winroth, Anders, *The Conversion of Scandinavia: Vikings, Merchants, and Missionaries in the Remaking of Northern Europe*. Yale University Press 2012.

Index

Aalborg 45, 80, 176
Abel, King of Denmark (r. 1250–1252) 133–136
Æbelholt 74, 172, 225
Absalon, Bishop of Roskilde and Archbishop of Lund 46–47, 64, 74, 100, 214, 222, 225
Åby 103
Adalbert, Archbishop of Hamburg-Bremen 45
Adalstein, King of England (r. 924–939) 17
Adam of Bremen 1, 15, 20, 22, 49, 53–54, 63, 277
Adele of Flanders, Queen of Denmark 16
Adolf III, Count of Holstein 123
Aesop 294
Afonso II, King of Portugal (r. 1211–1223) 142
Africa 73, 211
Åge Sparre, Archbishop of Lund 246
Agnes, daughter of King Erik IV Ploughpenny of Denmark 79, 134, 139
Åker in Vang 152
Akershus 204, 240, 243
Al-Andalus 101
Åland Islands 121, 177
Albert, Bishop of Riga 125–126
Albert II, Count of Mecklenburg 155
Albert III of Mecklenburg, King of Sweden (r. 1363–1389) 77, 158, 169, 231–233
Albert IV, Count of Mecklenburg 158
Albert of Orlamünde, Count of Holstein 123, 125
Albertus Pictor 254, 289
Alcuin 41
Alexander III, King of Scotland 131, 299
Alexander III, Pope (r. 1159–1181) 28, 63, 72, 125
Alexander VI, Pope (r. 1492–1503) 173, 255
Alexander Nevsky, Prince of Novgorod (r. 1236–1240, 1241–1256, 1258–1259) 129
Alfonso X the Wise, King of Castile and Leon (r. 1252–1284) 144
Algot 224

Ælnoth 84
Alskog 290
Alsnö 136
Alvastra 31, 55, 72, 81
Amadeus VIII, Duke of Savoy 291
Amalfi 76
America 23, 26, 50, 110
Amsterdam 113, 283
Anatolia 180
Anders, Bishop of Oslo 164
Anders Sunesen, Archbishop of Lund 46, 57–58, 63, 79, 160, 182, 222, 225–226, 258
Ångermanland 21
Ansgar 1, 42–43, 53, 71
Antoninus of Florence 217
Antvorskov 76
Arabic territory 92, 272
Aragon 237
Arboga 64–65, 169, 281, 285
Århus 43, 45, 74, 139, 185, 198, 224
Ari Þorgilsson 26
Aristotle 216, 294
Arkona 28, 46
Árni Þorláksson, Bishop of Skálholt 166
Arnold Klemensson 251
Arnold of Lübeck 123
Årsta 77
Arvassalo 282
Asia 196, 231, 273, 297
Aslak Bolt, Archbishop of Nidaros 196, 249
Asmild 74
Asser, Archbishop of Lund 45–46, 52
Asserbo 72
Assisi 77
Æthelred the Unready, King of England (r. 978–1016) 15
Atlantic Sea / territory 1–2, 7, 22, 25, 35, 45, 49, 51, 59, 72, 85, 92, 94, 120, 130–131, 133, 136, 194, 238, 249, 271, 277–278
Augsburg 283
Auðunn Þorbergsson, Bishop of Hólar 166
Aura 152

308 *Index*

Avignon 73, 153, 157, 160, 162–163, 168, 177, 179, 226, 231, 244, 282
Axel Pedersen Thott 234

Bäckarskog 75
Båhus 204
Baltic Sea / territory 1–2, 7, 16–17, 21–22, 38, 46–47, 55–56, 72, 76–77, 85, 92, 119–123, 125–126, 128–129, 138, 155, 157, 159–160, 165, 167, 169, 180, 182, 186–187, 193–194, 199, 201, 215, 221, 223, 232–233, 236, 238, 247, 249, 251, 254, 270–273, 276–278, 281, 283–284, 288, 291, 294
Bard 264
Basel 57, 245, 251
Bastrup 37, 99
Bede the Venerable 214
Benedict IX, Pope (r. 1032–1048) 45
Benedictus Magnus 189
Berengaria of Portugal, Queen of Denmark 124
Bergen 20, 28–29, 38, 49–50, 64, 71–74, 78, 92, 96, 100, 104, 130, 133, 145, 159, 165, 185, 187–188, 191, 196, 202, 204–205, 226, 249, 270, 284–285, 299
Bergman, Ingmar 289
Bergslagen 235–236, 280–281
Bernard of Clairvaux 46, 55, 72, 74, 182
Bernardus of Pavia 63
Bernt Notke 198, 290
Bero, Bishop of Finland 169
Bero Magni 224
Biörn, King of Birka 21
Birger 189
Birger, Archbishop of Uppsala 64
Birger Jarl 129, 135–138, 167–168, 170
Birger Magnusson, King of Sweden (r. 1290–1318) 154–155
Birger Månsson, Bishop of Västerås 177
Birger Persson 179
Birgitta Birgersdotter, Saint 71–73, 75, 111, 157, 160, 168–169, 172–175, 177–181, 211, 217, 224, 231–232, 249–251, 263, 265, 297–298
Birka 21, 53, 184–185, 272
Bissen, Vilhelm 47
Bjernede 99
Black Plough 27
Black Sea 40, 235
Blanche of Namur, Queen of Sweden 179
Blekinge 10, 59, 121, 125, 147
Blot-Sweyn, King in Sweden (r. *c.* 1100) 22, 31, 175
Bodil, Queen of Denmark 16, 45
Bohemia 159, 223, 235–236, 251, 275
Bohuslän 59, 277

Bologna 62, 143, 220, 222, 224, 226
Boniface IX, Pope (r. 1389–1404) 180, 230–231, 233
Borg 152
Borgarting 145, 152
Borgholm 204
Børglum 45, 75
Bornholm 99–100, 126, 147, 204, 232
Bornhöved 128–129
Botulf Botulfsson 62, 258
Bouvines 124, 126
Bratthalid 26
Bremen 1, 15, 20–22, 42, 44, 45–46, 48–49, 51–54, 63, 82, 277
Bromma 99
Brother Gauling 125
Bruges 270
Brunkeberg 221, 238
Brynolf Algotsson, Bishop of Skara 173, 251–252
Buddha 297
Bugislav of Pomerania *see* Eric of Pomerania
Bugislav IX of Pomerania 235
Burgundy 239
Byzantium 1, 7, 15–17, 21, 38, 100–101, 103–104, 128, 272, 292

Cambridge 220
Canada 24, 131, 194
Canterbury 213
Canute IV, Saint, King of Denmark (r. 1080–1086) 15–16, 45, 54, 172, 174–176, 211, 217, 269, 284
Canute V Magnussen, King of Denmark (r. 1146–1157) 27
Canute VI, King of Denmark (r. 1182–1202) 15, 28–29, 44, 120, 123, 147, 264
Canute Ericsson, King of Sweden (r. 1167–1196) 31, 103, 140
Canute Lavard, Saint 27–29, 45–46, 126, 172–173, 217, 298–299
Canute the Great, King of England, Denmark and Norway (r. 1019–1035) 15, 19, 44–45, 72
Castile 144, 237
Catherine Ulfsdotter 173–174, 178–179, 251–252
Catillus, Bishop of Finland 169
Central Asia 196
Charlemagne, Emperor (r. 800–814) 16, 41, 216
Charles IV, German Emperor 222
Charles V, German Emperor 242
Charles of Flanders, son of King Canute VI of Denmark 16
Chartreuse 72
Chiquart Amiczon 291

Chiusi 62
Christ 13, 22, 40, 58, 62, 72, 99, 101–103, 115, 173, 175, 177, 180, 206–207, 210–211, 232, 244, 248, 257–260, 265, 269, 289–290
Christian I, Union King (r. Denmark 1448–1481; Norway 1450–1481; Sweden 1457–1464) 177, 221, 231, 237–239, 245–246, 254, 252, 282
Christian II, Union King (r. 1513–1523) 240–243, 246, 249, 253, 294
Christian III, King of Denmark 243, 249–250, 288, 301
Christian V, King of Denmark (r. 1670–1699) 147
Christiern Pedersen 297
Christina Gyldenstierna 241
Christopher I, King of Denmark (r. 1252–1259) 134–135, 161
Christopher II, King of Denmark (r. 1320–1332) 141, 155–156, 162
Christopher Columbus 110
Christopher of Bavaria, Union King (r. 1440–1448) 149, 236–237, 245, 251, 292
Christopher of Oldenburg, Count 243, 294
Citeaux 72
Clairvaux 46, 55, 72, 74, 161, 182
Clemens Ragvaldus 61
Clement V, Pope (r. 1305–1314) 63, 75
Clermont 180
Cluny 22
Cologne 72, 134, 158, 176, 222
Conrad II, King of Germany, Emperor (r. 1024–1039) 44
Constance 57, 78, 180, 244–245, 251
Constantine, Roman Emperor (r. 306–337) 268
Constantinople 21, 41, 59, 272
Copenhagen 47, 70, 79–80, 100, 108, 132, 148, 185, 187, 219–221, 237, 242–243, 245–247, 252, 288, 293
Corvey 9
Curland 125
Cyprus 16, 157, 282

Dagmar, Queen of Denmark 104
Dalarna 148–149, 152, 235, 238
Dalby 45, 74
Dalhem 210
Dannenberg 128
Dante Alighieri 139
Daugava 125
Denmark 1, 9–10, 12–18, 20–23, 27–31, 33–39, 41–46, 49, 54–55, 59, 61, 64–65, 67, 72, 74, 76–80, 82, 84–85, 87, 89, 92–93, 96–104, 110, 113, 120–130, 132–137, 139–143, 147–148, 150–163, 165, 168–169, 172–175, 177–178, 180, 182, 184–188, 191–197, 200–205, 208, 211, 214–218, 220–221, 224–225, 229, 231, 233–243, 245–247, 249–253, 258, 263–264, 270–272, 278, 284–286, 289, 291–294, 297–300
Didrik Pinning 278
Dorothea of Brandenburg, Union Queen 221, 237, 246
Dublin 121
Dueholm 76

Ebbe 127
Ebo, Archbishop of Reims 42
Edgar the Peaceful, King of England (r. 959–975) 48
Egil Skallagrímsson 105
Eidsivating 145, 152
Eidsvoll 152
Eirik, Archbishop of Nidaros 74
Elbe 12, 42, 125, 128, 182
Elmelunde 208
Enea Silvio Piccolomini *see* Pius II
Engelbrekt Engelbrektsen 235–236, 251
England 1, 7, 10, 14–19, 21–22, 26, 34, 37, 41, 44–45, 47–48, 51, 53, 59, 66, 71, 73, 84, 92, 96, 99–101, 124, 133, 140, 142, 153, 176, 180, 182, 186, 192–193, 196, 203–206, 211, 213–214, 218, 220, 222, 224, 231, 234, 238–239, 245, 258, 272–273, 276, 278, 290, 292, 295
Enköping 169
Erasmus of Rotterdam 294
Erfurt 222, 224
Eric, Bishop of Gardar 25
Eric I Ejegod, King of Denmark (r. 1095–1103) 16, 27, 45
Eric II Emune, King of Denmark (r. 1134–1137) 27, 45–46
Eric II Magnusson the Priesthater, King of Norway (r. 1273–1299) 154, 159, 164, 299
Eric III Lam, King of Denmark (r. 1137–1146) 27
Eric IV Ploughpenny, King of Denmark (r. 1241–1250) 79, 133–134, 137, 139, 147, 161
Eric V Klipping, King of Denmark (r. 1259–1286) 133, 137–139, 161–162
Eric VI Menved, King of Denmark (r. 1286–1319) 122, 154–156, 162, 193
Eric IX Jedvarsson, Saint, King of Sweden (r. 1150–1160) 31–32, 54–56, 167–168, 173, 175–176, 182, 211, 217, 238
Eric X Knutson, King of Sweden (r. 1208–1216) 140
Eric XI Ericsson, King of Sweden (r. 1234–1250) 135

310 *Index*

Eric Magnusson, Duke of Södermanland 154, 164, 215
Eric of Pomerania, Union King (r. 1397–1439) 67, 79, 141, 158, 186, 221, 229, 233–237, 245, 247, 249, 251, 271
Eric Segersäll, King of Sweden (r. c. 970–995) 22
Eric the Red 24, 26
Ericus Nicolai 295
Erling, Earl of Norway 29–30, 50
Ertholmen 232
Esger Juul, Archbishop of Lund 155, 162
Eskil, Archbishop of Lund 28, 46, 55, 72, 74
Eskilsø 74, 225
Eskilstuna 53, 76, 81, 195
Esrom 72
Estonia 1, 59, 72–73, 77, 79, 120–121, 125–128, 157, 182, 198, 201, 214–215, 239
Estrid 15
Eufemia, Duchess of Mecklenburg 155
Eufemia of Rügen, Queen of Norway 154, 216
Eugene III, Pope (r. 1145–1153) 49
Eugene IV, Pope (r. 1431–1447) 245
Europe 1–2, 7, 10, 15–18, 24, 26, 28, 33, 37–38, 41, 43–45, 53, 55, 57, 62, 66, 71–73, 75–76, 79, 82, 85, 87–88, 90, 92–93, 96, 99, 102–103, 106, 108, 110–114, 119, 121, 123–126, 128–129, 131–133, 136–137, 139–140, 142–145, 150, 153, 157, 160, 164, 173, 176, 180, 184–187, 192–194, 196, 198–199, 206–207, 213–214, 216, 219–220, 222, 230–232, 234–236, 244–246, 250, 263, 270, 272–273, 275–276, 280–283, 286, 290–292, 294–295, 297, 300–301
Eystein I, King of Norway (r. c. 1142–1157) 29
Eystein Erlendsson, Archbishop of Nidaros 50–52, 166

Faaborg 80, 286
Falkenberg 158
Falster 21, 85, 147
Falsterbo 270, 278–279
Falun 281
Fantoft 97
Faroe Islands 22, 30, 48–49, 59, 92, 130–131, 137, 159, 247, 278, 291
Fehmarn 85
Ferdinand, Count of Flanders 124
Ferrara 57
Florence 57, 217, 283
Finderup 133, 135
Finland 1, 32, 35, 41, 53, 55–57, 59, 62–63, 65–67, 72–73, 79, 85, 87, 89, 92, 98, 100–101, 104, 106, 109, 121–122, 125, 127, 129–130, 135, 148–150, 152, 154, 169–170, 172–175, 178, 182, 184–185, 187, 193, 195–196, 201–202, 204, 206, 217, 222, 232, 234, 238, 241, 254–255, 275, 285–286, 288–289, 291, 297–299
Finnmark 48, 165
Finnström 177
Finsta 179
Flanders 16, 92, 124, 211, 272, 286
Flatey-Helgafell 74
Flensburg 185, 234
Florence 57, 217, 240, 283
Folkvinus, Bishop of Finland 56, 169
Fortun 97
Fotevik 27, 31, 46
France 1, 34, 41, 46–47, 61, 72–75, 79–80, 100–101, 110, 124, 140, 160–161, 163, 168–169, 180, 193, 196, 202, 203–204, 206, 211, 216, 218, 220, 222, 224, 225, 231, 244, 250, 262, 264, 267, 286, 291–292, 295
Francis of Assisi 77–78
Franciscus Gonzaga 245–246
Fraugde 286
Frederick I, King of Denmark (r. 1523–1533) 242–243
Frederick I Barbarossa, German Emperor (r. 1152–1190) 119
Frederick II, German Emperor (r. 1212–1250) 119, 124–125, 128
Frederick III, German Emperor (r. 1452–1493) 239
Friesland 41–42, 125, 134, 239
Frösön 10
Frostating 145, 152
Funen 12, 16, 38, 59, 140, 147, 152, 204, 289

Gardar 49, 132, 185
Gaute Ivarsson, Archbishop of Nidaros 176
Gävle 185
Gavnø 79
Gaza 207
Gdansk 159, 281
Gelasius, Pope (r. 492–496) 73
Genoa 217
Gerhard III, Count of Holstein 156
Germany 1, 12–13, 16, 18, 20–22, 26–28, 33, 38, 41–42, 44–46, 49, 51–52, 59, 62, 64, 66, 69, 71–74, 76, 85, 92, 100, 103–105, 110–113, 119–120, 123–126, 128–129, 136, 140, 144, 148, 151, 155–158, 163, 165, 168, 173, 178, 180, 182, 184, 189, 192–193, 196, 199–200, 203–204, 206–207, 211, 213–214, 216, 218, 220–225, 232–235, 237, 239, 244–245, 247, 249, 270, 272, 278, 281, 283, 285, 288–292, 294–295, 300

Gisle, Bishop of Linköping 55
Gizur, Bishop of Skálholt 51
Gjorslev 288
Glimmingehus 288
Godfred, King of Denmark (r. c. 904–910) 42
Gorm the Old, King of Denmark (r. mid-10th century) 13, 42
Göta 137
Götaland 21–22, 31, 38, 53, 140, 148, 152, 175, 178, 202
Gotland 38, 61, 77, 101–102, 130, 143, 148, 152, 156–158, 186–187, 197–199, 202, 205, 209–210, 232–234, 236–237, 270, 272, 290, 300
Gotskalk 122
Gottröra 62
Granada 182
Grathe 27, 33
Gratian 62, 143
Greece 41, 198, 240, 235, 291, 294, 300
Greenland 1, 24–25, 45, 48–50, 59, 72, 74, 76, 85, 92, 100, 106, 112, 130–132, 143, 185, 194, 211, 231, 238, 247, 277, 297
Gregorius Turonis 176
Gregory I, Pope (r. 590–604) 298
Gregory VII, Pope (r. 1973–1085) 41, 265
Gregory IX, Pope (r. 1227–1241) 63, 77, 167, 171, 225–226, 257
Gregory XI 160
Greifswald 223
Grenoble 72
Grimkell 48
Gripsholm 72, 254
Gudmundus Gerss 68
Guilielmus Caorsin 294
Gulating 145, 147, 152
Gulet 152
Gunhild 104
Gustav I Vasa, King of Sweden (r. 1523–1560) 242–243, 253–255, 287, 301
Gustav II Adolf, King of Sweden (r. 1611–1632) 150
Gustav Trolle, Archbishop of Uppsala 177, 241, 246, 253

Haakon I the Good, King of Norway (r. c. 935–960) 17, 48, 145
Haakon III Sverresson, King of Norway (r. 1202–1204) 51, 163
Haakon IV Haakonsson, King of Norway (r. 1217–1263) 24, 130–131, 137, 165, 204–205
Haakon V Magnussen, King of Norway (r. 1299–1319) 139, 154, 164–165
Haakon VI Magnussen, King of Norway (r. 1343–1380) 157–158, 250, 263
Haakon Erlingsson, Bishop of Bergen 226
Haakon Sigurdsson, Earl of Lade (r. c. 970–995) 17–18
Hadrian IV, Pope (r. 1154–1159) 49, 54, 58, 74
Hafliði Másson 147
Hagby 74
Halland 10, 59, 126, 137, 147, 155, 194
Hålogaland 17, 19
Hälsingland 21, 53, 148–149, 152
Halsnøy 74
Haltdalen 97
Halvard 10
Hamar 49, 74, 164
Hamburg 18, 42, 45–46, 48, 51–53, 63, 82, 123
Hamburg-Bremen see Bremen, see Hamburg
Hämeenlinna 129, 204
Hammershus 204
Hans Brask, Bishop of Linköping 66, 252–253
Hans Tausen 247
Harald, King of England (r. 1014–1018?) 15
Harald Bluetooth, King of Denmark (r. c. 958–985) 9–10, 12–14, 17–18, 22, 42–44, 99, 192
Harald Fairhair, King of Norway (r. c. 871–933) 17
Harald Gille, King of Norway (r. c. 1130–1136) 28
Harald Hardrada, King of Norway (r. 1046–1066) 15, 21
Harald Klak, King of Denmark (r. 9th century) 12, 42
Härjedalen 59
Härkeberga 254, 289
Håtuna 154
Hebrides 49, 59, 130–131, 137, 163, 247
Hedeby 42–43, 184–185, 272
Heidelberg 222
Helmold of Bosau 27
Helsingborg 157–158, 162, 186
Helsingør 176, 186
Helvig of Schleswig, Queen of Denmark 156
Hemming 223
Hemming, Bishop of Turku 65, 173, 217, 252, 255
Hemming Gadh, Electus of Linköping 177, 252
Henning Podebusk 158
Henrik Harpestreng 108, 292–293
Henrik Krummedige 240
Henry, Bishop of Finland 32, 55–56, 169, 172, 174–176, 217, 298
Henry, Count of Schwerin 126–129
Henry II, King of England (r. 1154–1189) 213
Henry V, King of England (r. 1413–1422) 234

312 *Index*

Henry of Livonia 215
Henry of Segusio 262
Henry the Lion, Duke of Saxony 270
Hermann 103
Hermannus Hartlevi 177
Herrevad 72, 136
Heyredal 70
Hippo 73
Hjørungavåg 18
Högsäter 263
Hólar 24, 49, 52, 74, 166, 197, 249
Holland *see* Netherlands
Holmger Knutsson 135
Holstein 122–124, 128, 134, 155–158, 233–234, 236, 239, 247, 272
Holy Land 29, 45, 75–76, 79, 99, 128, 177, 180–181, 215
Holy Roman Empire *see* Germany
Høm 97–98
Homer 294
Honorius III, Pope (r. 1216–1227) 77–79, 128, 225
Hordaland 17, 290
Hored, Bishop of Schleswig 43
Horik II, King of Denmark (r. 850s–860s/870s?) 42
Horsens 76
Hostiensis *see* Henry of Segusio
Hrafn Sveinbjarnarson 108
Huguccio 63
Humbert of Romans 295
Hungary 75, 235, 275

Iberian Peninsula 75, 101, 160, 180, 182, 220, 289
Ibsen, Henrik 240
Iceland 1, 10, 22–24, 26, 45, 48–49, 51–52, 59, 67, 72, 74, 85, 87, 89, 92, 94, 100–101, 104–106, 108, 130–131, 133, 136–137, 143, 145, 147, 150, 152–153, 165–166, 172, 177, 180, 184–185, 194, 196–197, 199, 204, 214, 216–217, 226, 238–239, 247, 249–251, 264–265, 273, 275, 277–278, 291–292, 297, 300
Ii 66
Ikšķile 125
India 136, 196
Inge, King in Götaland (r. *c.* 1110–1125) 31
Inge the Elder, King in Sweden (r. *c.* 1080–1084 and 1087–1105) 22, 31
Inge the Hunchback, King of Norway (r. 1136–1161) 29
Ingeborg Axelsdotter Thott 234
Ingeborg Bengtsdotter 179
Ingeborg Ericsdotter, Duchess of Finland 154–155

Ingeborg Haakonsdotter, Queen of Norway 154–156, 164
Ingeborg Magnusdotter, Queen of Denmark 154
Ingeborg of Denmark, Queen of France 124, 264
Ingeborg Valdemarsdotter 158
Ingelheim 12, 43
Ingólfr Arnarson 23
Ingrid Elovsdotter of Skänninge 79, 173, 251–252
Innocent III, Pope (r. 1198–1216) 51, 57, 63, 80, 119, 124, 140, 222
Innocent IV, Pope (r. 1243–1254) 61, 77, 167, 170
Innocent VIII, Pope (r. 1484–1492) 173
Ireland 17, 22–23, 28, 136
Isle of Man 49, 130–131, 163, 247
Isleif, Bishop of Skálholt 51
Italy 13, 59, 61–62, 72–73, 101, 110–111, 139, 160, 193, 217, 220, 272, 289, 291–292, 294–295
Ivan, Grand Prince of Moscow 238

Jacobus de Varagine, Archbishop of Genoa 217
Jadwiga 235
Jakob Erlandsen, Archbishop of Lund 161–162, 217
Jakob Ulfsson, Archbishop of Uppsala 173, 252–253
James II, King of Scotland 239
Jämtland 10, 21
Jan Hus 223
Jarimar, Ruler of Rügen 126
Jaroslav, King of Kiev 19
Järvamaa 127
Jean de Gerson 267, 295
Jelling 9, 13–14
Jens Andersen Beldenak, Bishop of Odense 240–241
Jens Bostrup, Archbishop of Lund 245
Jens Grand, Archbishop of Lund 162, 168, 193
Jerusalem 16, 20–21, 45, 75–76, 79, 99, 119, 128, 157, 164, 173–174, 176–177, 180, 182, 189–190, 215, 231, 235, 248, 266
Jesus *see* Christ
Johan Håkansson, Archbishop of Uppsala 251
Johann Snell 294
Johannes Angelus Arcimboldus 70
Johannes Bengedans 292
Johannes Elavi 225
Johannes Gerechini, Archbishop of Uppsala, Bishop of Skálholt 67, 250–251
Johannes Gutenberg 291

Johannes Johannis 225
Johannes Kalenskæ 282
Johannes Nicholai de Dacia 223
Johannes Petri 177
Johannes Werth 221
John, Union King (r. 1481–1513) 110, 238–240
John I Sverkersson, King of Sweden (r. 1216–1222) 127
John XIX, Pope (r. 1024–1032) 44
John XXII, Pope (r. 1316–1334) 63
John Lackland, King of England (r. 1199–1216) 124
John Paul II, Pope (r. 1978–2005) 52, 172
John Wyclif 258
Jon Birgersson, Bishop of Stavanger 49
Jon Hallordsson, Bishop of Skálholt 226
Jon Raude, Archbishop of Nidaros 145, 164
Jonas 207–208
Jöns Bengtsson, Archbishop of Uppsala 251–252
Jöns Budde 297
Jordanes 1
Jutland 10, 12–13, 16, 20, 27, 59, 73, 92, 103, 120, 133, 140, 147–148, 150, 152, 156, 158, 172, 186, 236, 243, 245, 247, 277–278
Jutta, daughter of King Erik IV Ploughpenny of Denmark 79, 134, 139

Kalmar 2, 67, 75, 78–79, 100, 122, 141, 163, 165, 185, 193, 205, 220, 229–230, 233–234, 236–240, 243, 247, 249–253, 255, 270, 278, 285, 294, 301
Kalundborg 38, 186, 205
Kanutus de Arusia 224
Kanutus Molle 178–179
Karelia 123, 168, 180, 229, 253
Karl Knutson Bonde, King of Sweden (r. 1448–1457, 1464–1465, 1467–1470) 237, 252
Karl Sverkersson, King of Sweden (r. c. 1158–1167) 31
Karl the Deaf, Duke 127
Kasimir of Pomerania 126
Kattegat 38
Kemi 275
Ketilsfjord 74
Kiev 7, 19
Kimito 68
Kingdom of Jerusalem *see* Jerusalem
Kinsarvik 290
Kirkwall 131
Knud Porse, Duke of Halland 155–156
Knut Alvsson 240
Kolding 188
Kökar 255

Kokemäki 65
Konghelle 78, 165
Konrad Bitz, Bishop of Turku 254
Konrad von Jungingen 232
Koroinen 169–170, 206
Kuggmaren 121
Kuli 9–10
Kungälv 74
Kuusisto 206, 288

Ladoga 129–130, 272
Lalli 56
Landskrona 79, 130
L'Anse aux Meadows 194
Laon 74
Lapland 40, 170
Lars Sunesson Vit 67
Latvia 77, 214–215
Laurentius 241
Laurentius Johannis 81–82
Laurentius Misener 195
Leif the Lucky 26
Leipzig 221, 223, 295
Leo IX, Pope (r. 1049–1054) 48
Leofdag, Bishop of Ribe 43
Leon 144
Limfjorden 77–78
Limoges 211–212
Linköping 31, 53, 55, 66, 78, 127, 166–167, 173, 185, 217, 251–253
Lisbjerg 103
Lisbon 182
Lithuania 233, 235, 237
Livonia 77, 125, 186, 215
Lödöse 224
Lofoten 277
Logtun in Frosta 152
Lolland 10, 73, 147
London 270
Lönnroth, Erik 230
Lothar I, German Emperor (r. 817–855) 12
Lothar III, German Emperor (r. 1125–1137) 27
Louis the Pious, Frankish Emperor (r. 814–840) 21, 42
Louis XI, King of France (r. 1461–1483) 75
Louvre 124
Lübeck 123, 126, 186, 199, 237, 243, 270–271, 280–281
Lund 28, 35, 45–47, 49, 52, 55, 57–59, 63–64, 72, 74, 76, 78–79, 96, 102–103, 130–131, 139, 147, 152, 155–156, 160–163, 167–168, 182, 185, 189, 193, 214–215, 219, 222–226, 230, 236, 241, 245–246, 253, 286–287, 300
Lüneburg 276
Lydia 192
Lyø 127

Lyon 57, 160
Lyrskov Moor 20
Lyse 50, 72

Macharius Magnussen 223
Madonna *see* Saint Mary
Magdeburg 74
Magnus, son of King Niels of Denmark, King in Götaland (r. 1120s–1134) 27–28, 31
Magnus, son of King Olaf Haraldsson of Norway 19–21
Magnus II Henriksson, King of Sweden (r. 1160–1161) 31, 54
Magnus III Barefoot, King of Norway (r. 1093–1103) 28
Magnus III Birgersson, King of Sweden (r. 1275–1290) 136, 154
Magnus IV Ericsson, King of Sweden (r. (1319) 1331/1332–1363) 72, 139, 148–150, 154–158, 163–165, 169, 179, 193, 197, 232, 282, 297
Magnus IV Sigurdsson, King of Norway (r. 1130–1139) 28–29
Magnus V Erlingsson, King of Norway (r. 1163/4–1184) 29–30, 50–51, 64, 140
Magnus VI Haakonsson 'the Law-mender', King of Norway (r. 1263–1280) 131, 136–137, 141, 145, 164, 166, 205, 214
Magnus Grito 178
Magnus Ladulås *see* Magnus III Birgersson
Magnus Nicolai, Bishop of Turku 65, 68, 176
Magnus Tavast, Bishop of Turku 66, 177, 254
Mälaren 21, 53, 125, 184, 272, 281
Malbork *see* Marienburg
Malmö 80, 185, 270
Malta 76
Maren Hemmingsdatter 80
Margaret I, Union Queen (r. 1175–1412) 77, 158–159, 163, 165, 169, 229–234, 245, 247, 249–251, 263
Margaret Fridkulla, Queen of Denmark 31
Margaret of Denmark, Queen of Scotland 239
Margaret of Scotland, Queen of Norway 299
Margarete 231
Mariager 73, 247
Maribo 73, 185, 187, 204, 247
Marienburg 76
Marinus de Fregano 58
Marstrand 78, 165
Martin V, Pope (r. 1417–1431) 67, 244, 248, 251
Martin Luther 69, 174, 244–245, 246–247, 254, 291, 300
Martin Mogensen 162
Maschenholt 76
Masku 255, 282

Mats Gregersson, Bishop of Strängnäs 173, 253
Matthias of Ribe 79
Maxentius, Roman Emperor (r. 306–312) 174
Mecklenburg 126, 155, 232
Mediterranean 92, 128–129, 196, 268, 272
Meinhard 125
Merete Ulfsdotter 220
Michael Nicolai 176, 263–264
Middle East 126, 128, 297
Minsk 31
Möðruvellir 74
Möja 181
Montpellier 80
Moscow 238
Mount Carmel 79

Naantali 73, 79, 83, 110, 185, 187, 255, 297
Nakskov 80
Nanne Kerling 81–82
Naples 220
Närke 148, 152
Nävelsjö 212
Near East 75, 99
Nebuchadnezzar, King of Babylon (r. 605–562 BC) 157
Netherlands 73, 92, 238, 273, 290
Neva 129–130
Newfoundland 194, 277
Niccolò Machiavelli 240, 294
Nicholas Breakspear, Cardinal *see* Hadrian IV
Nicholaus Drukken 223
Nicolaus Johannis 224
Nicopolis 231
Nidaros 17, 19–20, 28–31, 46, 48–52, 55, 59, 61, 64, 74, 78, 96, 99–100, 107, 130–131, 133, 145, 163–165, 176–178, 185, 191, 196, 202–203, 209, 211, 225, 230–231, 237, 247–250, 257, 268, 270, 300
Niels, Duke of Halland 126
Niels, King of Denmark (r. 1104–1134) 27, 31, 45, 140
Niels Ebbesen 156
Niels Skave, Bishop of Roskilde 67
Niels Stigsen, Bishop of Roskilde 133, 161
Nils Allesson, Archbishop of Uppsala 62, 64
Nils Hermansson, Bishop of Linköping 173, 178, 217, 251
Nils Kettilsson, Archbishop of Uppsala 62
Nils Ragvaldsson, Archbishop of Uppsala 221, 251
Normandy 15, 19, 48, 84, 96, 224
Norrland 21, 90
North Sea / territory 14–17, 38, 239, 270, 272–273, 276–277, 283
Norway 1, 7, 9–10, 12–15, 17–24, 26–31, 34–38, 41, 45–52, 54–55, 59, 61, 64–65,

70, 72, 74–76, 78–79, 85, 87, 89–90,
  92–94, 96–101, 103–105, 107–108,
  120–123, 125, 129–137, 139–143,
  145–148, 150, 152–159, 163–166, 169,
  172–173, 175–176, 178, 181–182,
  184–187, 191–197, 200–205, 210–211,
  213–217, 225–226, 229, 231–235,
  237–241, 243, 247–250, 257, 263–265,
  270, 272–273, 276–277, 281, 284, 288,
  290–291, 297–301
Nöteborg 130, 170
Nousiainen 289
Novgorod 7, 101, 129–130, 170, 270, 272,
  282
Nuuk 26
Nyborg 38, 204, 270
Nydala 31, 55, 72
Nyköping 154–155, 204, 270, 281

Odense 16, 27, 45, 76, 78, 116, 161, 174,
  176, 185, 240, 286, 294
Oder 20
Ogier the Dane 216
Old Uppsala 53–54, 167
Oldenburg 237, 243, 252, 294
Olaf I Tryggvason, King of Norway
  (r. c. 995–999) 18, 26, 37, 48–49, 51, 192
Olaf II Haraldsson, Saint, King of Norway
  (r. 1015–1028) 10, 18–21, 30, 48, 51,
  54, 74, 99, 137, 145, 164, 170, 172–173,
  175–178, 199, 211, 217, 248, 269, 288, 298
Olaf III Kyrre, King of Norway (r. 1067–1093)
  49
Olaf II/IV Haakonsson, King of
  Denmark (r. 1376–1387), King of Norway
  (r. 1380–1387) 158–159, 165, 229
Öland 38, 100
Olavus Magni, Bishop of Turku 177, 222
Olof Björnsson, Archbishop of Uppsala 168
Olof Larsson, Archbishop of Uppsala 251
Olof Skötkonung, King of Sweden
  (r. c. 995–1022) 22, 192
Olof Svärd 66
Ølst 103
Øresund 10, 18, 158, 186, 271, 277–278
Orkney Islands 48–49, 59, 130–131, 142,
  159, 239, 247
Örlygsstaðir 24
Oslo 18, 38, 49, 64, 78, 142, 145, 164–165,
  184, 197, 240
Östergötland 21, 31, 53, 148, 152, 178
Østerlars 99
Östman 10
Ostrobothnia 129
Otto I, German Emperor (r. 936–73) 42
Otto IV, German Emperor (1209–1218)
  123–125

Otto, brother of King Valdemar IV of
  Denmark 157
Otto Olafsson, Bishop of Västerås 173
Ottomans *see* Turkey
Öved 74
Oxford 220, 222

Pälkäne 109
Papal States 160, 177
Paris 52, 62–63, 74, 79, 162, 196, 202,
  219–226, 267, 295
Paschal II, Pope (r. 1099–1118) 16, 45
Paul II, Pope (r. 1464–1472) 172, 177
Paul III, Pope (r. 1534–1549) 61
Peder Jensen, Archbishop of Lund 162–163
Peder Lykke 245
Peder Månsson, Bishop of Västerås 177, 292
Peder Sunesen, Bishop of Roskilde 46, 225
Perth 131
Peter 223
Peter Lombard 216
Peter the Venerable 22
Petrus de Abo 226
Petrus Olavi 225
Philip II Augustus, King of France
  (r. 1180–1223) 124, 264
Philip IV, King of France (r. 1285–1314) 75
Philippa of England, Union Queen 193,
  234–235
Pisa 244
Pius II, Pope (r. 1458–1464) 235
Poland 20, 22, 74, 76, 182, 233, 235,
  237, 273
Pomerania 67, 79, 126, 141, 158, 186, 221,
  229, 233–236, 245, 247, 249, 251, 279
Poppo 43–44
Portugal 124, 142, 272, 277, 292
Poul Helgesen 80, 246–247, 294
Prague 143, 220, 222–224
Prémontré 74
Provence 179
Prussia 76, 153, 186
Publius Flavius Vegetius Renatus 292

Raasepori 254
Radulf, Bishop of Ribe 35, 295
Ragnhild 178
Ragnvald, King of Svealand 31
Ragvaldus, Bishop of Finland 169
Randers 80
Ratzeburg 71
Rauma 255
Ravninge 13
Raymundus de Penyaforte 63
Reginbrand, Bishop of Århus 43
Reims 42
Reykjavik 23, 147

Rhine 214, 272
Rhodes 76, 294
Ribe 12, 35, 42–43, 45, 76, 78–79, 102, 151, 162, 185, 195, 197, 200, 247, 285–286, 295, 300
Richard I the Lionheart, King of England (r. 1189–1199) 215
Riga 67, 122, 125, 126, 281
Rikissa, Queen of Norway 137
Rikissa, Queen of Sweden 31
Rimbert, Archbishop of Bremen 21, 53
Rimbo 259
Ringsted 28–29, 46, 97–98, 104, 134, 152, 155
Rinna 178
Robert the Monk 215
Rodulfus, Bishop of Finland 56, 169
Rogaland 17
Rök 105
Roman Empire 2, 34, 40, 96, 143, 184, 192, 214–215, 220, 240–241, 292, 300
Rome 41, 44–45, 57, 71, 73, 80, 139, 160, 162–165, 169, 174–177, 179–180, 211, 220, 222, 224, 230–231, 244–245, 247, 250, 254, 266, 282, 292, 298
Roskilde 27, 45–46, 67, 74, 78–79, 96, 121, 133–134, 139, 142, 147–148, 161, 185, 197, 202, 219, 223, 225, 282, 288
Rostock 199, 223, 225
Rotebro 238
Rouen 19
Rügen 28, 46, 59, 76, 126, 154, 161
Russia 31, 61, 79, 122, 125, 129–130, 132–133, 165, 169–170, 185, 214, 231–232, 237–238, 242, 255, 272, 278
Ryd 215, 294

Saaremaa 125, 127, 182
Saint Andrews 49, 247
Saint Ansgar *see* Ansgar
Saint Anthony 174, 176
Saint Augustine of Hippo 73–74, 80, 167, 190
Saint Benedict 71
Saint Birgitta *see* Birgitta Birgersdotter
Saint Botulf 269
Saint Botvid 53, 172, 175
Saint Bruno of Cologne 72
Saint Canute *see* Canute IV
Saint Canute Lavard *see* Canute Lavard
Saint Catherine of Alexandria 174
Saint Catherine of Siena 172
Saint Catherine of Vadstena *see* Catherine Ulfsdotter
Saint Clare of Assisi 77
Saint David 172
Saint Dominic 78
Saint Eric *see* Eric Jedvarsson
Saint Eskil 53, 172, 175
Saint Francis *see* Francis of Assisi
Saint George 80–81, 290
Saint Gregory of Tours 214
Saint Henry *see* Henry, Bishop of Finland
Saint James the Great 175, 178
Saint John the Evangelist 175
Saint Kjeld of Viborg 172, 175
Saint Lawrence 99, 172, 175
Saint Lucy 172, 174, 265
Saint Luke the Evangelist 175
Saint Mark the Evangelist 175
Saint Mary 16, 20, 65, 101, 103, 142, 175, 180, 197, 204, 206, 208–211, 218, 256, 260, 269
Saint Mary Magdalene 179
Saint Matthew the Evangelist 175
Saint Mechtild 297
Saint Michael 75, 269
Saint Norbert of Xanten 74
Saint Olaf *see* Olaf Haraldsson
Saint Paul 175, 177
Saint Peter 15, 80, 169, 175, 177, 180, 244
Saint Petersburg 129
Saint Sigfrid 53, 175, 181
Saint Staffan 53
Saint Swithun 176
Saint Thomas Aquinas 111, 172
Saint Thomas Becket 213
Saint Þorlakur *see* Þorlákur Þorhallason
Saint Ursula 176
Saint Viktor 74
Saint Villads 172
Saladin 215
Salerno 108, 111
Sámi/Sápmi 1, 40, 104, 106, 112, 130, 132–133, 165, 170, 231, 249, 291, 297, 300
Samsø 156
Samson 207
Santiago de Compostela 79, 164, 173–174, 176, 178–179, 211
Satakunta 55
Savonia 255
Saxo Grammaticus 1, 13, 33, 46, 55, 214–215
Saxony 9, 120, 238–239, 270
Scania 10, 12, 27, 46, 59, 72, 74, 92–93, 101–102, 122–123, 130, 147–148, 152, 155–158, 161–162, 195, 270, 273, 275, 278–279, 285, 288, 299
Schleswig 27, 34, 42–43, 45, 59, 82, 103, 107, 123, 126, 134–135, 156, 184, 186, 189, 194–195, 200, 233–236, 239, 243, 247, 272, 280, 294
Schwerin 124, 126–127

Index 317

Scotland 23, 49, 59, 131, 133, 153, 163, 220, 237, 239, 247, 299
Selje 50, 72, 98
Shetland Islands 48–49, 59, 130–131, 239, 247
Sicily 21, 29, 119, 273
Sigefredus, Bishop of Norwegians 48
Sigersholm 37
Sigismund von Luxembourg, King of Hungary (r. 1387–1437), King of Germany (r. 1410–1437), German Emperor (r. 1433–1437) 75, 234–235
Sigtuna 22, 53, 125, 169, 185, 204, 272
Sigurd, Archbishop of Nidaros 166
Sigurd Slembe, King of Norway (r. 1135–1139) 28
Sigurd I Magnusson Jorsalafare, King of Norway (r. 1103–1130) 28–29, 181–182
Sigurd II Munn, King of Norway (r. 1136–1155) 28–30
Silves 182
Sixtus IV, Pope (r. 1471–1484) 221, 246–247
Skálholt 24, 49, 51–52, 67, 74, 166, 172, 226, 249–251
Skänninge 64, 79, 167, 169, 173, 251–252
Skanør 278
Skara 53, 74, 166–167, 169, 173, 224–225, 241, 251–253, 295
Skíringssal 184–155
Skriða 74
Slagelse 76
Småland 22, 148, 175
Snorri Sturluson 19, 24, 37, 105, 145, 215
Søborg 99, 123
Söderby-Karl 91, 208
Söderköping 64, 80, 169
Södermanland 21, 53, 148–149, 152, 154, 175, 215
Södertörn 53
Sodor Islands 130, 247
Sofia, Queen of Denmark 27, 137, 139
Somero 67
Sønderborg 243
Sorø 67, 72
Spain 61, 101, 178, 216, 237, 289
Sparrsätra 135
Sprogø 38
Staffan 234
Stäket 241
Stamford Bridge 15, 21
Stavanger 49, 74, 176, 203, 225
Stefan, Archbishop of Uppsala 55
Steinvikholm 288
Sten Sture the Elder 72, 76, 221, 234, 238, 254, 290
Sten Sture the Younger 241, 253

Stephen, King of England (r. 1135–1154) 26
Stiklestad 19, 21, 48
Stockholm 21, 53, 76, 78, 99, 115, 121, 138, 148, 150, 158, 173, 181, 185, 187, 189, 195, 198, 204, 212, 221, 230, 232, 236–239, 241–243, 246, 253, 268, 270, 281, 285–286, 290, 294
Storebælt 38
Stralsund 158, 271
Strängnäs 53, 142, 166, 173, 241, 253
Suen Stærke 125
Sueno Huso 71
Svante Nilsson Sture, Regent of Sweden 240
Svealand 21–22, 31, 53, 140, 148
Svendstrup 76, 84
Sverker the Elder, King of Sweden (r. c. 1130–1156) 31–32, 55
Sverre Sigurdsson, King of Norway (r. 1184–1202) 30, 34, 51, 142, 159, 163
Svold 18
Swanogh Olaffzdother 70
Sweden 1, 7, 9, 10, 15, 18–19, 21–23, 31–38, 41–42, 45–46, 52–56, 59, 62, 64–65, 71–81, 84–85, 87, 89, 91–94, 96–101, 103–105, 111, 113, 115, 120–122, 125–127, 129–130, 133–143, 145, 148–160, 163–170, 172–175, 177–182, 184–185, 191–195, 197–198, 200–205, 208–209, 211–212, 214–217, 220–221, 224–225, 229–243, 246, 249–255, 258, 263, 265, 269, 271–273, 280–282, 284–292, 294–301
Swenwngh Helghessen 70
Sweyn I Forkbeard, King of Denmark (r. c. 985–1014) 13–17, 18, 22
Sweyn II Estridsen, King of Denmark (r. 1047–1076) 15–16, 33, 45
Sweyn III Grathe, King of Denmark (r. 1146–1157) 27, 32
Sweyn, Prince of Denmark 180
Sweyn, son of King Canute the Great 19
Sweyn the Sacrificer see Blot-Sweyn
Switzerland 289
Syria 173, 196

Täby 254, 289
Tacitus 83
Tälje 64
Tallinn 121, 126–127, 182, 187, 198, 201, 239, 284
Tamdrup 44
Tårnborg 38
Tavastland 129–130, 170, 182
Thangbrand 51
Theodoric, Bishop of Estonia 126
Theodoric, King of Ostrogoths (r. 475–526) 105

318 *Index*

Thidemannus Ulfhardi 177
Thjodhild 26
Thomas, Bishop of Finland 63, 169
Thuo de Vibergia 224
Thyra, Queen of Denmark 13
Tiber 174
Tidericus 198–199
Þingeyrar 52
Þingvellir 23, 147, 153
Tommarp 74
Tommerup 195
Tønsberg 38, 64, 75, 78, 99, 145, 164–165, 185, 205
Tord Pedersson (Bonde), Archbishop of Uppsala 252
Tord Räv 264
Tore 10
Tore, Bishop of Hamar 74
Torfinn, Bishop of Hamar 164
Torgel Knutsson 129
Þorlákur Þorhallason, Bishop of Skálholt 52, 74, 172, 217
Törnevalla 115
Torpo 97
Toulouse 220
Tromsø 132, 165
Trøndelag 17–19, 21, 48
Trondenes 165
Trondheim *see* Nidaros
Turin 175
Turkey 192, 231, 235, 251, 294
Turku 53, 55, 61, 64–65, 68, 81, 130, 167, 169–170, 173, 176–177, 179, 185, 187, 204, 217, 221–222, 226, 252, 254–255, 266, 270, 282, 286, 288
Tvilum 74
Þykkivibær 52, 74, 172

Udlængen 121
Ugolino di Conti *see* Gregory IX
Ulf, Father of Sweyn Estridsen 15
Ulf Gudmarsson 179, 263
Ulfhild, Queen of Denmark and Sweden 31
Úlfljótr 147
Ulrik 120
Ulvila 150, 289
Unni, Archbishop of Hamburg-Bremen 42–43, 53
Uppland 22, 62, 74, 148–150, 152, 179, 288
Uppsala 32, 40, 53–55, 59, 61–62, 64, 67, 75, 108, 129, 166–170, 176–177, 183, 202, 221, 230, 237, 241, 246, 250–252, 254, 286, 294–295, 298
Urban II, Pope (r. 1088–1099) 180

Urban V, Pope (r. 1362–1370) 73, 162, 169, 244
Urnes 103
Utstein 74

Vä 74, 101, 195
Vadstena 71, 73, 110, 169, 173–174, 178–180, 204, 211, 215, 224, 231, 240, 254, 295, 297
Valdemar, son of King Abel of Denmark 134
Valdemar I, King of Denmark (r. 1157–1182) 27–29, 38–39, 46, 76, 137, 140, 264
Valdemar II 'the Victorious', King of Denmark (r. 1202–1241) 74, 77, 122–126, 133, 135, 141–142, 147, 161, 182
Valdemar III, King of Denmark (r. 1326–1329) 156
Valdemar IV Atterdag, King of Denmark (r. 1320–1375) 77, 156–157, 162–163, 165, 182, 201, 245, 250
Valdemar Birgersson, King of Sweden (r. 1250–1275) 134–135, 139, 168
Valdemar Haakonson 137
Valdemar Knudsen, Bishop of Schleswig 82, 123
Valdemar Magnusson, Duke of Finland 154
Vardøy 132
Värmland 148, 152
Varne 76
Varnhem 71, 81, 138
Västerås 53, 166, 169, 173, 177, 241, 254
Västergötland 21–22, 53, 148, 152, 175
Västmanland 21, 148
Vättern 21, 31, 38
Växjö 53, 167, 251
Vegetius *see* Publius Flavius Vegetius Renatus
Vejle 64, 161
Veng 72
Vestervig 45, 74
Vestfold 10, 18
Viborg 45, 74, 76, 78, 152, 172, 175, 185, 224
Vienna 222, 224, 245
Vienne 57, 63
Vik 288
Viken 10, 18
Vilhelm of Æbelholt 74, 172, 225
Vincent Henningsson, Bishop of Skara 253
Viðey 74
Virgin Mary *see* Saint Mary
Visby 78, 148, 156–157, 185–187, 197–199, 205, 236, 270
Visingsö 31, 38
Vitslav, Prince of Rügen 126

Volodar, Prince of Minsk 31
Vordingborg 38, 126, 186, 205, 271
Vosborg 99
Vreta 55, 98
Vyborg 61, 79, 170, 185, 204, 238, 255

Wendic territory 20
Westrobothnia 129
Widukind 9
William of Sabina 58, 64, 130, 167
William the Conqueror, King of England (r. 1066–1087) 15

Willibrord 42
Wismar 182
Wittenberg 247
Wladyslaw II, King of Poland-Lithuania-Hungary (r. 1377–1434) 235
Wolf 159

Yolanda, Princess of Jerusalem 128
York 21, 48, 99

Zealand 10, 12, 37–38, 59, 75–76, 99, 147, 152, 194, 285

For Product Safety Concerns and Information please contact our EU representative GPSR@taylorandfrancis.com
Taylor & Francis Verlag GmbH, Kaufingerstraße 24, 80331 München, Germany

www.ingramcontent.com/pod-product-compliance
Lightning Source LLC
Chambersburg PA
CBHW060303010526

44108CB00042B/2625